Angel Sanctuary

story and art by Kaori Yuki   vol.11

The Story Thus Far

High school boy Setsuna Mudo's life is hellish. He's always been a troublemaker, but his worst sin was falling incestuously in love with his beautiful sister Sara. But his troubles are preordained—Setsuna is the reincarnation of the Lady Alexiel, an angel who rebelled against Heaven and led the demons of Hell in a revolt. Her punishment was to be reborn into tragic life after tragic life. This time, her life is as Setsuna.

Setsuna's body, left behind on Earth while he searched Hell for his beloved Sara's soul, has died. When Setsuna returned from Hell along the Meidou path of reincarnation, he reemerged on Earth in the body of the Angel Alexiel. Now Setsuna is determined to brave the gates of Heaven in order to retrieve his sister.

Unfortunately, before Setsuna could look for Sara, he had to return once again to Hell—this time to rescue a friend. Kurai agreed to become the Demon Lord Lucifer's bride in return for Setsuna getting his original body back. Kurai didn't know, however, that the Demon's resurrection elixir would have made Setsuna a mindless slave, and as a Demon bride she would have become a sacrifice. Setsuna goes through several trials before he manages to find a way to crash the infernal wedding. All hell breaks loose as Setsuna manages to find Kurai.

Meanwhile, the Angel of Death and Earth, Uriel, has called the other elemental angels together in order to revive Setsuna's original body. Angel of Air, Raphael, may be able to perform this task, but at what cost?

Contents

Angel Sanctuary™

story and art by **Kaori Yuki**
vol.11

Angel Sanctuary

Vol. 11
Shôjo Edition

STORY AND ART BY KAORI YUKI

Translation/Alexis Kirsch
English Adaptation/Matt Segale
Touch-up & Lettering/James Hudnall
Cover, Graphics & Design/Izumi Evers
Editors/Pancha Diaz & Nancy Thistlethwaite

Managing Editor/Annette Roman
Director of Production/Noboru Watanabe
Vice President of Publishing/Alvin Lu
Sr. Director of Acquisitions/Rika Inouye
VP of Sales & Marketing/Liza Coppola
Publisher/Hyoe Narita

Printed in Canada.

Published by VIZ Media, LLC
P.O. Box 77010
San Francisco, CA 94107

Shôjo Edition
10 9 8 7 6 5 4 3 2 1
First printing, November 2005

www.viz.com
store.viz.com

PARENTAL ADVISORY
ANGEL SANCTUARY is rated T+ for Older Teen and is recommended for ages 16 and up. This volume contains violence and mature situations.

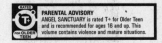

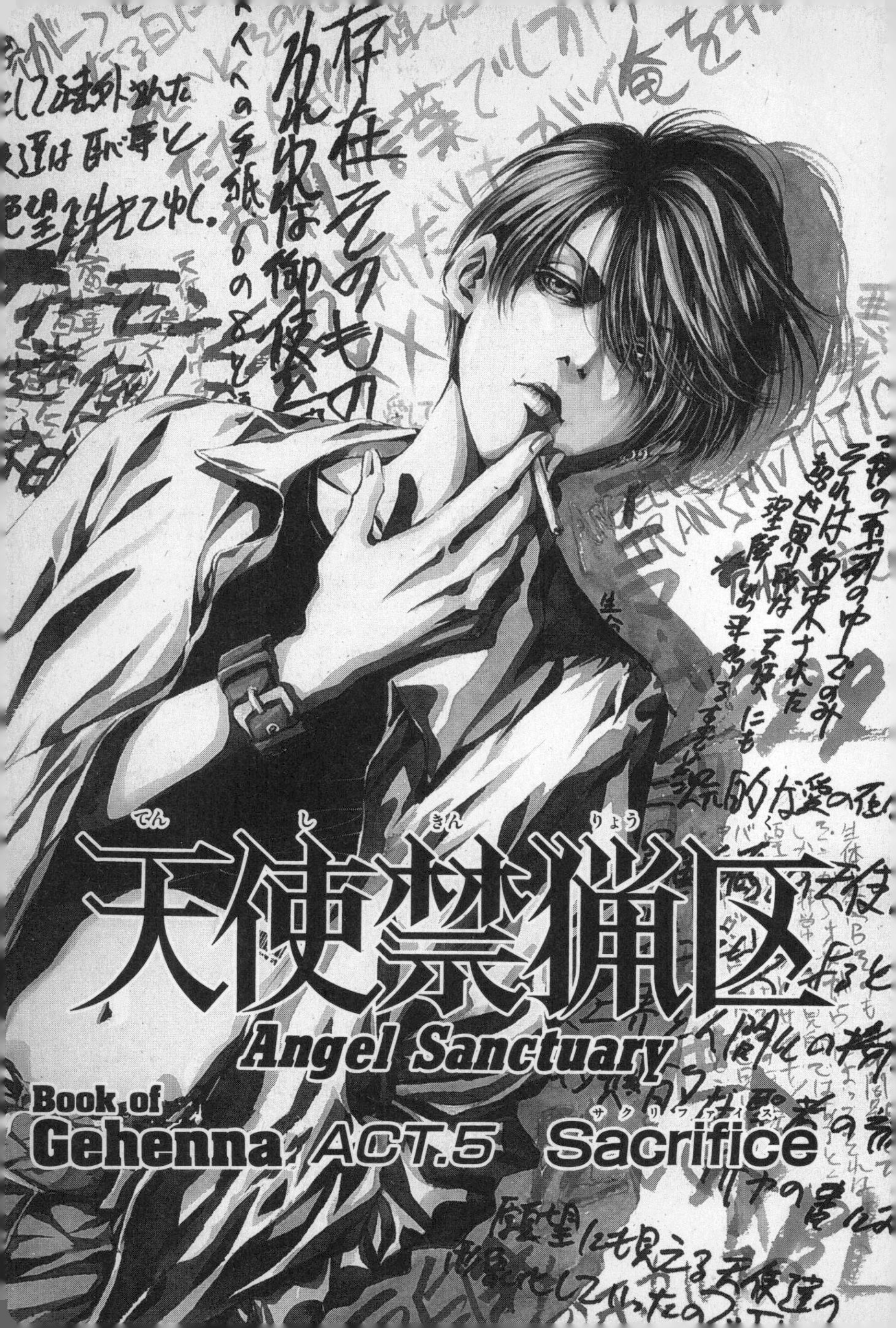
天使禁猟区
Angel Sanctuary
Book of Gehenna ACT.5 Sacrifice

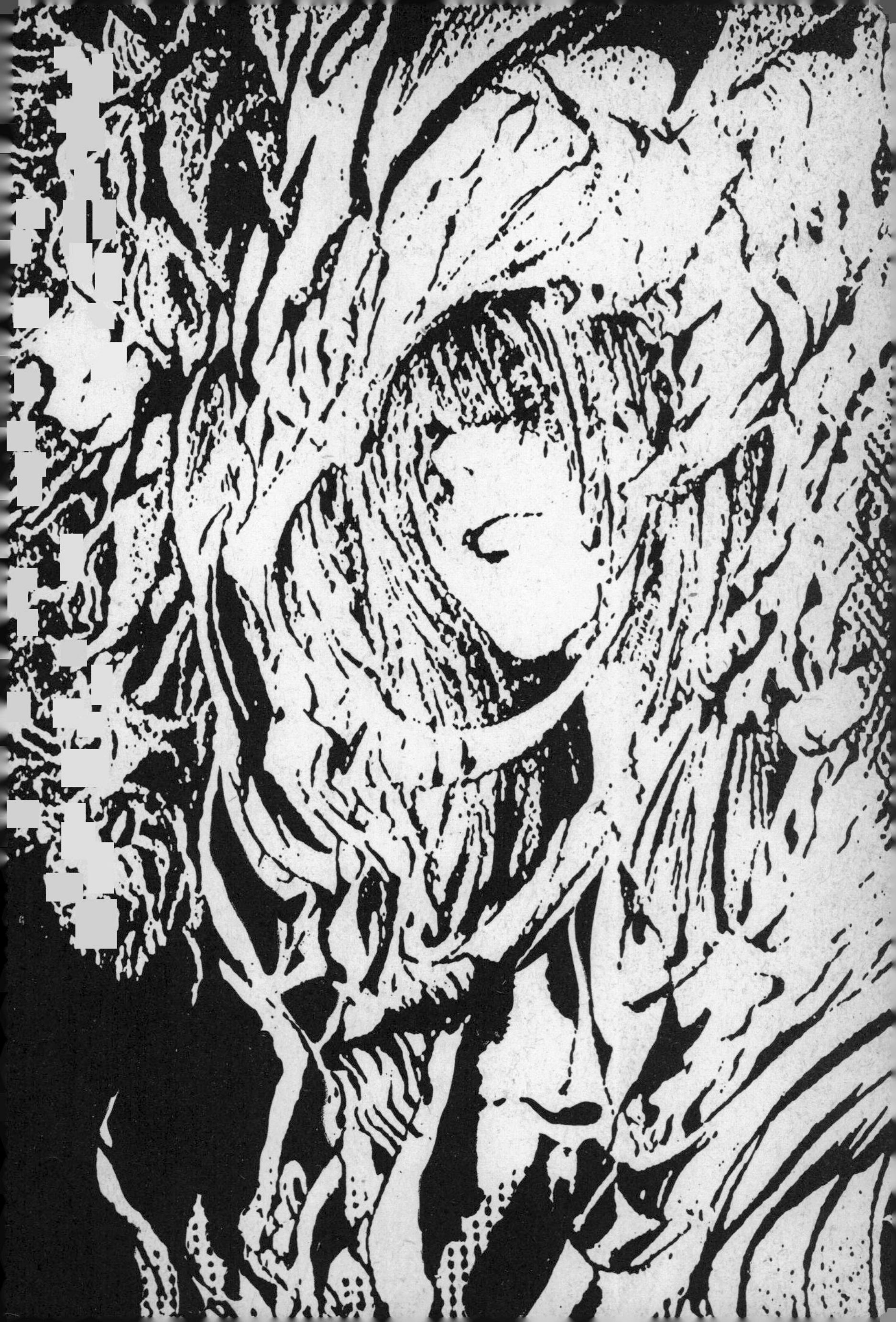

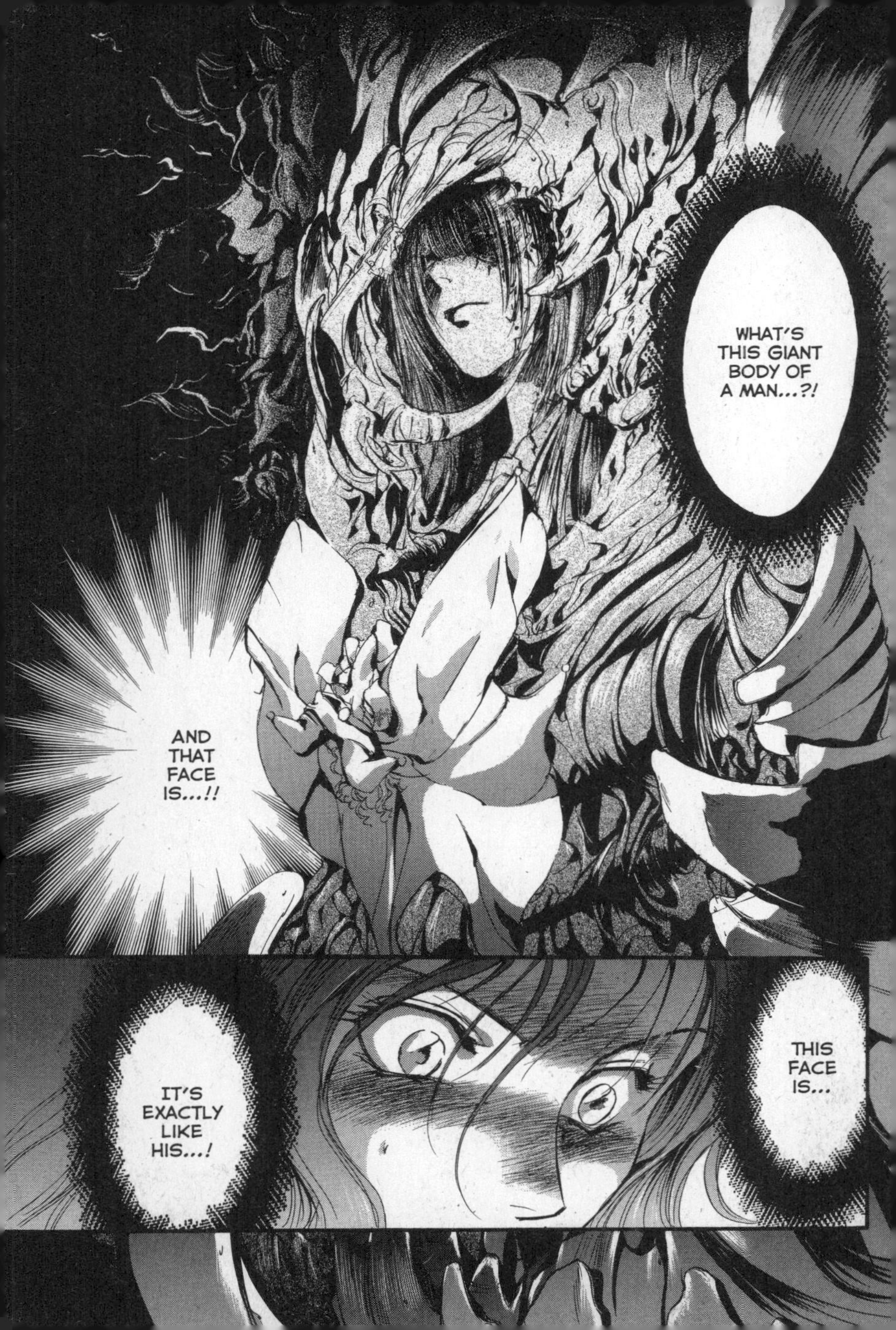
WHAT'S THIS GIANT BODY OF A MAN...?!
AND THAT FACE IS...!!
THIS FACE IS...
IT'S EXACTLY LIKE HIS...!

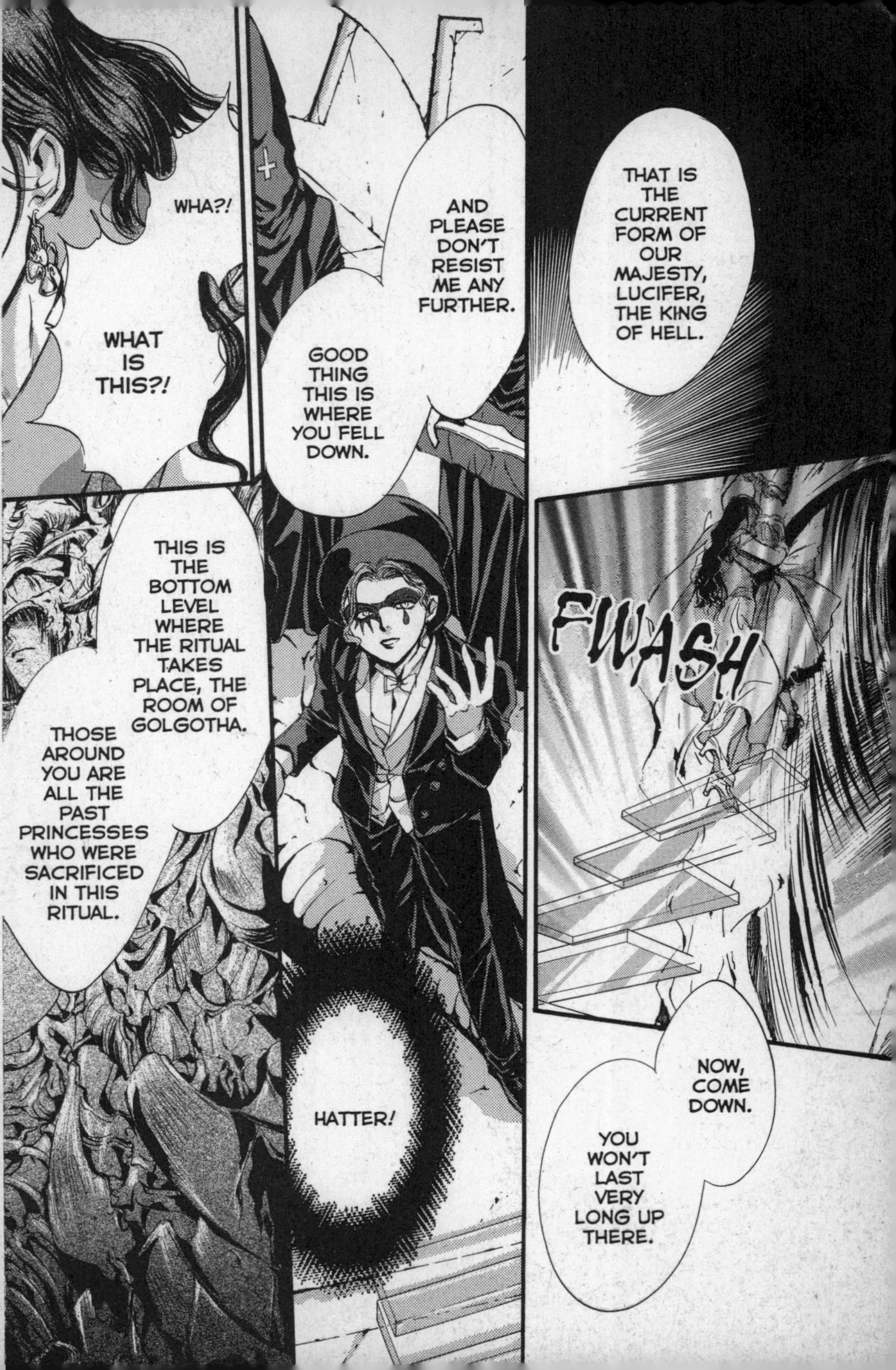
THAT IS THE CURRENT FORM OF OUR MAJESTY, LUCIFER, THE KING OF HELL.
FWASH
NOW, COME DOWN.
YOU WON'T LAST VERY LONG UP THERE.
AND PLEASE DON'T RESIST ME ANY FURTHER.
GOOD THING THIS IS WHERE YOU FELL DOWN.
WHA?!
WHAT IS THIS?!
HATTER!
THIS IS THE BOTTOM LEVEL WHERE THE RITUAL TAKES PLACE, THE ROOM OF GOLGOTHA.
THOSE AROUND YOU ARE ALL THE PAST PRINCESSES WHO WERE SACRIFICED IN THIS RITUAL.

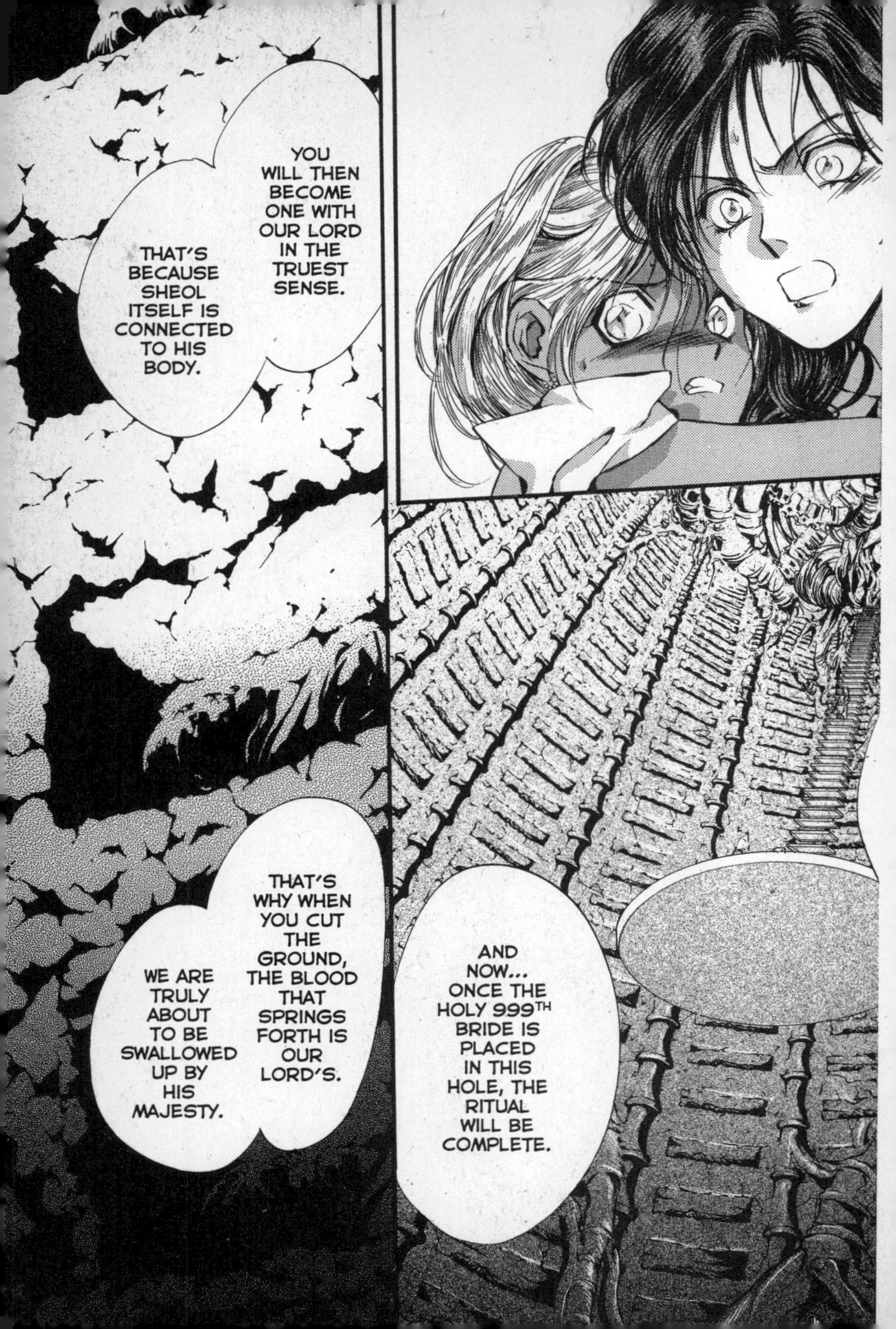
AND NOW... ONCE THE HOLY 999TH BRIDE IS PLACED IN THIS HOLE, THE RITUAL WILL BE COMPLETE.
YOU WILL THEN BECOME ONE WITH OUR LORD IN THE TRUEST SENSE.
THAT'S BECAUSE SHEOL ITSELF IS CONNECTED TO HIS BODY.
THAT'S WHY WHEN YOU CUT THE GROUND, THE BLOOD THAT SPRINGS FORTH IS OUR LORD'S.
WE ARE TRULY ABOUT TO BE SWALLOWED UP BY HIS MAJESTY.

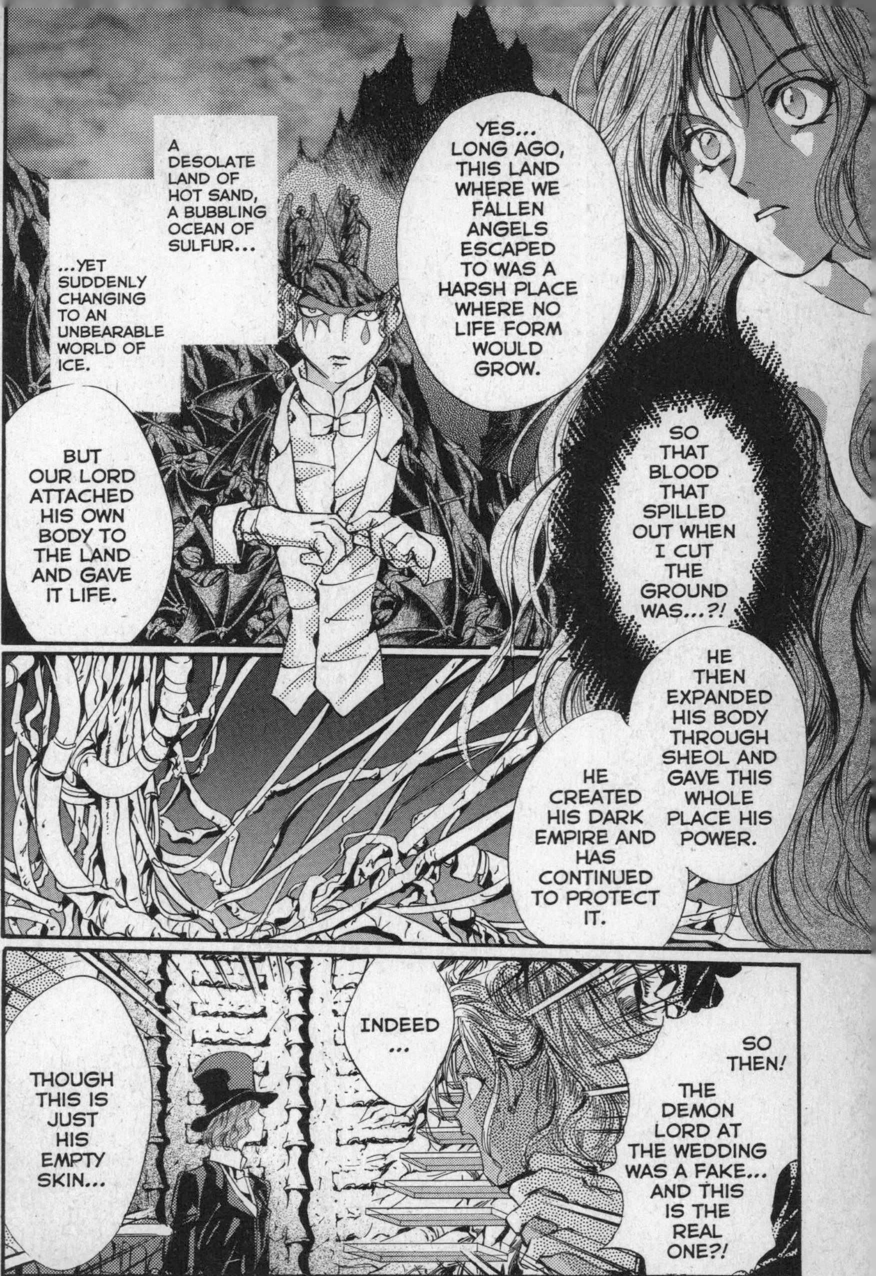
YES... LONG AGO, THIS LAND WHERE WE FALLEN ANGELS ESCAPED TO WAS A HARSH PLACE WHERE NO LIFE FORM WOULD GROW.
A DESOLATE LAND OF HOT SAND, A BUBBLING OCEAN OF SULFUR...
...YET SUDDENLY CHANGING TO AN UNBEARABLE WORLD OF ICE.
BUT OUR LORD ATTACHED HIS OWN BODY TO THE LAND AND GAVE IT LIFE.
SO THAT BLOOD THAT SPILLED OUT WHEN I CUT THE GROUND WAS...?!
HE THEN EXPANDED HIS BODY THROUGH SHEOL AND GAVE THIS WHOLE PLACE HIS POWER.
HE CREATED HIS DARK EMPIRE AND HAS CONTINUED TO PROTECT IT.
SO THEN!
THE DEMON LORD AT THE WEDDING WAS A FAKE... AND THIS IS THE REAL ONE?!
INDEED...
THOUGH THIS IS JUST HIS EMPTY SKIN...

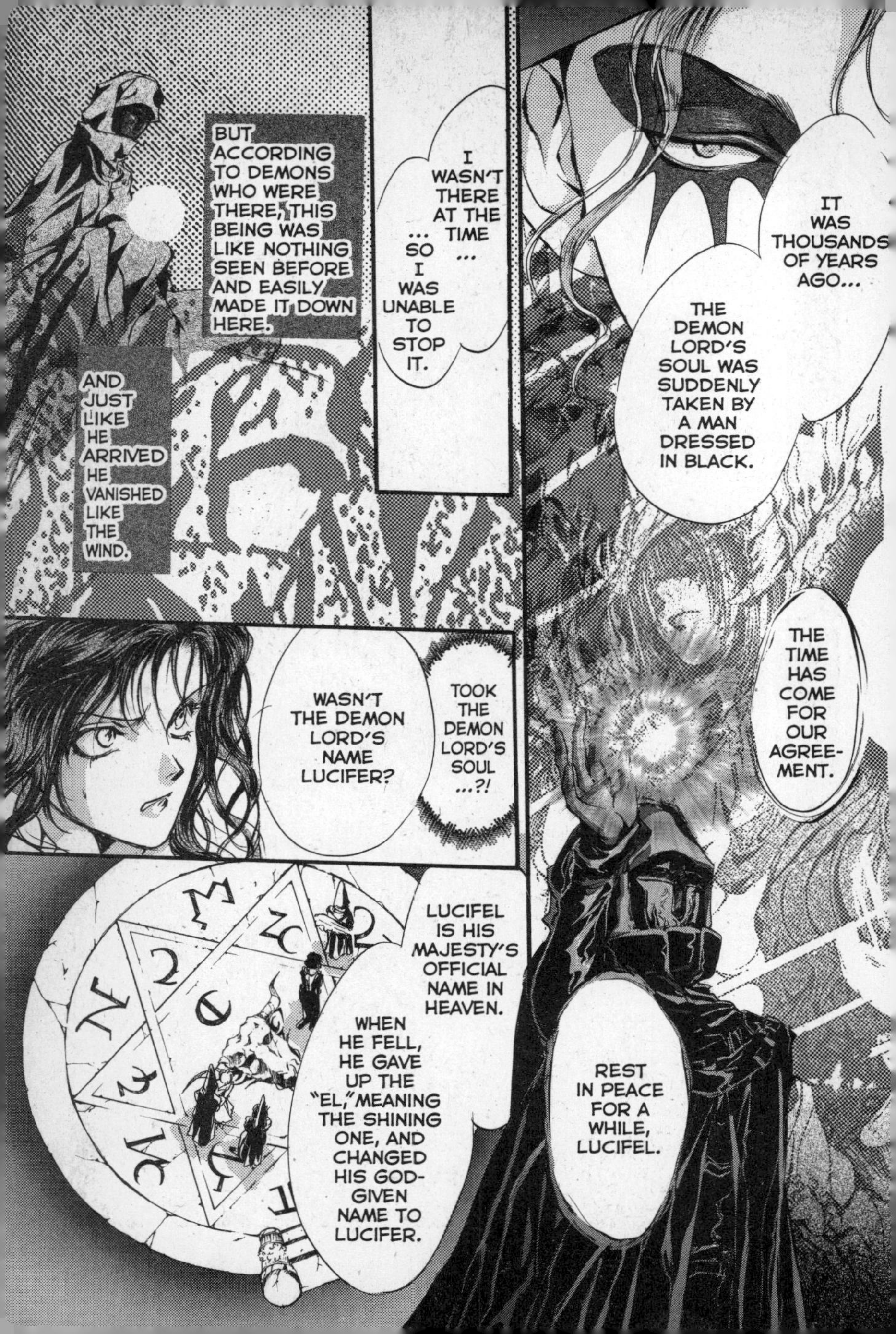
IT WAS THOUSANDS OF YEARS AGO...
THE DEMON LORD'S SOUL WAS SUDDENLY TAKEN BY A MAN DRESSED IN BLACK.
THE TIME HAS COME FOR OUR AGREEMENT.
REST IN PEACE FOR A WHILE, LUCIFEL.
I WASN'T THERE AT THE TIME ... ... SO I WAS UNABLE TO STOP IT.
BUT ACCORDING TO DEMONS WHO WERE THERE, THIS BEING WAS LIKE NOTHING SEEN BEFORE AND EASILY MADE IT DOWN HERE.
AND JUST LIKE HE ARRIVED HE VANISHED LIKE THE WIND.
TOOK THE DEMON LORD'S SOUL ...?!
WASN'T THE DEMON LORD'S NAME LUCIFER?
LUCIFEL IS HIS MAJESTY'S OFFICIAL NAME IN HEAVEN.
WHEN HE FELL, HE GAVE UP THE "EL," MEANING THE SHINING ONE, AND CHANGED HIS GOD-GIVEN NAME TO LUCIFER.

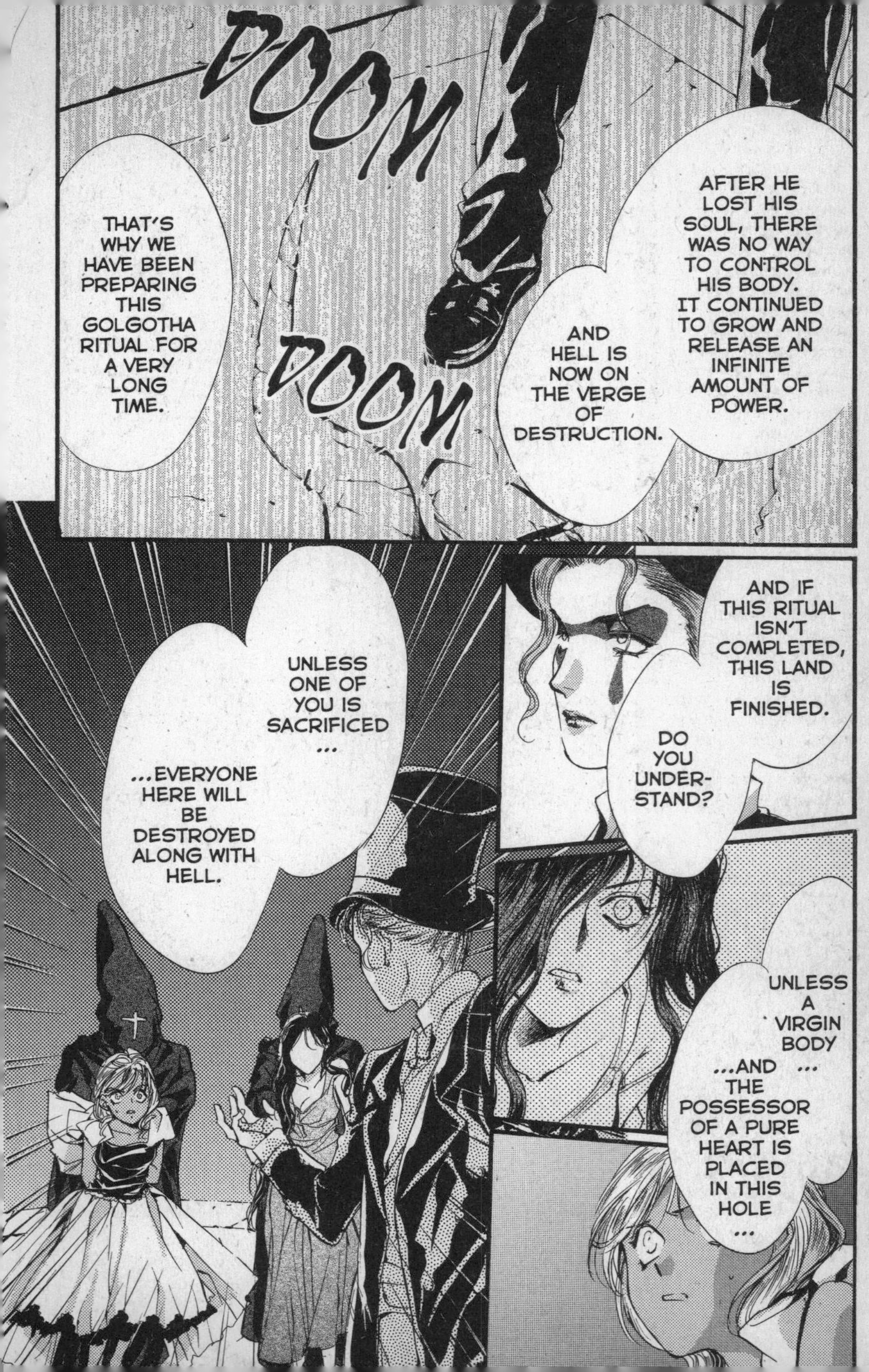
AFTER HE LOST HIS SOUL, THERE WAS NO WAY TO CONTROL HIS BODY. IT CONTINUED TO GROW AND RELEASE AN INFINITE AMOUNT OF POWER.
AND HELL IS NOW ON THE VERGE OF DESTRUCTION.
DOOM
DOOM
THAT'S WHY WE HAVE BEEN PREPARING THIS GOLGOTHA RITUAL FOR A VERY LONG TIME.
AND IF THIS RITUAL ISN'T COMPLETED, THIS LAND IS FINISHED.
DO YOU UNDER-STAND?
UNLESS A VIRGIN BODY ...
...AND THE POSSESSOR OF A PURE HEART IS PLACED IN THIS HOLE ...
UNLESS ONE OF YOU IS SACRIFICED ...
...EVERYONE HERE WILL BE DESTROYED ALONG WITH HELL.

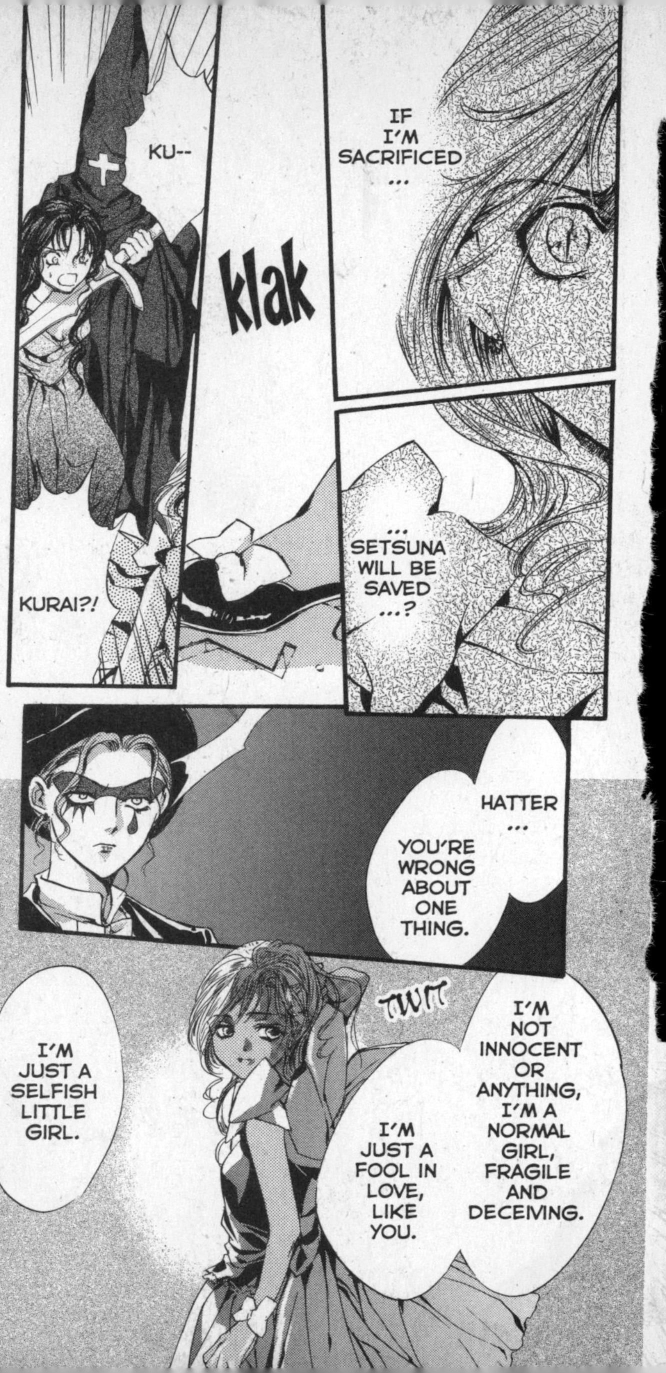
IF I'M SACRIFICED ...
... SETSUNA WILL BE SAVED ...?
KU--
klak
KURAI?!
HATTER ...
YOU'RE WRONG ABOUT ONE THING.
I'M NOT INNOCENT OR ANYTHING, I'M A NORMAL GIRL, FRAGILE AND DECEIVING.
I'M JUST A FOOL IN LOVE, LIKE YOU.
I'M JUST A SELFISH LITTLE GIRL.

We meet again. It's AS book 11! You'll see a picture of Astaroth below, but he won't be appearing in this book. I did receive cosplay pictures of both Astaroth and Hatter. The Astaroth one was so wonderful. And Hatter was kind of cute! Lord Astaroth scored pretty well in the character poll we ran in the magazine for someone who didn't appear much. I guess it was worth me talking about him a lot... Or maybe many people actually like him. Anyway, this saga reaches the climax in the next chapter... Well, I mean, it's over. And as always I didn't have enough pages and had to cram everything together. Well, enjoy reading it. Yeah.

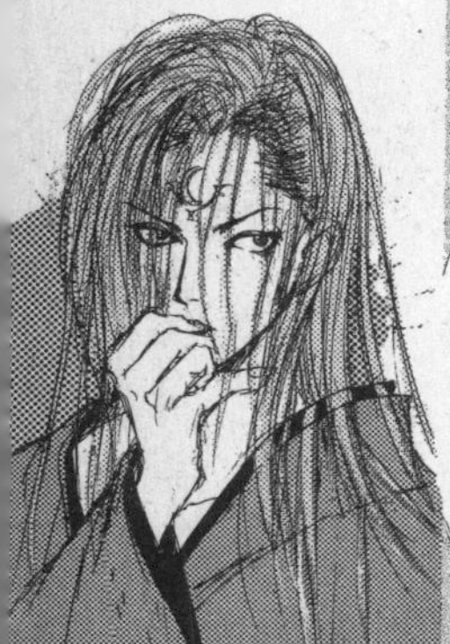

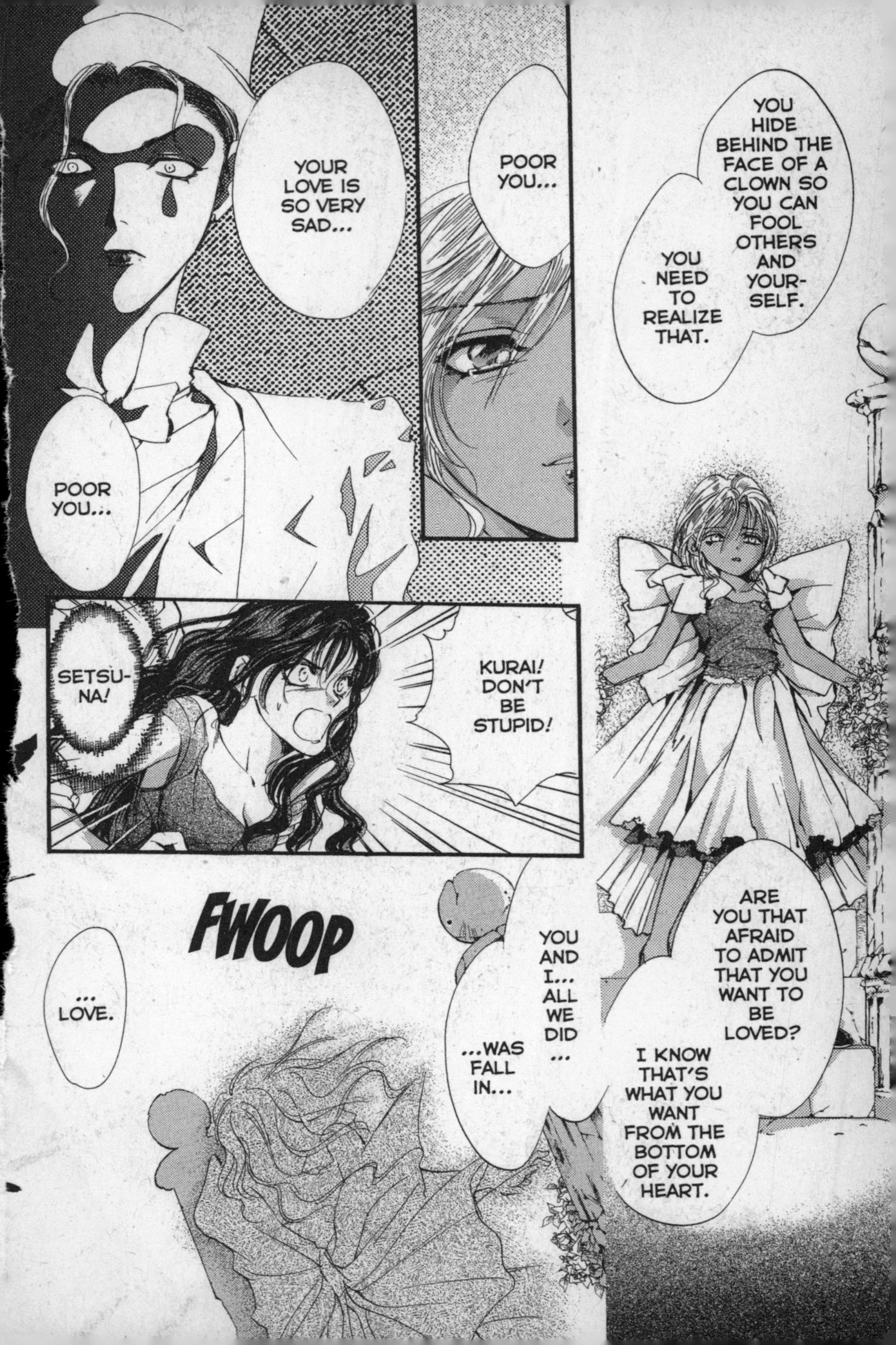
YOU HIDE BEHIND THE FACE OF A CLOWN SO YOU CAN FOOL OTHERS AND YOURSELF.
YOU NEED TO REALIZE THAT.
POOR YOU...
YOUR LOVE IS SO VERY SAD...
POOR YOU...
KURAI! DON'T BE STUPID!
SETSU-NA!
ARE YOU THAT AFRAID TO ADMIT THAT YOU WANT TO BE LOVED?
I KNOW THAT'S WHAT YOU WANT FROM THE BOTTOM OF YOUR HEART.
YOU AND I... ALL WE DID...
...WAS FALL IN...
FWOOP
...LOVE.

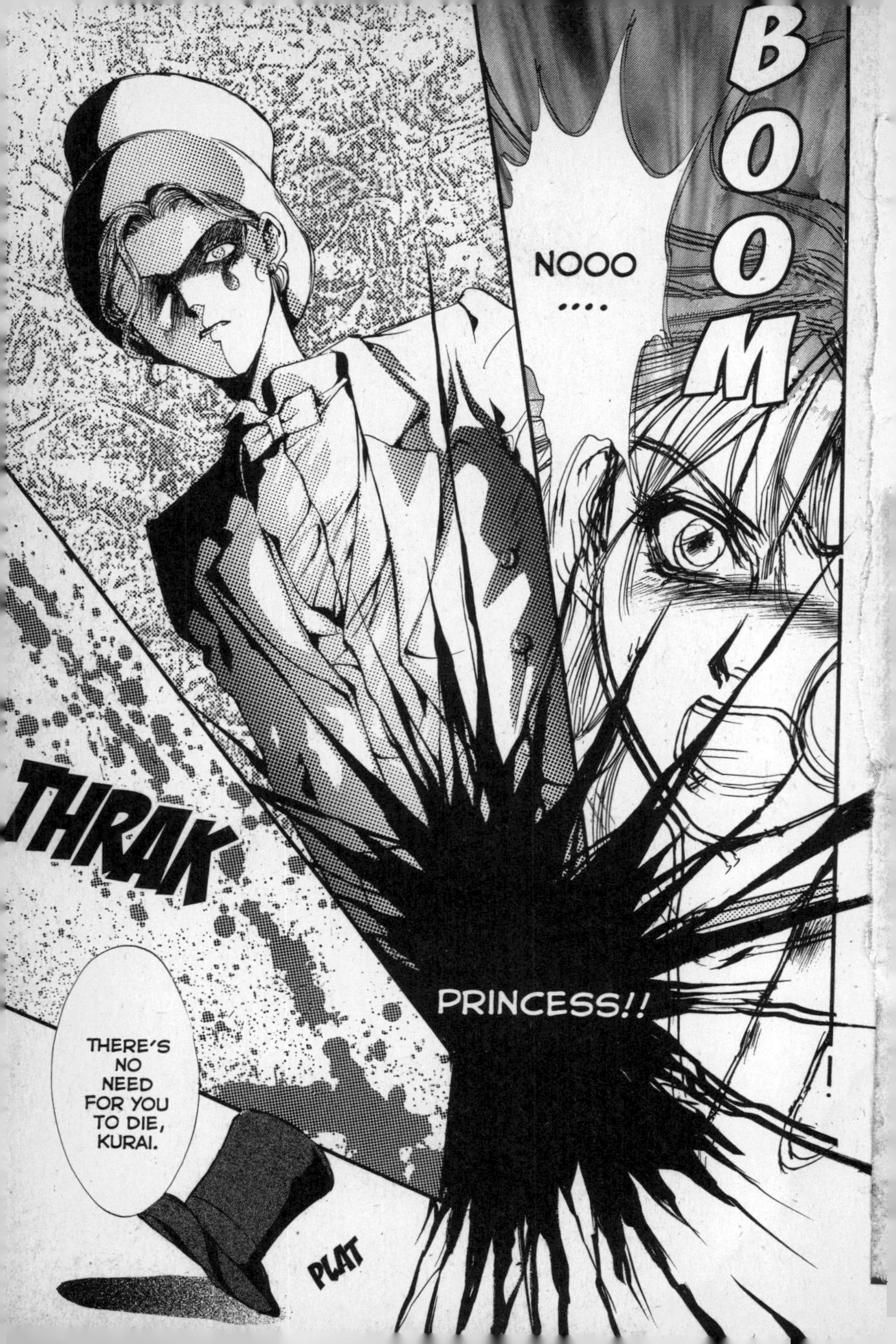
BOOM
NOOO ....
PRINCESS!!
!
THRAK
THERE'S NO NEED FOR YOU TO DIE, KURAI.
PLAT

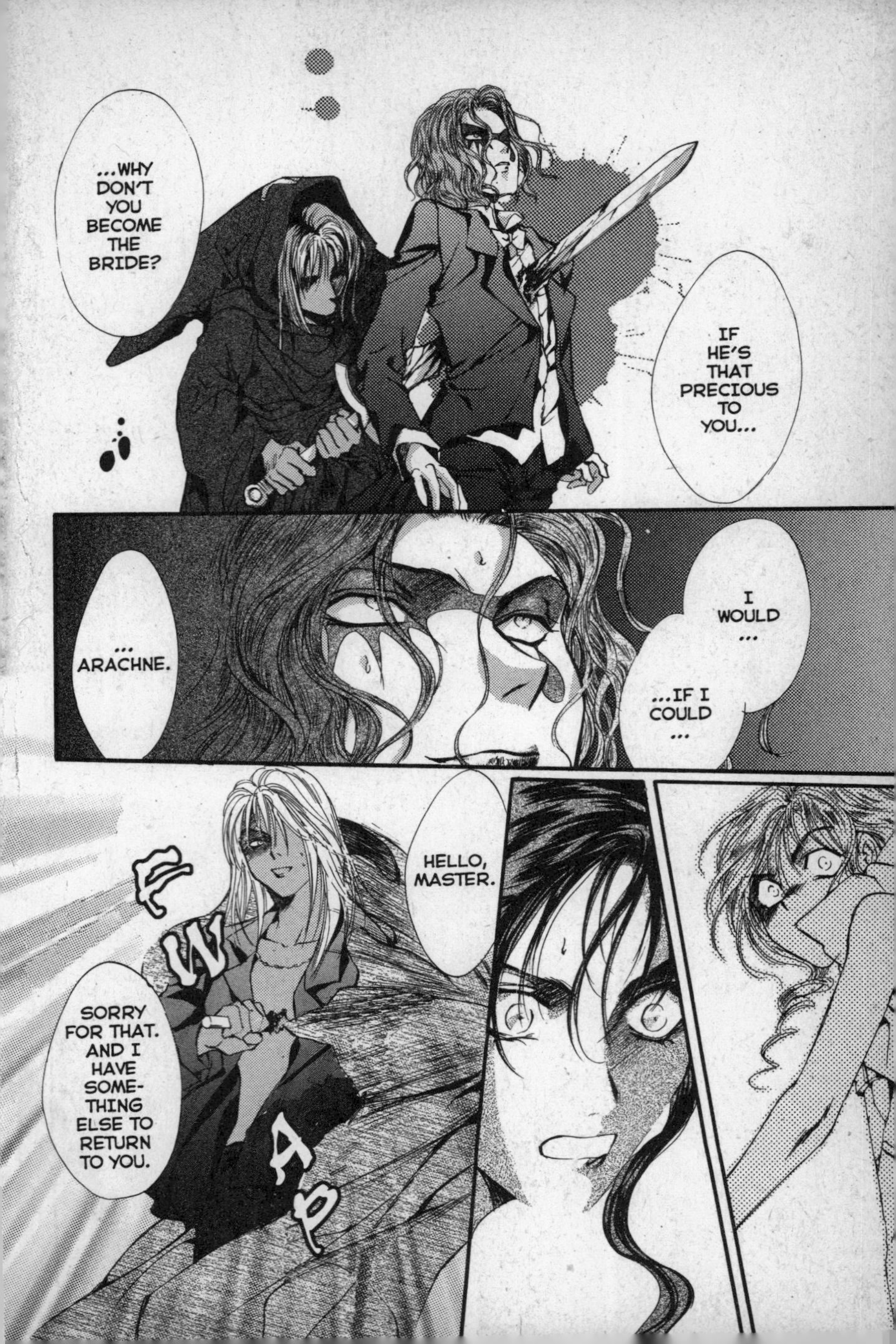
IF HE'S THAT PRECIOUS TO YOU...
...WHY DON'T YOU BECOME THE BRIDE?
I WOULD ...
...IF I COULD ...
... ARACHNE.
HELLO, MASTER.
SORRY FOR THAT. AND I HAVE SOME-THING ELSE TO RETURN TO YOU.

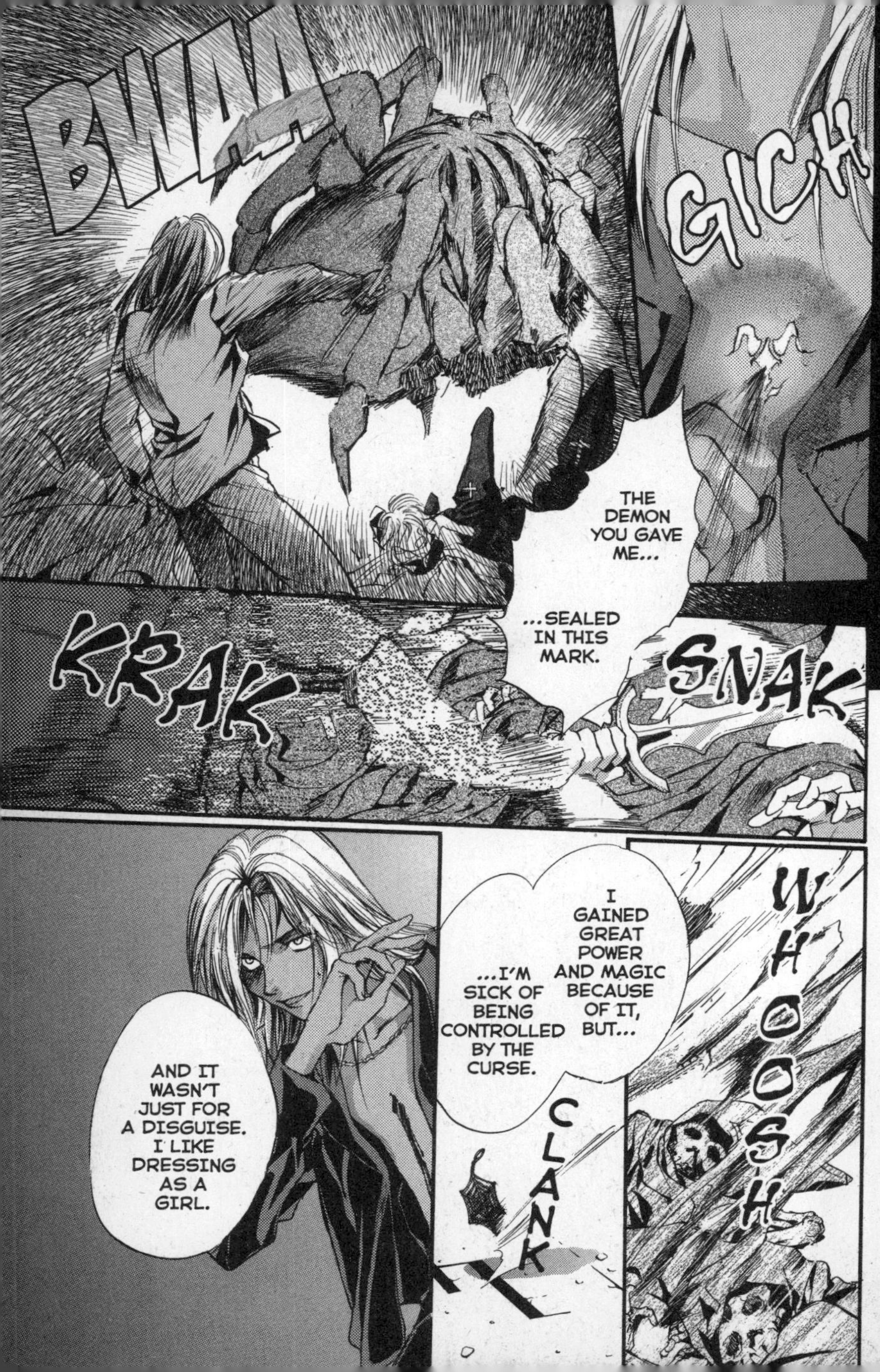
GICH
THE DEMON YOU GAVE ME...
BWAAA
...SEALED IN THIS MARK.
SNAK
KRAK
WHOOSH
I GAINED GREAT POWER AND MAGIC BECAUSE OF IT, BUT...
...I'M SICK OF BEING CONTROLLED BY THE CURSE.
CLANK
AND IT WASN'T JUST FOR A DISGUISE. I LIKE DRESSING AS A GIRL.

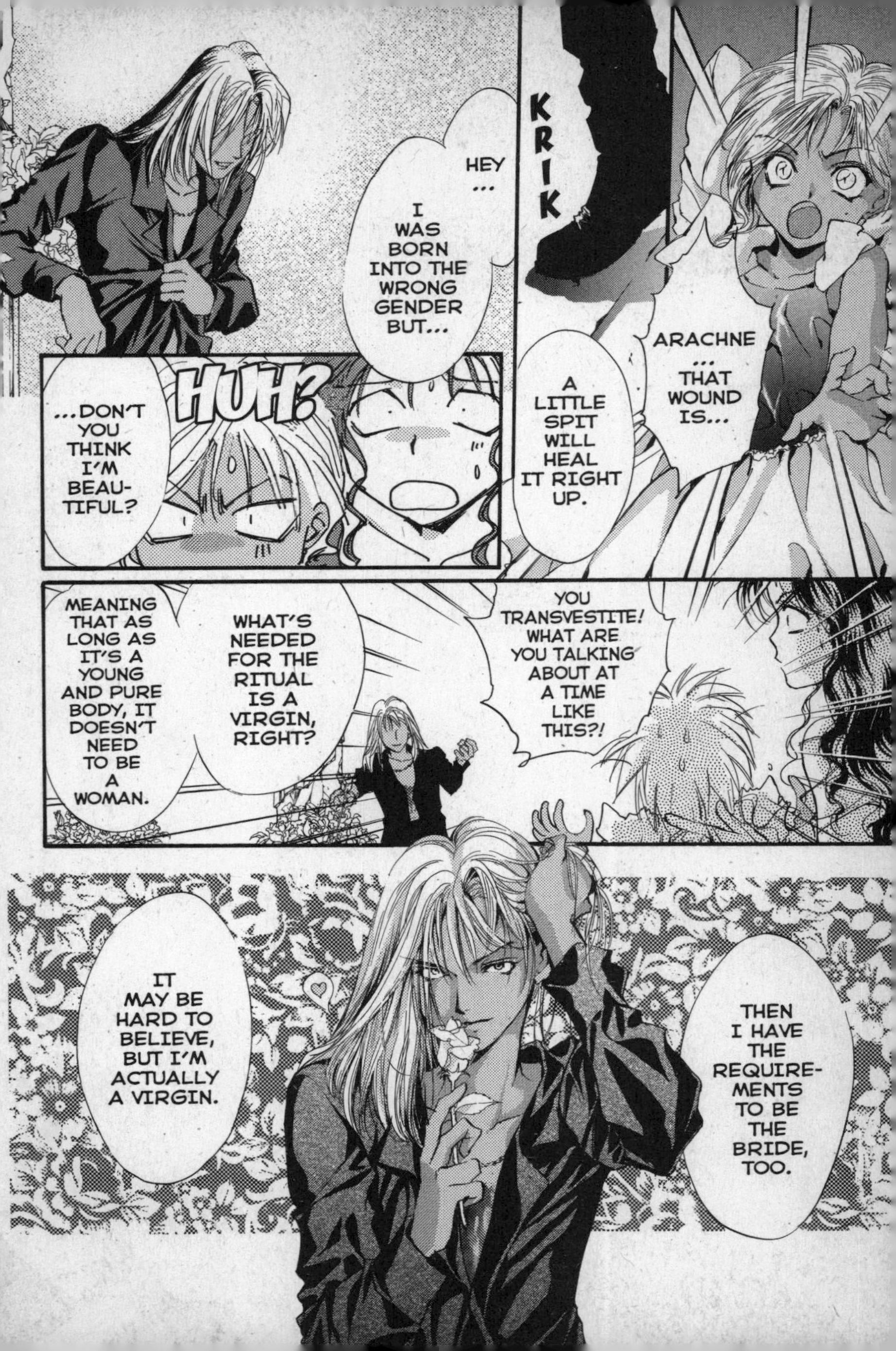
KRIK
ARACHNE ... THAT WOUND IS...
A LITTLE SPIT WILL HEAL IT RIGHT UP.
HEY ...
I WAS BORN INTO THE WRONG GENDER BUT...
HUH?
...DON'T YOU THINK I'M BEAUTIFUL?
YOU TRANSVESTITE! WHAT ARE YOU TALKING ABOUT AT A TIME LIKE THIS?!
WHAT'S NEEDED FOR THE RITUAL IS A VIRGIN, RIGHT?
MEANING THAT AS LONG AS IT'S A YOUNG AND PURE BODY, IT DOESN'T NEED TO BE A WOMAN.
IT MAY BE HARD TO BELIEVE, BUT I'M ACTUALLY A VIRGIN.
THEN I HAVE THE REQUIREMENTS TO BE THE BRIDE, TOO.

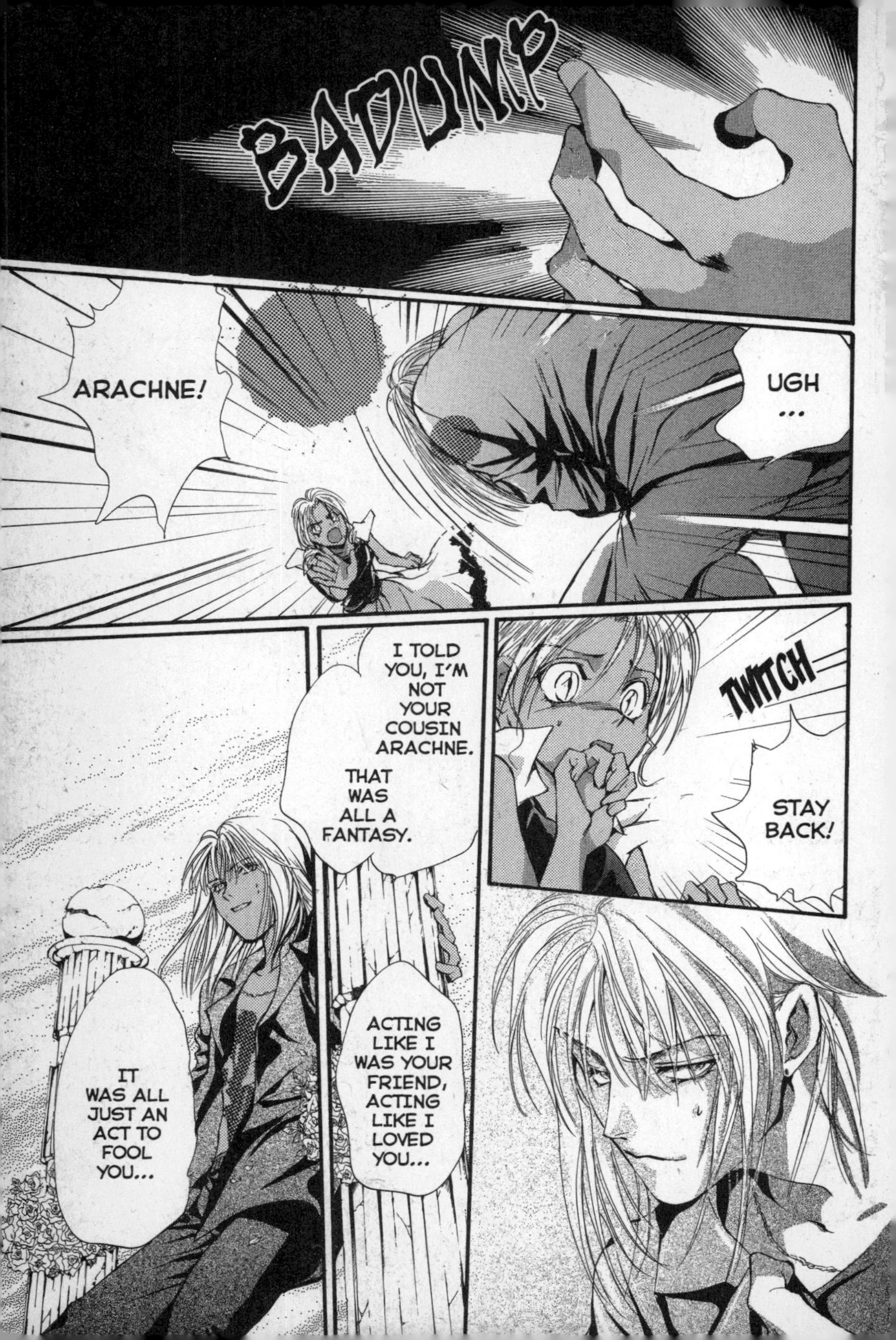
BADUMP
UGH ...
ARACHNE!
TWITCH
STAY BACK!
I TOLD YOU, I'M NOT YOUR COUSIN ARACHNE.
THAT WAS ALL A FANTASY.
ACTING LIKE I WAS YOUR FRIEND, ACTING LIKE I LOVED YOU...
IT WAS ALL JUST AN ACT TO FOOL YOU...

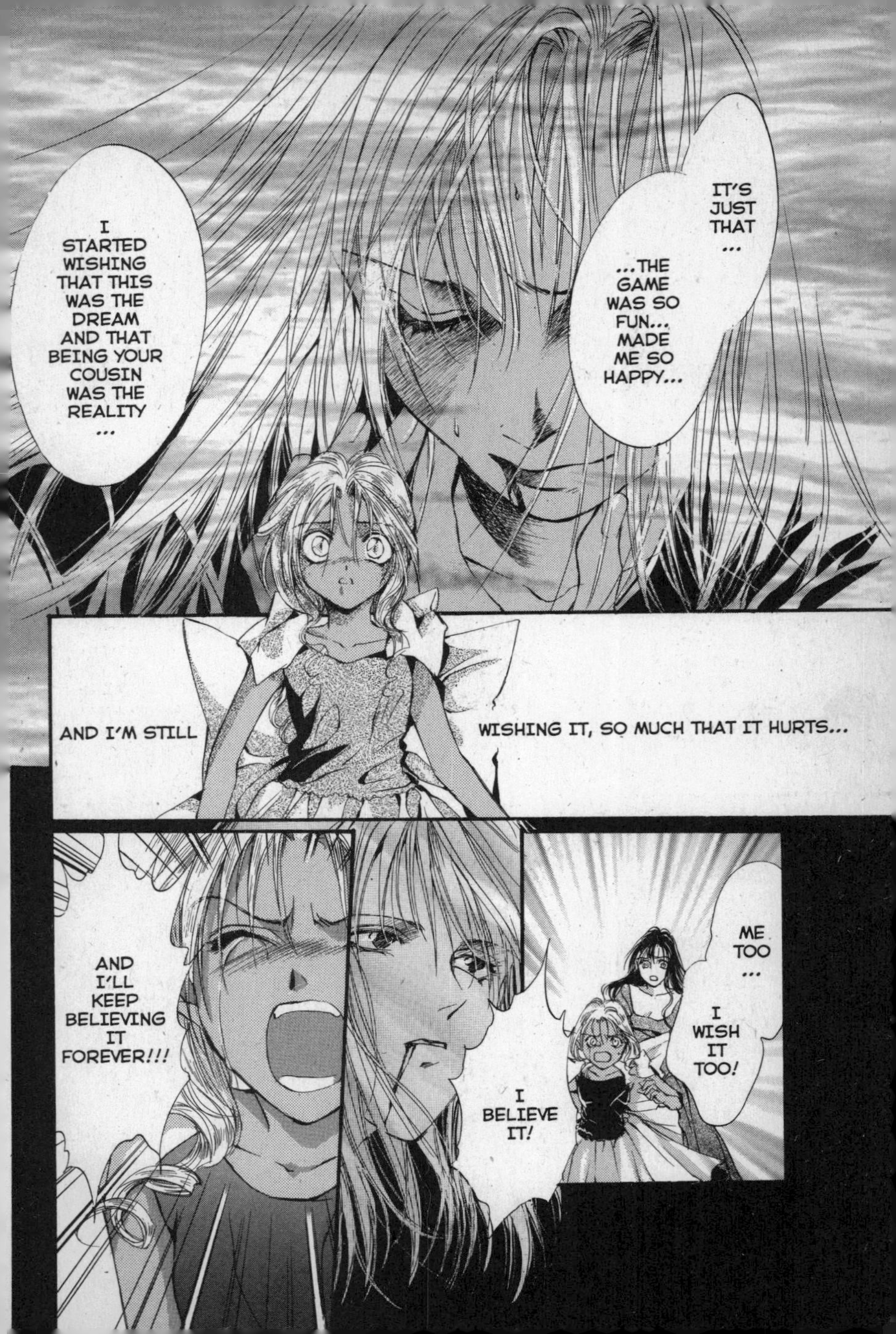
IT'S JUST THAT ...
...THE GAME WAS SO FUN... MADE ME SO HAPPY...
I STARTED WISHING THAT THIS WAS THE DREAM AND THAT BEING YOUR COUSIN WAS THE REALITY ...
AND I'M STILL
WISHING IT, SO MUCH THAT IT HURTS...
ME TOO ...
I WISH IT TOO!
I BELIEVE IT!
AND I'LL KEEP BELIEVING IT FOREVER!!!

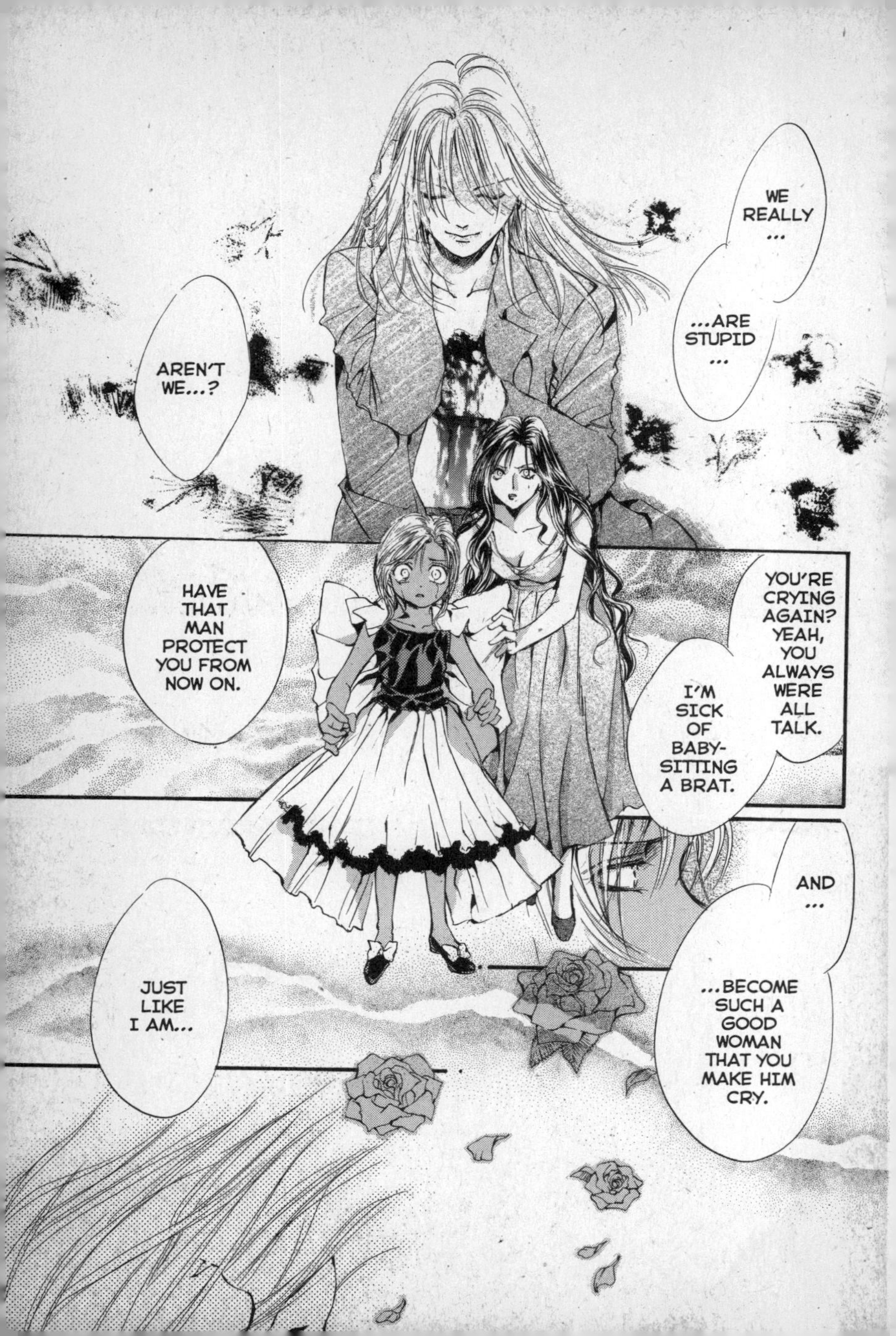
WE REALLY ...
...ARE STUPID ...
AREN'T WE...?
YOU'RE CRYING AGAIN? YEAH, YOU ALWAYS WERE ALL TALK.
I'M SICK OF BABY-SITTING A BRAT.
HAVE THAT MAN PROTECT YOU FROM NOW ON.
AND ...
...BECOME SUCH A GOOD WOMAN THAT YOU MAKE HIM CRY.
JUST LIKE I AM...

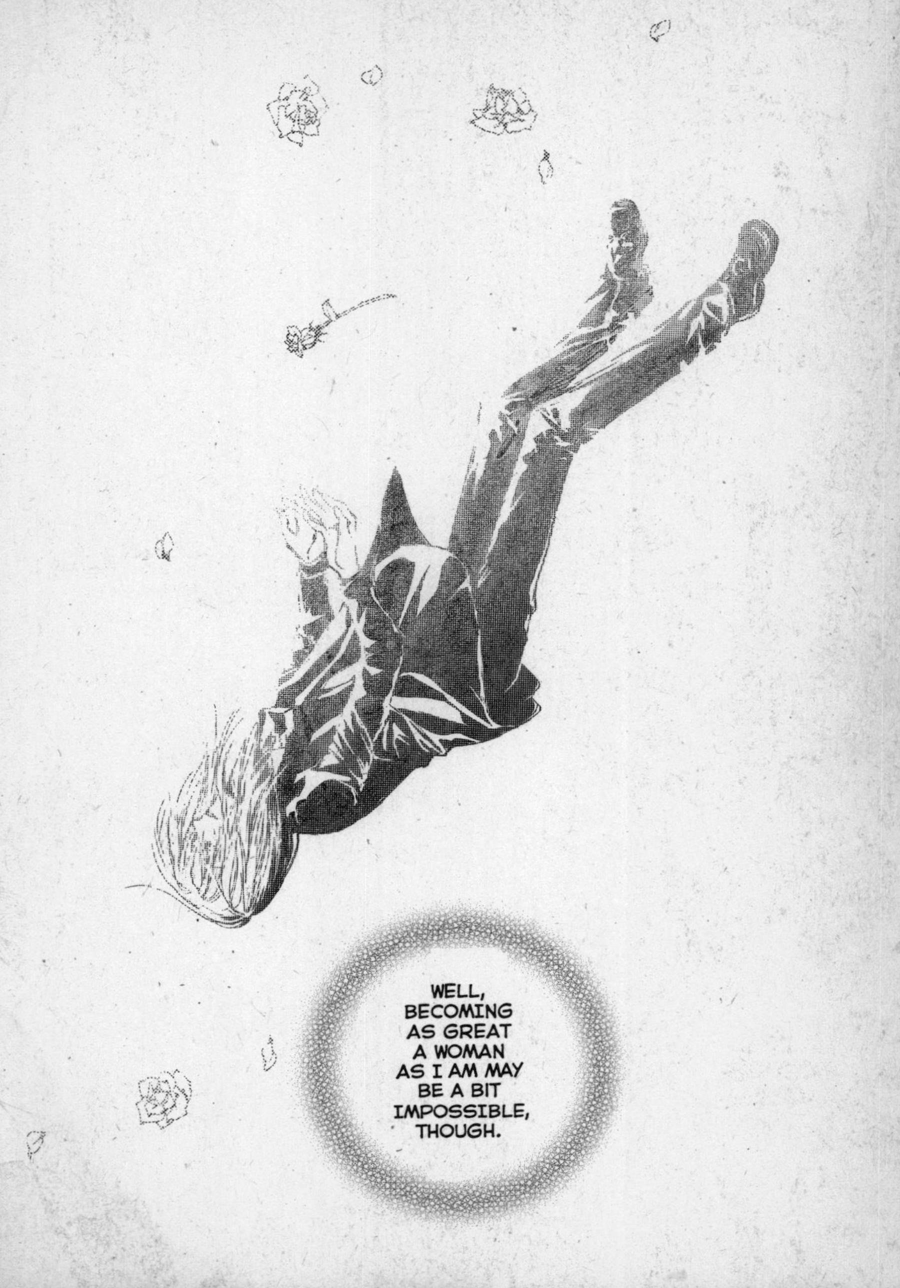
WELL, BECOMING AS GREAT A WOMAN AS I AM MAY BE A BIT IMPOSSIBLE, THOUGH.

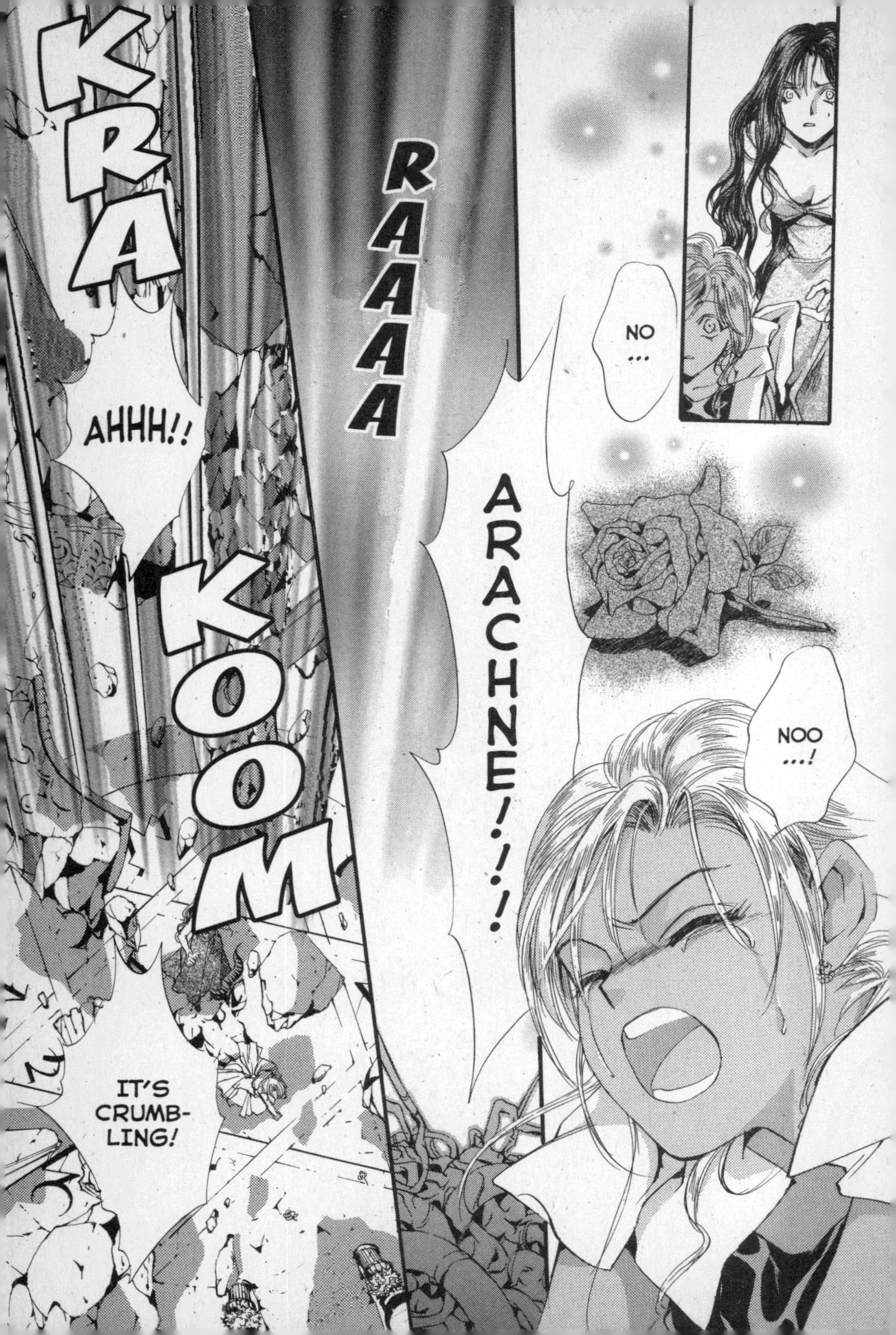
NO ...
NOO ...!
ARACHNE!!!
RAAAA
KRA
AHHH!!
KOOM
IT'S CRUMBLING!

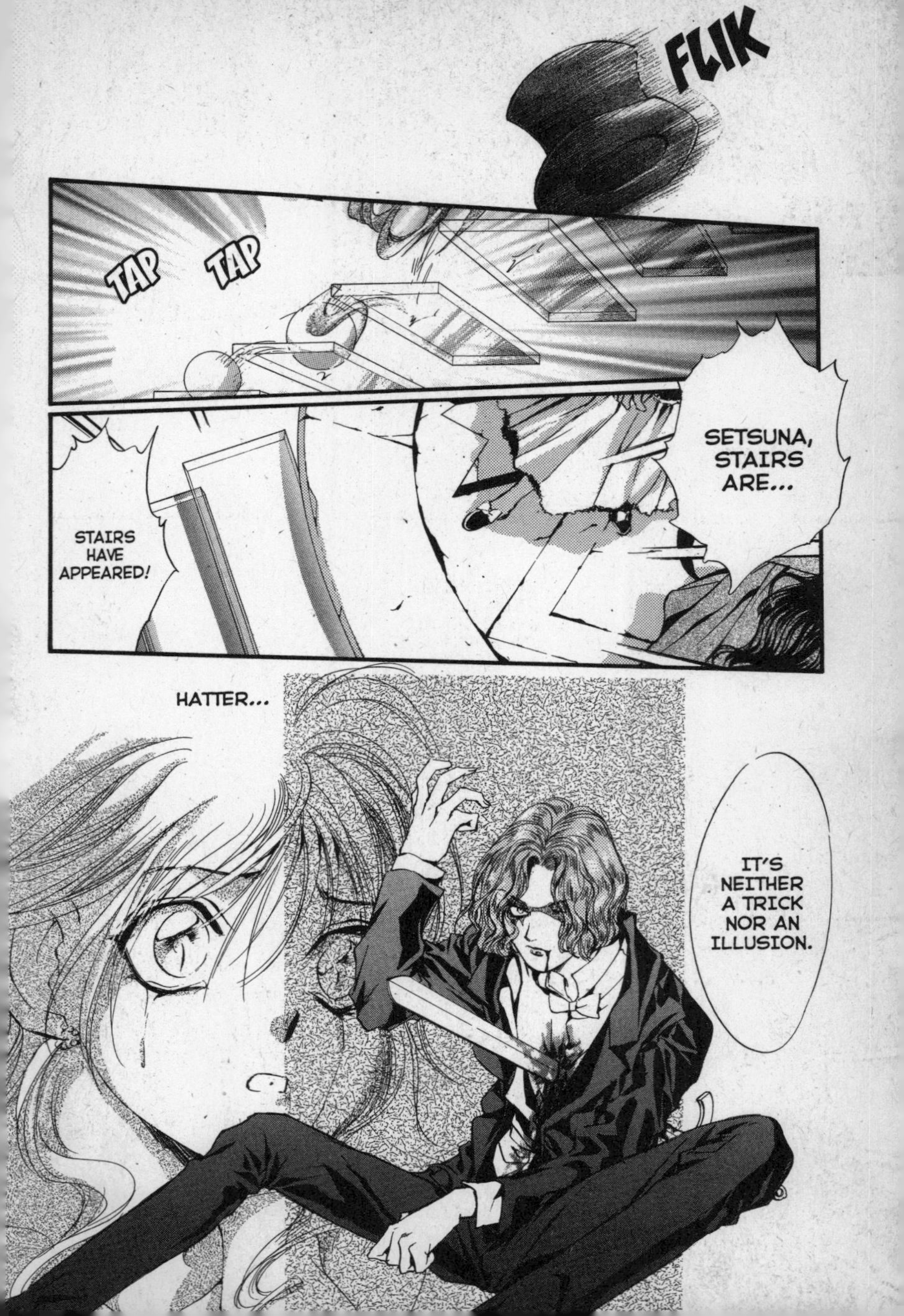
FLIK
TAP TAP
SETSUNA, STAIRS ARE...
STAIRS HAVE APPEARED!
IT'S NEITHER A TRICK NOR AN ILLUSION.
HATTER...

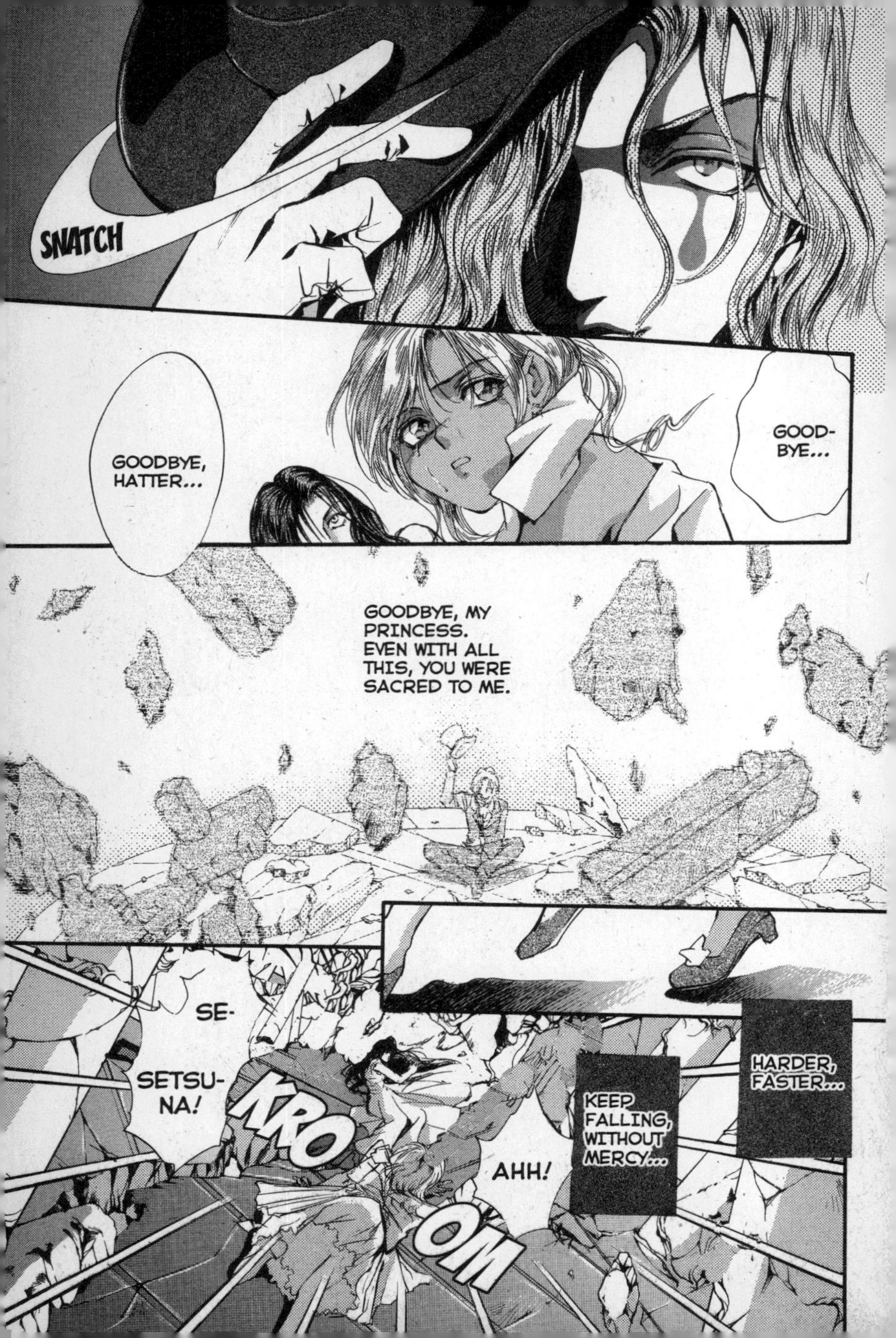
SNATCH
GOOD-BYE...
GOODBYE, HATTER...
GOODBYE, MY PRINCESS. EVEN WITH ALL THIS, YOU WERE SACRED TO ME.
HARDER, FASTER...
KEEP FALLING, WITHOUT MERCY...
SE-
SETSU-NA!
KROOM
AHH!

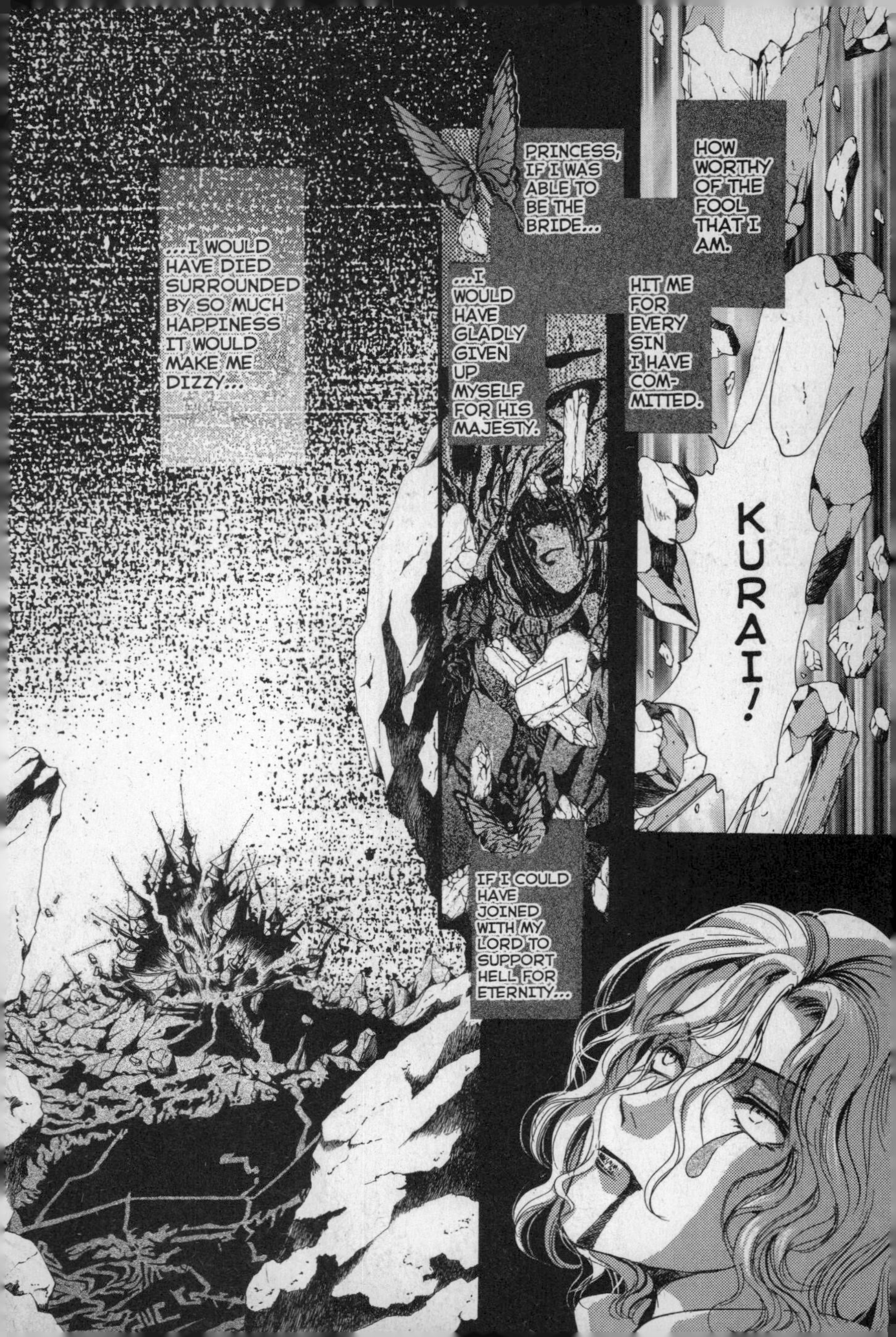
HOW WORTHY OF THE FOOL THAT I AM.
HIT ME FOR EVERY SIN I HAVE COM-MITTED.
KURAI!
PRINCESS, IF I WAS ABLE TO BE THE BRIDE...
...I WOULD HAVE GLADLY GIVEN UP MYSELF FOR HIS MAJESTY.
IF I COULD HAVE JOINED WITH MY LORD TO SUPPORT HELL FOR ETERNITY...
...I WOULD HAVE DIED SURROUNDED BY SO MUCH HAPPINESS IT WOULD MAKE ME DIZZY...

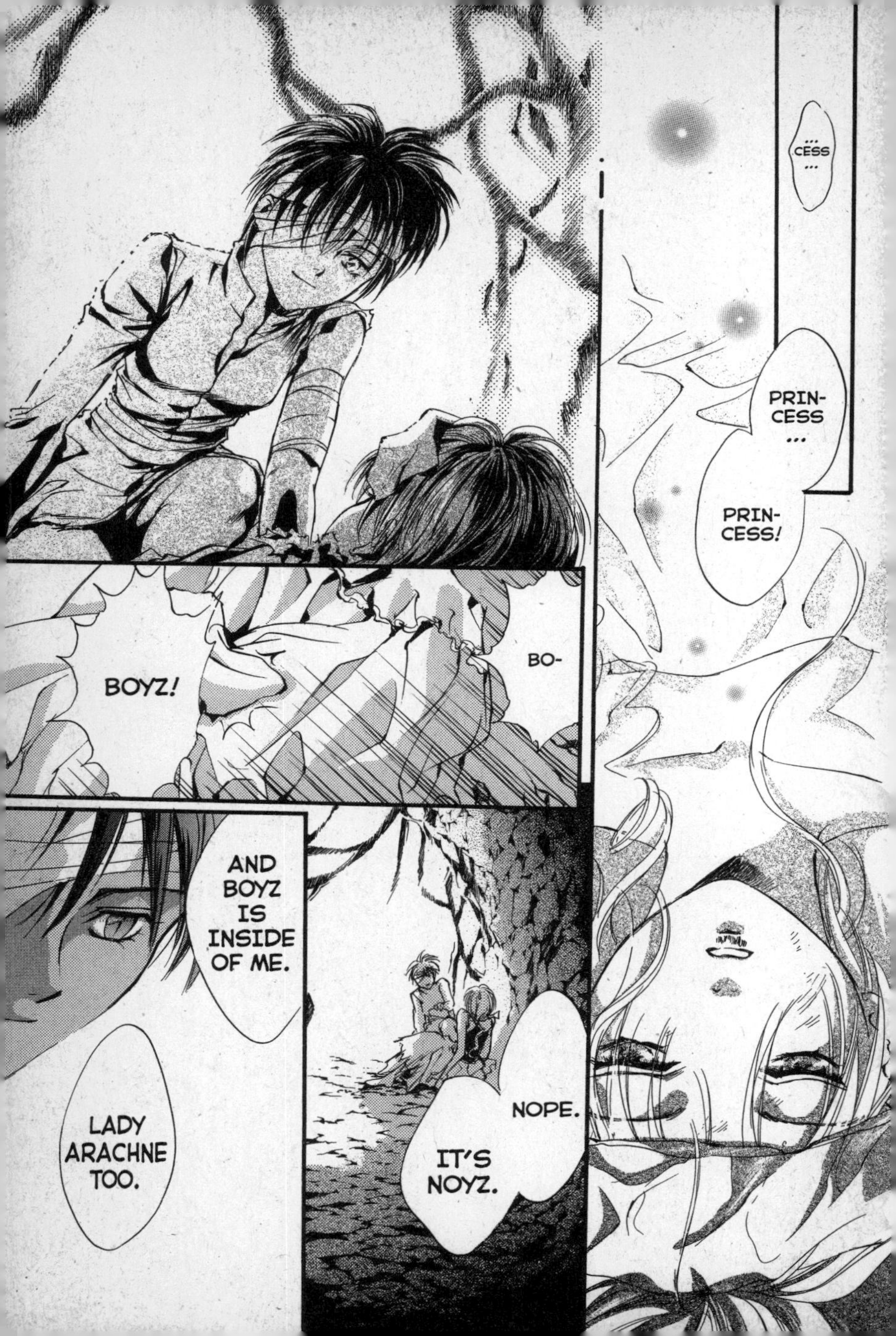
...CESS...
PRINCESS...
PRINCESS!
BO-
BOYZ!
NOPE.
IT'S NOYZ.
AND BOYZ IS INSIDE OF ME.
LADY ARACHNE TOO.

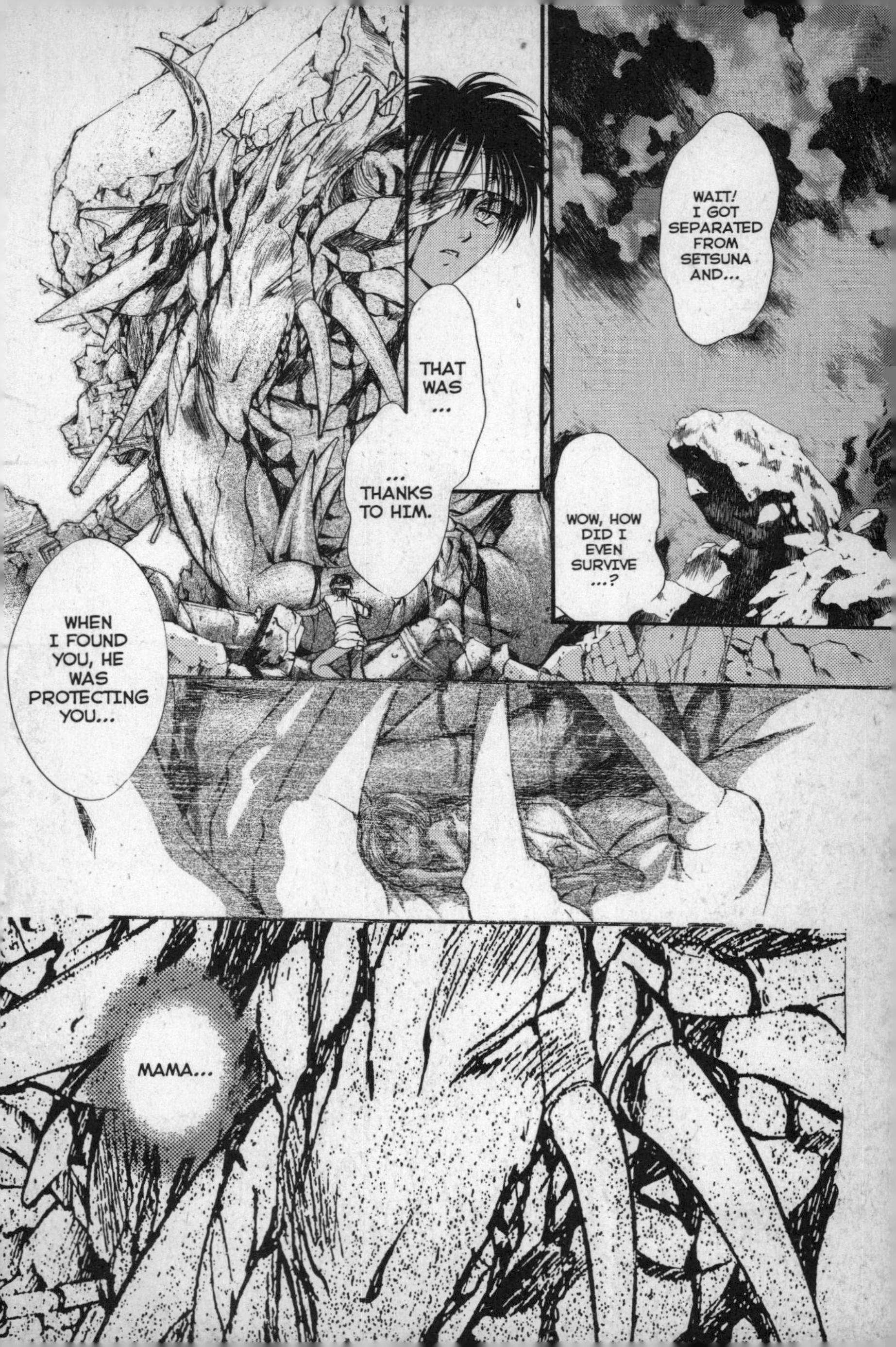
WAIT! I GOT SEPARATED FROM SETSUNA AND...
WOW, HOW DID I EVEN SURVIVE ...?
THAT WAS ...
... THANKS TO HIM.
WHEN I FOUND YOU, HE WAS PROTECTING YOU...
MAMA...

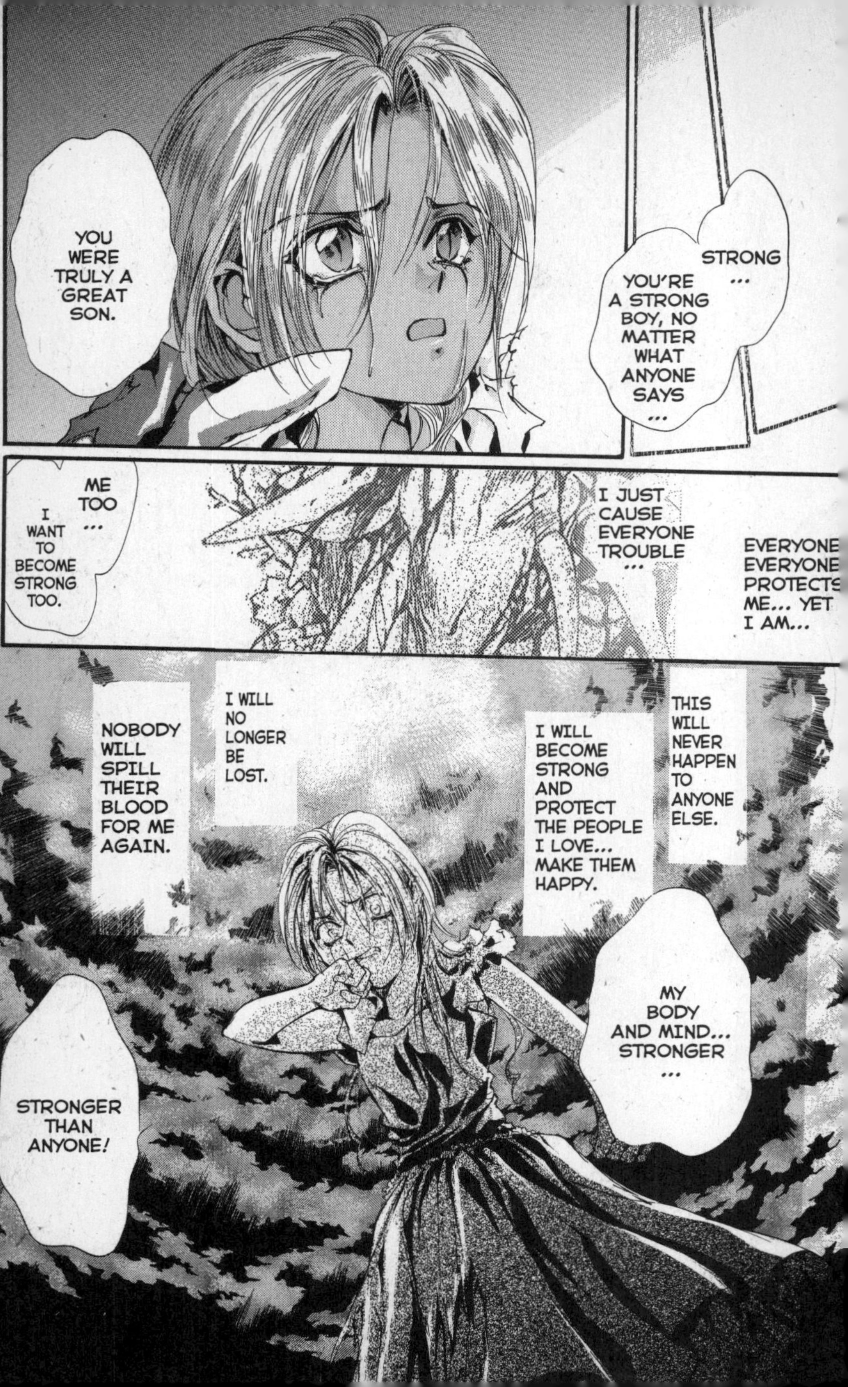
STRONG ...
YOU'RE A STRONG BOY, NO MATTER WHAT ANYONE SAYS ...
YOU WERE TRULY A GREAT SON.
EVERYONE EVERYONE PROTECTS ME... YET I AM...
I JUST CAUSE EVERYONE TROUBLE ...
ME TOO ...
I WANT TO BECOME STRONG TOO.
THIS WILL NEVER HAPPEN TO ANYONE ELSE.
I WILL BECOME STRONG AND PROTECT THE PEOPLE I LOVE... MAKE THEM HAPPY.
I WILL NO LONGER BE LOST.
NOBODY WILL SPILL THEIR BLOOD FOR ME AGAIN.
MY BODY AND MIND... STRONGER ...
STRONGER THAN ANYONE!

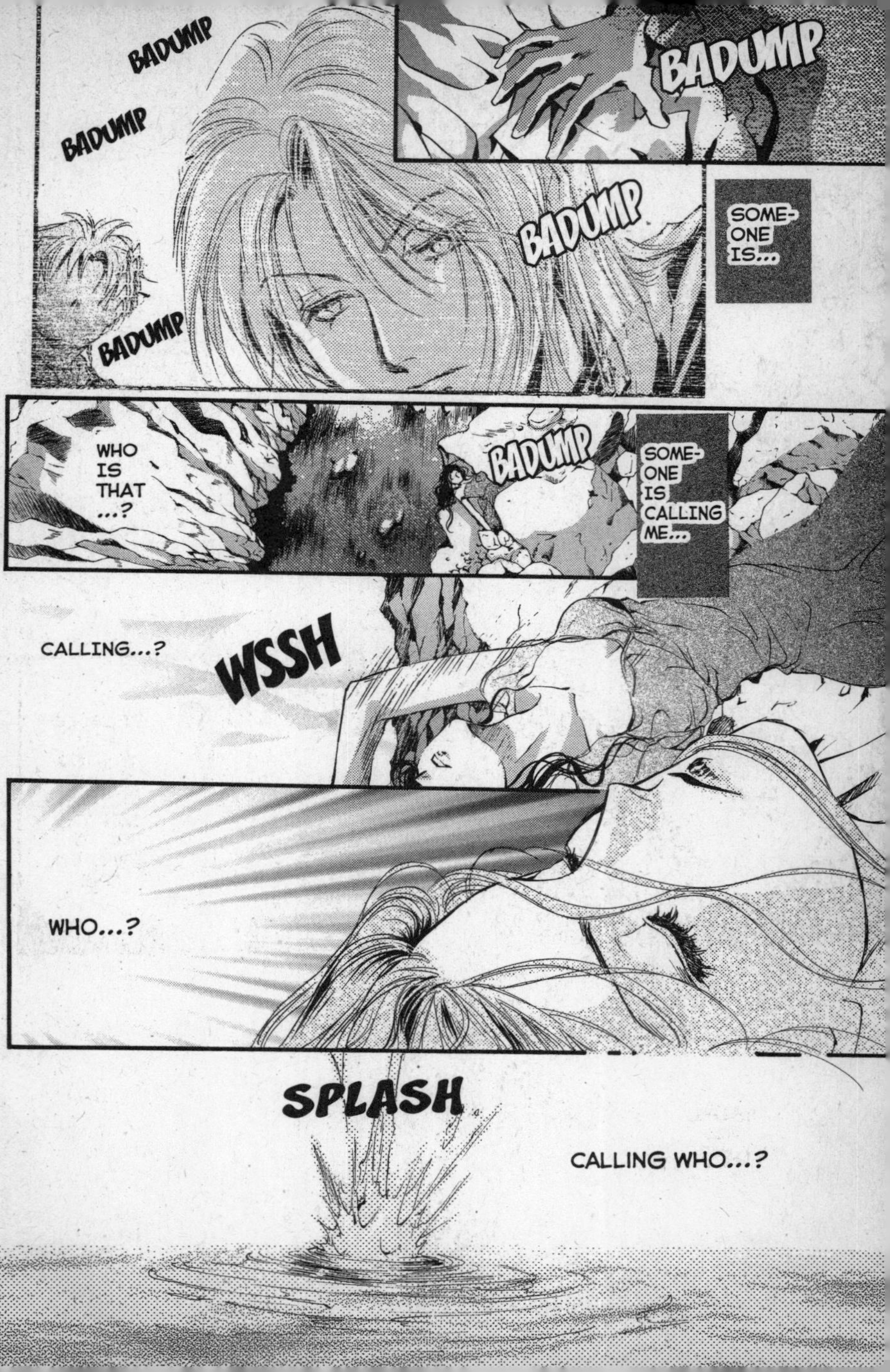
BADUMP
SOME-ONE IS...
BADUMP
BADUMP
BADUMP
BADUMP
SOME-ONE IS CALLING ME...
BADUMP
WHO IS THAT ...?
WSSH
CALLING...?
WHO...?
SPLASH
CALLING WHO...?

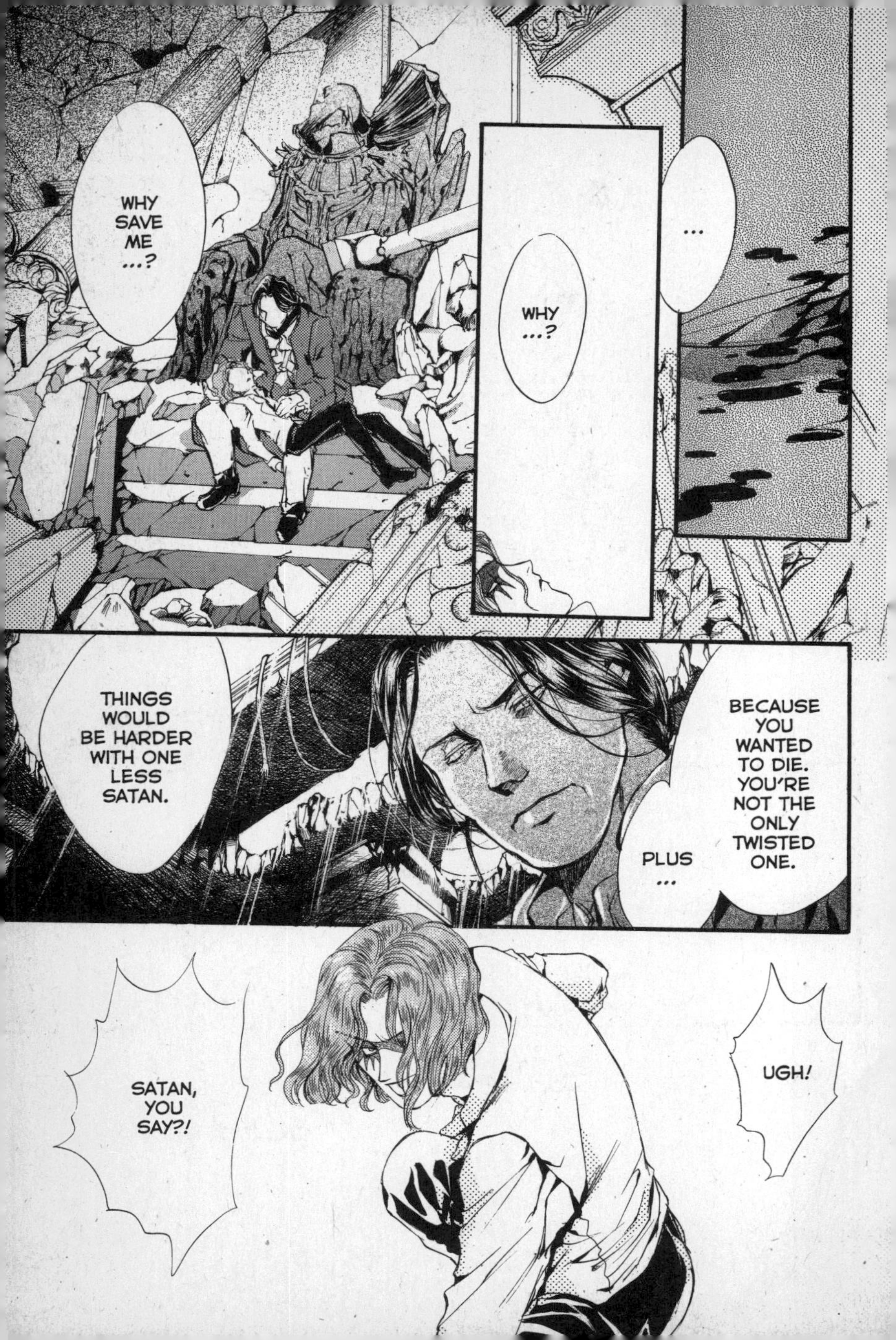
...
WHY ...?
WHY SAVE ME ...?
BECAUSE YOU WANTED TO DIE. YOU'RE NOT THE ONLY TWISTED ONE.
PLUS ...
THINGS WOULD BE HARDER WITH ONE LESS SATAN.
UGH!
SATAN, YOU SAY?!

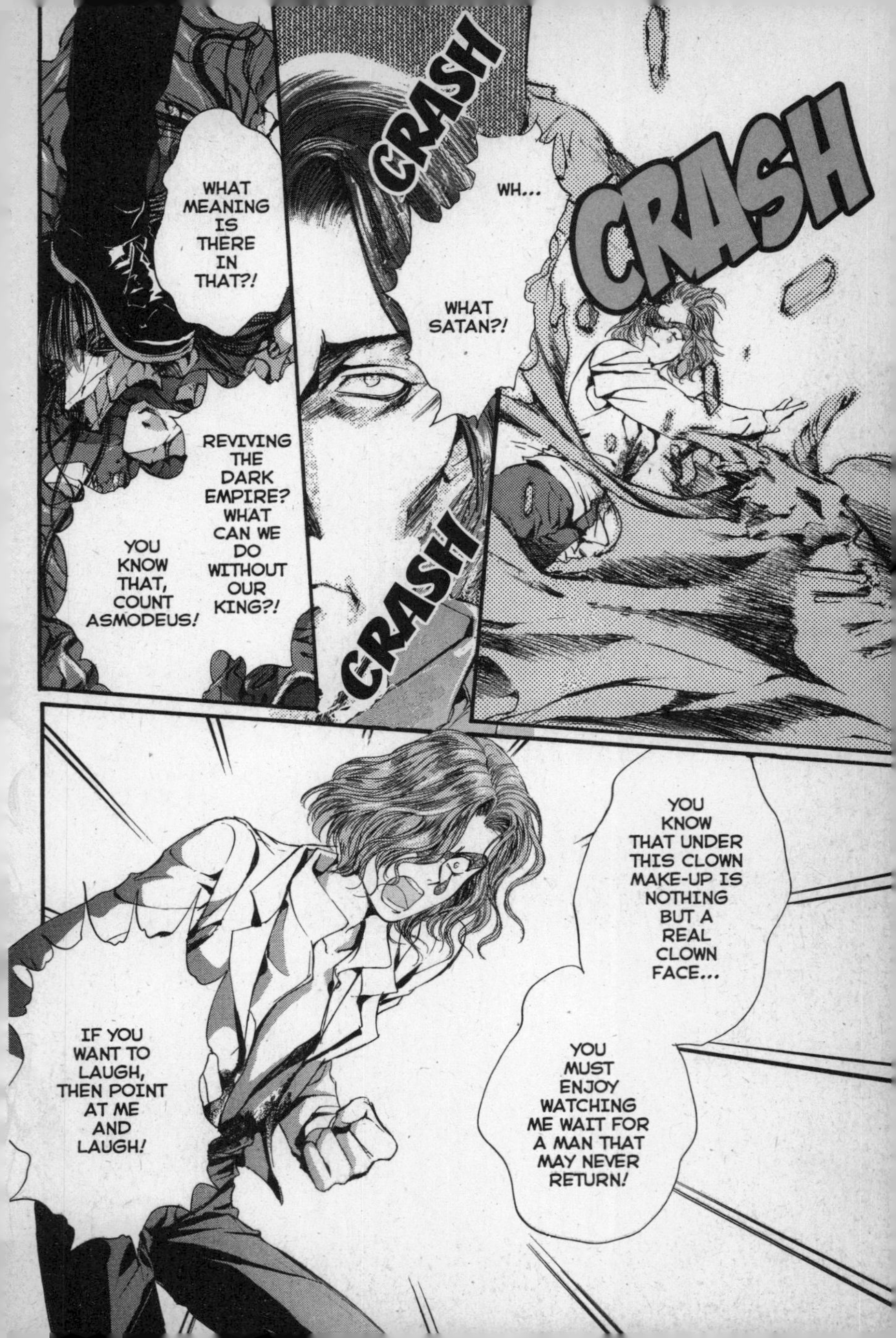
CRASH
WH...
CRASH
WHAT SATAN?!
CRASH
WHAT MEANING IS THERE IN THAT?!
REVIVING THE DARK EMPIRE? WHAT CAN WE DO WITHOUT OUR KING?!
YOU KNOW THAT, COUNT ASMODEUS!
YOU KNOW THAT UNDER THIS CLOWN MAKE-UP IS NOTHING BUT A REAL CLOWN FACE...
YOU MUST ENJOY WATCHING ME WAIT FOR A MAN THAT MAY NEVER RETURN!
IF YOU WANT TO LAUGH, THEN POINT AT ME AND LAUGH!

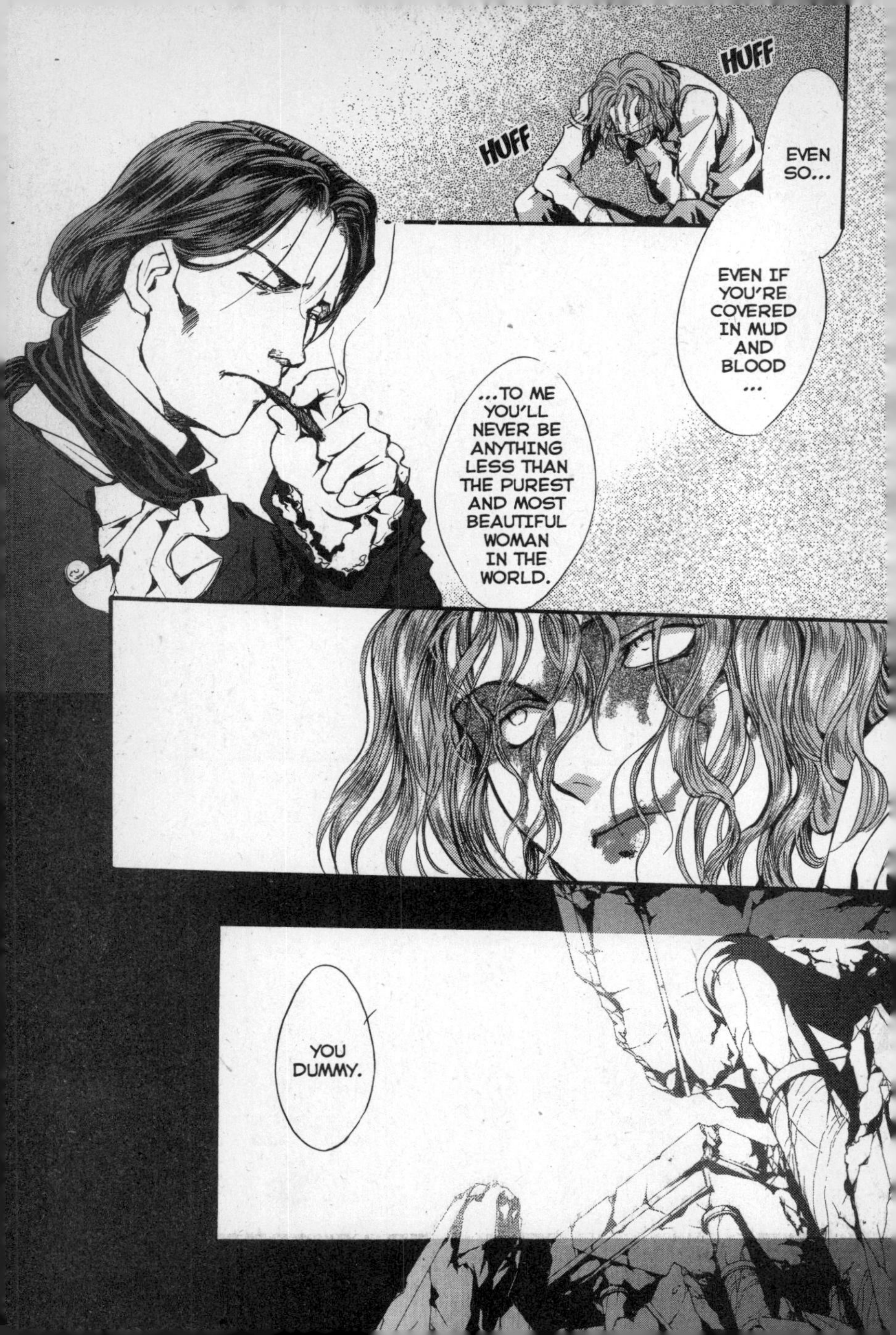
HUFF
HUFF
EVEN SO...
EVEN IF YOU'RE COVERED IN MUD AND BLOOD ...
...TO ME YOU'LL NEVER BE ANYTHING LESS THAN THE PUREST AND MOST BEAUTIFUL WOMAN IN THE WORLD.
YOU DUMMY.

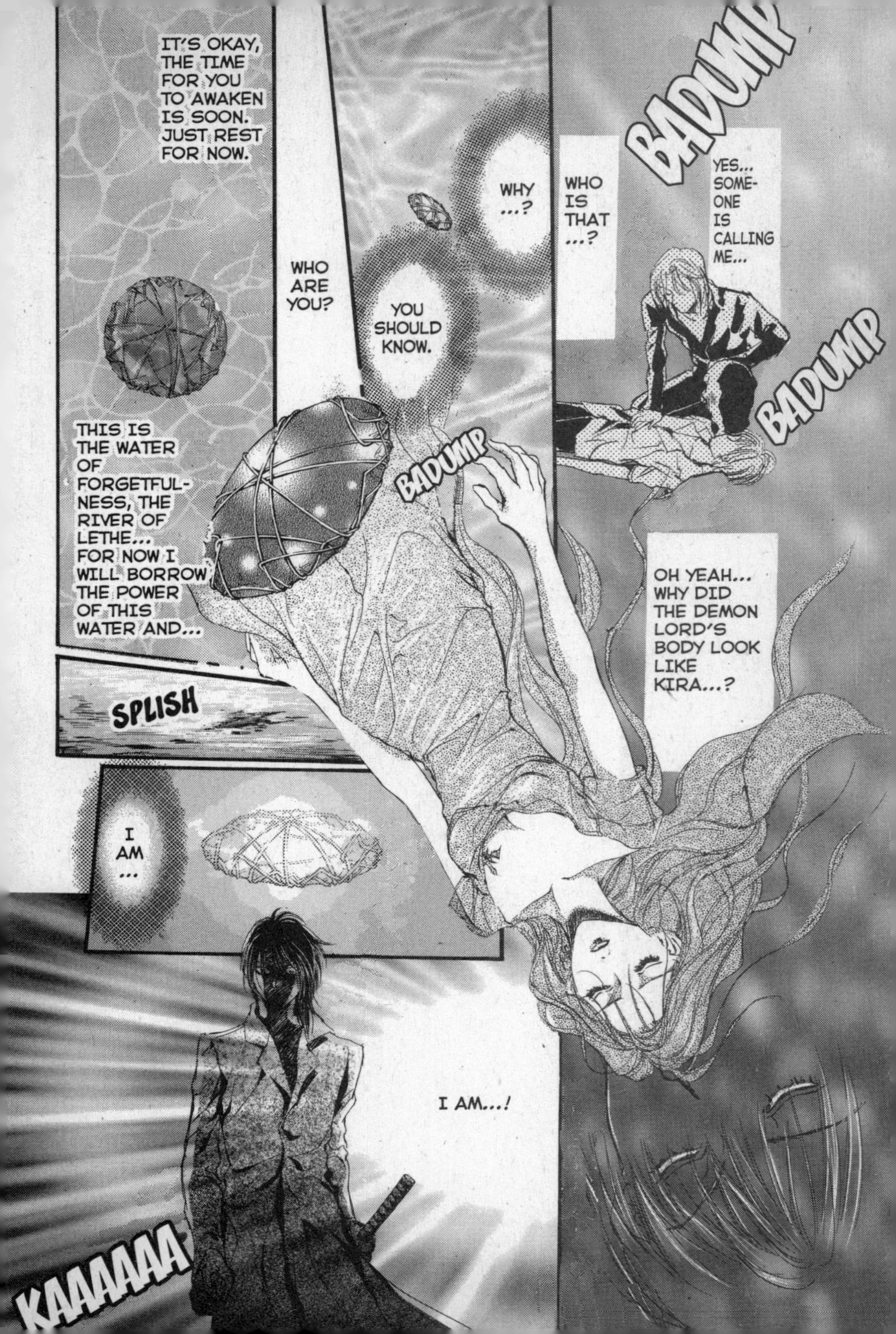
BADUMP
YES... SOMEONE IS CALLING ME...
BADUMP
WHO IS THAT ...?
WHY ...?
YOU SHOULD KNOW.
WHO ARE YOU?
IT'S OKAY, THE TIME FOR YOU TO AWAKEN IS SOON. JUST REST FOR NOW.
THIS IS THE WATER OF FORGETFULNESS, THE RIVER OF LETHE... FOR NOW I WILL BORROW THE POWER OF THIS WATER AND...
BADUMP
OH YEAH... WHY DID THE DEMON LORD'S BODY LOOK LIKE KIRA...?
SPLISH
I AM ...
I AM...!
KAAAAAA

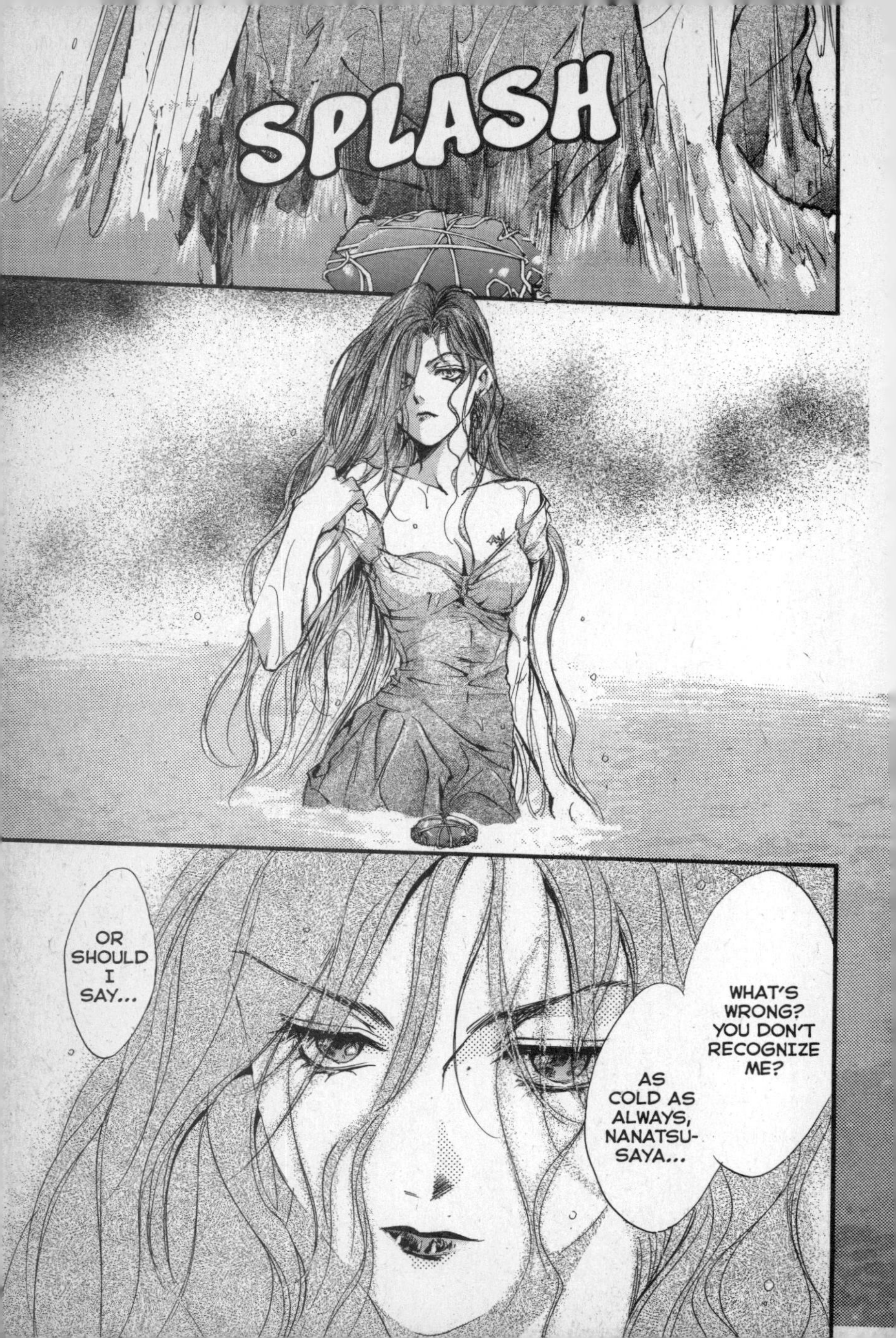
SPLASH
WHAT'S WRONG? YOU DON'T RECOGNIZE ME?
AS COLD AS ALWAYS, NANATSU-SAYA...
OR SHOULD I SAY...

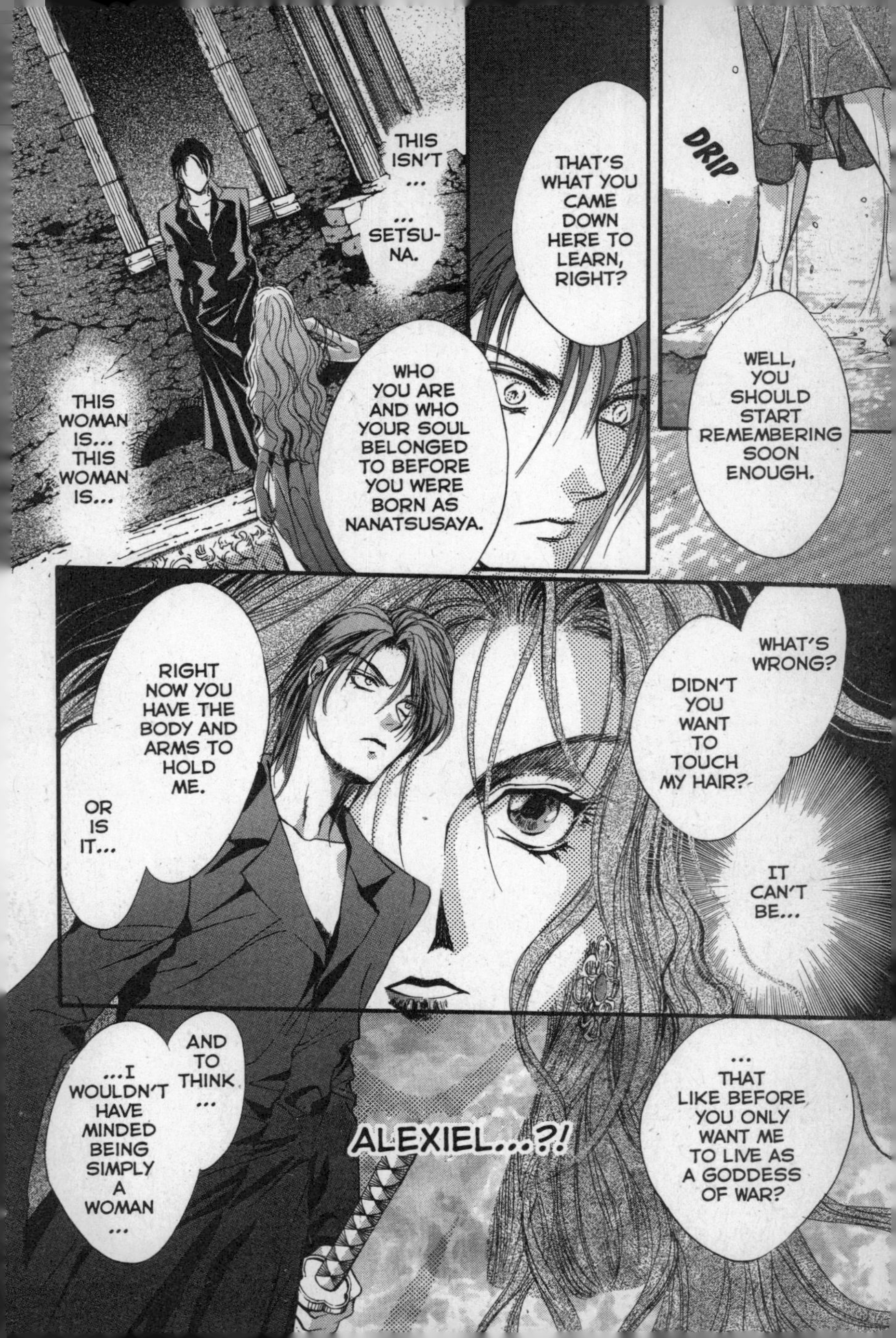
DRIP
WELL, YOU SHOULD START REMEMBERING SOON ENOUGH.
THAT'S WHAT YOU CAME DOWN HERE TO LEARN, RIGHT?
WHO YOU ARE AND WHO YOUR SOUL BELONGED TO BEFORE YOU WERE BORN AS NANATSUSAYA.
THIS ISN'T ...
... SETSU-NA.
THIS WOMAN IS... THIS WOMAN IS...
WHAT'S WRONG?
DIDN'T YOU WANT TO TOUCH MY HAIR?
IT CAN'T BE...
RIGHT NOW YOU HAVE THE BODY AND ARMS TO HOLD ME.
OR IS IT...
... THAT LIKE BEFORE YOU ONLY WANT ME TO LIVE AS A GODDESS OF WAR?
ALEXIEL...?!
AND TO THINK ...
...I WOULDN'T HAVE MINDED BEING SIMPLY A WOMAN ...

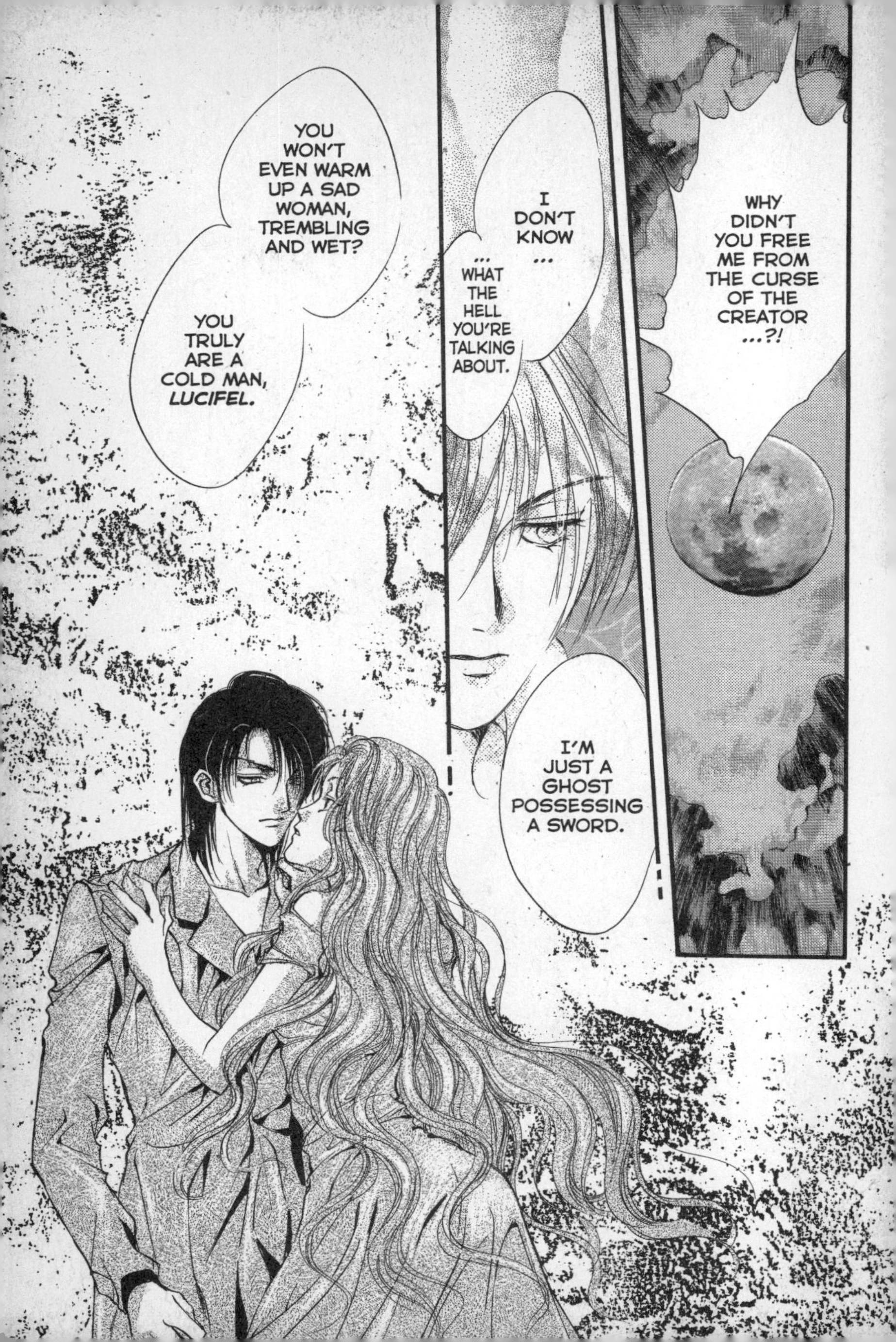
WHY DIDN'T YOU FREE ME FROM THE CURSE OF THE CREATOR ...?!
I DON'T KNOW ...
... WHAT THE HELL YOU'RE TALKING ABOUT.
I'M JUST A GHOST POSSESSING A SWORD.
YOU WON'T EVEN WARM UP A SAD WOMAN, TREMBLING AND WET?
YOU TRULY ARE A COLD MAN, *LUCIFEL.*

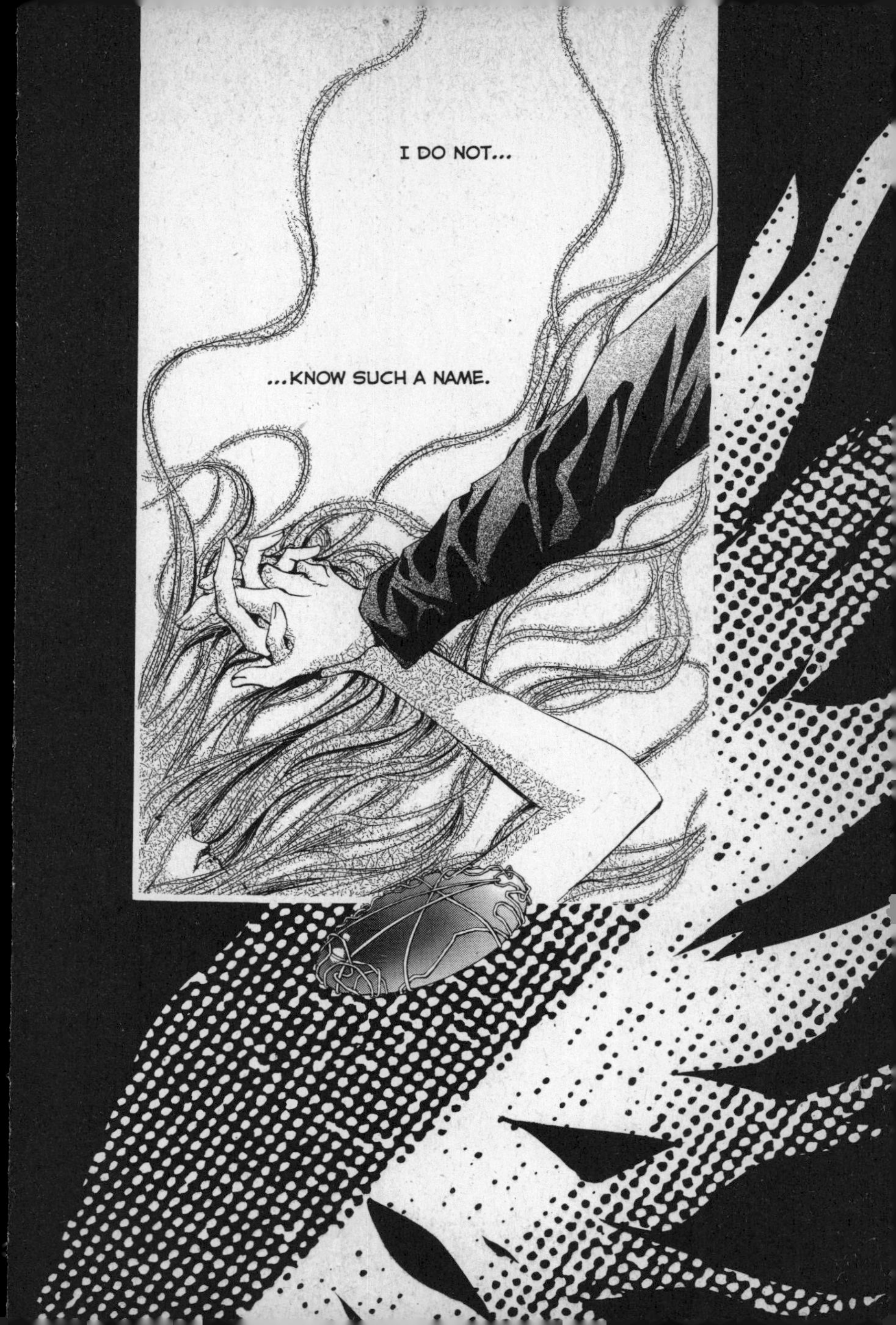
I DO NOT...
...KNOW SUCH A NAME.

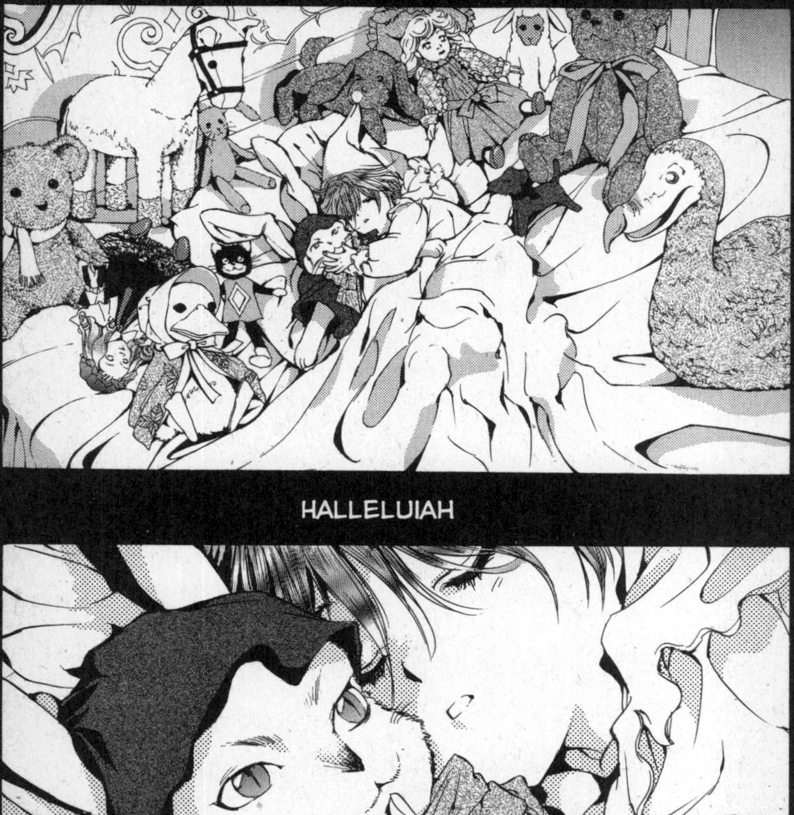
HALLELUIAH
SALVATION AND GLORY ARE THE WILL OF GOD, RECEIVE HIS JUDGMENT AND BECOME RIGHTEOUS

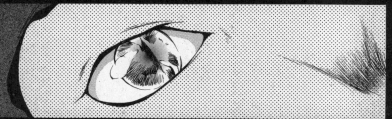

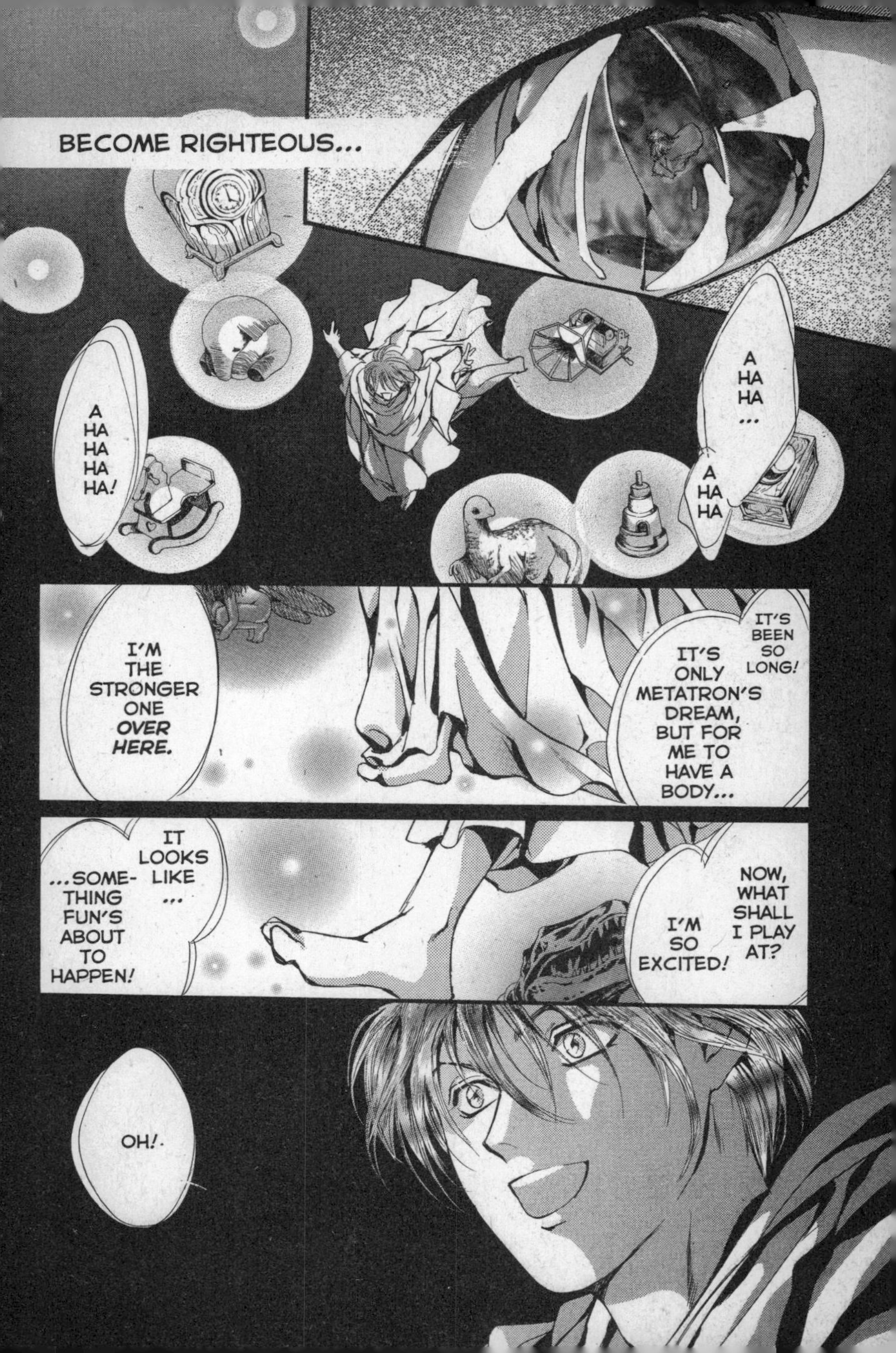
BECOME RIGHTEOUS...
A HA HA...
A HA HA
A HA HA HA HA!
IT'S BEEN SO LONG!
IT'S ONLY METATRON'S DREAM, BUT FOR ME TO HAVE A BODY...
I'M THE STRONGER ONE *OVER HERE.*
NOW, WHAT SHALL I PLAY AT?
I'M SO EXCITED!
IT LOOKS LIKE...
...SOME-THING FUN'S ABOUT TO HAPPEN!
OH!.

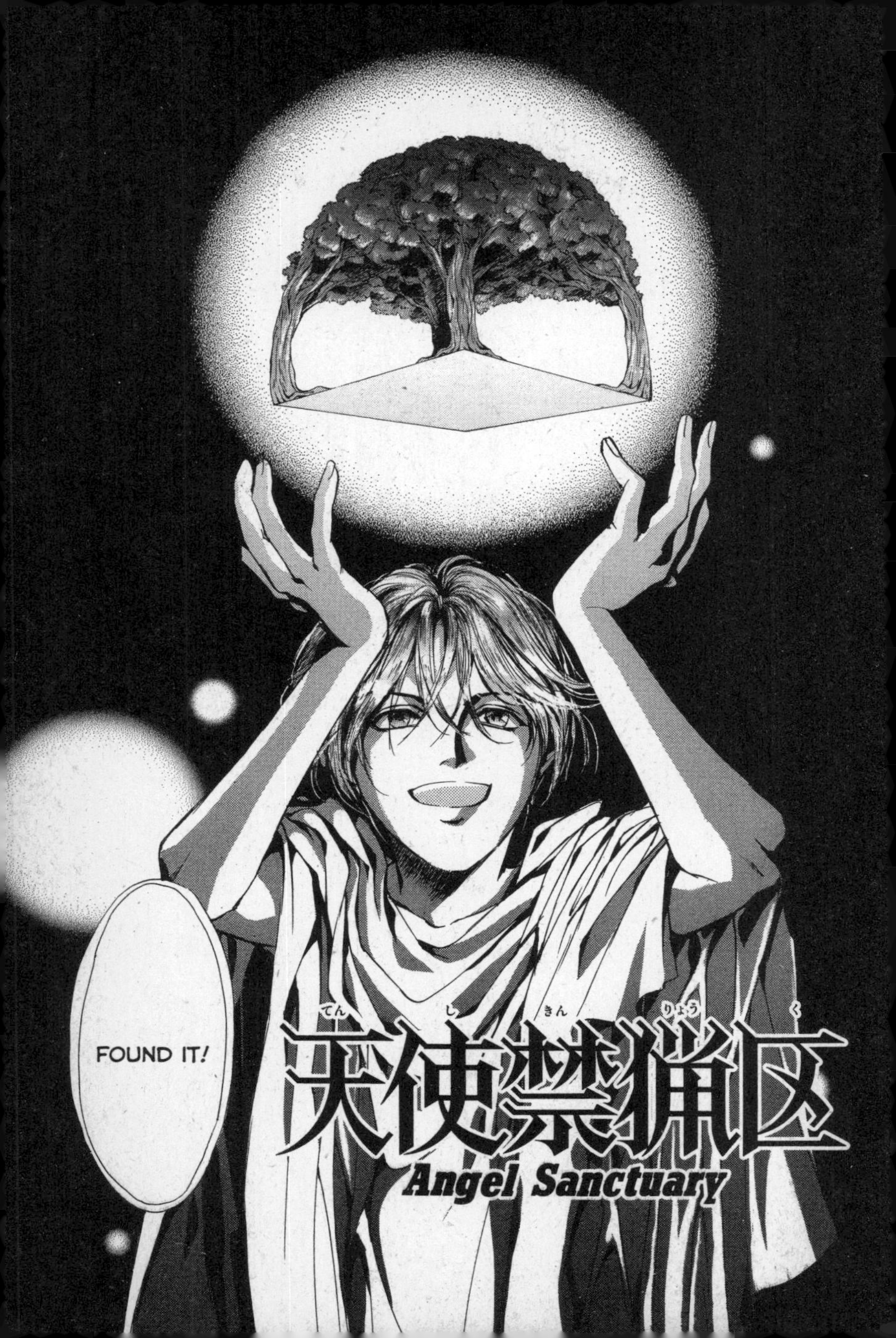
FOUND IT!
てん し きん りょう く
天使禁猟区
Angel Sanctuary

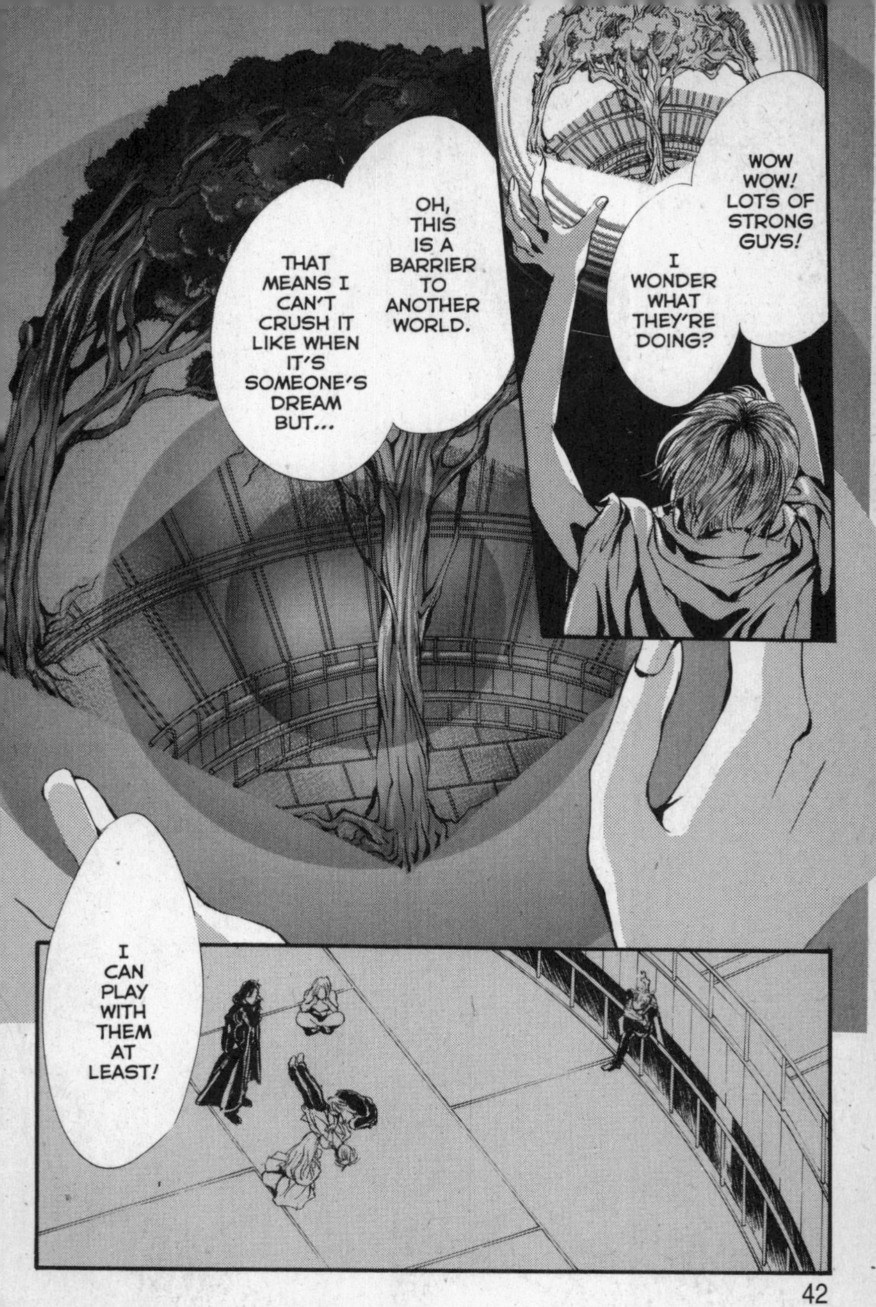
WOW WOW! LOTS OF STRONG GUYS!
I WONDER WHAT THEY'RE DOING?
OH, THIS IS A BARRIER TO ANOTHER WORLD.
THAT MEANS I CAN'T CRUSH IT LIKE WHEN IT'S SOMEONE'S DREAM BUT...
I CAN PLAY WITH THEM AT LEAST!

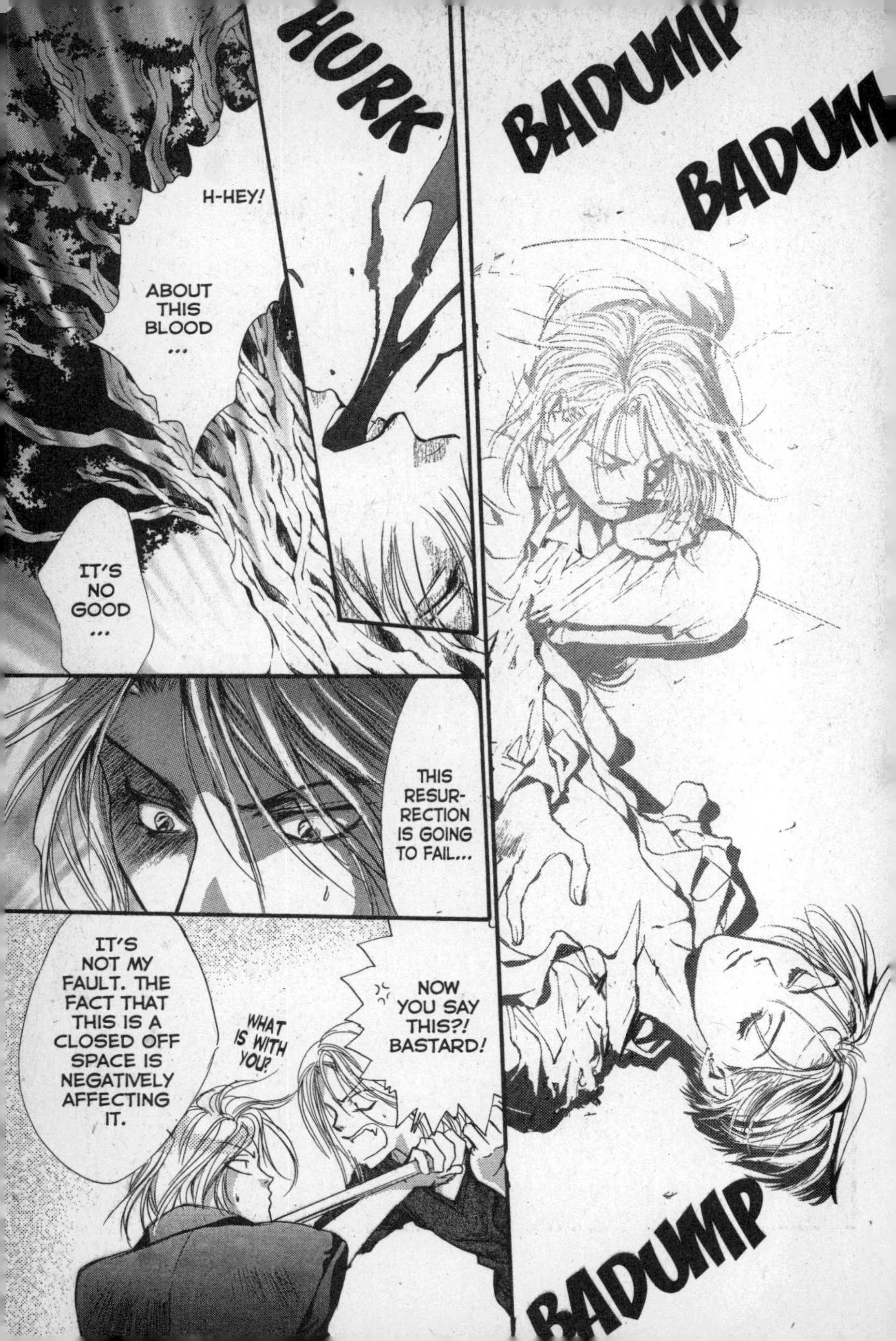
BADUMP
BADUMP
BADUMP
HURK
H-HEY!
ABOUT THIS BLOOD...
IT'S NO GOOD...
THIS RESURRECTION IS GOING TO FAIL...
NOW YOU SAY THIS?! BASTARD!
WHAT IS WITH YOU?
IT'S NOT MY FAULT. THE FACT THAT THIS IS A CLOSED OFF SPACE IS NEGATIVELY AFFECTING IT.

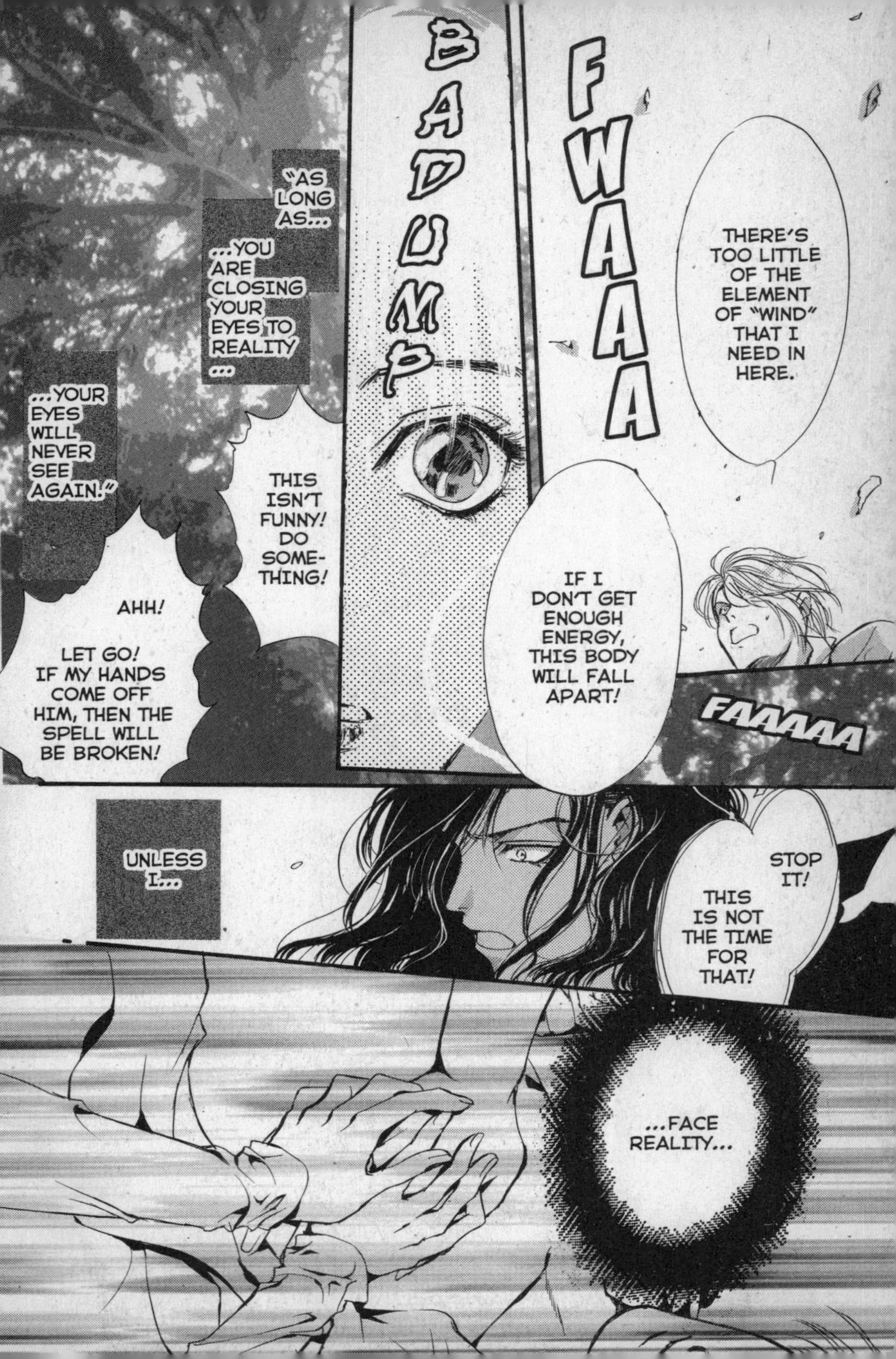
FWAAAA
THERE'S TOO LITTLE OF THE ELEMENT OF "WIND" THAT I NEED IN HERE.
IF I DON'T GET ENOUGH ENERGY, THIS BODY WILL FALL APART!
FAAAAAA
BADUMP
"AS LONG AS...
...YOU ARE CLOSING YOUR EYES TO REALITY...
...YOUR EYES WILL NEVER SEE AGAIN."
THIS ISN'T FUNNY! DO SOME-THING!
AHH!
LET GO! IF MY HANDS COME OFF HIM, THEN THE SPELL WILL BE BROKEN!
STOP IT! THIS IS NOT THE TIME FOR THAT!
UNLESS I...
...FACE REALITY...

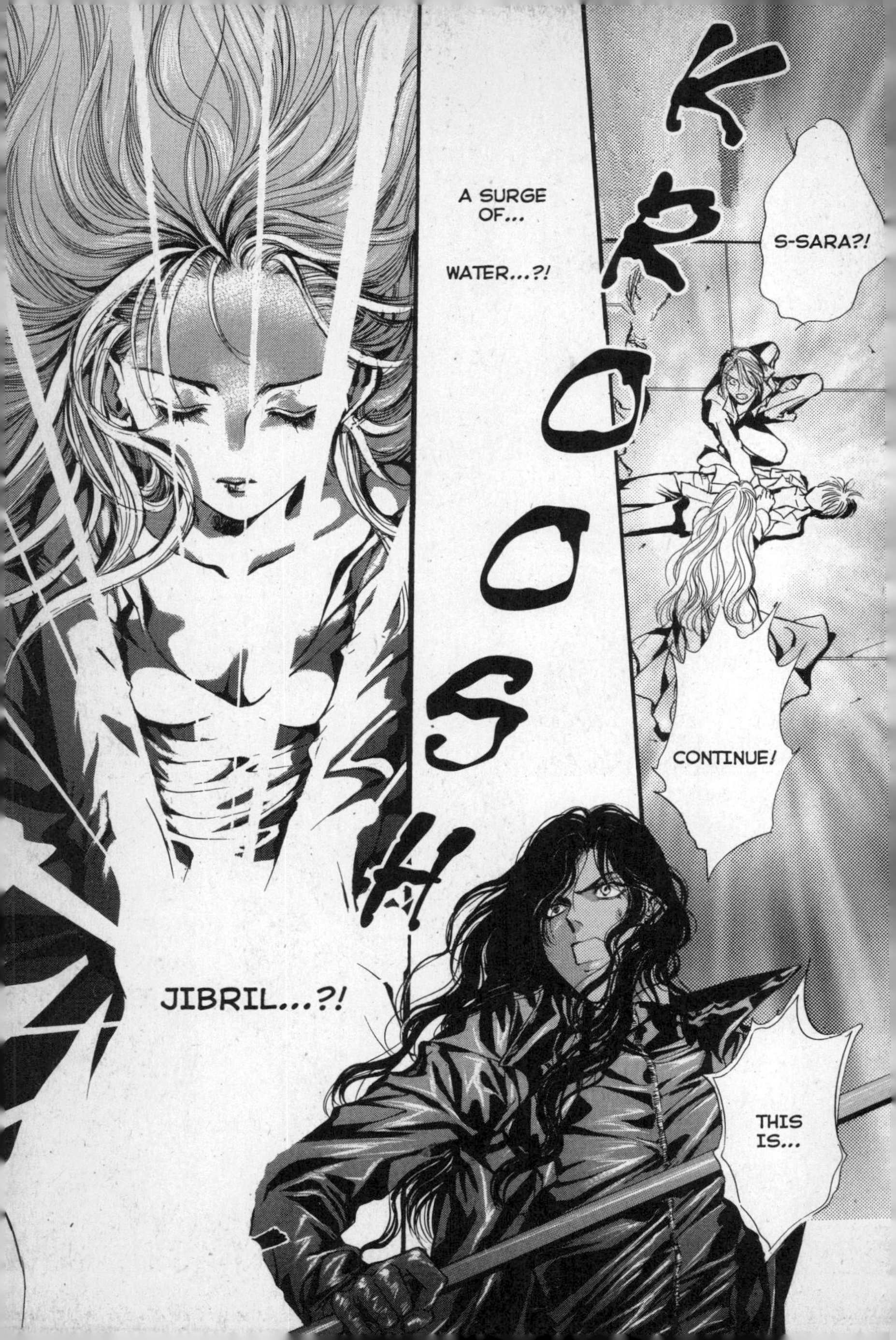
S-SARA?!
KROOOSH!
A SURGE OF...
WATER...?!
CONTINUE!
THIS IS...
JIBRIL...?!

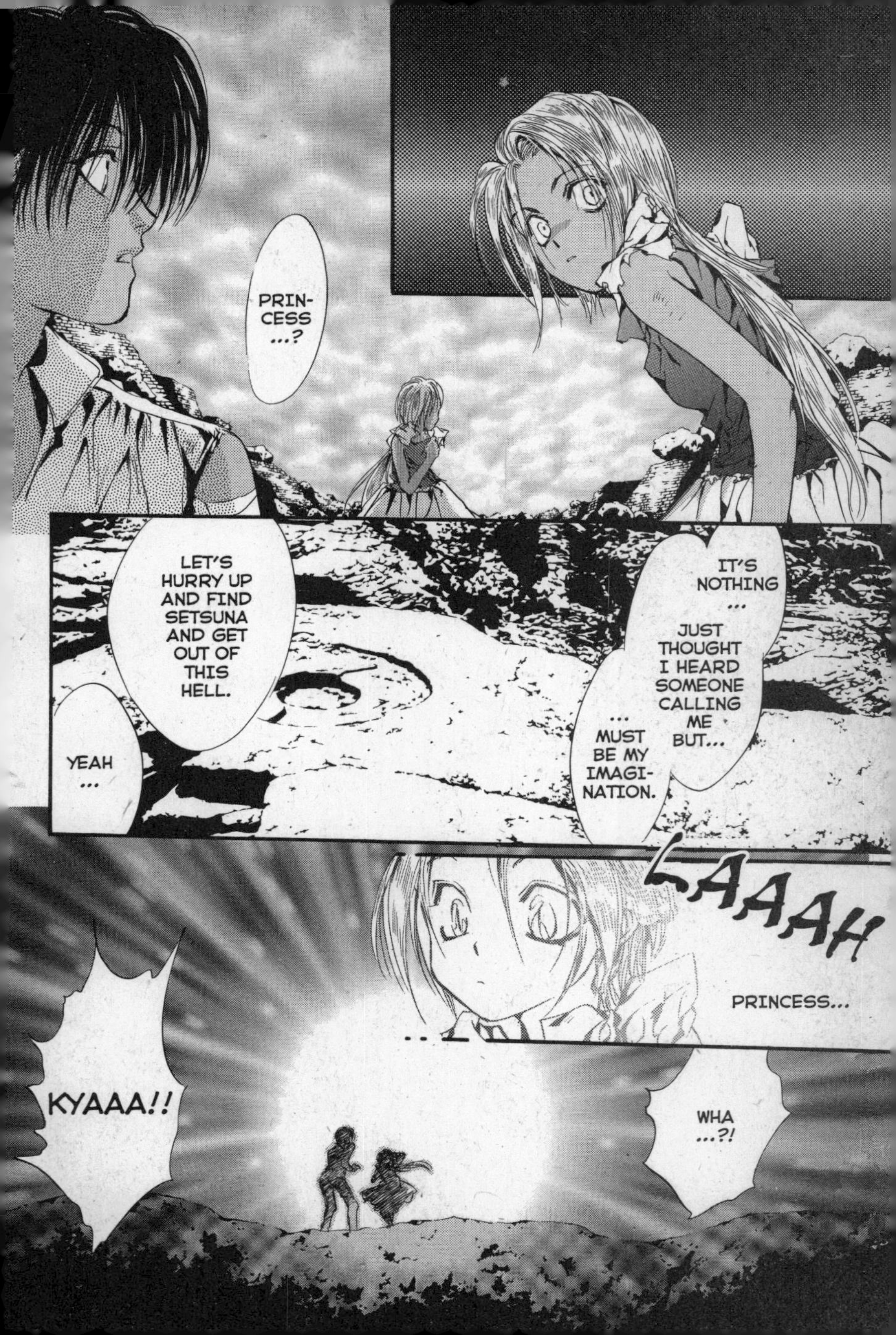

PRIN-CESS ...?
IT'S NOTHING ... JUST THOUGHT I HEARD SOMEONE CALLING ME BUT...
... MUST BE MY IMAGI-NATION.
LET'S HURRY UP AND FIND SETSUNA AND GET OUT OF THIS HELL.
YEAH ...
LAAAH
PRINCESS...
WHA ...?!
KYAAA!!

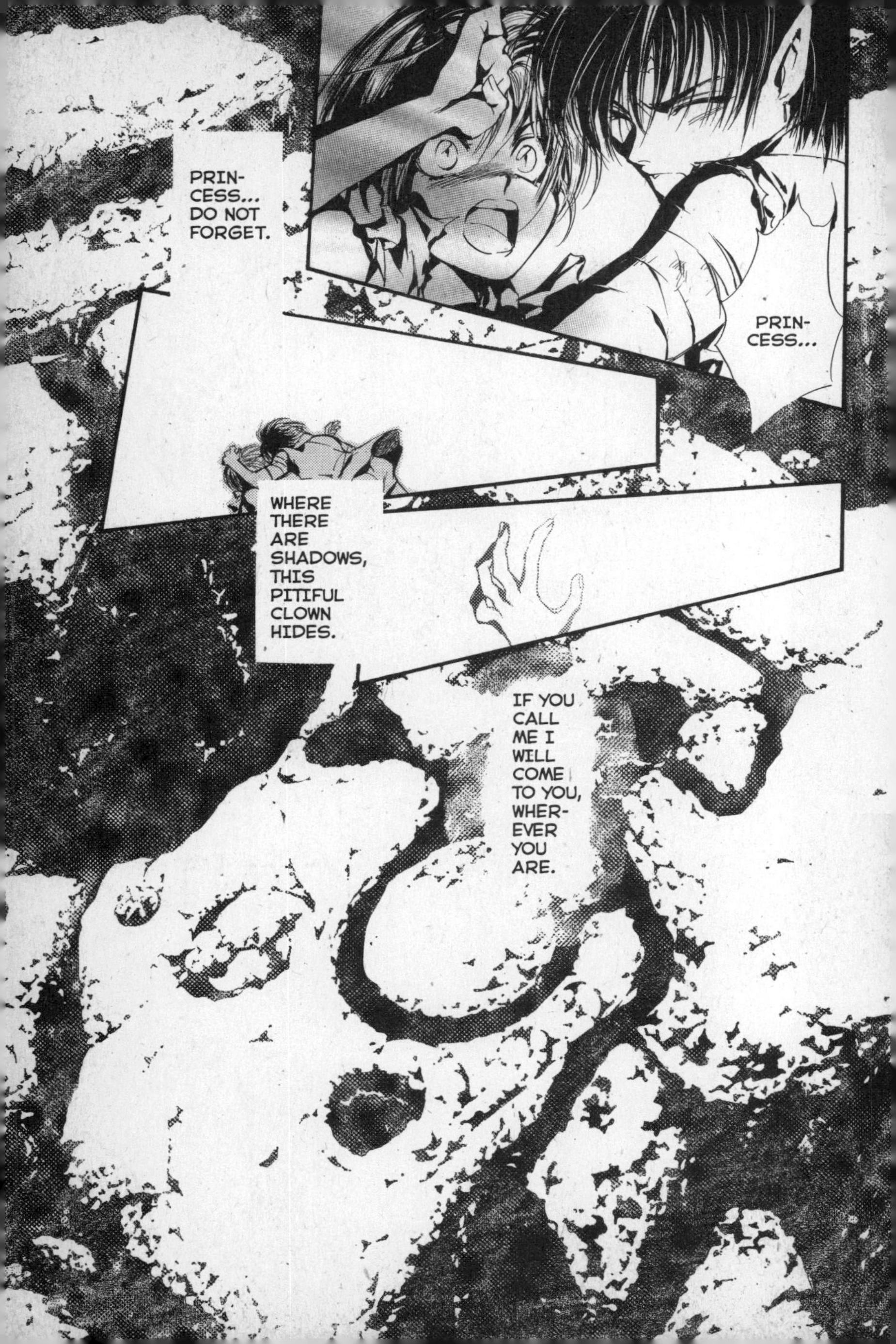
PRIN-
CESS...
PRIN-
CESS...
DO NOT
FORGET.
WHERE THERE ARE SHADOWS, THIS PITIFUL CLOWN HIDES.
IF YOU CALL ME I WILL COME TO YOU, WHER-EVER YOU ARE.

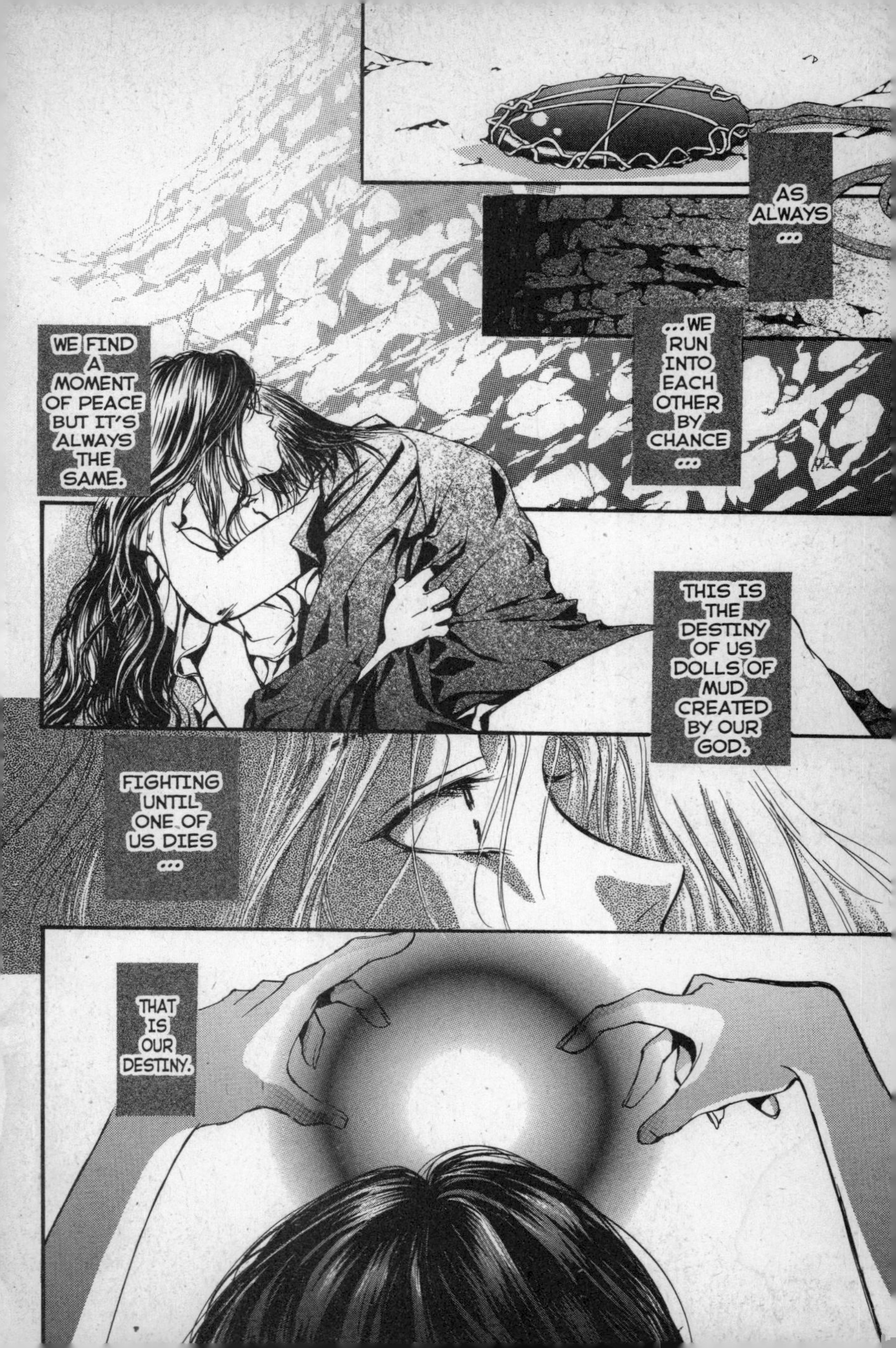
AS ALWAYS...
...WE RUN INTO EACH OTHER BY CHANCE...
WE FIND A MOMENT OF PEACE BUT IT'S ALWAYS THE SAME.
THIS IS THE DESTINY OF US DOLLS OF MUD CREATED BY OUR GOD.
FIGHTING UNTIL ONE OF US DIES...
THAT IS OUR DESTINY.

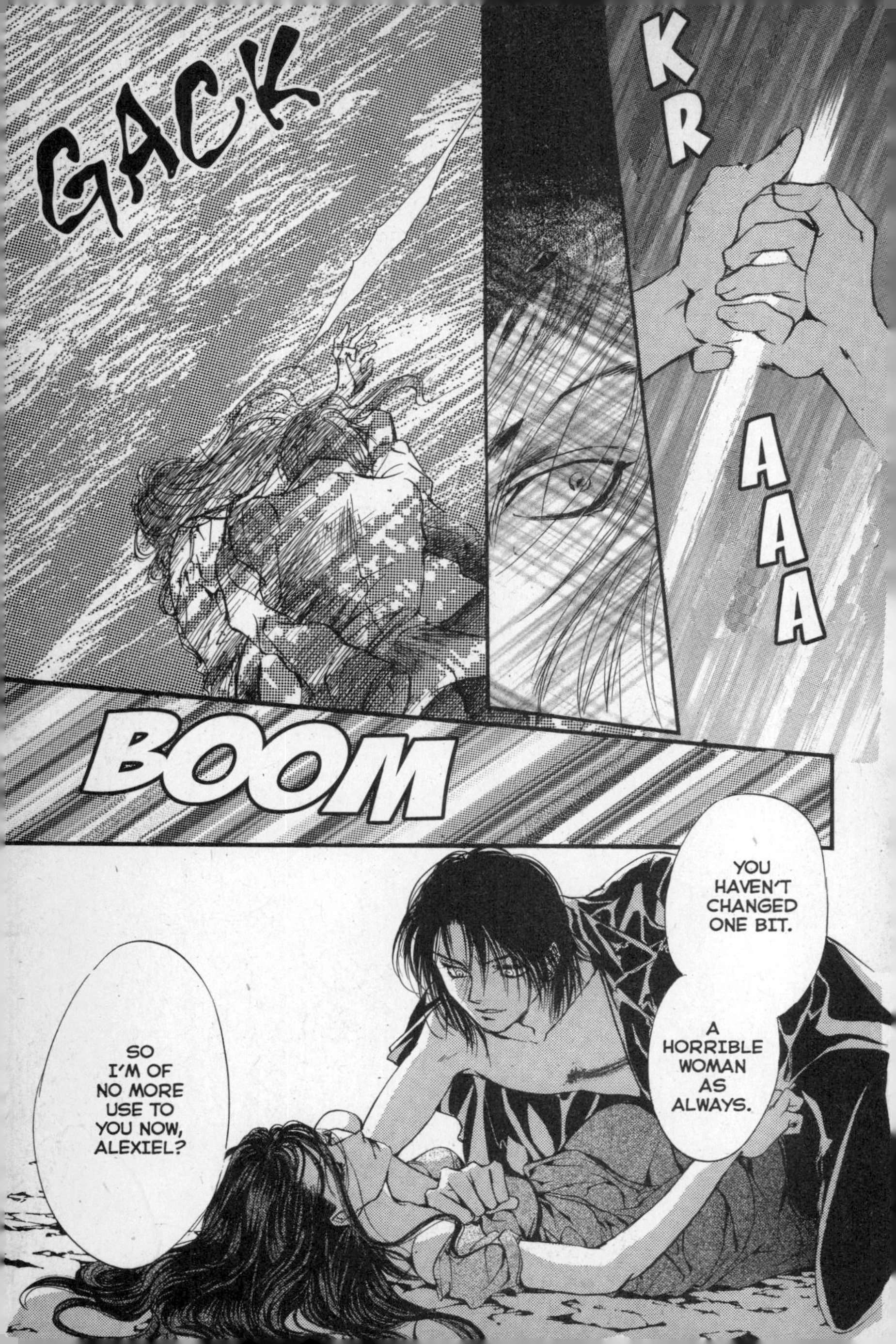
KR
AAA
GACK
BOOM
YOU HAVEN'T CHANGED ONE BIT.
A HORRIBLE WOMAN AS ALWAYS.
SO I'M OF NO MORE USE TO YOU NOW, ALEXIEL?

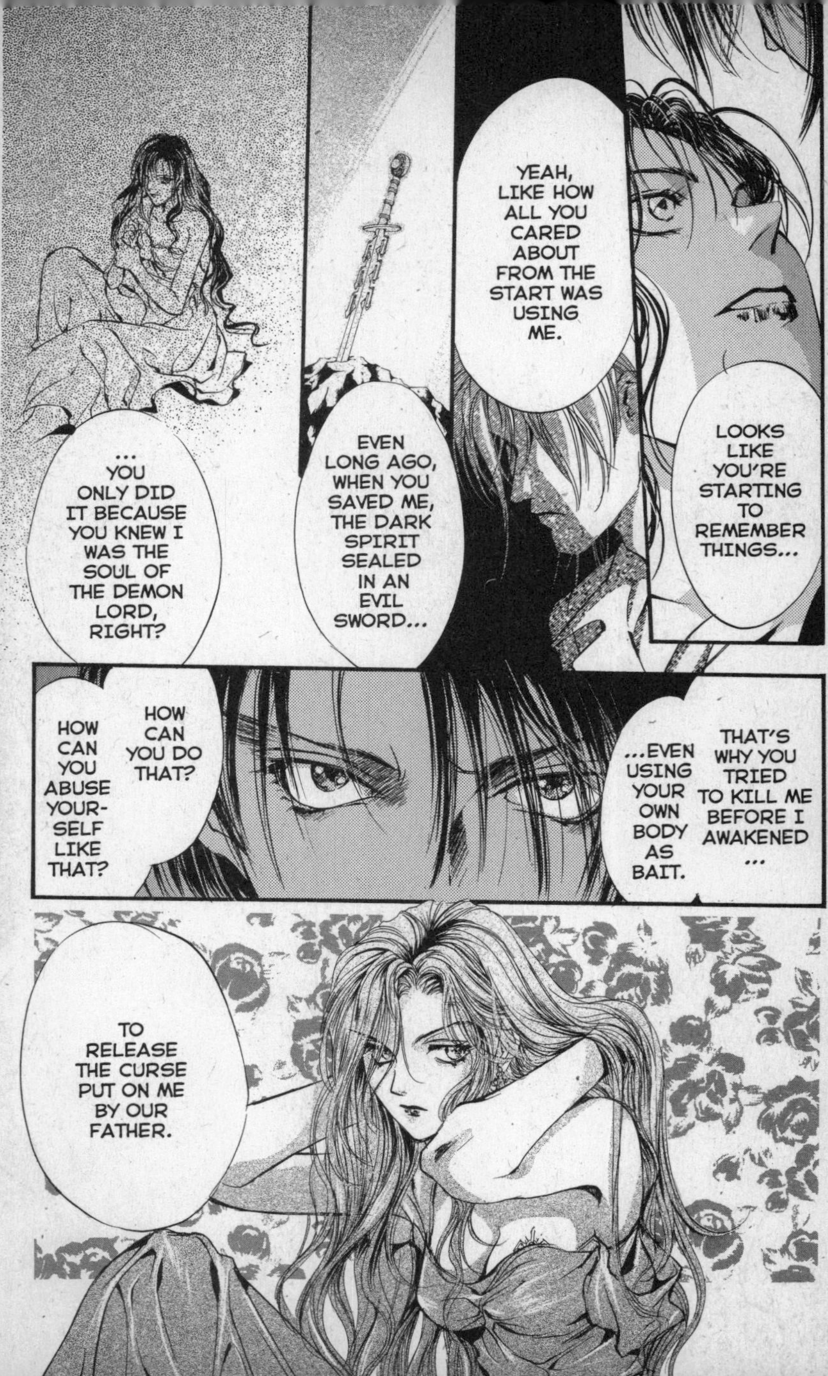
LOOKS LIKE YOU'RE STARTING TO REMEMBER THINGS...
YEAH, LIKE HOW ALL YOU CARED ABOUT FROM THE START WAS USING ME.
EVEN LONG AGO, WHEN YOU SAVED ME, THE DARK SPIRIT SEALED IN AN EVIL SWORD...
...YOU ONLY DID IT BECAUSE YOU KNEW I WAS THE SOUL OF THE DEMON LORD, RIGHT?
THAT'S WHY YOU TRIED TO KILL ME BEFORE I AWAKENED...
...EVEN USING YOUR OWN BODY AS BAIT.
HOW CAN YOU DO THAT?
HOW CAN YOU ABUSE YOURSELF LIKE THAT?
TO RELEASE THE CURSE PUT ON ME BY OUR FATHER.

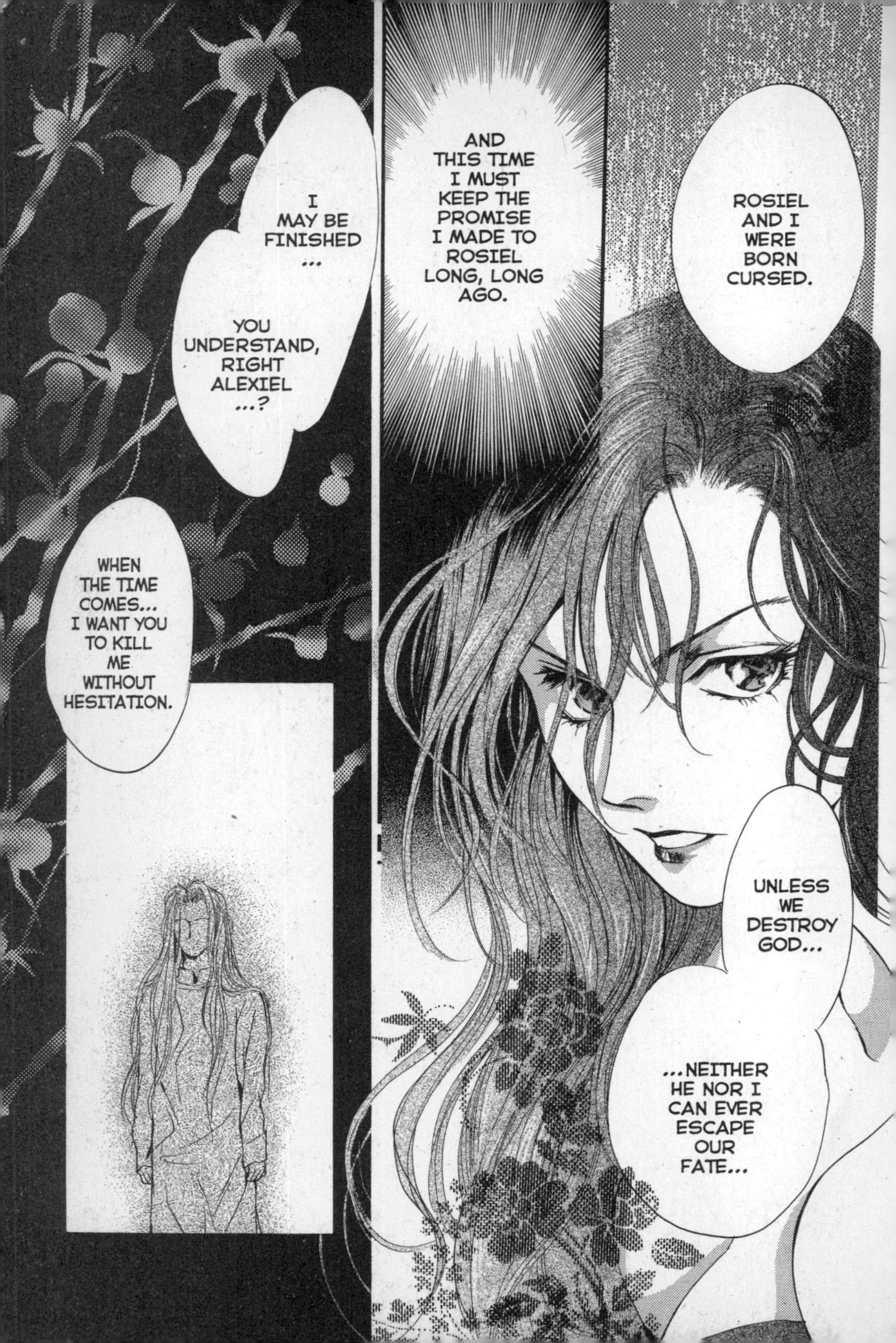
ROSIEL AND I WERE BORN CURSED.
UNLESS WE DESTROY GOD...
...NEITHER HE NOR I CAN EVER ESCAPE OUR FATE...
AND THIS TIME I MUST KEEP THE PROMISE I MADE TO ROSIEL LONG, LONG AGO.
I MAY BE FINISHED ...
YOU UNDERSTAND, RIGHT ALEXIEL ...?
WHEN THE TIME COMES... I WANT YOU TO KILL ME WITHOUT HESITATION.

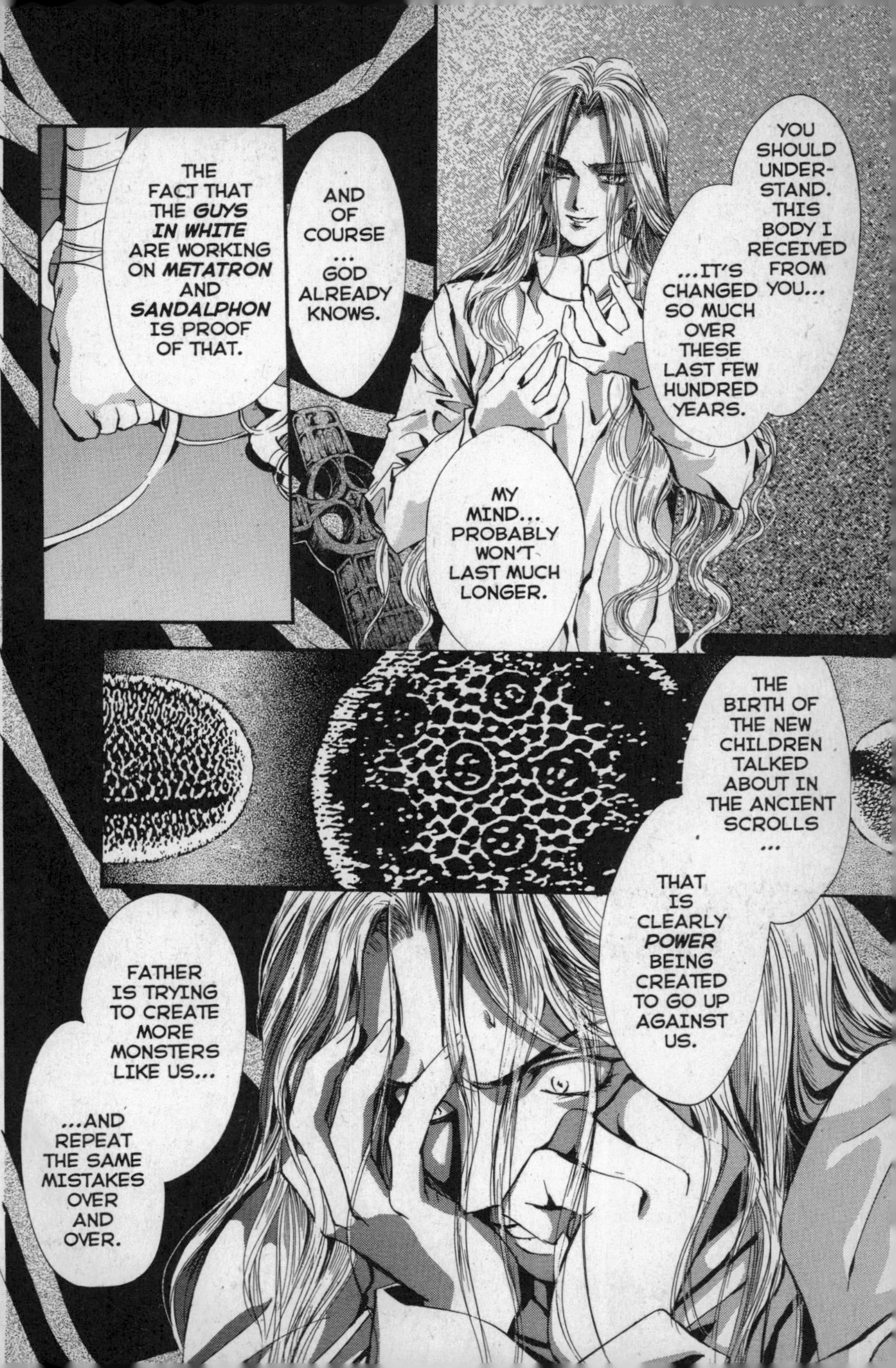
YOU SHOULD UNDERSTAND. THIS BODY I RECEIVED FROM YOU...
...IT'S CHANGED SO MUCH OVER THESE LAST FEW HUNDRED YEARS.
MY MIND... PROBABLY WON'T LAST MUCH LONGER.
AND OF COURSE ... GOD ALREADY KNOWS.
THE FACT THAT THE *GUYS IN WHITE* ARE WORKING ON *METATRON* AND *SANDALPHON* IS PROOF OF THAT.
THE BIRTH OF THE NEW CHILDREN TALKED ABOUT IN THE ANCIENT SCROLLS ...
THAT IS CLEARLY *POWER* BEING CREATED TO GO UP AGAINST US.
FATHER IS TRYING TO CREATE MORE MONSTERS LIKE US...
...AND REPEAT THE SAME MISTAKES OVER AND OVER.

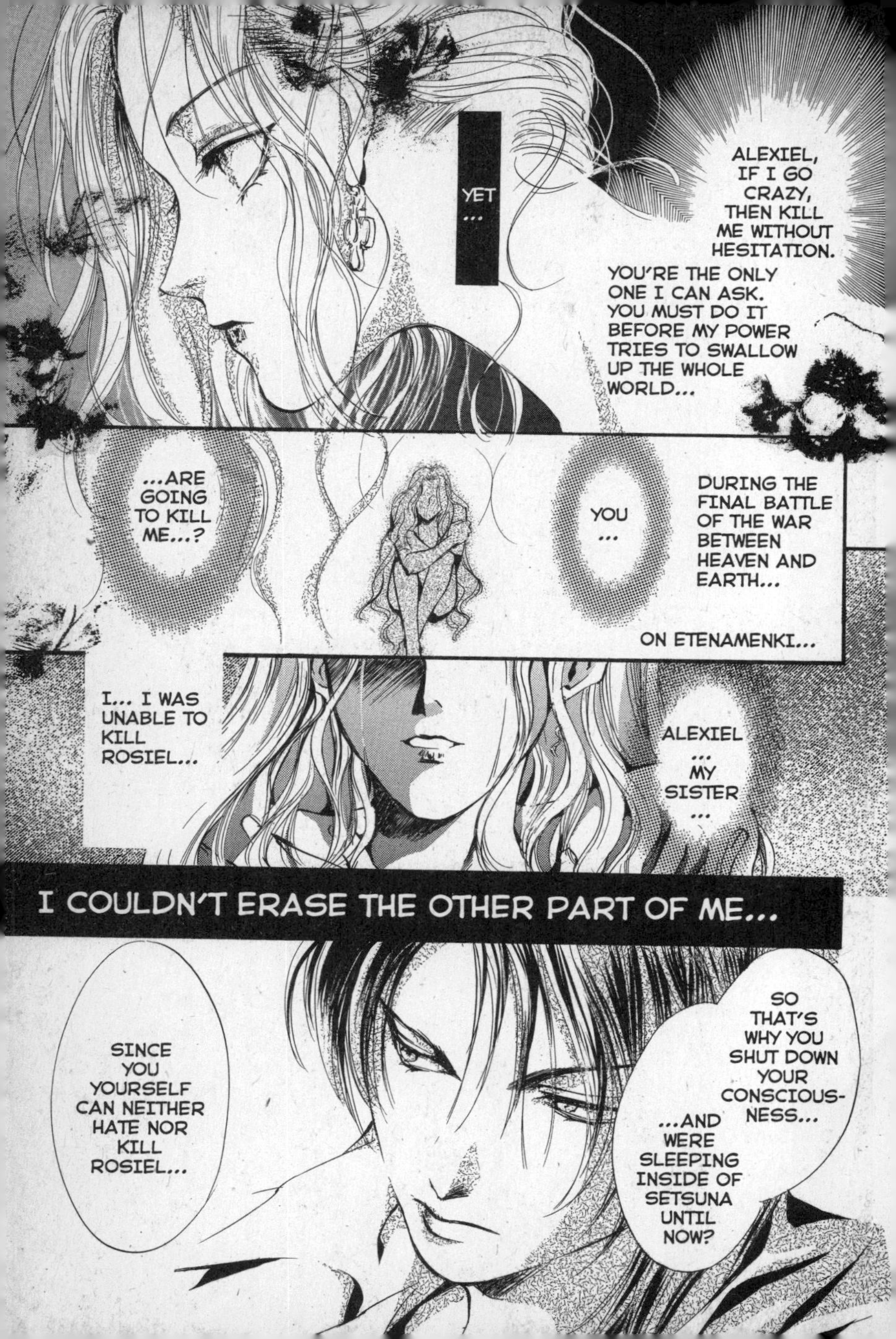
ALEXIEL, IF I GO CRAZY, THEN KILL ME WITHOUT HESITATION.
YOU'RE THE ONLY ONE I CAN ASK. YOU MUST DO IT BEFORE MY POWER TRIES TO SWALLOW UP THE WHOLE WORLD...
YET ...
DURING THE FINAL BATTLE OF THE WAR BETWEEN HEAVEN AND EARTH...
ON ETENAMENKI...
YOU ...
...ARE GOING TO KILL ME...?
ALEXIEL ... MY SISTER ...
I... I WAS UNABLE TO KILL ROSIEL...
I COULDN'T ERASE THE OTHER PART OF ME...
SO THAT'S WHY YOU SHUT DOWN YOUR CONSCIOUS-NESS...
...AND WERE SLEEPING INSIDE OF SETSUNA UNTIL NOW?
SINCE YOU YOURSELF CAN NEITHER HATE NOR KILL ROSIEL...

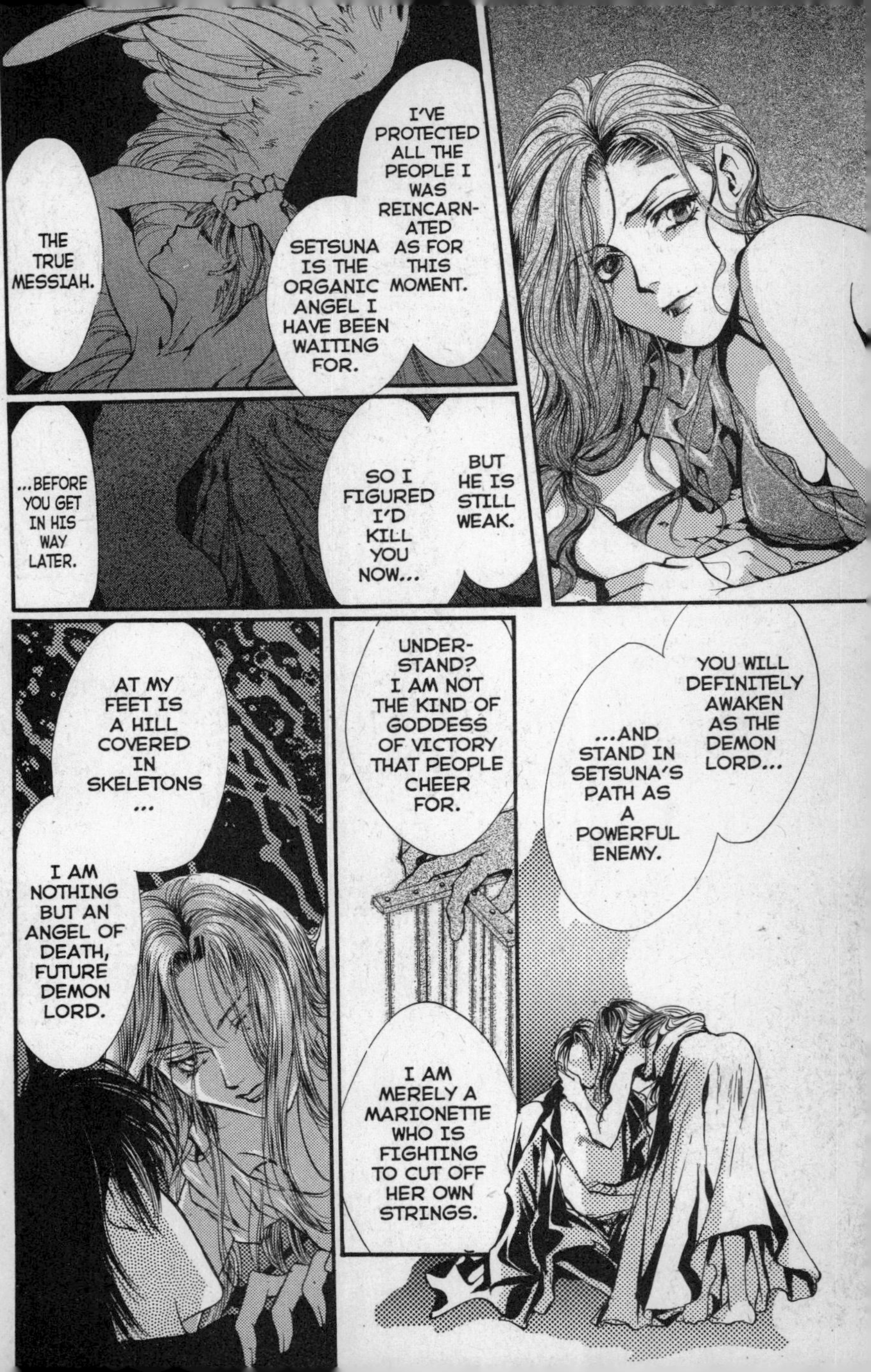
I'VE PROTECTED ALL THE PEOPLE I WAS REINCARNATED AS FOR THIS MOMENT.
SETSUNA IS THE ORGANIC ANGEL I HAVE BEEN WAITING FOR.
THE TRUE MESSIAH.
BUT HE IS STILL WEAK.
SO I FIGURED I'D KILL YOU NOW...
...BEFORE YOU GET IN HIS WAY LATER.
YOU WILL DEFINITELY AWAKEN AS THE DEMON LORD...
...AND STAND IN SETSUNA'S PATH AS A POWERFUL ENEMY.
UNDERSTAND? I AM NOT THE KIND OF GODDESS OF VICTORY THAT PEOPLE CHEER FOR.
I AM MERELY A MARIONETTE WHO IS FIGHTING TO CUT OFF HER OWN STRINGS.
AT MY FEET IS A HILL COVERED IN SKELETONS ...
I AM NOTHING BUT AN ANGEL OF DEATH, FUTURE DEMON LORD.

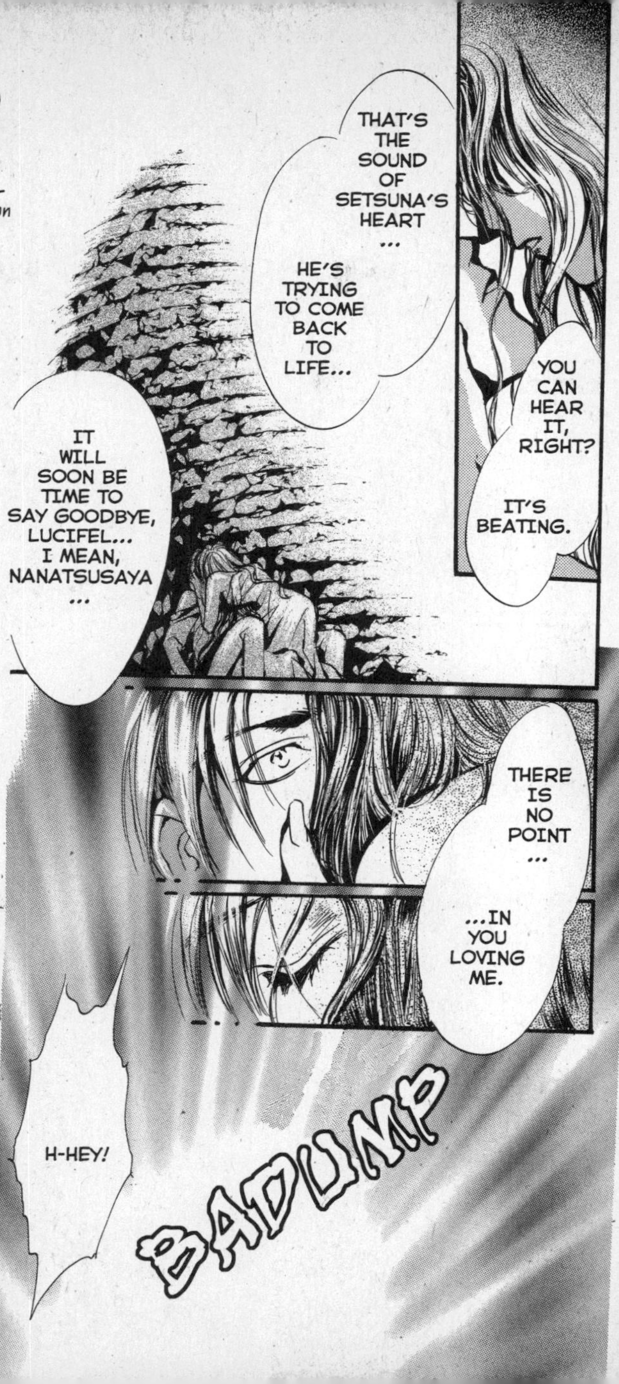
YOU CAN HEAR IT, RIGHT?
IT'S BEATING.
THAT'S THE SOUND OF SETSUNA'S HEART...
HE'S TRYING TO COME BACK TO LIFE...
IT WILL SOON BE TIME TO SAY GOODBYE, LUCIFEL... I MEAN, NANATSUSAYA...
THERE IS NO POINT...
...IN YOU LOVING ME.
BADUMP
H-HEY!

This arc sure was long... After this chapter is the three-page teaser that ran in the magazine. It shows a glimpse of a few things that will happen in the future, and I got a lot of questions like "what does this mean?!" and "(blank) is going to die?!" Plus, since it says "Final Chapter," I got a lot of "please don't end it"... And many people mistook the characters in some panels. Like one person thought that Katan on the second page was Raphael... Made me sad. Well, it is the final chapter, but it's going to be a very, very long chapter. I swear!

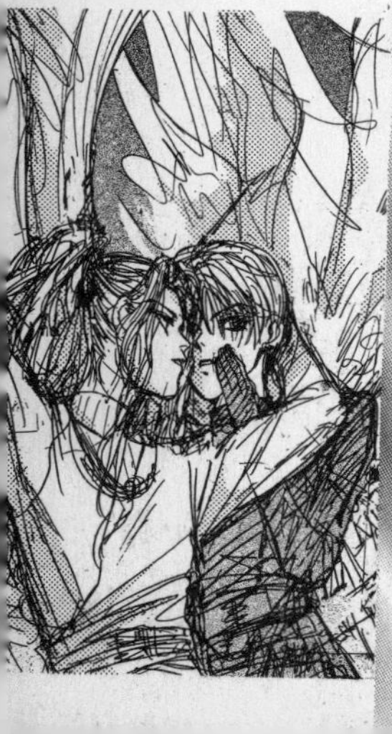

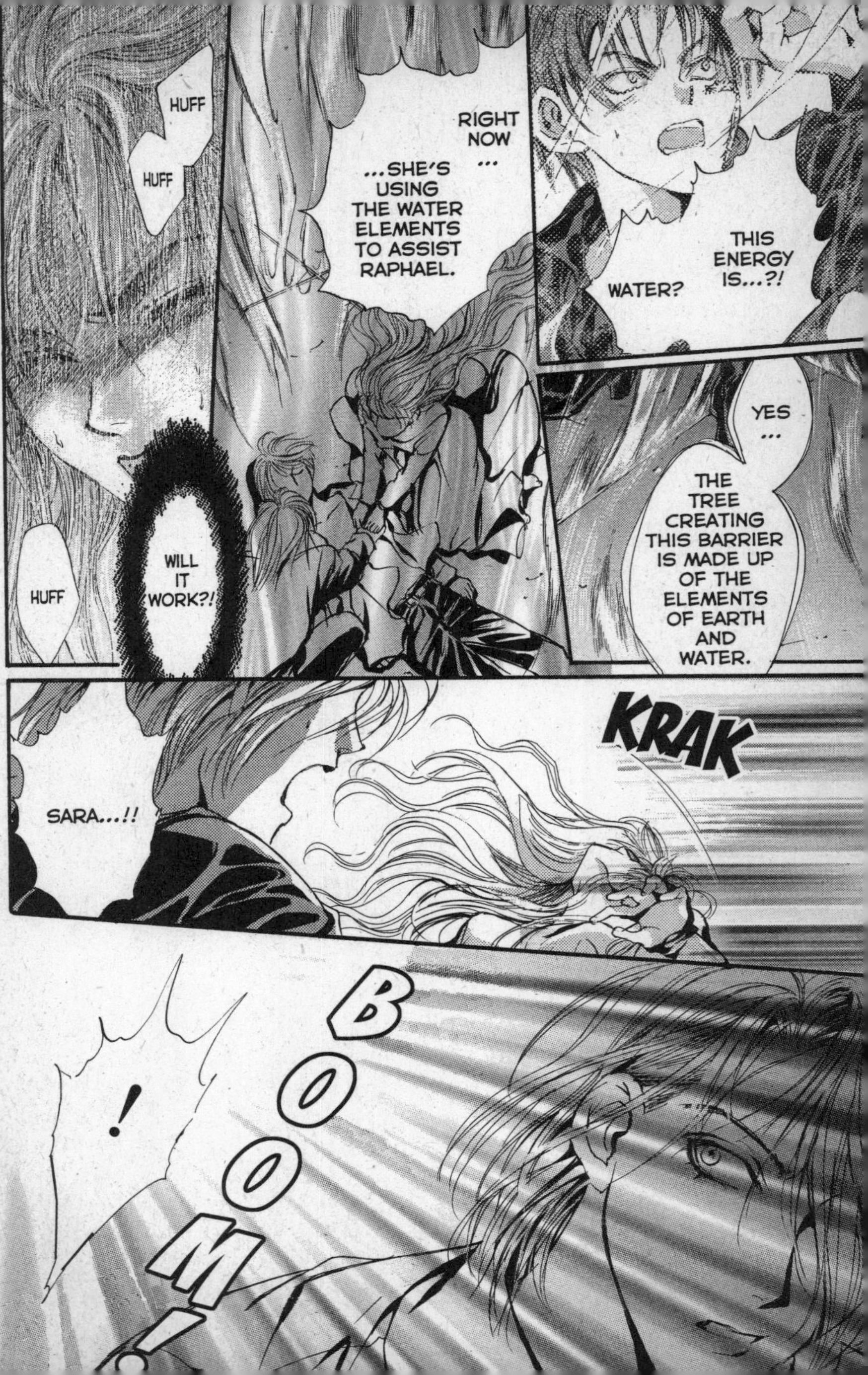
THIS ENERGY IS...?!
WATER?
YES ...
THE TREE CREATING THIS BARRIER IS MADE UP OF THE ELEMENTS OF EARTH AND WATER.
RIGHT NOW ...
...SHE'S USING THE WATER ELEMENTS TO ASSIST RAPHAEL.
WILL IT WORK?!
HUFF
HUFF
HUFF
KRAK
SARA...!!
BOOOM!
!

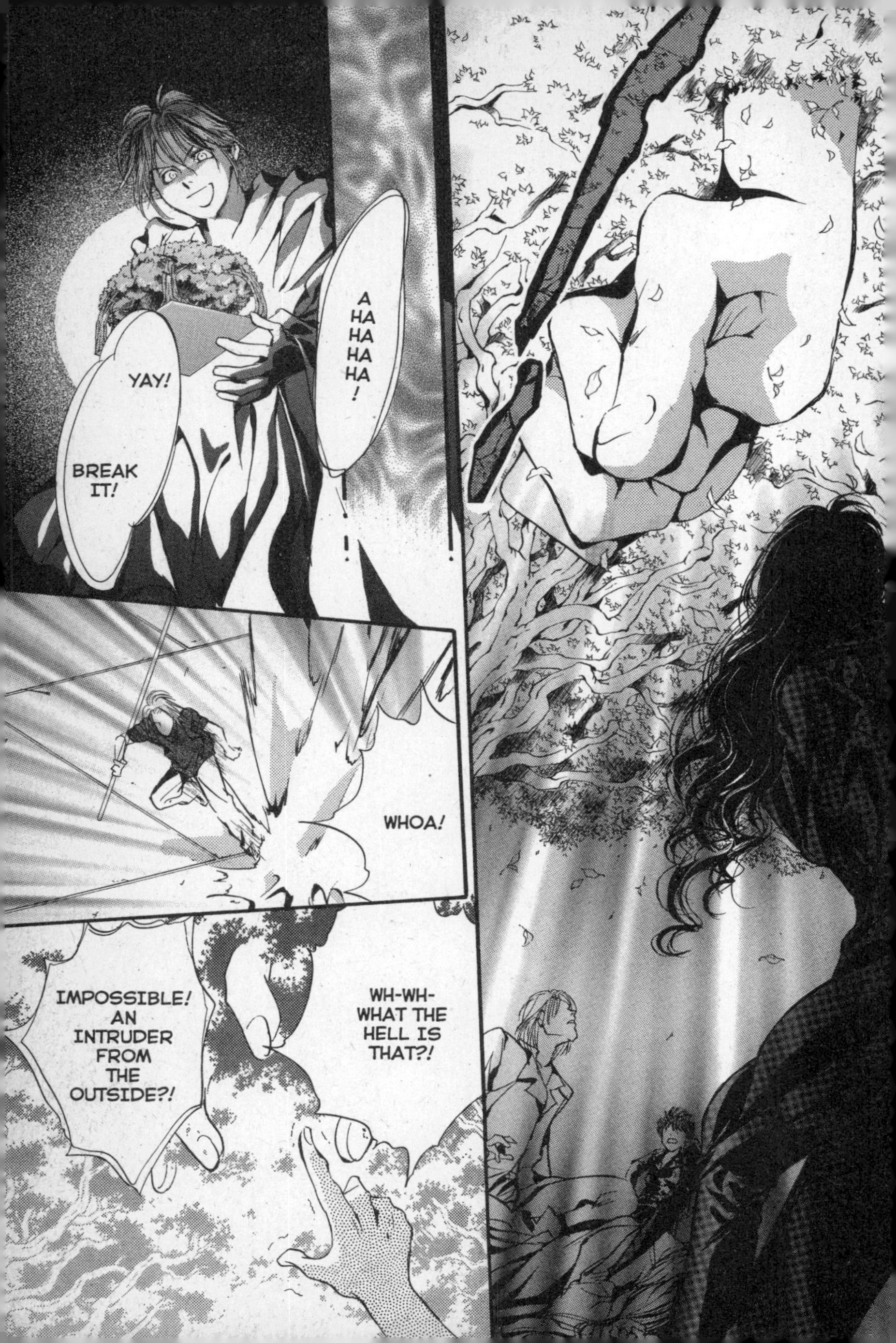
A HA HA HA HA!
YAY!
BREAK IT!
WHOA!
WH-WH-WHAT THE HELL IS THAT?!
IMPOSSIBLE! AN INTRUDER FROM THE OUTSIDE?!

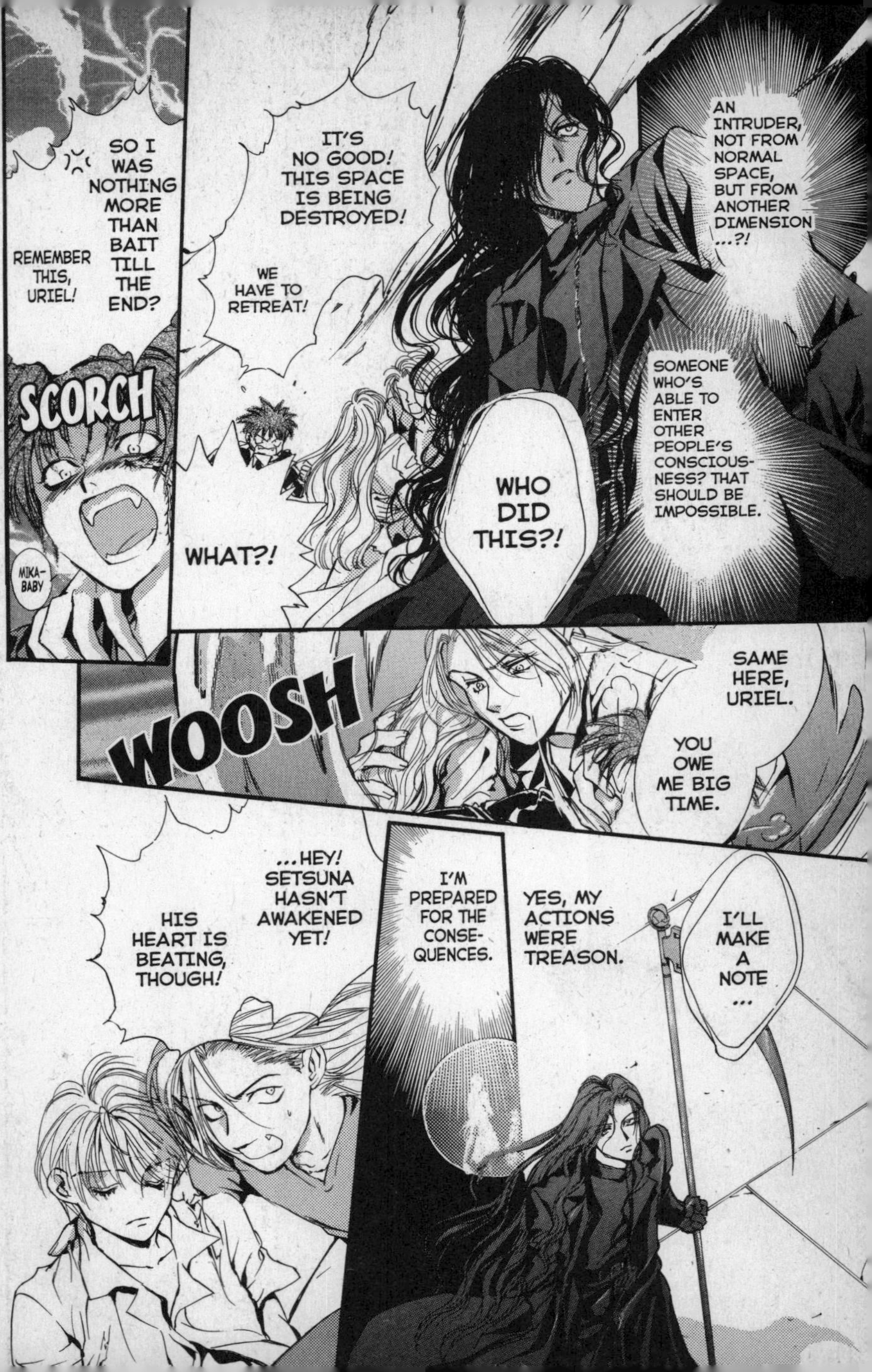
AN INTRUDER, NOT FROM NORMAL SPACE, BUT FROM ANOTHER DIMENSION ...?!
SOMEONE WHO'S ABLE TO ENTER OTHER PEOPLE'S CONSCIOUS-NESS? THAT SHOULD BE IMPOSSIBLE.
WHO DID THIS?!
IT'S NO GOOD! THIS SPACE IS BEING DESTROYED!
WE HAVE TO RETREAT!
WHAT?!
SO I WAS NOTHING MORE THAN BAIT TILL THE END?
REMEMBER THIS, URIEL!
SCORCH
MIKA-BABY
SAME HERE, URIEL.
YOU OWE ME BIG TIME.
WOOSH
I'LL MAKE A NOTE ...
YES, MY ACTIONS WERE TREASON.
I'M PREPARED FOR THE CONSE-QUENCES.
...HEY! SETSUNA HASN'T AWAKENED YET!
HIS HEART IS BEATING, THOUGH!

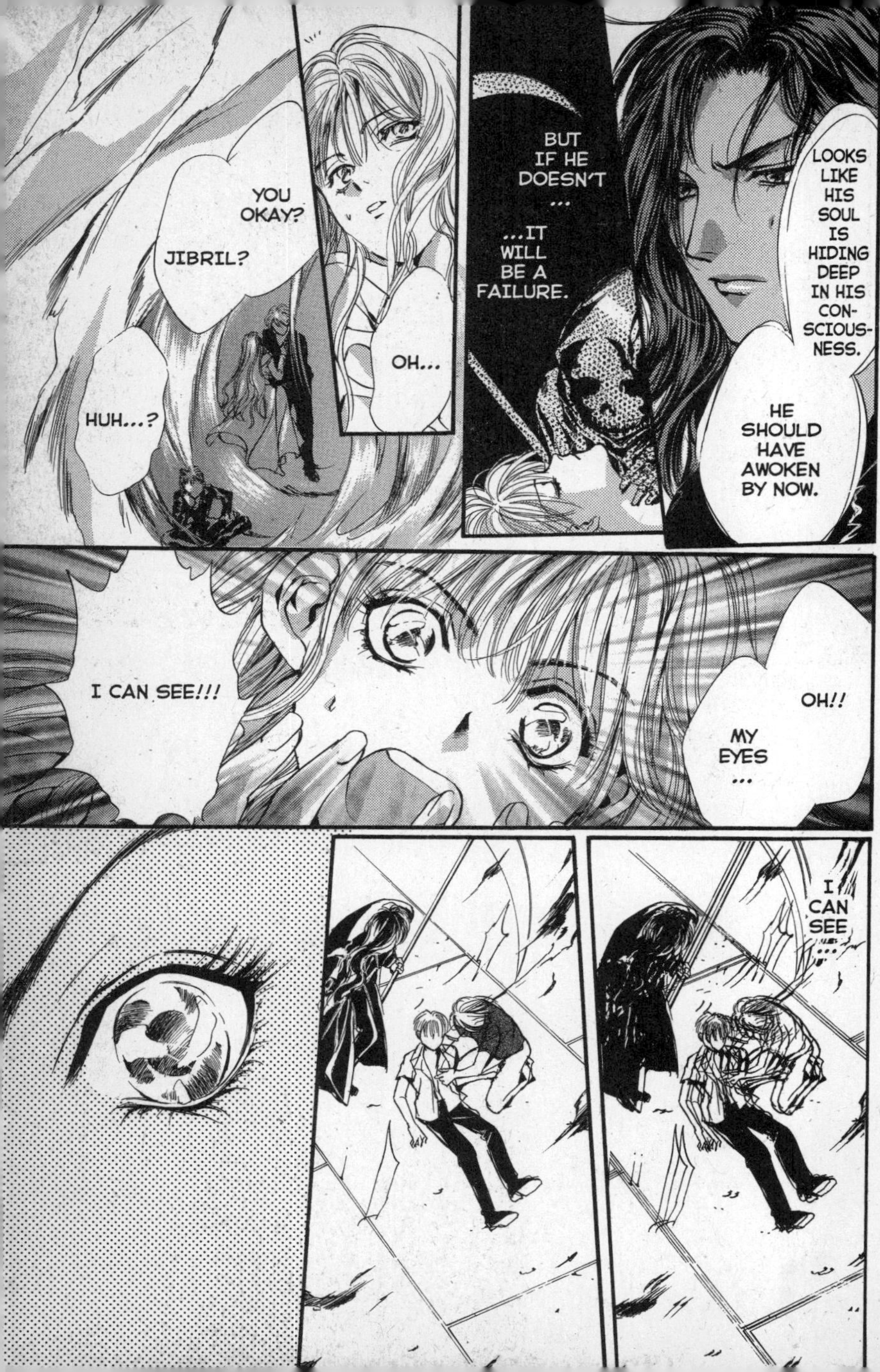

LOOKS LIKE HIS SOUL IS HIDING DEEP IN HIS CONSCIOUSNESS.
HE SHOULD HAVE AWOKEN BY NOW.
BUT IF HE DOESN'T ...
...IT WILL BE A FAILURE.
YOU OKAY? JIBRIL?
OH...
HUH...?
OH!!
MY EYES ...
I CAN SEE!!!
I CAN SEE ...

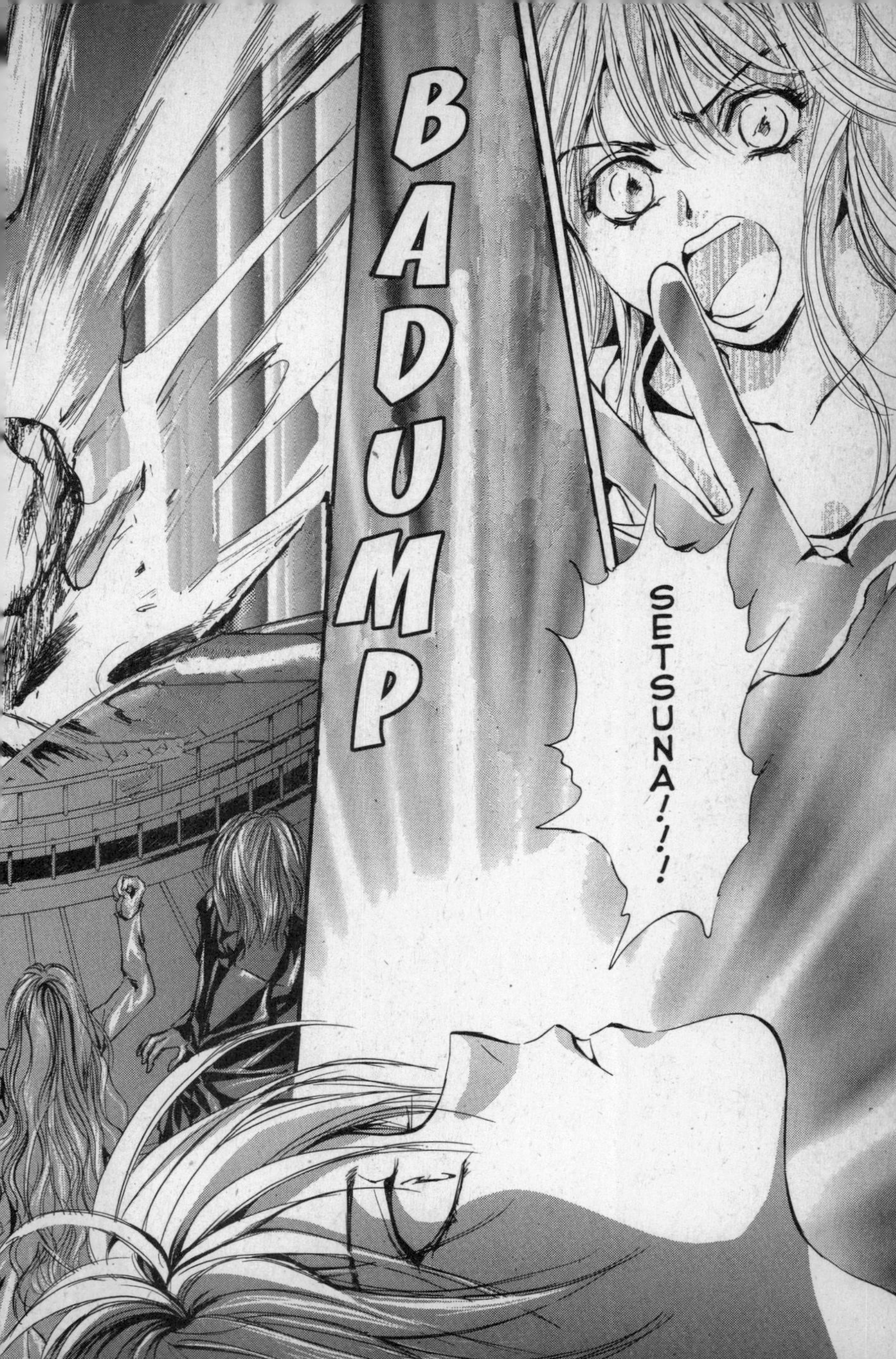
BADUMP
SETSUNA!!!!

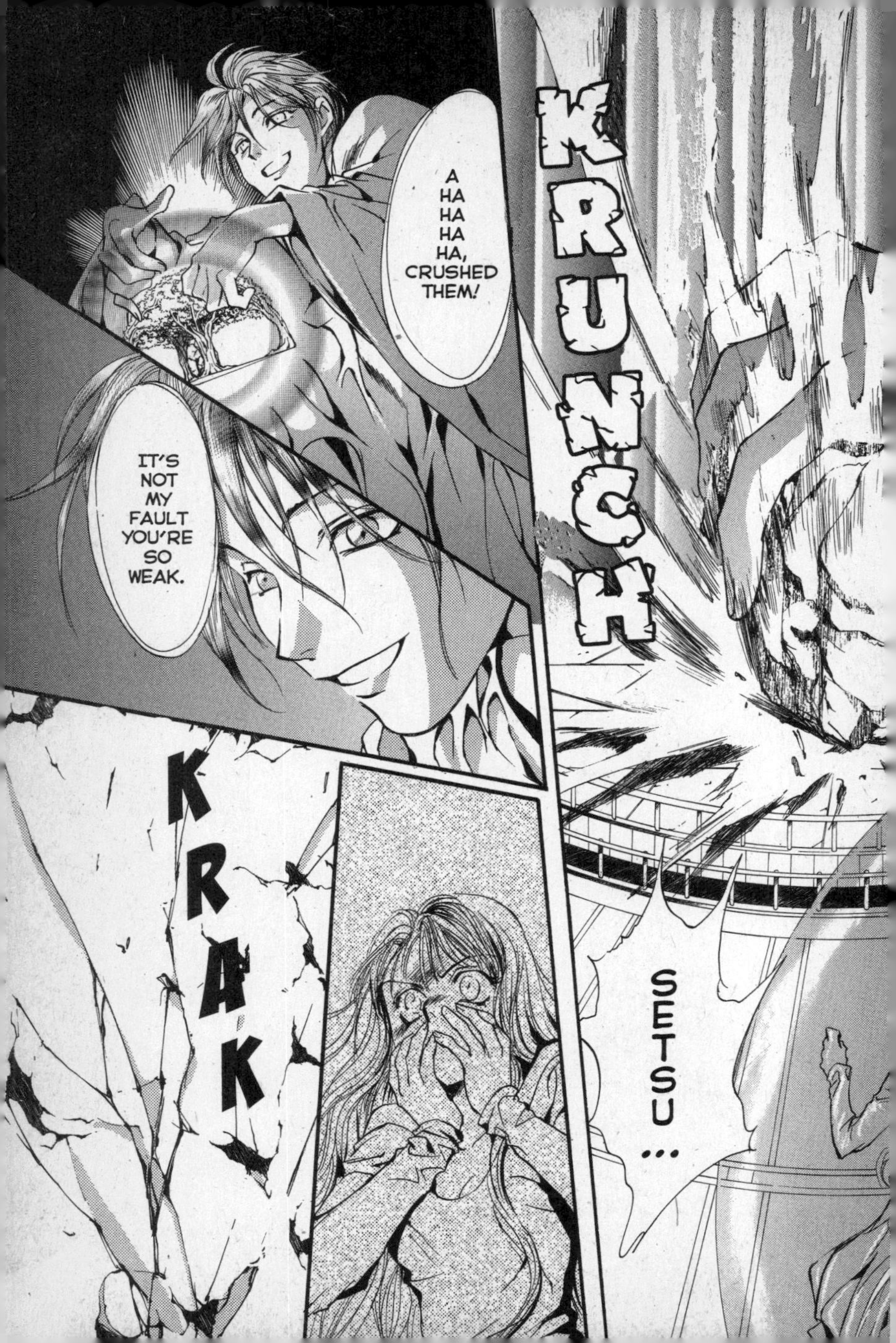
KRUNCH
A HA HA HA HA, CRUSHED THEM!
IT'S NOT MY FAULT YOU'RE SO WEAK.
SETSU...
KRAK

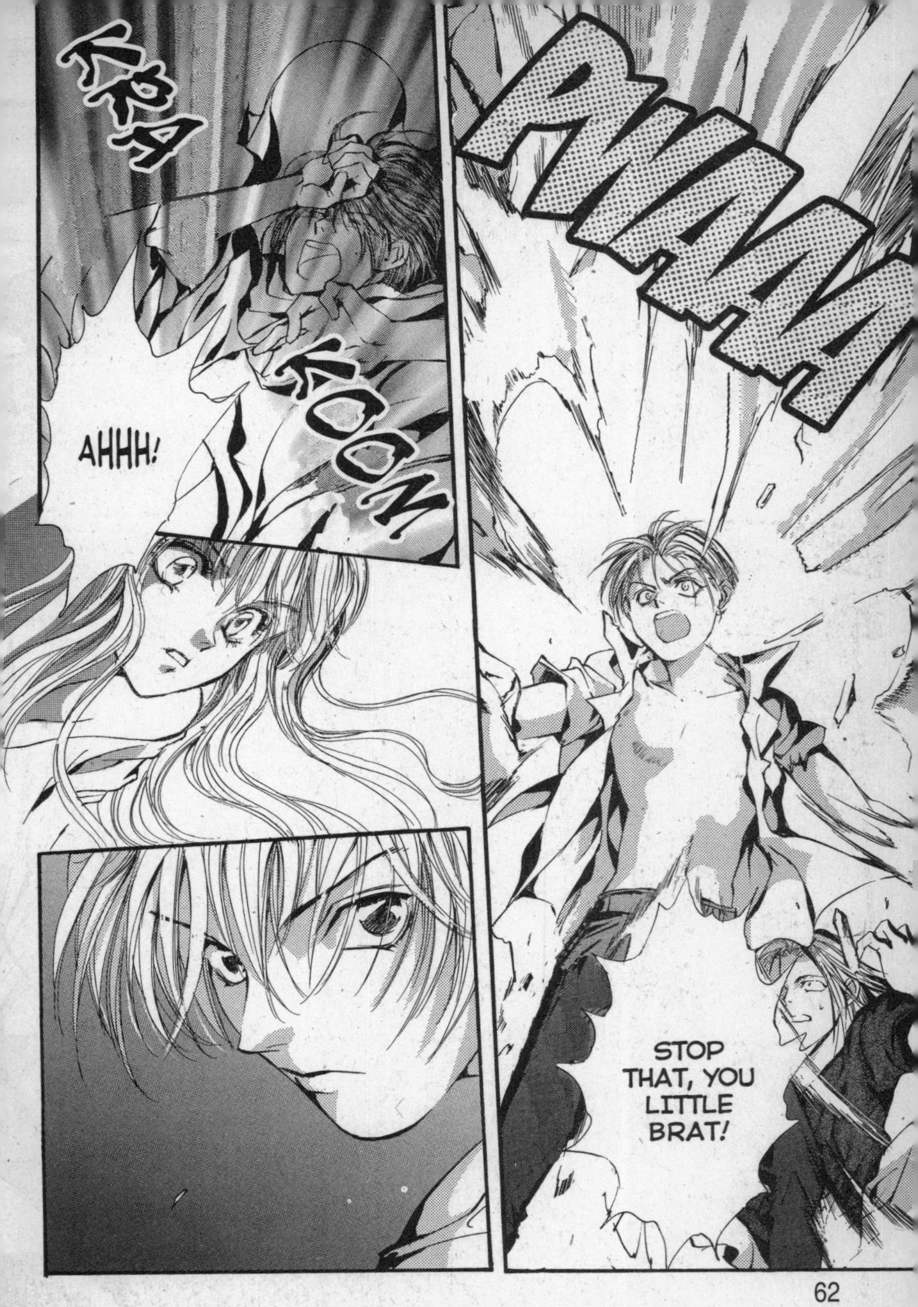
STOP THAT, YOU LITTLE BRAT!
KRA
KOOM!
AHHH!

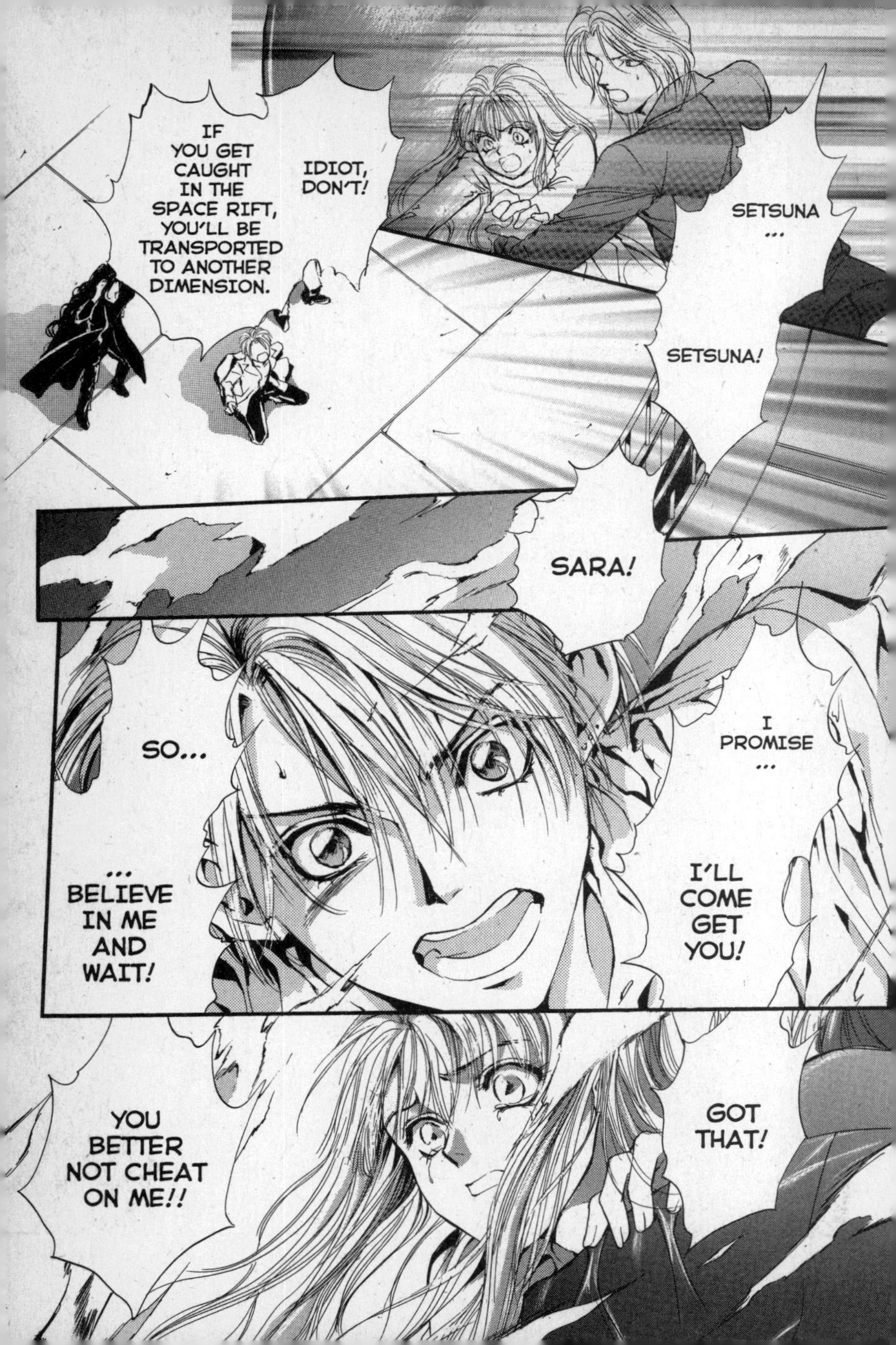
SETSUNA ...
IDIOT, DON'T!
IF YOU GET CAUGHT IN THE SPACE RIFT, YOU'LL BE TRANSPORTED TO ANOTHER DIMENSION.
SETSUNA!
SARA!
I PROMISE ...
I'LL COME GET YOU!
SO...
... BELIEVE IN ME AND WAIT!
GOT THAT!
YOU BETTER NOT CHEAT ON ME!!

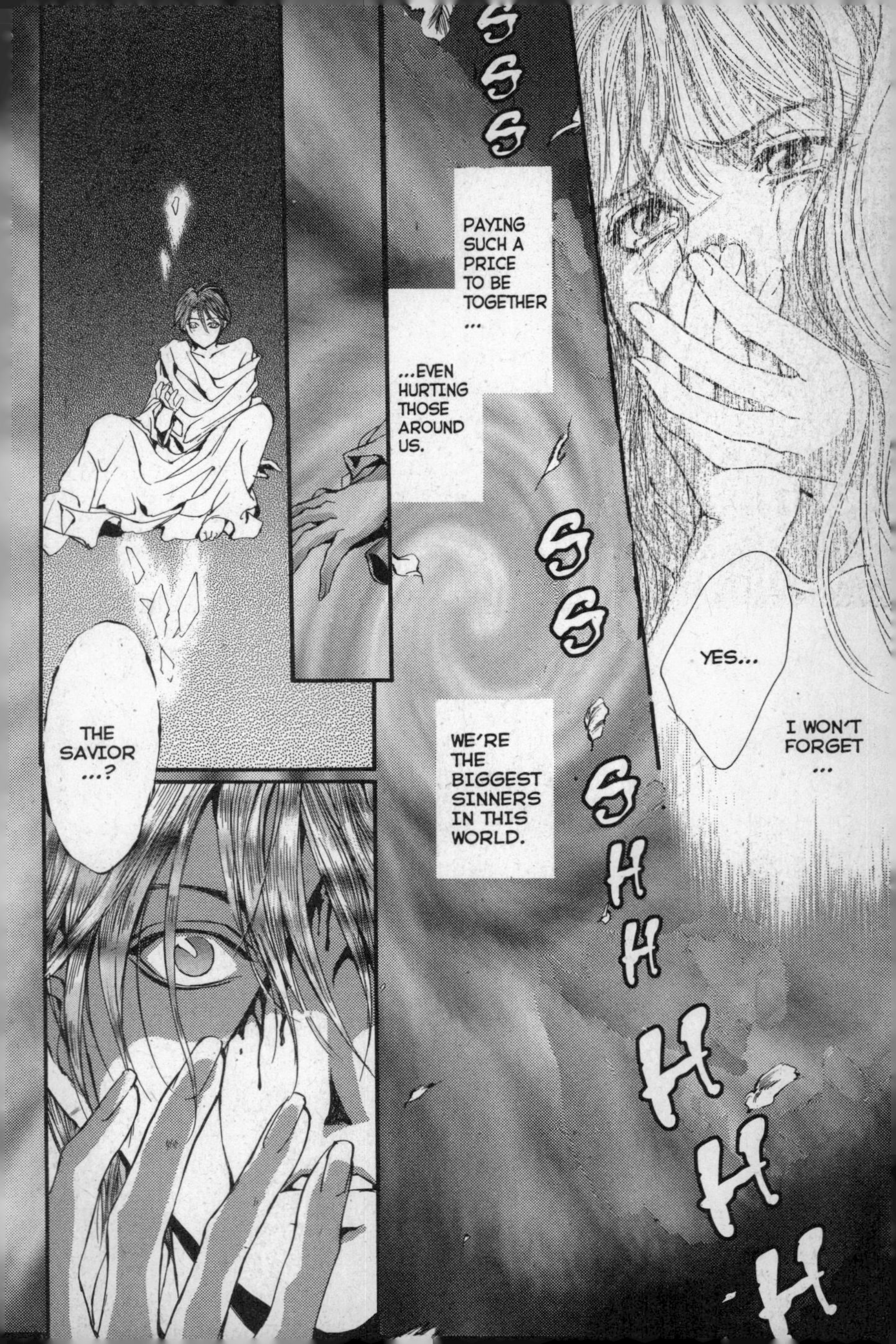
YES...
I WON'T FORGET ...
SSSSSSHHHHHH
PAYING SUCH A PRICE TO BE TOGETHER ...
...EVEN HURTING THOSE AROUND US.
WE'RE THE BIGGEST SINNERS IN THIS WORLD.
THE SAVIOR ...?

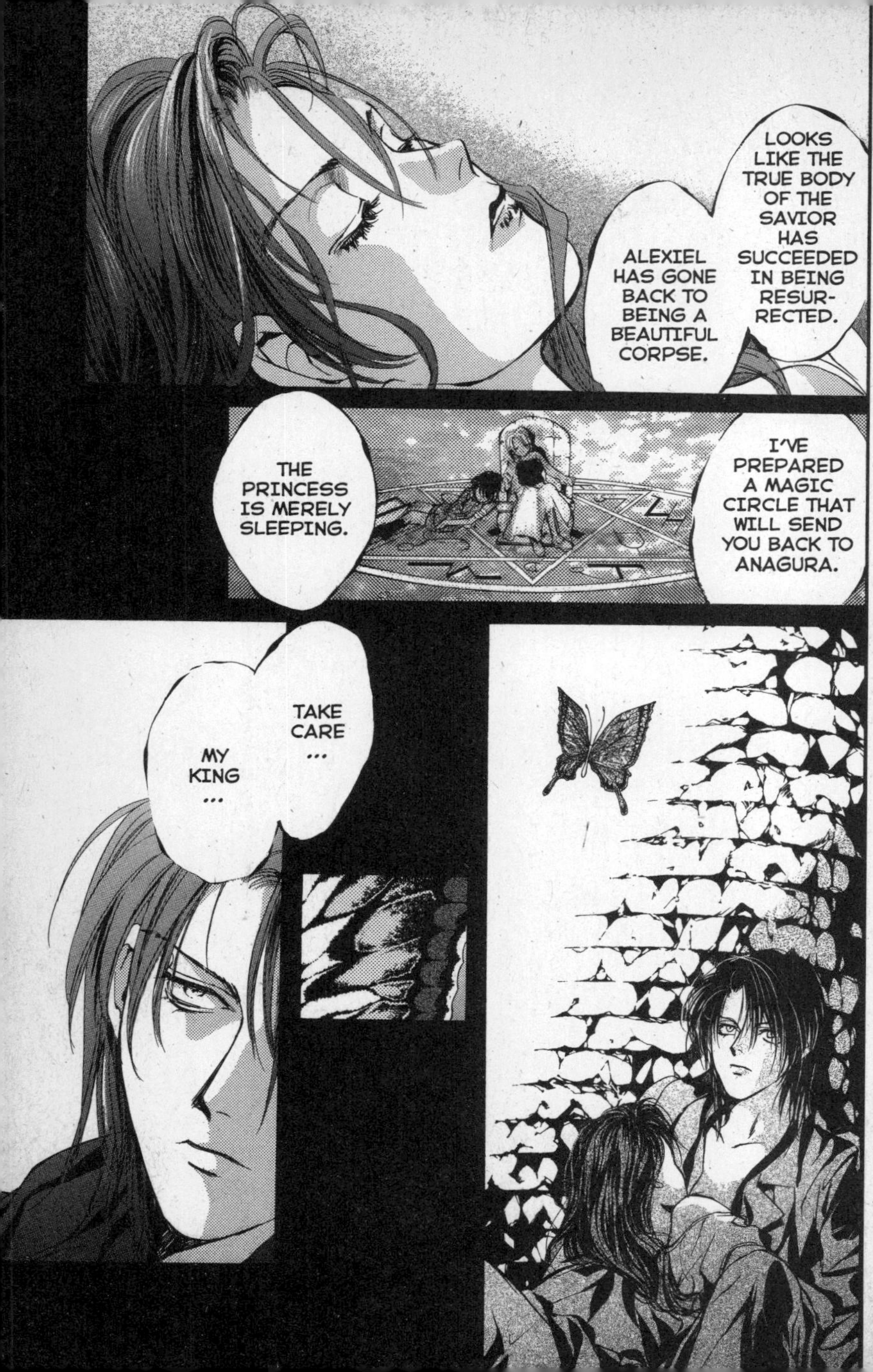
LOOKS LIKE THE TRUE BODY OF THE SAVIOR HAS SUCCEEDED IN BEING RESUR-RECTED.
ALEXIEL HAS GONE BACK TO BEING A BEAUTIFUL CORPSE.
I'VE PREPARED A MAGIC CIRCLE THAT WILL SEND YOU BACK TO ANAGURA.
THE PRINCESS IS MERELY SLEEPING.
TAKE CARE ...
MY KING ...

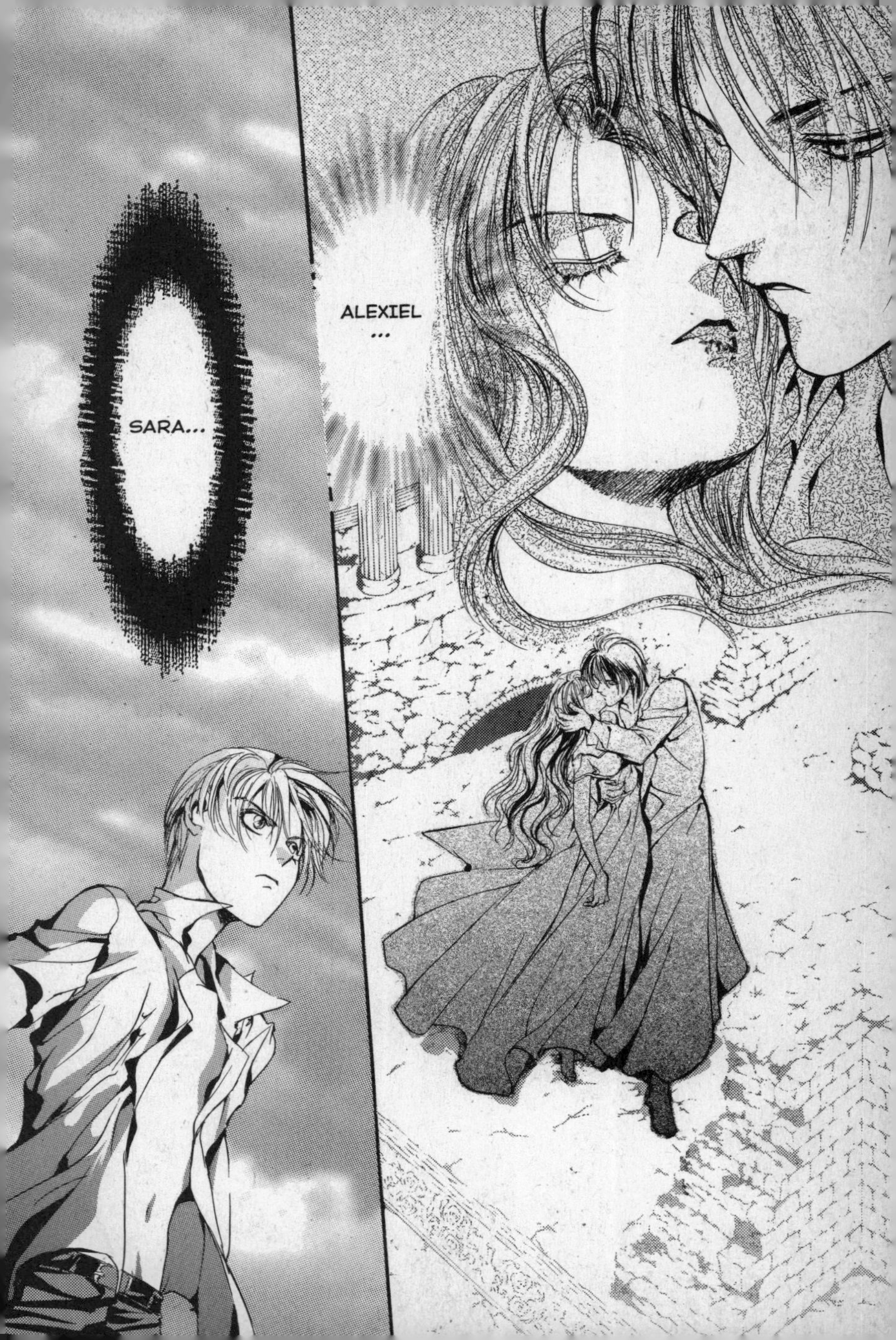
ALEXIEL
...
SARA...

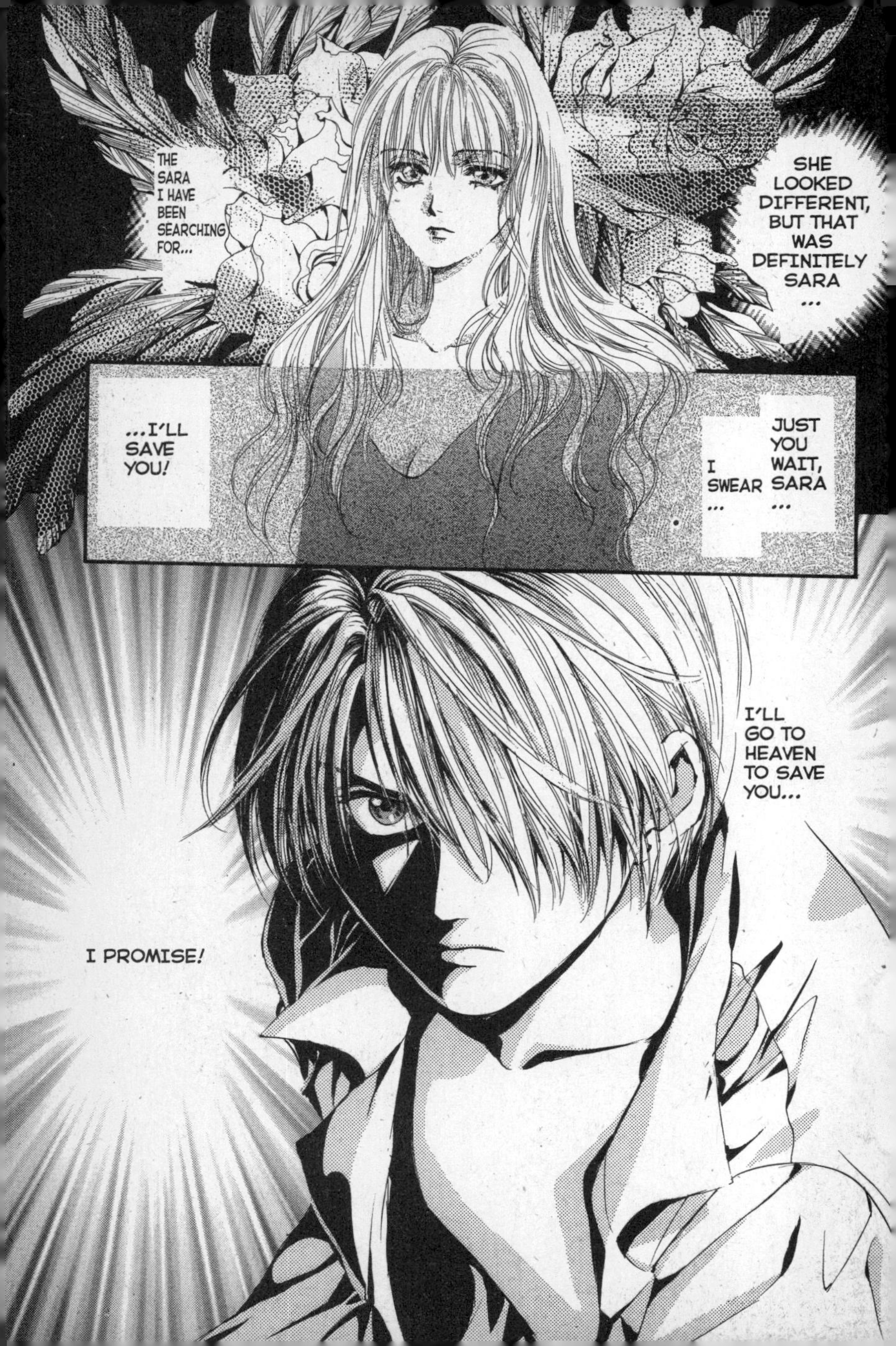
SHE LOOKED DIFFERENT, BUT THAT WAS DEFINITELY SARA ...
THE SARA I HAVE BEEN SEARCHING FOR...
JUST YOU WAIT, SARA ...
I SWEAR ...
...I'LL SAVE YOU!
I'LL GO TO HEAVEN TO SAVE YOU...
I PROMISE!

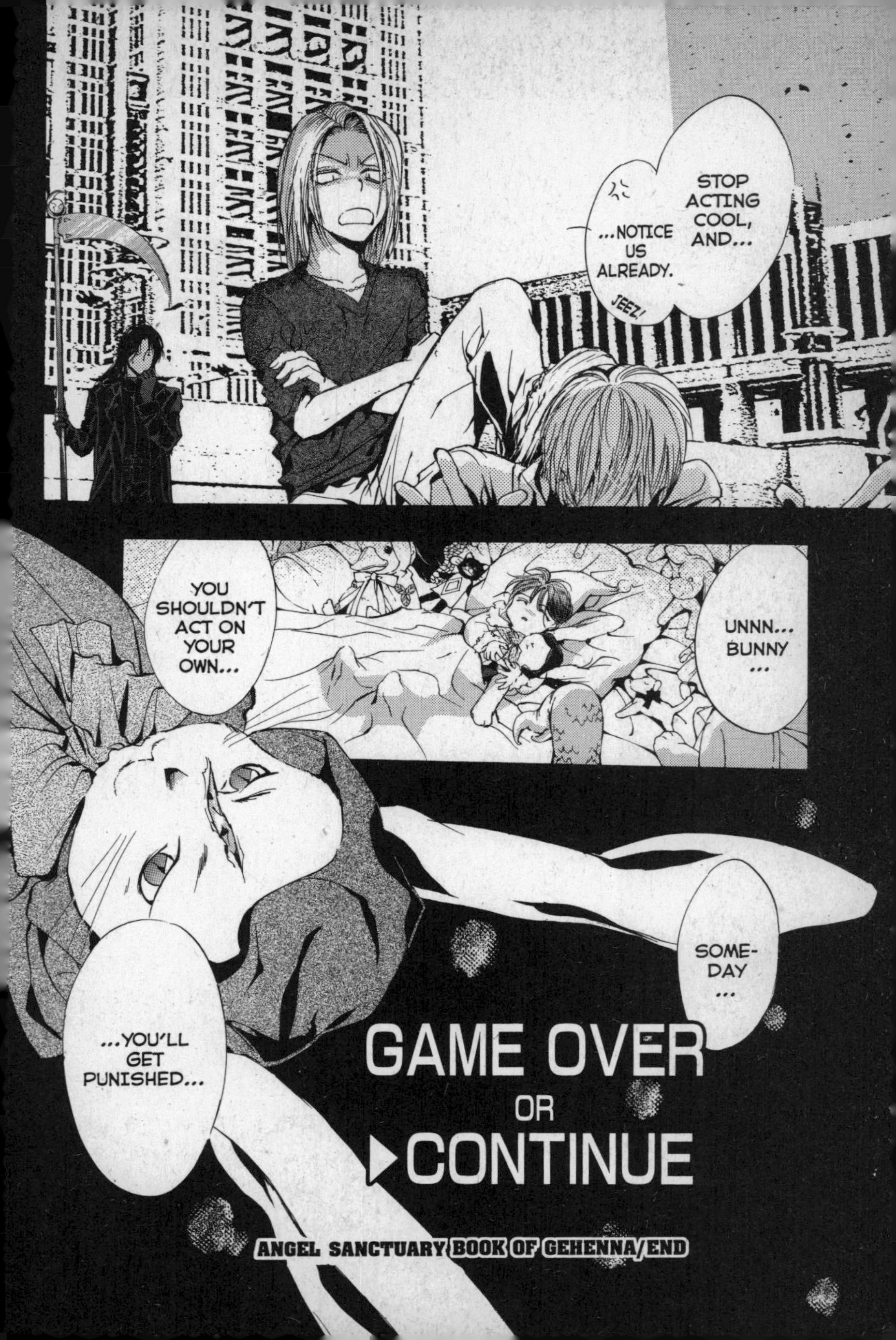
STOP ACTING COOL, AND...
...NOTICE US ALREADY.
JEEZ!
UNNN... BUNNY ...
YOU SHOULDN'T ACT ON YOUR OWN...
SOME-DAY ...
...YOU'LL GET PUNISHED...
GAME OVER
OR
▶CONTINUE
ANGEL SANCTUARY BOOK OF GEHENNA/END

ANGEL SANCTUARY BOOK OF HEAVEN PREVIEW

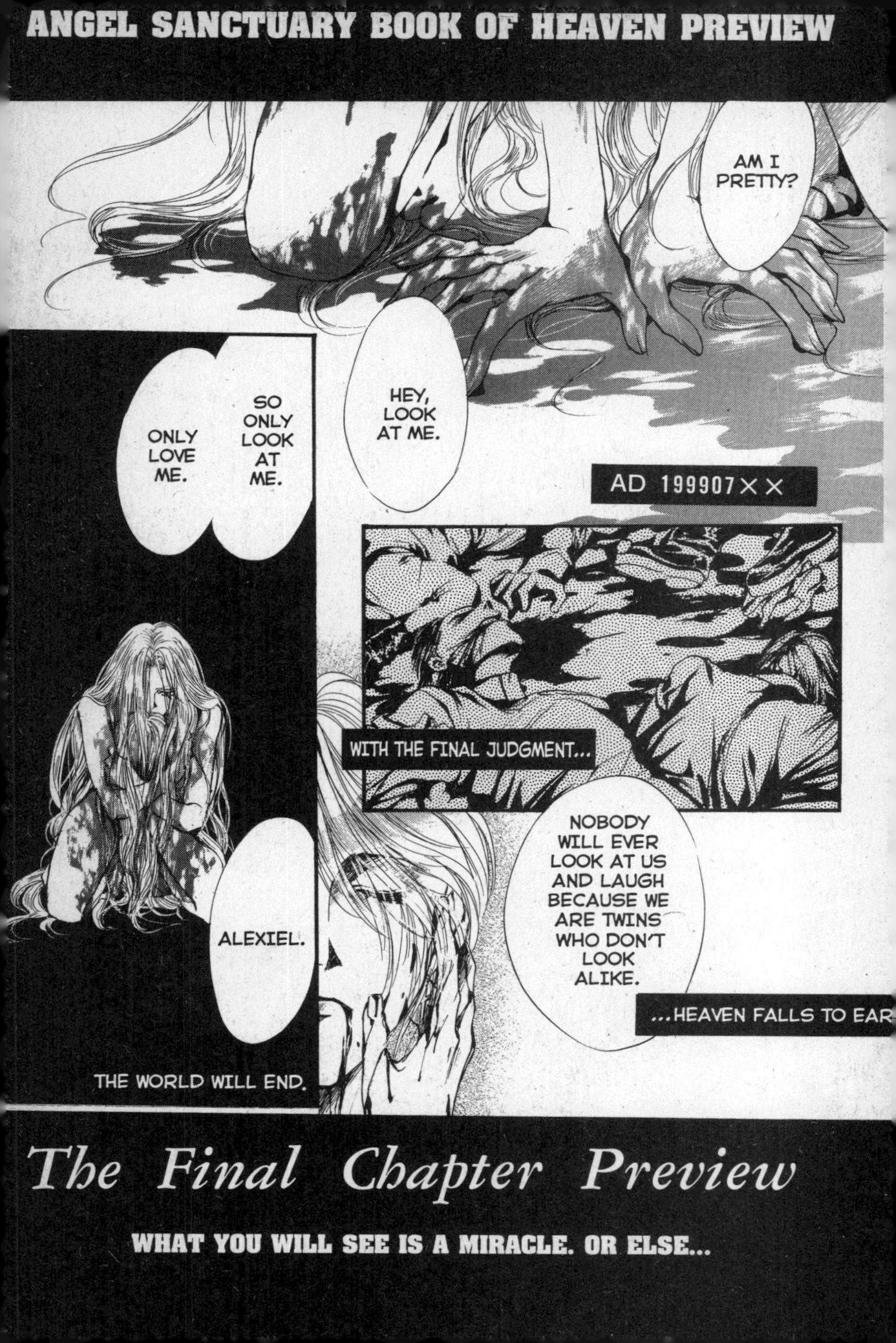
AM I PRETTY?
HEY, LOOK AT ME.
AD 199907××
WITH THE FINAL JUDGMENT...
NOBODY WILL EVER LOOK AT US AND LAUGH BECAUSE WE ARE TWINS WHO DON'T LOOK ALIKE.
...HEAVEN FALLS TO EAR
SO ONLY LOOK AT ME.
ONLY LOVE ME.
ALEXIEL.
THE WORLD WILL END.

The Final Chapter Preview

WHAT YOU WILL SEE IS A MIRACLE. OR ELSE...

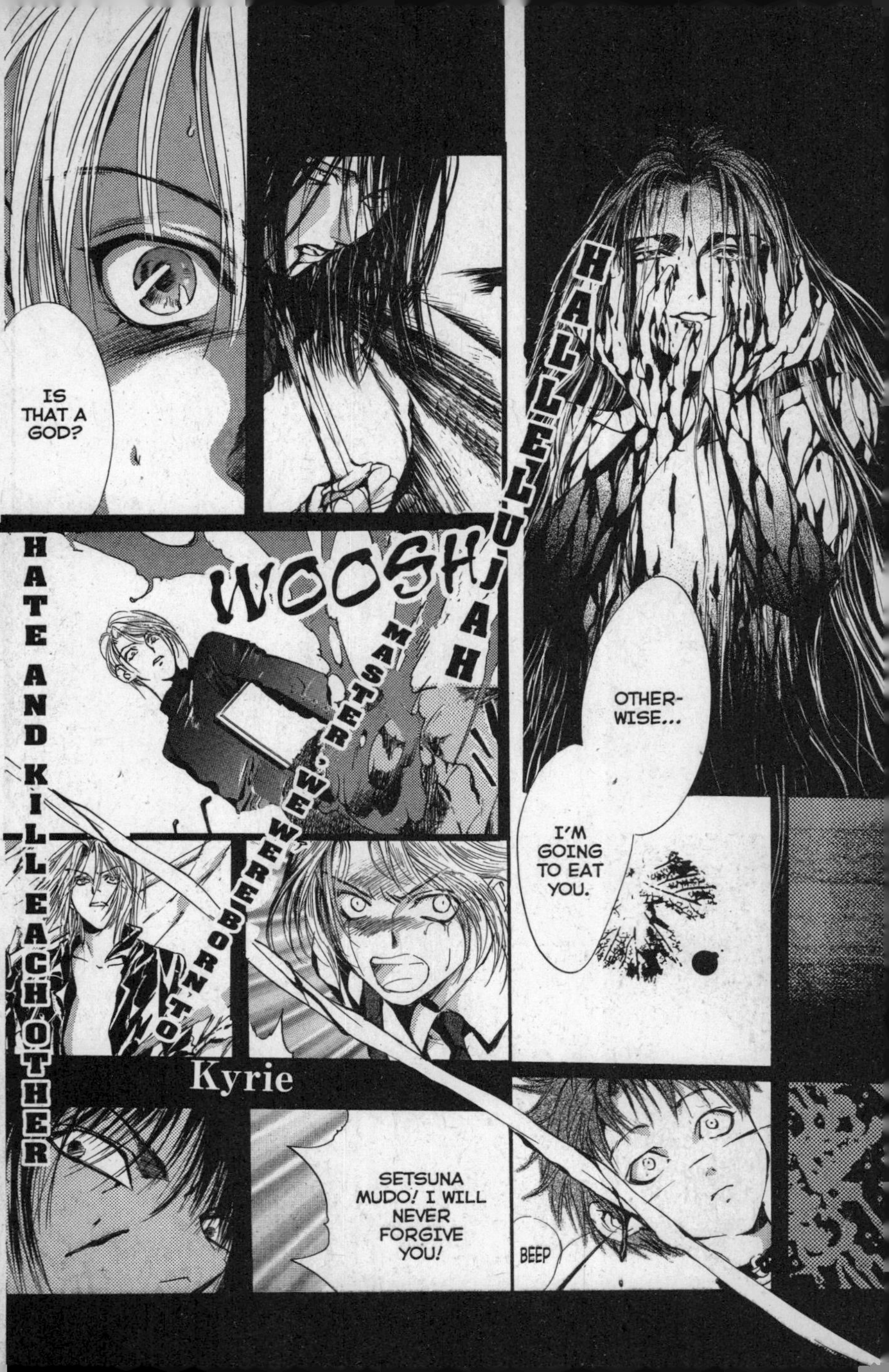
HALLELUJAH
OTHER-WISE...
I'M GOING TO EAT YOU.
IS THAT A GOD?
WOOSH
MASTER, WE WERE BORN TO
HATE AND KILL EACH OTHER
Kyrie
BEEP
SETSUNA MUDO! I WILL NEVER FORGIVE YOU!

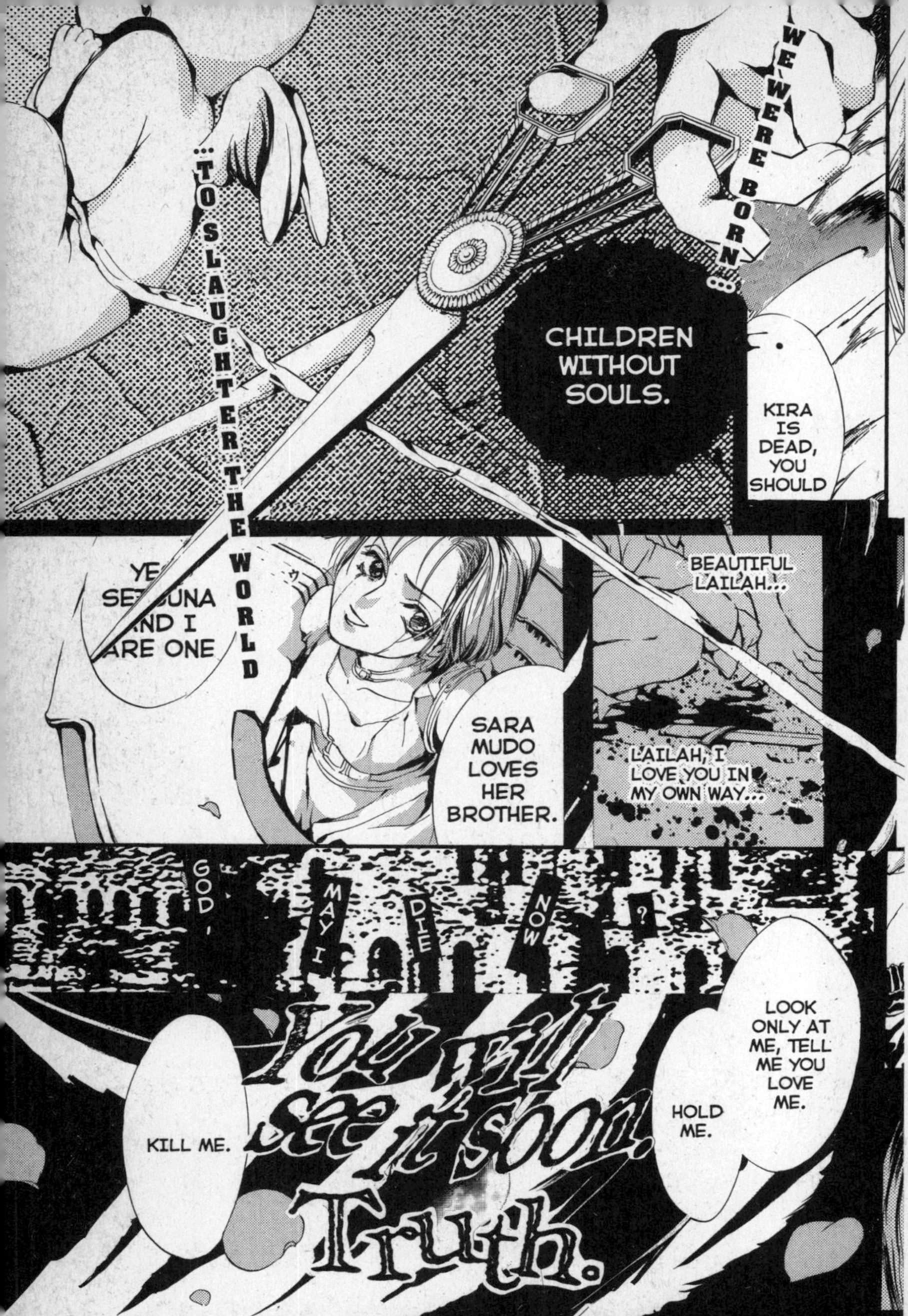
WE WERE BORN...
KIRA IS DEAD, YOU SHOULD
CHILDREN WITHOUT SOULS.
...TO SLAUGHTER THE WORLD
BEAUTIFUL LAILAH...
LAILAH, I LOVE YOU IN MY OWN WAY...
SARA MUDO LOVES HER BROTHER.
YE… SE UNA AND I ARE ONE
GOD, MAY I DIE NOW?
LOOK ONLY AT ME, TELL ME YOU LOVE ME.
HOLD ME.
KILL ME.
You will see it soon. Truth.

ANGEL SANCTUARY BOOK OF HEAVEN PREVIEW END

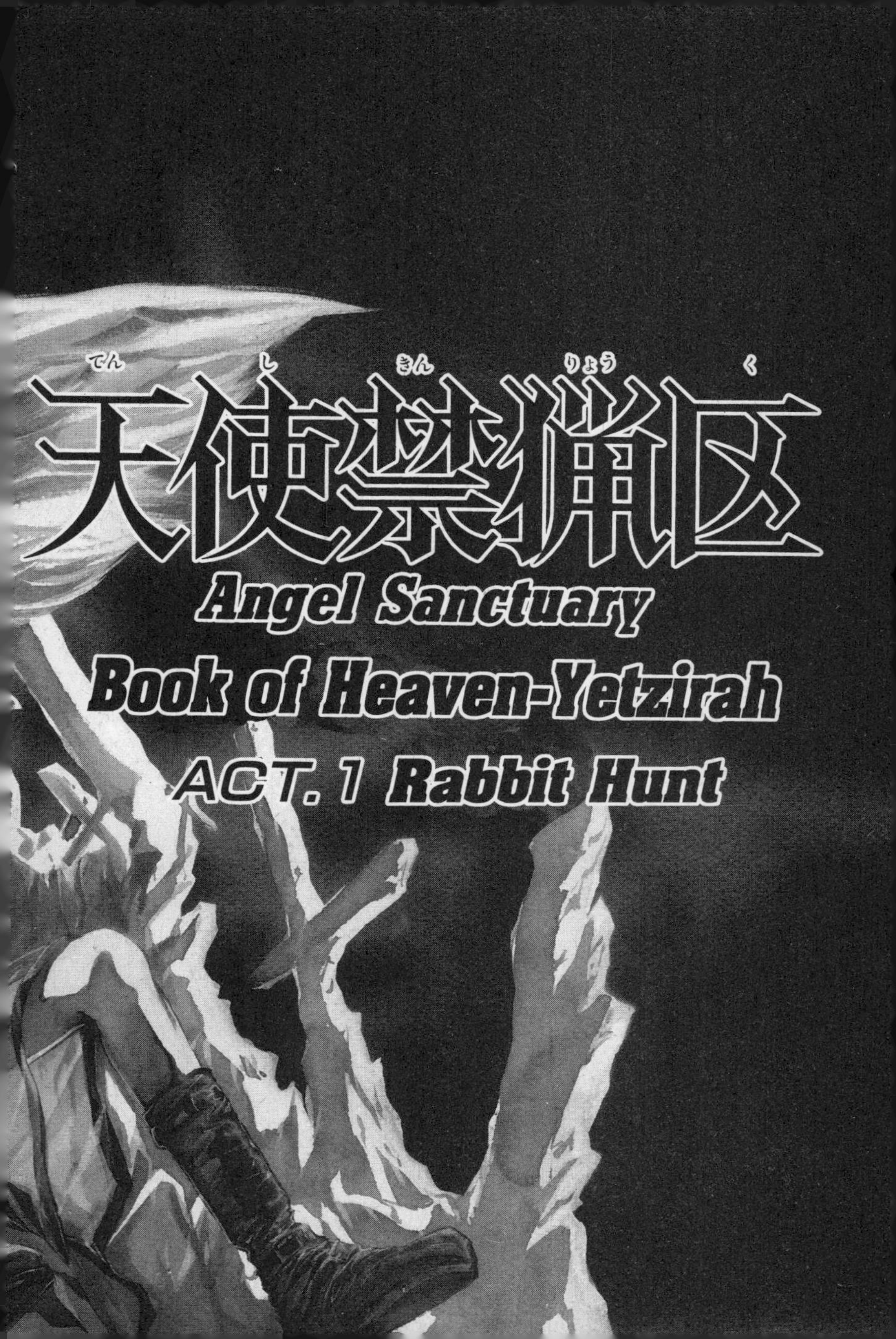

天使禁猟区
Angel Sanctuary
Book of Heaven-Yetzirah
ACT. 1 Rabbit Hunt

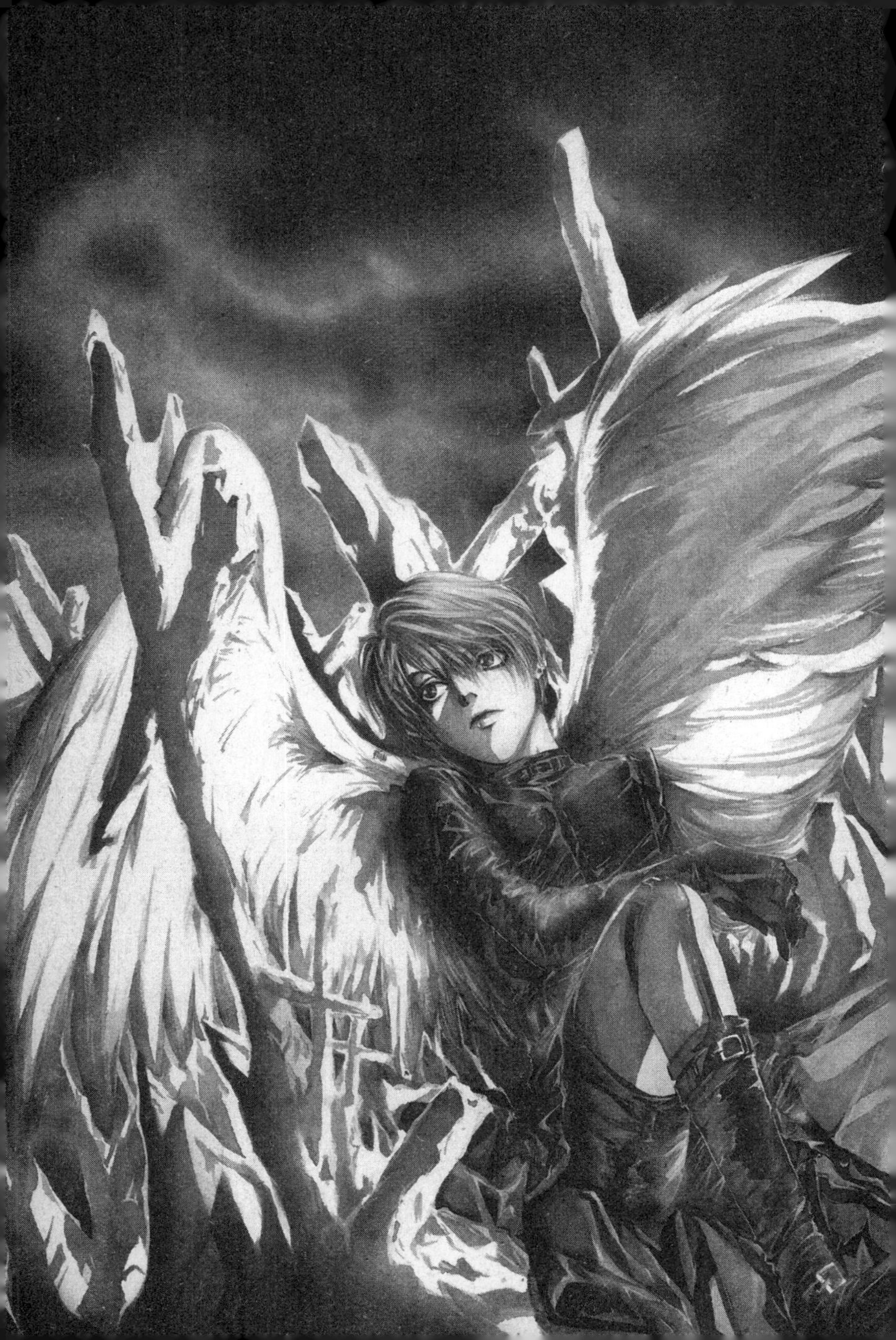

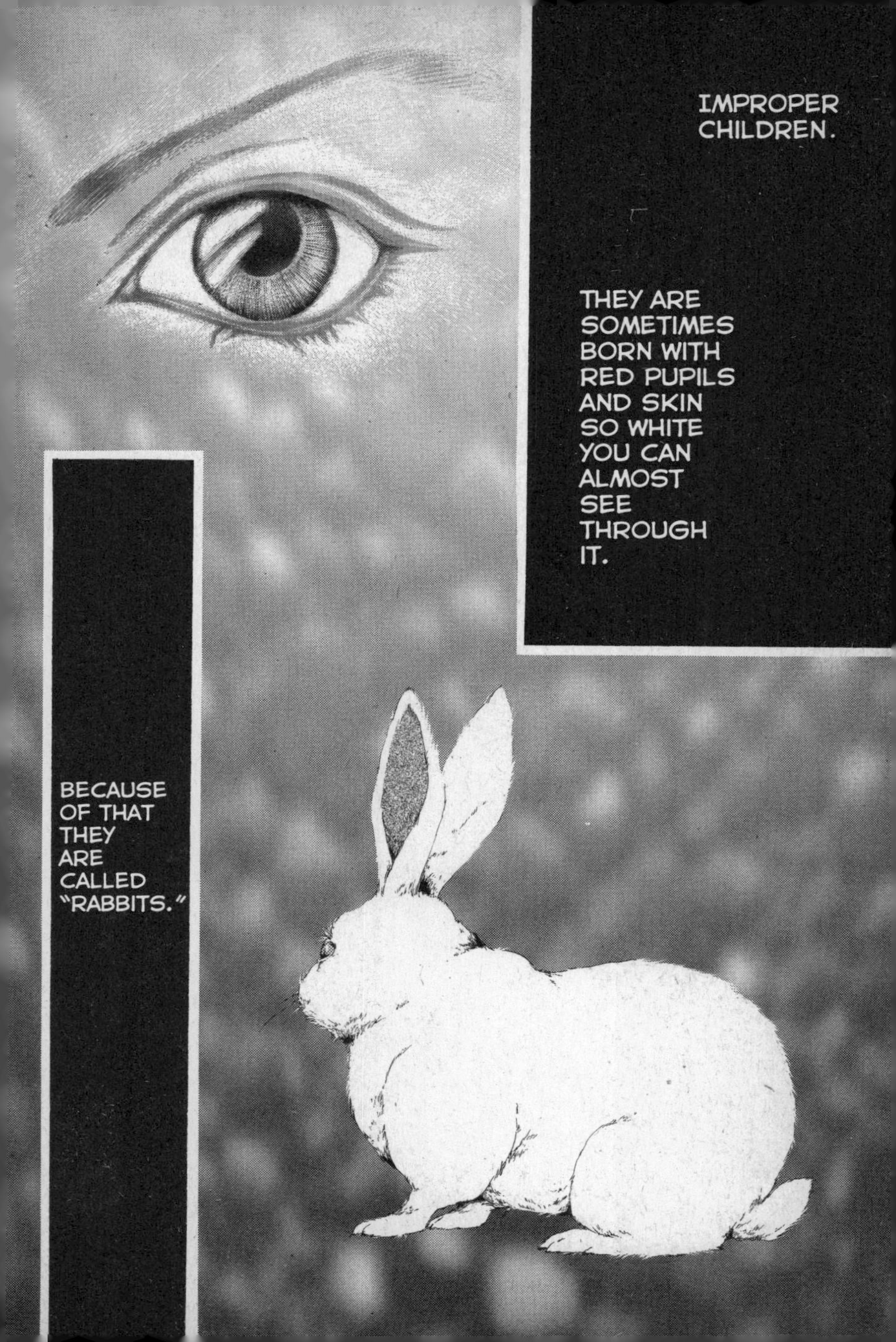
IMPROPER CHILDREN.
THEY ARE SOMETIMES BORN WITH RED PUPILS AND SKIN SO WHITE YOU CAN ALMOST SEE THROUGH IT.
BECAUSE OF THAT THEY ARE CALLED "RABBITS."

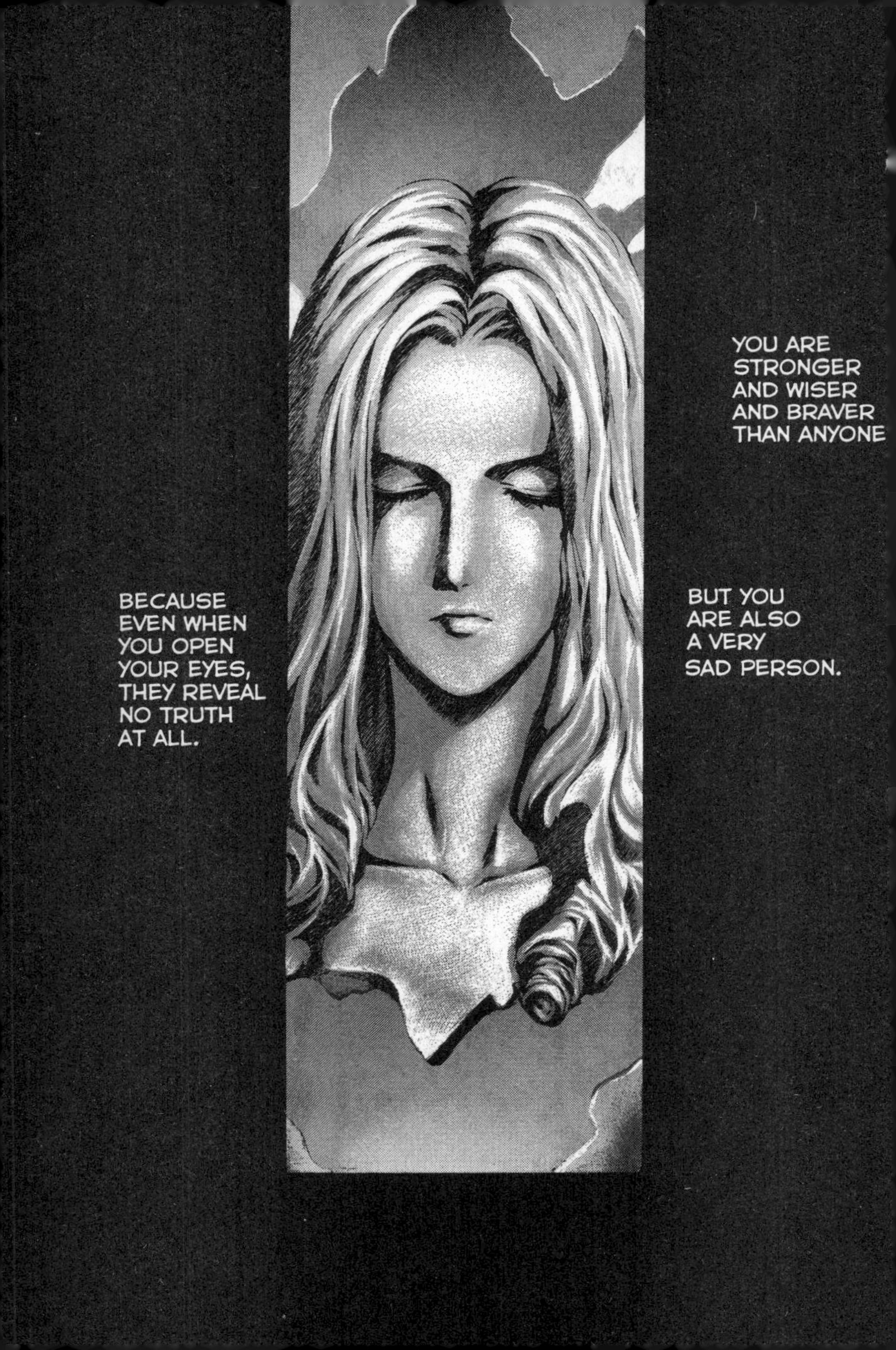
YOU ARE STRONGER AND WISER AND BRAVER THAN ANYONE
BUT YOU ARE ALSO A VERY SAD PERSON.
BECAUSE EVEN WHEN YOU OPEN YOUR EYES, THEY REVEAL NO TRUTH AT ALL.

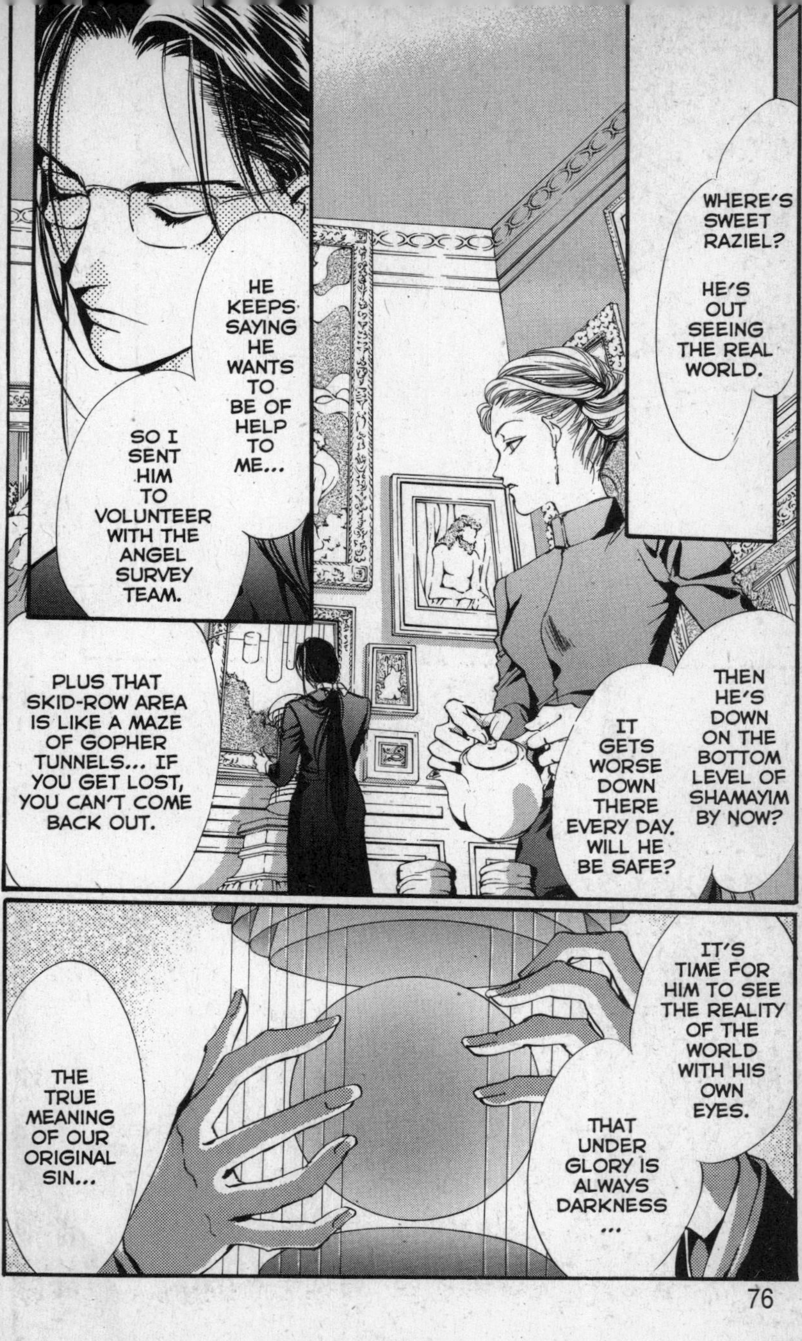
WHERE'S SWEET RAZIEL?
HE'S OUT SEEING THE REAL WORLD.
HE KEEPS SAYING HE WANTS TO BE OF HELP TO ME...
SO I SENT HIM TO VOLUNTEER WITH THE ANGEL SURVEY TEAM.
THEN HE'S DOWN ON THE BOTTOM LEVEL OF SHAMAYIM BY NOW?
IT GETS WORSE DOWN THERE EVERY DAY. WILL HE BE SAFE?
PLUS THAT SKID-ROW AREA IS LIKE A MAZE OF GOPHER TUNNELS... IF YOU GET LOST, YOU CAN'T COME BACK OUT.
IT'S TIME FOR HIM TO SEE THE REALITY OF THE WORLD WITH HIS OWN EYES.
THAT UNDER GLORY IS ALWAYS DARKNESS ...
THE TRUE MEANING OF OUR ORIGINAL SIN...

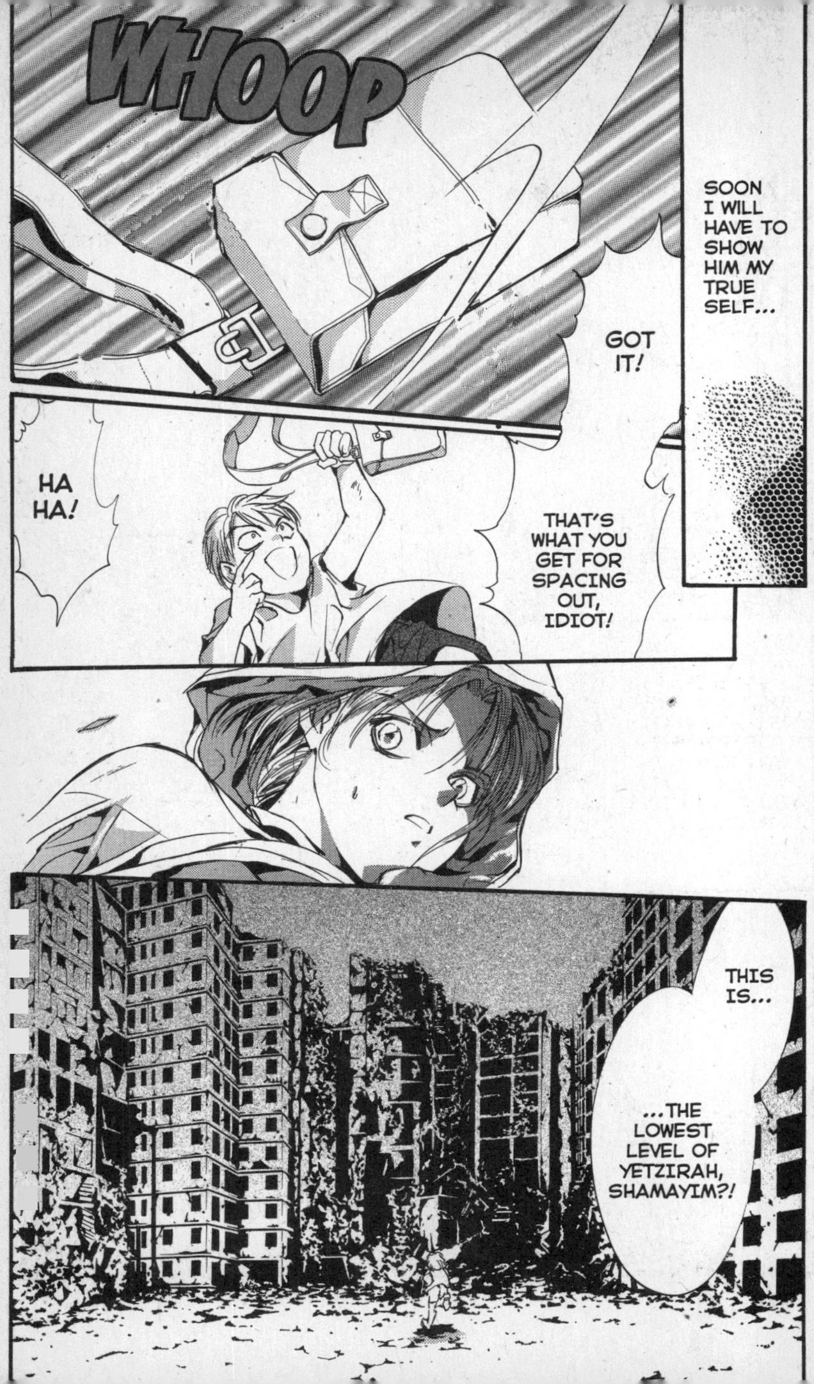
SOON I WILL HAVE TO SHOW HIM MY TRUE SELF...
WHOOP
GOT IT!
THAT'S WHAT YOU GET FOR SPACING OUT, IDIOT!
HA HA!
THIS IS...
...THE LOWEST LEVEL OF YETZIRAH, SHAMAYIM?!

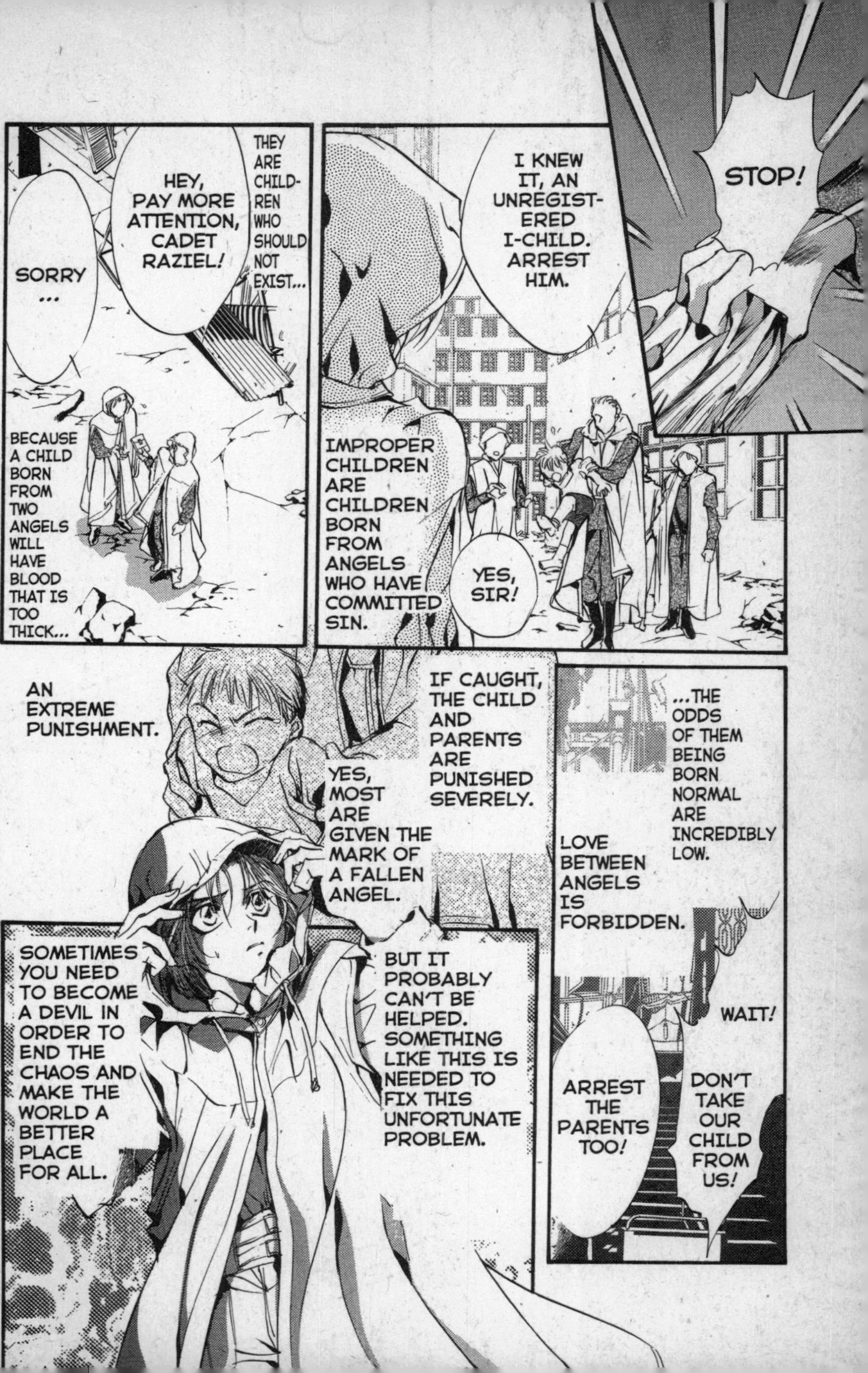
STOP!
I KNEW IT, AN UNREGISTERED I-CHILD. ARREST HIM.
IMPROPER CHILDREN ARE CHILDREN BORN FROM ANGELS WHO HAVE COMMITTED SIN.
YES, SIR!
THEY ARE CHILDREN WHO SHOULD NOT EXIST...
HEY, PAY MORE ATTENTION, CADET RAZIEL!
SORRY...
BECAUSE A CHILD BORN FROM TWO ANGELS WILL HAVE BLOOD THAT IS TOO THICK...
...THE ODDS OF THEM BEING BORN NORMAL ARE INCREDIBLY LOW.
LOVE BETWEEN ANGELS IS FORBIDDEN.
WAIT!
DON'T TAKE OUR CHILD FROM US!
ARREST THE PARENTS TOO!
IF CAUGHT, THE CHILD AND PARENTS ARE PUNISHED SEVERELY.
YES, MOST ARE GIVEN THE MARK OF A FALLEN ANGEL.
AN EXTREME PUNISHMENT.
BUT IT PROBABLY CAN'T BE HELPED. SOMETHING LIKE THIS IS NEEDED TO FIX THIS UNFORTUNATE PROBLEM.
SOMETIMES YOU NEED TO BECOME A DEVIL IN ORDER TO END THE CHAOS AND MAKE THE WORLD A BETTER PLACE FOR ALL.

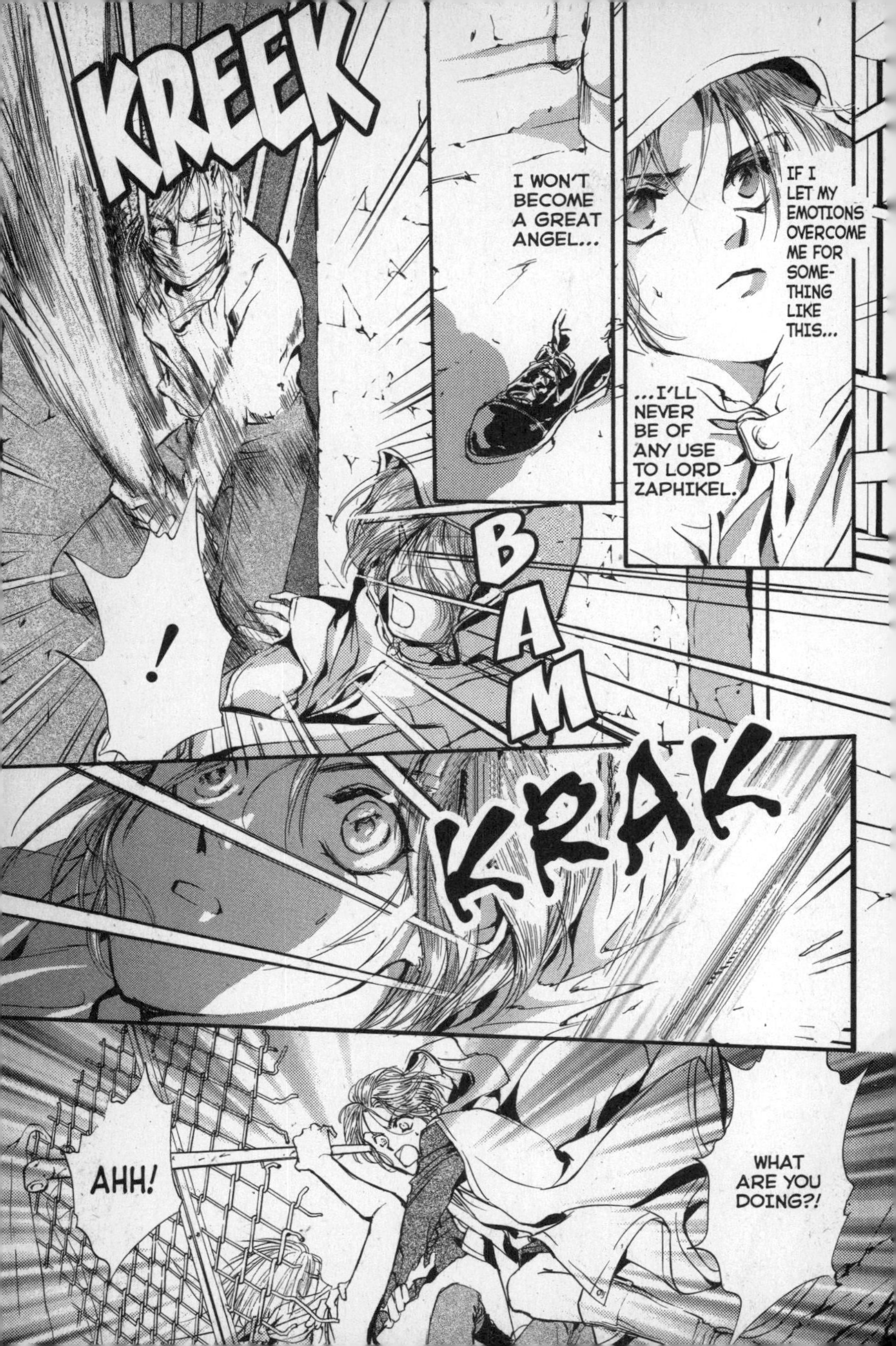
IF I LET MY EMOTIONS OVERCOME ME FOR SOME-THING LIKE THIS...
...I'LL NEVER BE OF ANY USE TO LORD ZAPHIKEL.
I WON'T BECOME A GREAT ANGEL...
KREEK
BAM
!
KRAK
WHAT ARE YOU DOING?!
AHH!

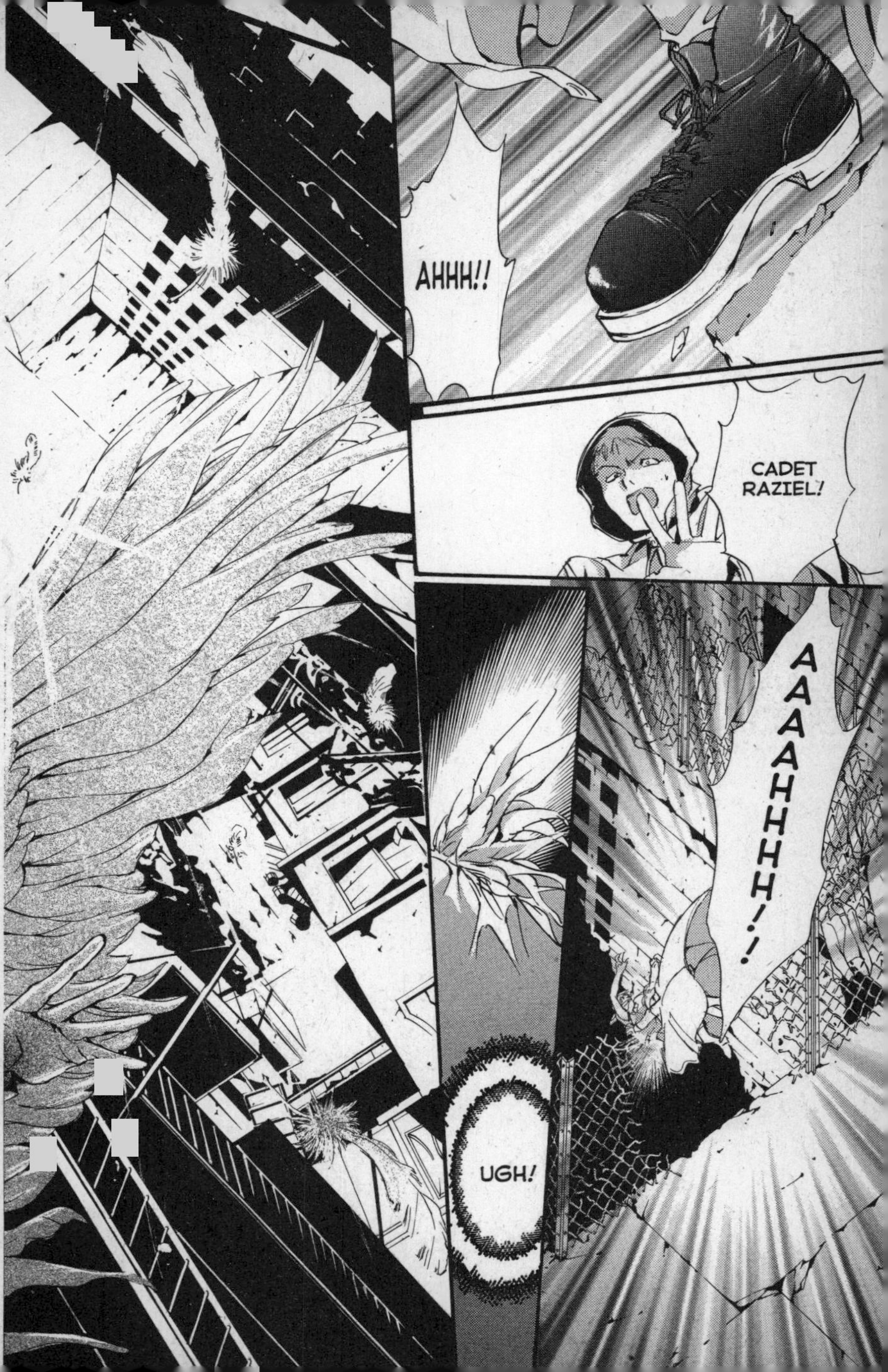
AHHH!!
CADET RAZIEL!
AAAAHHHH!!
UGH!

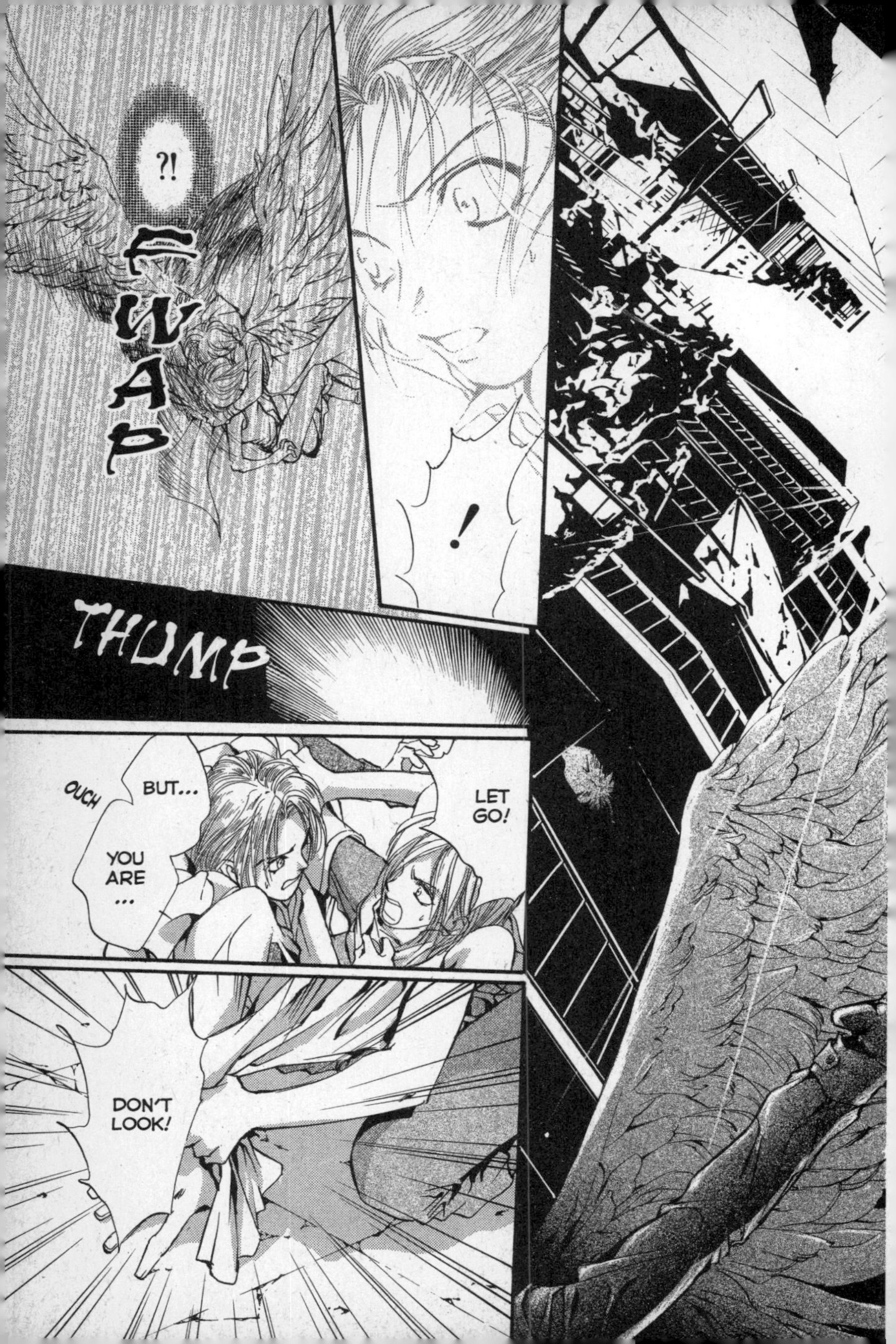
!
?!
FWAP
THUMP
LET GO!
BUT...
OUCH
YOU ARE ...
DON'T LOOK!

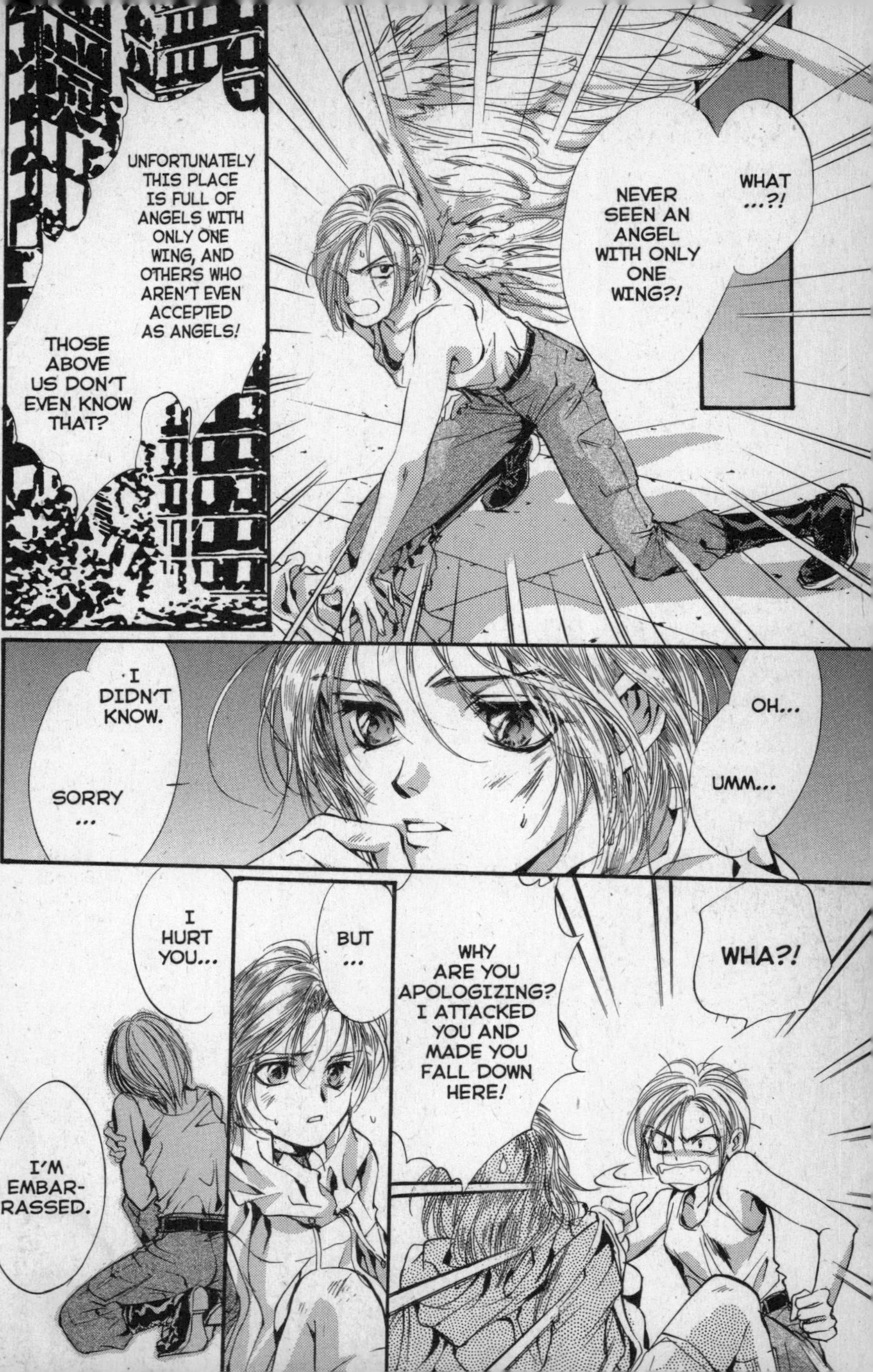
WHAT ...?!
NEVER SEEN AN ANGEL WITH ONLY ONE WING?!
UNFORTUNATELY THIS PLACE IS FULL OF ANGELS WITH ONLY ONE WING, AND OTHERS WHO AREN'T EVEN ACCEPTED AS ANGELS!
THOSE ABOVE US DON'T EVEN KNOW THAT?
OH...
UMM...
I DIDN'T KNOW.
SORRY ...
WHA?!
WHY ARE YOU APOLOGIZING? I ATTACKED YOU AND MADE YOU FALL DOWN HERE!
BUT ...
I HURT YOU...
I'M EMBARRASSED.

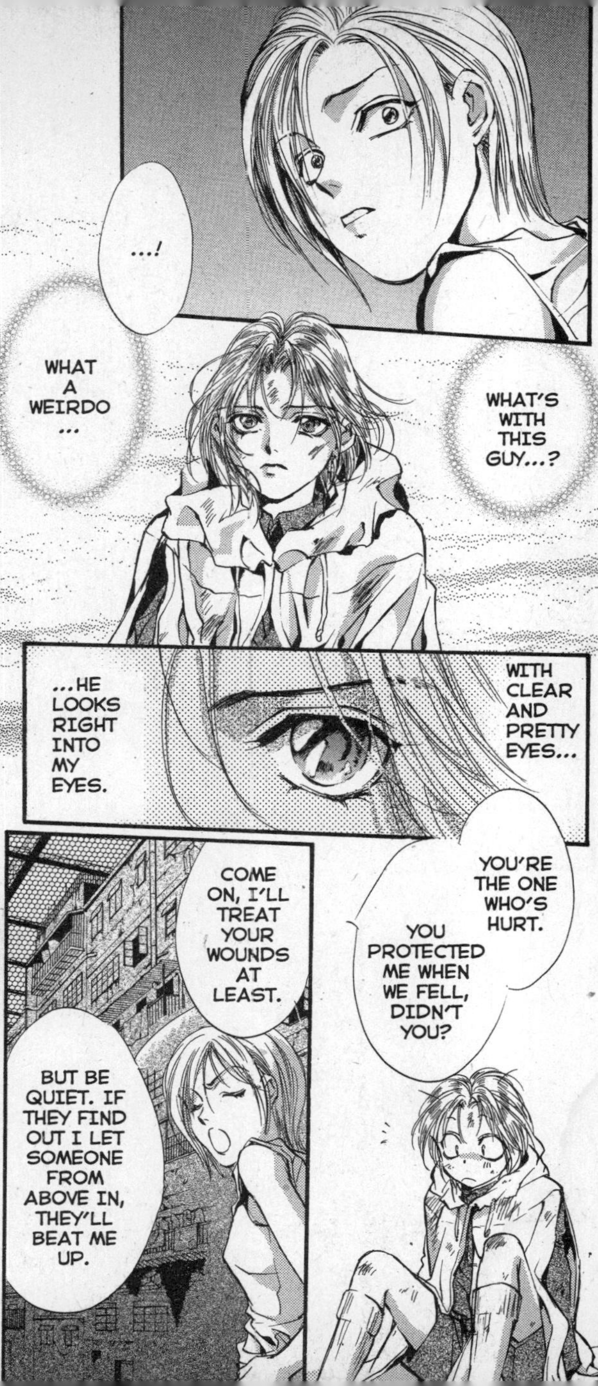
...!
WHAT'S WITH THIS GUY...?
WHAT A WEIRDO...
WITH CLEAR AND PRETTY EYES...
...HE LOOKS RIGHT INTO MY EYES.
YOU'RE THE ONE WHO'S HURT.
YOU PROTECTED ME WHEN WE FELL, DIDN'T YOU?
COME ON, I'LL TREAT YOUR WOUNDS AT LEAST.
BUT BE QUIET. IF THEY FIND OUT I LET SOMEONE FROM ABOVE IN, THEY'LL BEAT ME UP.

Heaven arc... Disappointed that I'm starting it with Raziel-kun? But I have to start it off with this. Umm... About the I-Children, it's not that they all have red eyes, just most of them. Some of them have the whites of their eyes colored red. Shateiel isn't an I-Child. Her character might be from the game "Linda Cube Again" which I was obsessed with for a while. Every day I would collect the animals in those ant hole-type dungeons. It was annoying but also very fun.

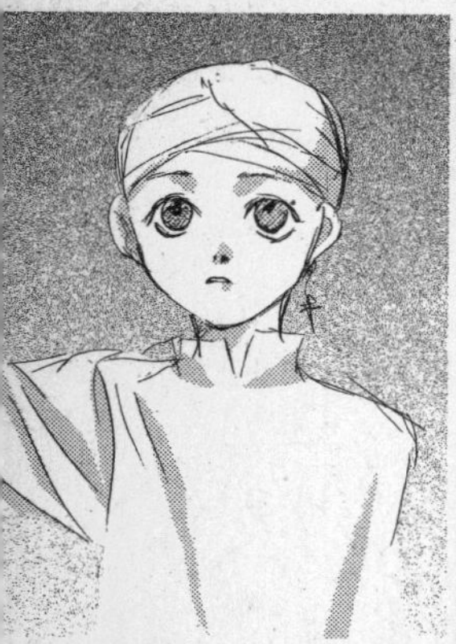

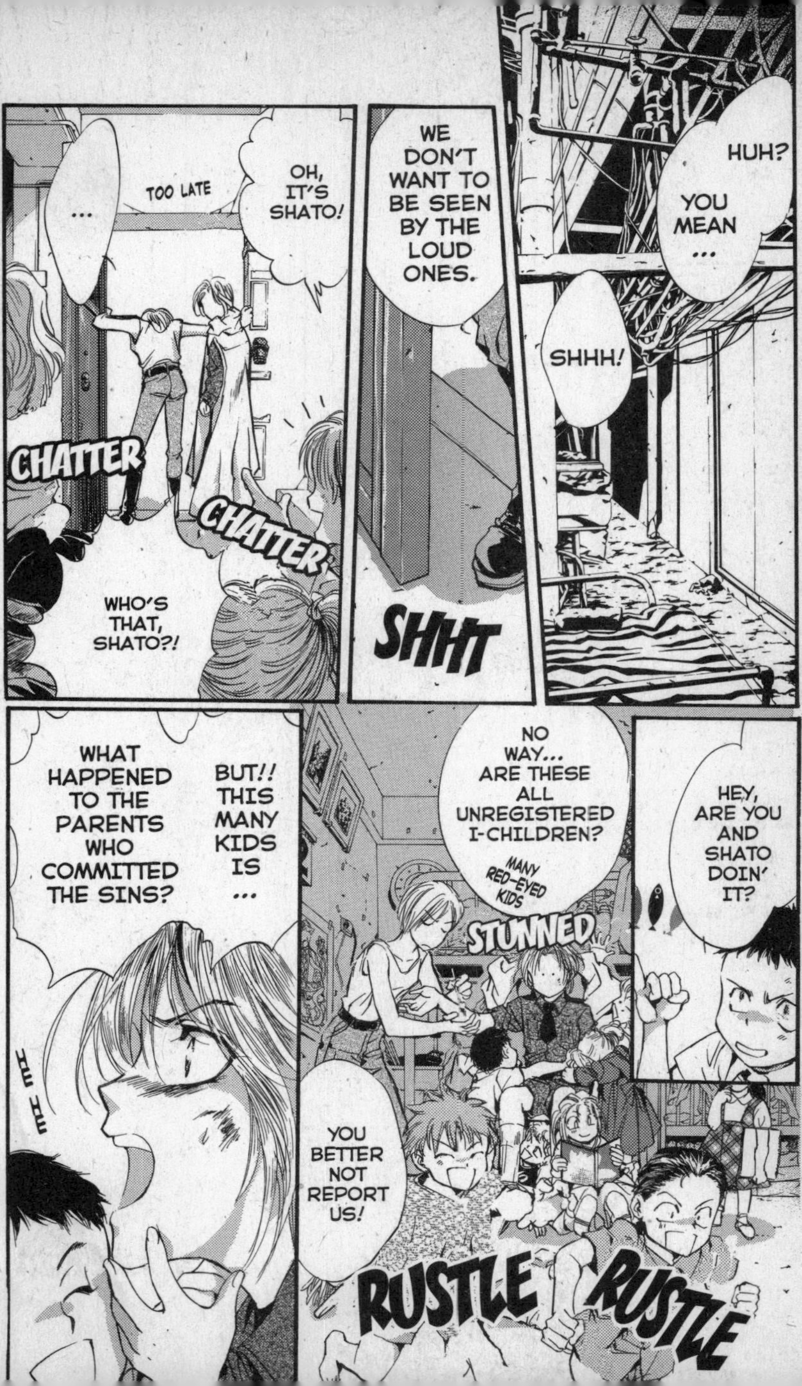
HUH?
YOU MEAN ...
SHHH!
WE DON'T WANT TO BE SEEN BY THE LOUD ONES.
SHHT
OH, IT'S SHATO!
TOO LATE
...
CHATTER
CHATTER
WHO'S THAT, SHATO?!
HEY, ARE YOU AND SHATO DOIN' IT?
NO WAY... ARE THESE ALL UNREGISTERED I-CHILDREN?
MANY RED-EYED KIDS
STUNNED
BUT!! THIS MANY KIDS IS ...
WHAT HAPPENED TO THE PARENTS WHO COMMITTED THE SINS?
HE HE
YOU BETTER NOT REPORT US!
RUSTLE
RUSTLE

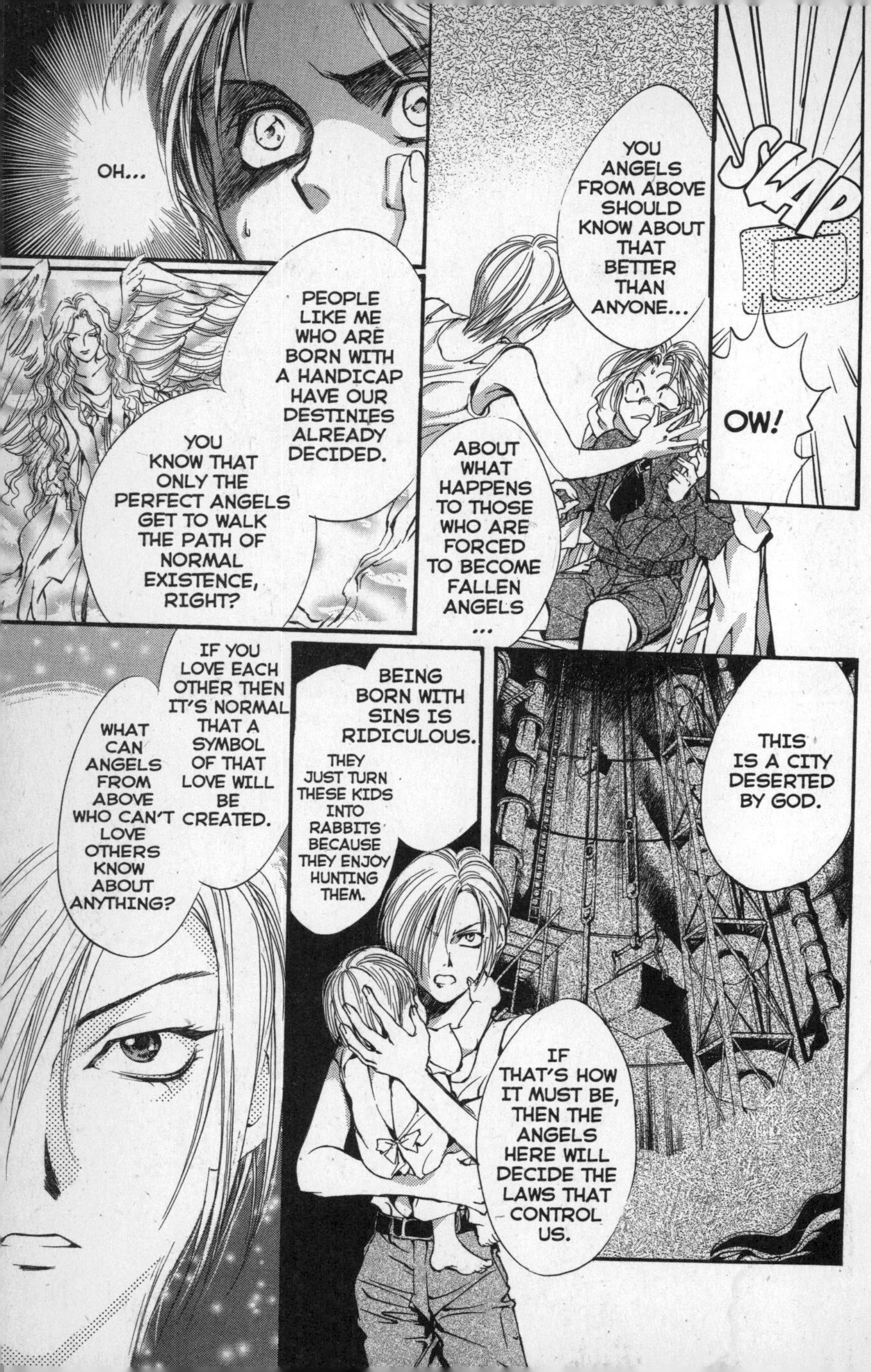
SLAP
OW!
YOU ANGELS FROM ABOVE SHOULD KNOW ABOUT THAT BETTER THAN ANYONE...
ABOUT WHAT HAPPENS TO THOSE WHO ARE FORCED TO BECOME FALLEN ANGELS ...
OH...
PEOPLE LIKE ME WHO ARE BORN WITH A HANDICAP HAVE OUR DESTINIES ALREADY DECIDED.
YOU KNOW THAT ONLY THE PERFECT ANGELS GET TO WALK THE PATH OF NORMAL EXISTENCE, RIGHT?
THIS IS A CITY DESERTED BY GOD.
BEING BORN WITH SINS IS RIDICULOUS.
THEY JUST TURN THESE KIDS INTO RABBITS BECAUSE THEY ENJOY HUNTING THEM.
IF THAT'S HOW IT MUST BE, THEN THE ANGELS HERE WILL DECIDE THE LAWS THAT CONTROL US.
IF YOU LOVE EACH OTHER THEN IT'S NORMAL THAT A SYMBOL OF THAT LOVE WILL BE CREATED.
WHAT CAN ANGELS FROM ABOVE WHO CAN'T LOVE OTHERS KNOW ABOUT ANYTHING?

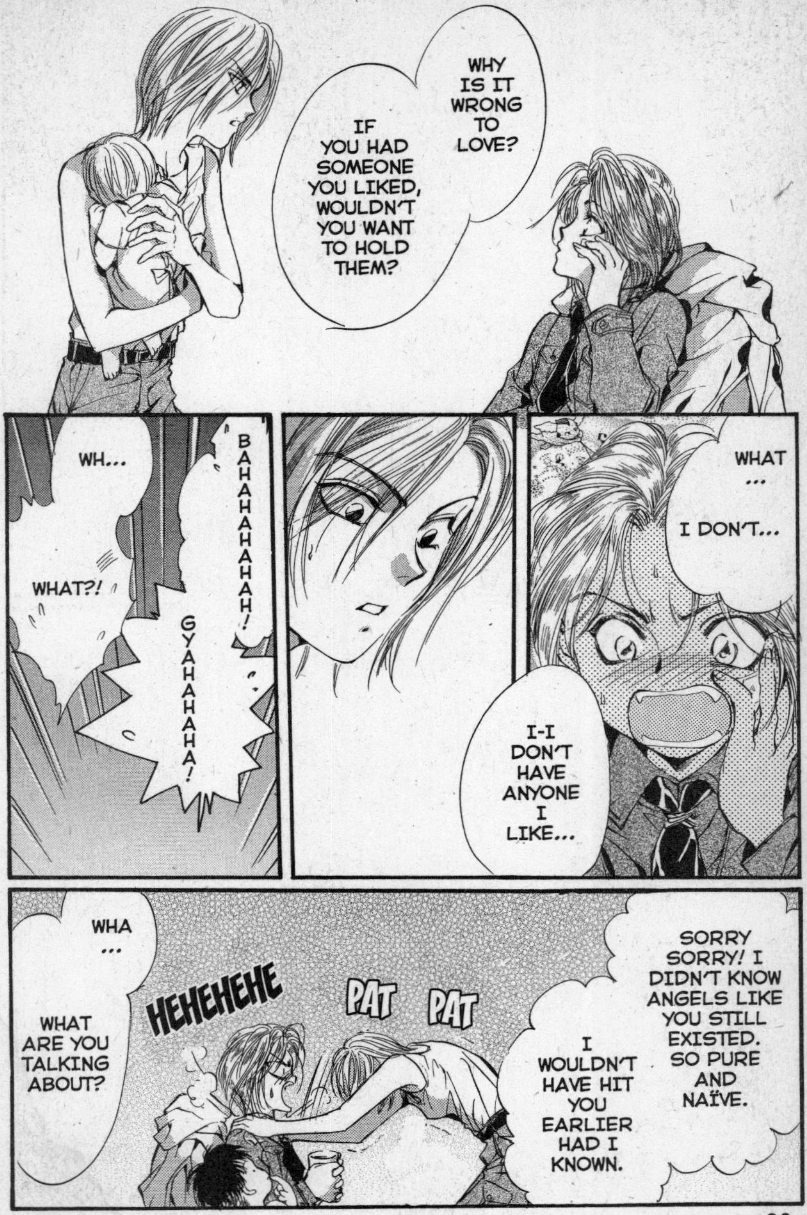
WHY IS IT WRONG TO LOVE?
IF YOU HAD SOMEONE YOU LIKED, WOULDN'T YOU WANT TO HOLD THEM?
WHAT ... I DON'T...
I-I DON'T HAVE ANYONE I LIKE...
BAHAHAHAHAHAH!
WH...
GYAHAHAHA!
WHAT?!
SORRY SORRY! I DIDN'T KNOW ANGELS LIKE YOU STILL EXISTED. SO PURE AND NAÏVE.
I WOULDN'T HAVE HIT YOU EARLIER HAD I KNOWN.
PAT PAT
HEHEHEHE
WHA ...
WHAT ARE YOU TALKING ABOUT?

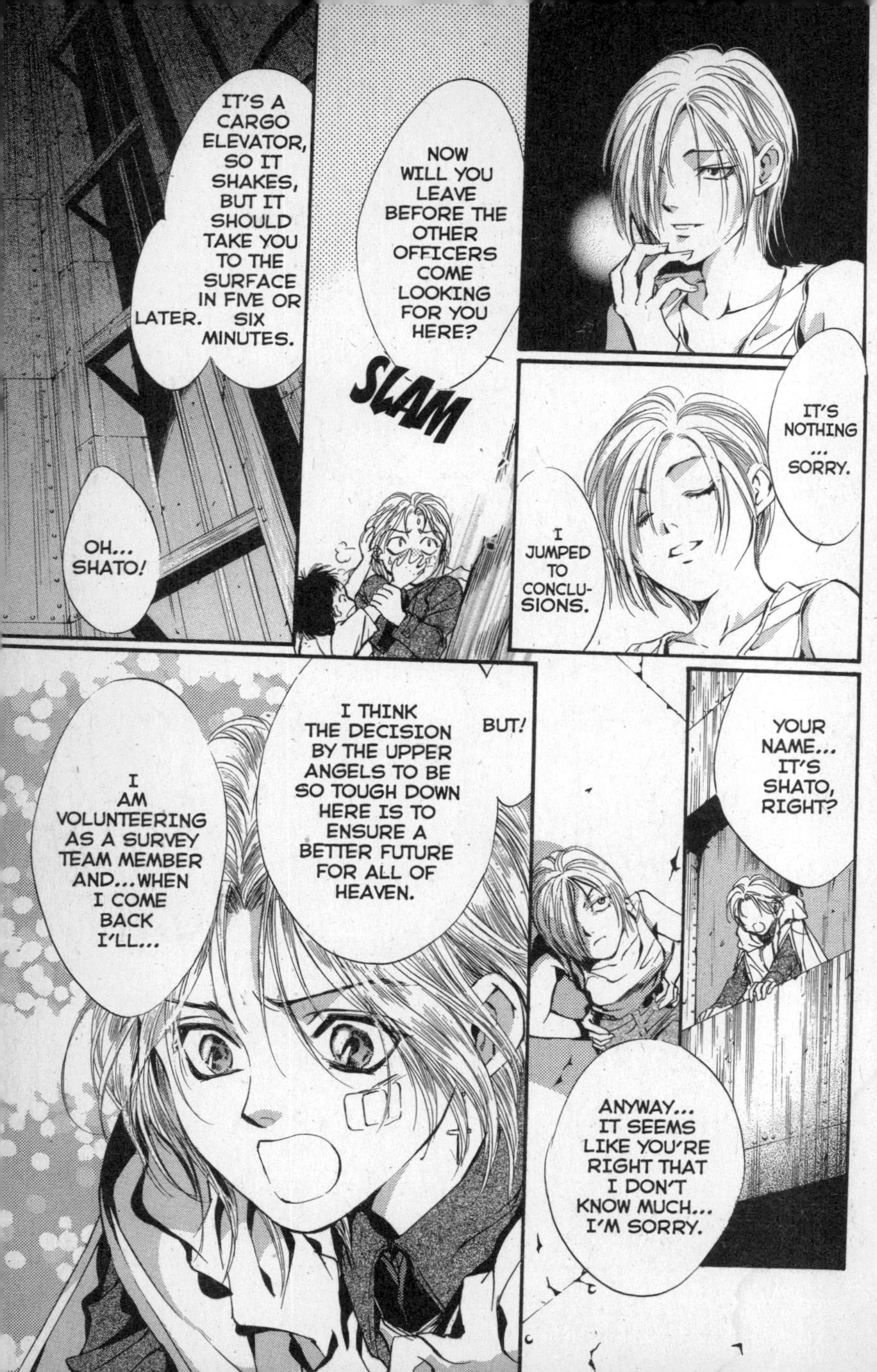
IT'S NOTHING ... SORRY.
I JUMPED TO CONCLUSIONS.
NOW WILL YOU LEAVE BEFORE THE OTHER OFFICERS COME LOOKING FOR YOU HERE?
SLAM
IT'S A CARGO ELEVATOR, SO IT SHAKES, BUT IT SHOULD TAKE YOU TO THE SURFACE IN FIVE OR SIX MINUTES.
LATER.
OH... SHATO!
YOUR NAME... IT'S SHATO, RIGHT?
ANYWAY... IT SEEMS LIKE YOU'RE RIGHT THAT I DON'T KNOW MUCH... I'M SORRY.
BUT!
I THINK THE DECISION BY THE UPPER ANGELS TO BE SO TOUGH DOWN HERE IS TO ENSURE A BETTER FUTURE FOR ALL OF HEAVEN.
I AM VOLUNTEERING AS A SURVEY TEAM MEMBER AND...WHEN I COME BACK I'LL...

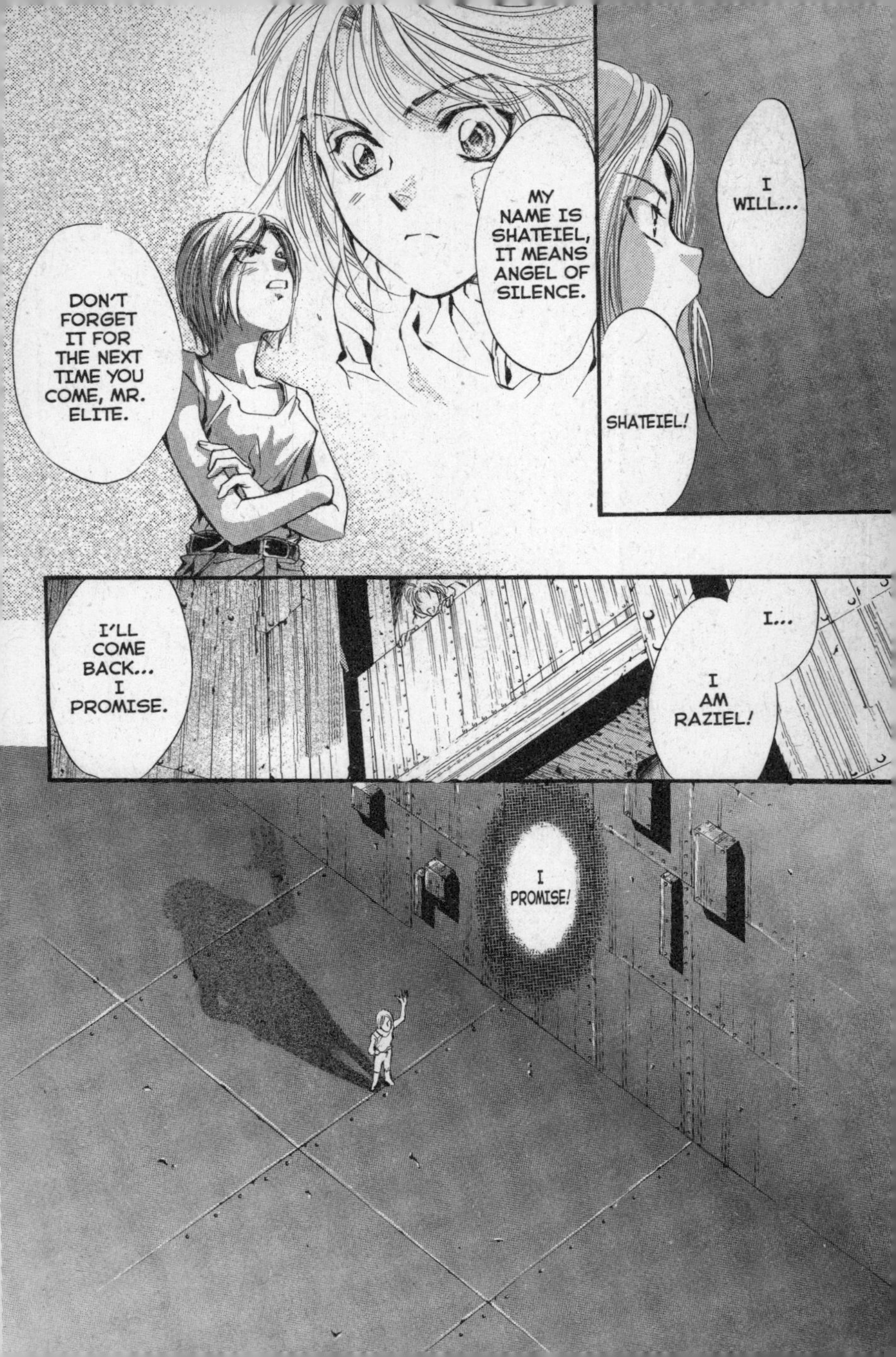
I WILL...
SHATEIEL!
MY NAME IS SHATEIEL, IT MEANS ANGEL OF SILENCE.
DON'T FORGET IT FOR THE NEXT TIME YOU COME, MR. ELITE.
I...
I AM RAZIEL!
I'LL COME BACK... I PROMISE.
I PROMISE!

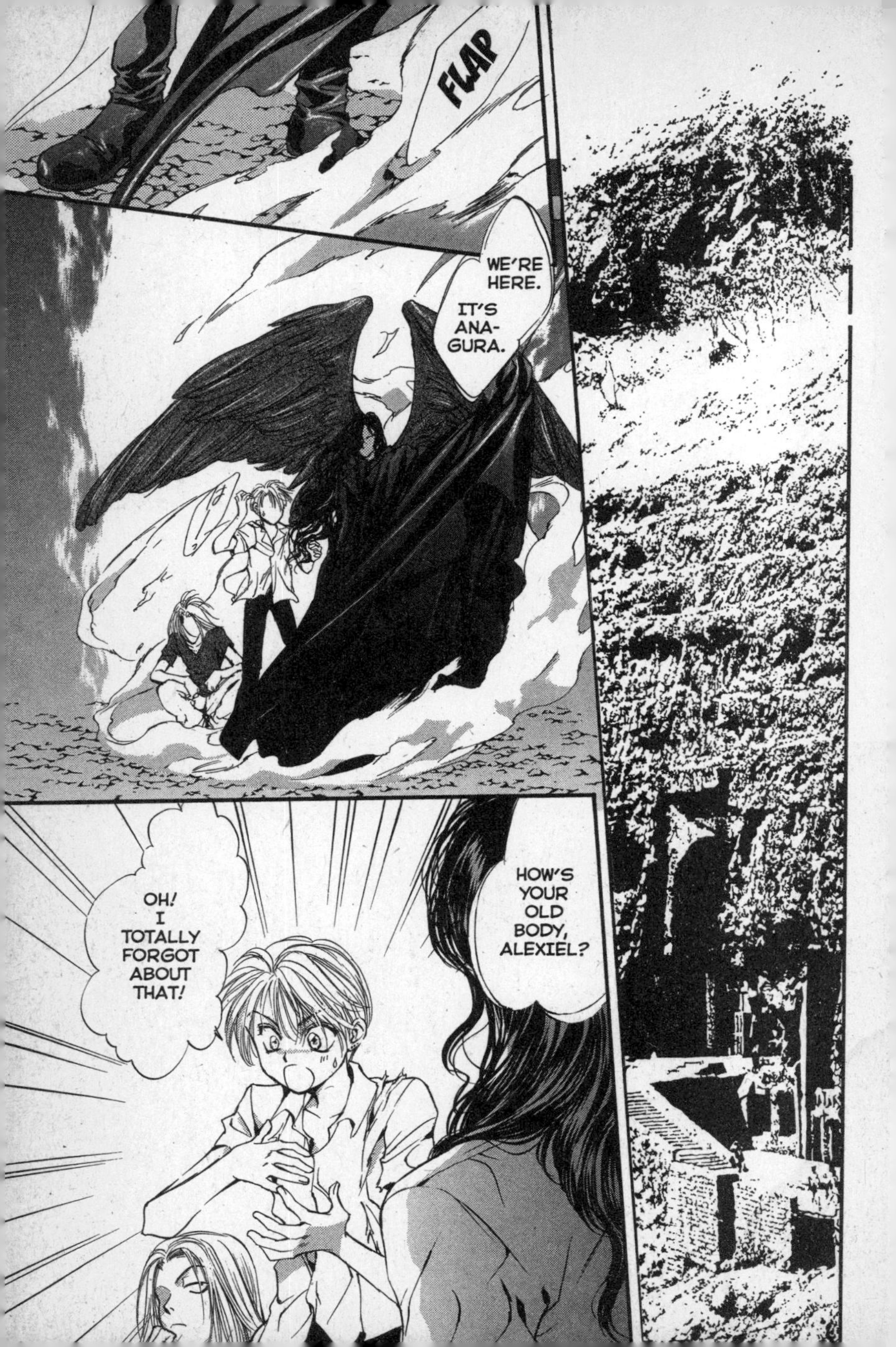
FLAP
WE'RE HERE. IT'S ANAGURA.
HOW'S YOUR OLD BODY, ALEXIEL?
OH! I TOTALLY FORGOT ABOUT THAT!

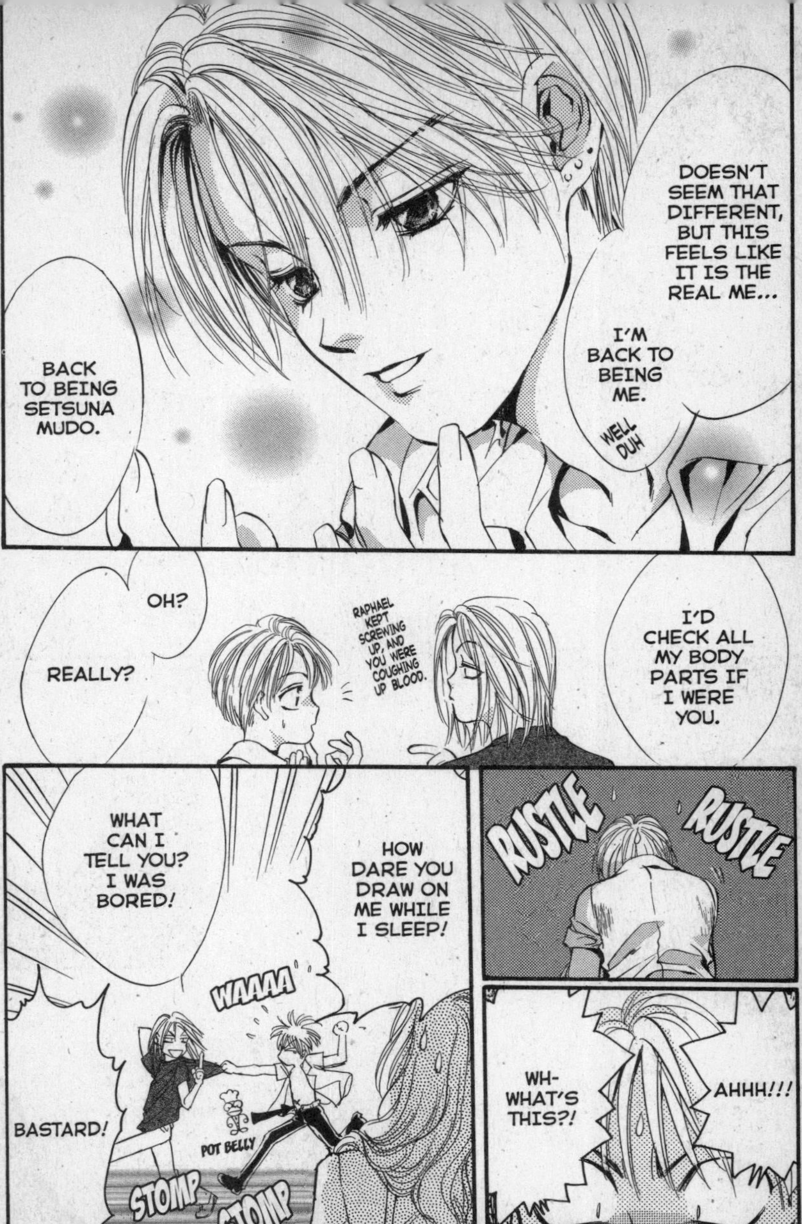
DOESN'T SEEM THAT DIFFERENT, BUT THIS FEELS LIKE IT IS THE REAL ME...
I'M BACK TO BEING ME.
WELL DUH
BACK TO BEING SETSUNA MUDO.
I'D CHECK ALL MY BODY PARTS IF I WERE YOU.
RAPHAEL KEPT SCREWING UP, AND YOU WERE COUGHING UP BLOOD.
OH?
REALLY?
RUSTLE
RUSTLE
AHHH!!!
WH-WHAT'S THIS?!
HOW DARE YOU DRAW ON ME WHILE I SLEEP!
WHAT CAN I TELL YOU? I WAS BORED!
WAAAA
BASTARD!
POT BELLY
STOMP
STOMP

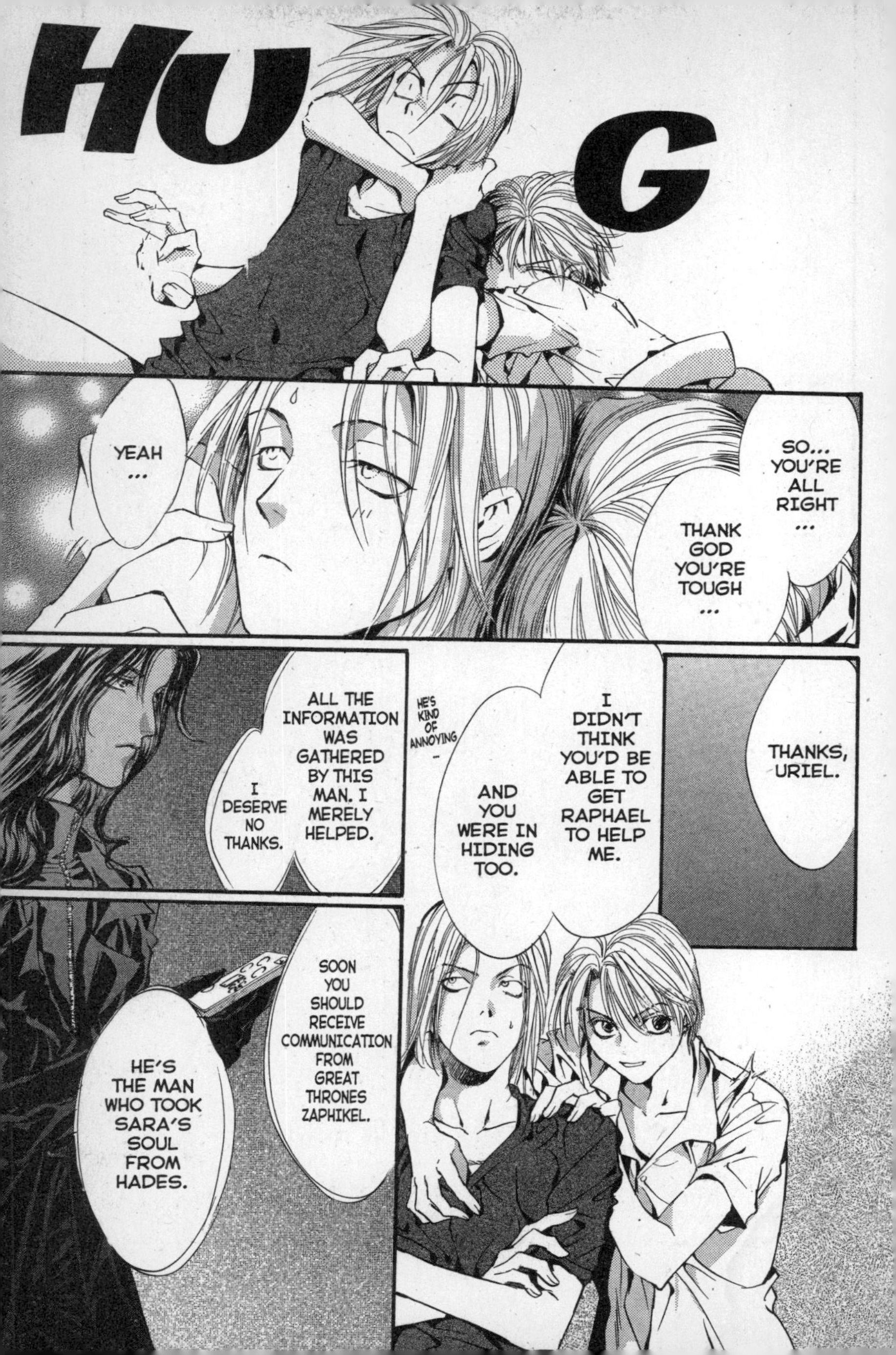
HUG
SO... YOU'RE ALL RIGHT ...
THANK GOD YOU'RE TOUGH ...
YEAH ...
THANKS, URIEL.
I DIDN'T THINK YOU'D BE ABLE TO GET RAPHAEL TO HELP ME.
AND YOU WERE IN HIDING TOO.
HE'S KIND OF ANNOYING –
ALL THE INFORMATION WAS GATHERED BY THIS MAN. I MERELY HELPED.
I DESERVE NO THANKS.
SOON YOU SHOULD RECEIVE COMMUNICATION FROM GREAT THRONES ZAPHIKEL.
HE'S THE MAN WHO TOOK SARA'S SOUL FROM HADES.

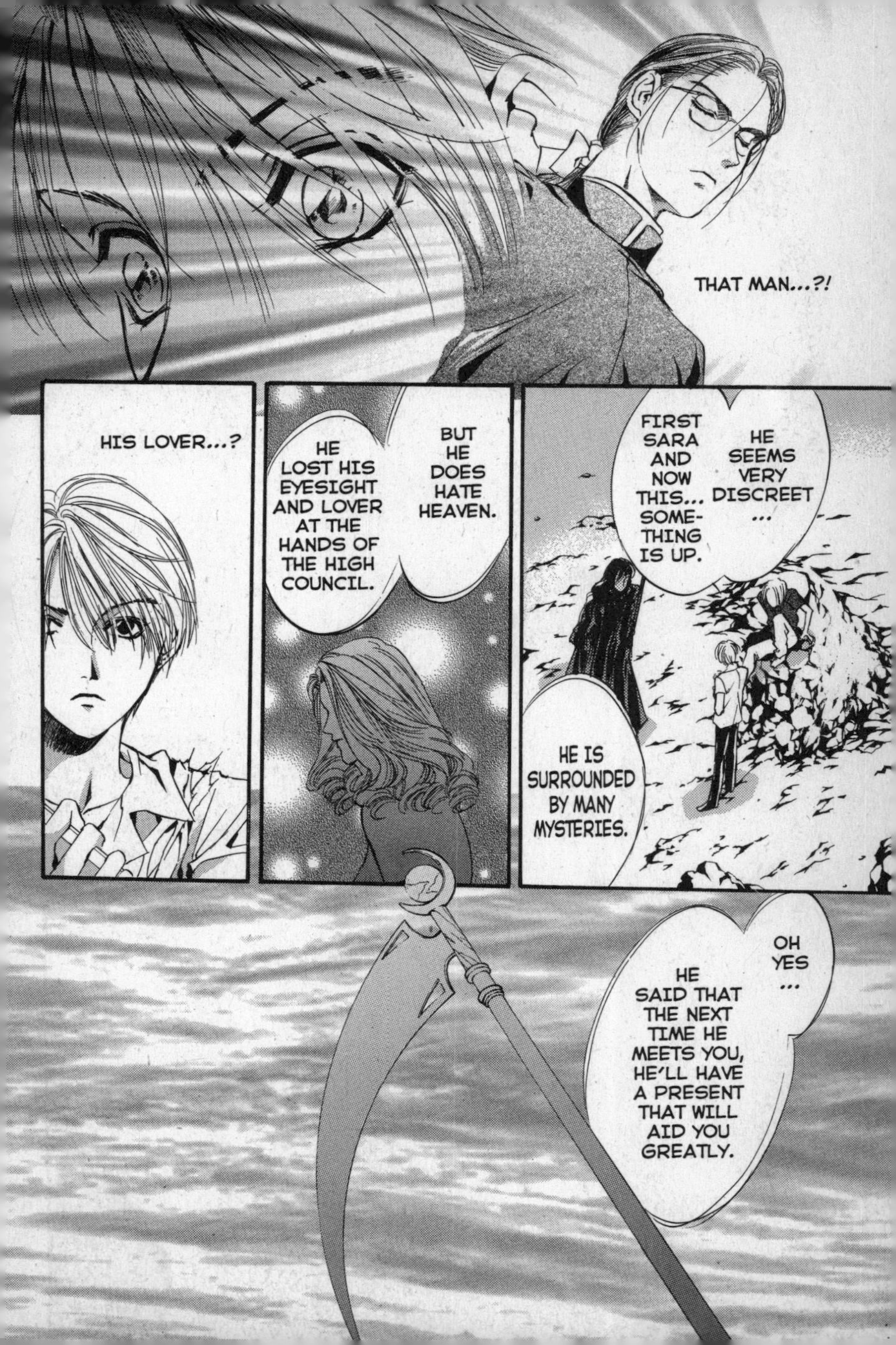
THAT MAN...?!
HE SEEMS VERY DISCREET ...
FIRST SARA AND NOW THIS... SOME-THING IS UP.
HE IS SURROUNDED BY MANY MYSTERIES.
BUT HE DOES HATE HEAVEN.
HE LOST HIS EYESIGHT AND LOVER AT THE HANDS OF THE HIGH COUNCIL.
HIS LOVER...?
OH YES ...
HE SAID THAT THE NEXT TIME HE MEETS YOU, HE'LL HAVE A PRESENT THAT WILL AID YOU GREATLY.

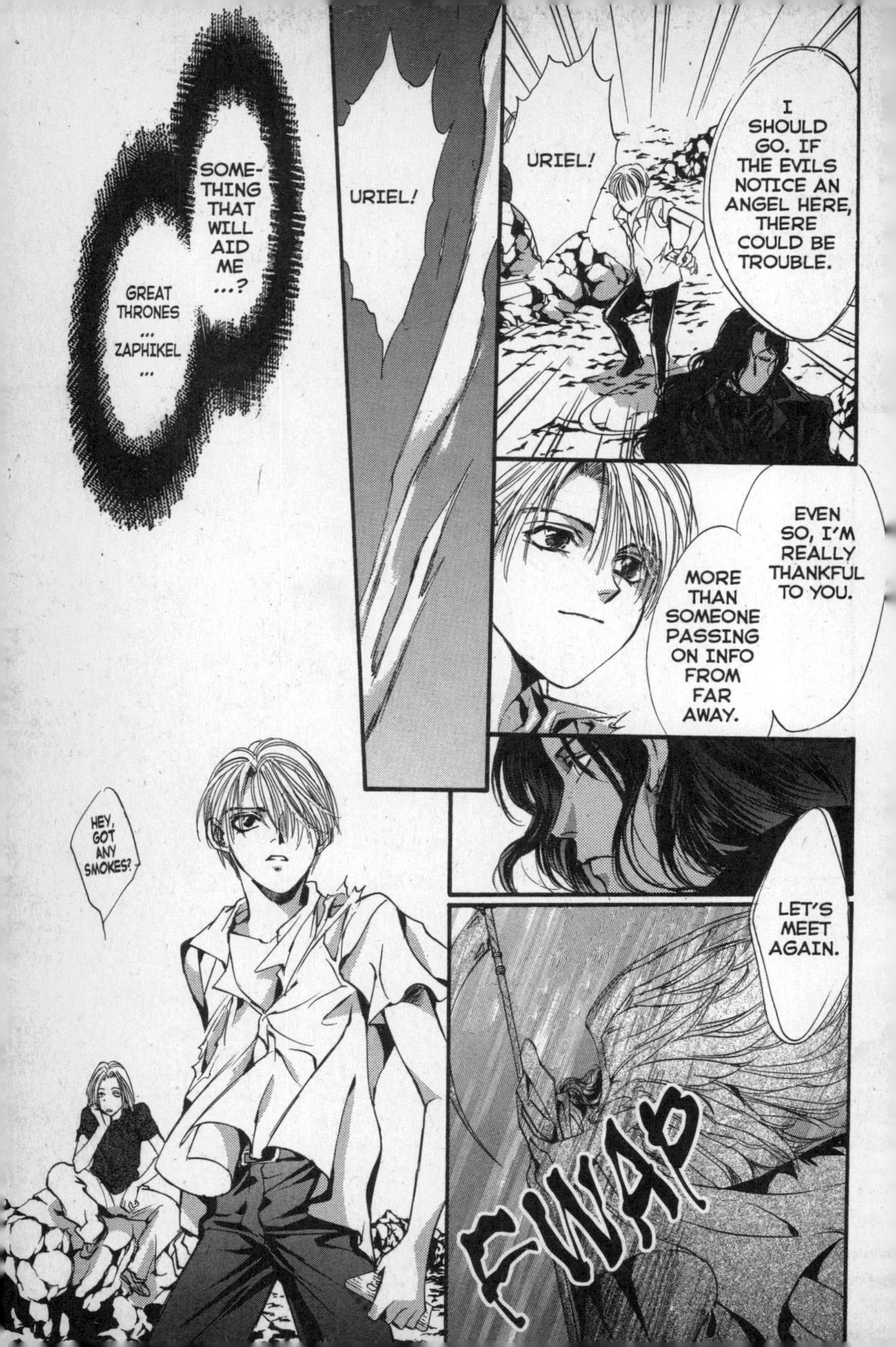
I SHOULD GO. IF THE EVILS NOTICE AN ANGEL HERE, THERE COULD BE TROUBLE.
URIEL!
EVEN SO, I'M REALLY THANKFUL TO YOU.
MORE THAN SOMEONE PASSING ON INFO FROM FAR AWAY.
LET'S MEET AGAIN.
FWAP
URIEL!
SOME-THING THAT WILL AID ME ...?
GREAT THRONES ... ZAPHIKEL ...
HEY, GOT ANY SMOKES?

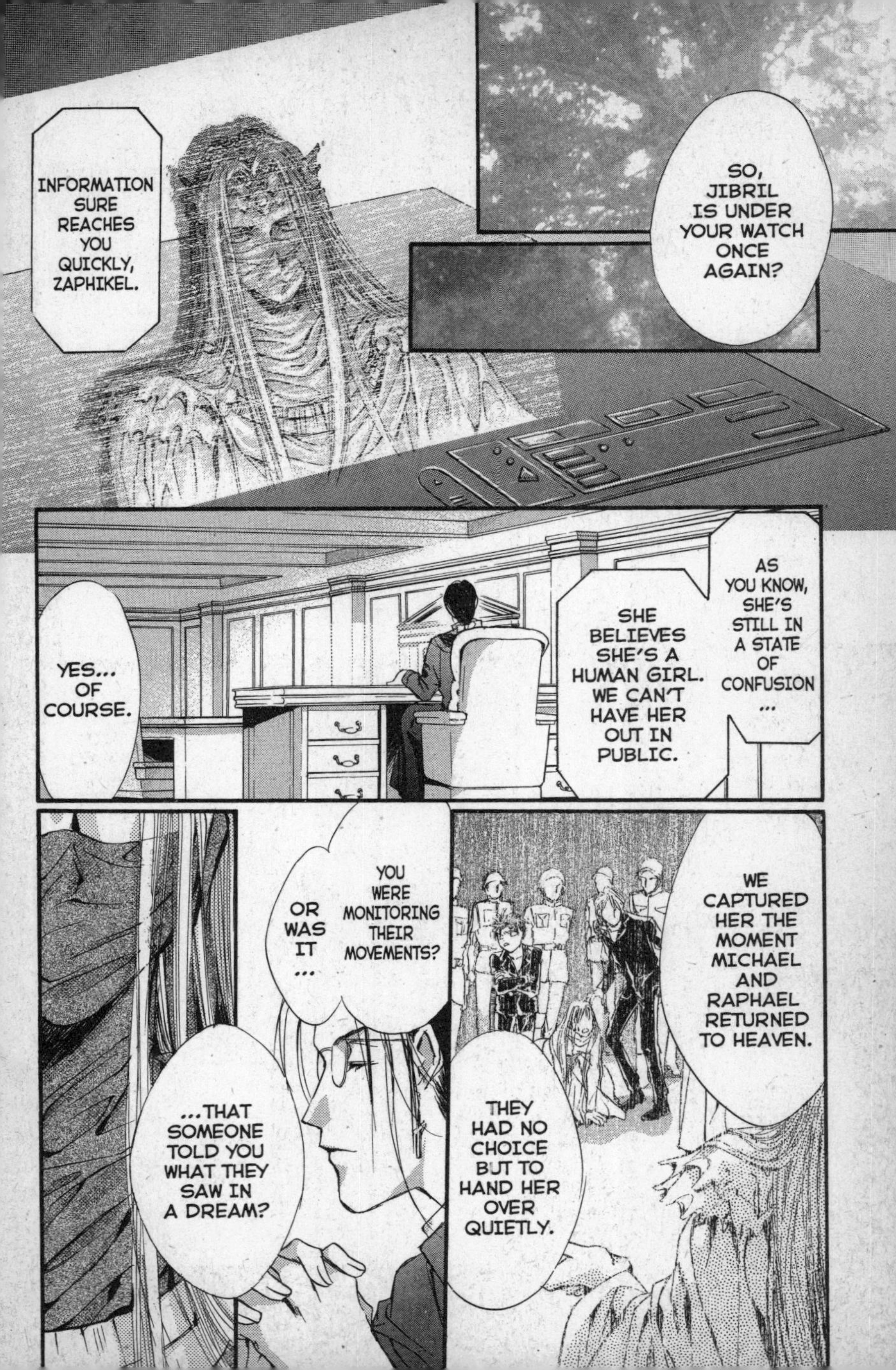
SO, JIBRIL IS UNDER YOUR WATCH ONCE AGAIN?
INFORMATION SURE REACHES YOU QUICKLY, ZAPHIKEL.
AS YOU KNOW, SHE'S STILL IN A STATE OF CONFUSION ...
SHE BELIEVES SHE'S A HUMAN GIRL. WE CAN'T HAVE HER OUT IN PUBLIC.
YES... OF COURSE.
WE CAPTURED HER THE MOMENT MICHAEL AND RAPHAEL RETURNED TO HEAVEN.
THEY HAD NO CHOICE BUT TO HAND HER OVER QUIETLY.
YOU WERE MONITORING THEIR MOVEMENTS?
OR WAS IT ...
...THAT SOMEONE TOLD YOU WHAT THEY SAW IN A DREAM?

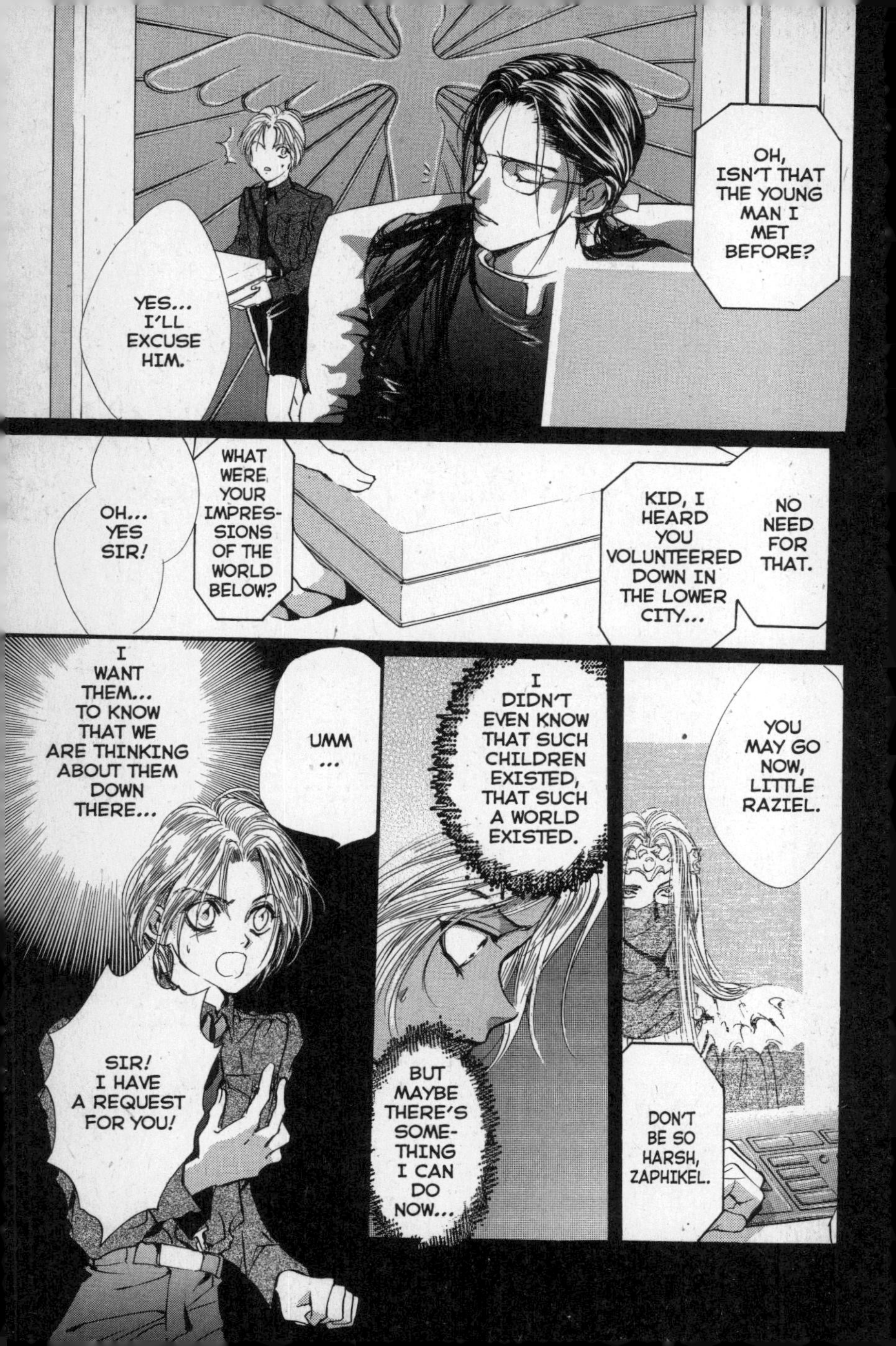
OH, ISN'T THAT THE YOUNG MAN I MET BEFORE?
YES... I'LL EXCUSE HIM.
NO NEED FOR THAT.
KID, I HEARD YOU VOLUNTEERED DOWN IN THE LOWER CITY...
WHAT WERE YOUR IMPRESSIONS OF THE WORLD BELOW?
OH... YES SIR!
YOU MAY GO NOW, LITTLE RAZIEL.
DON'T BE SO HARSH, ZAPHIKEL.
I DIDN'T EVEN KNOW THAT SUCH CHILDREN EXISTED, THAT SUCH A WORLD EXISTED.
BUT MAYBE THERE'S SOMETHING I CAN DO NOW...
UMM ...
I WANT THEM... TO KNOW THAT WE ARE THINKING ABOUT THEM DOWN THERE...
SIR! I HAVE A REQUEST FOR YOU!

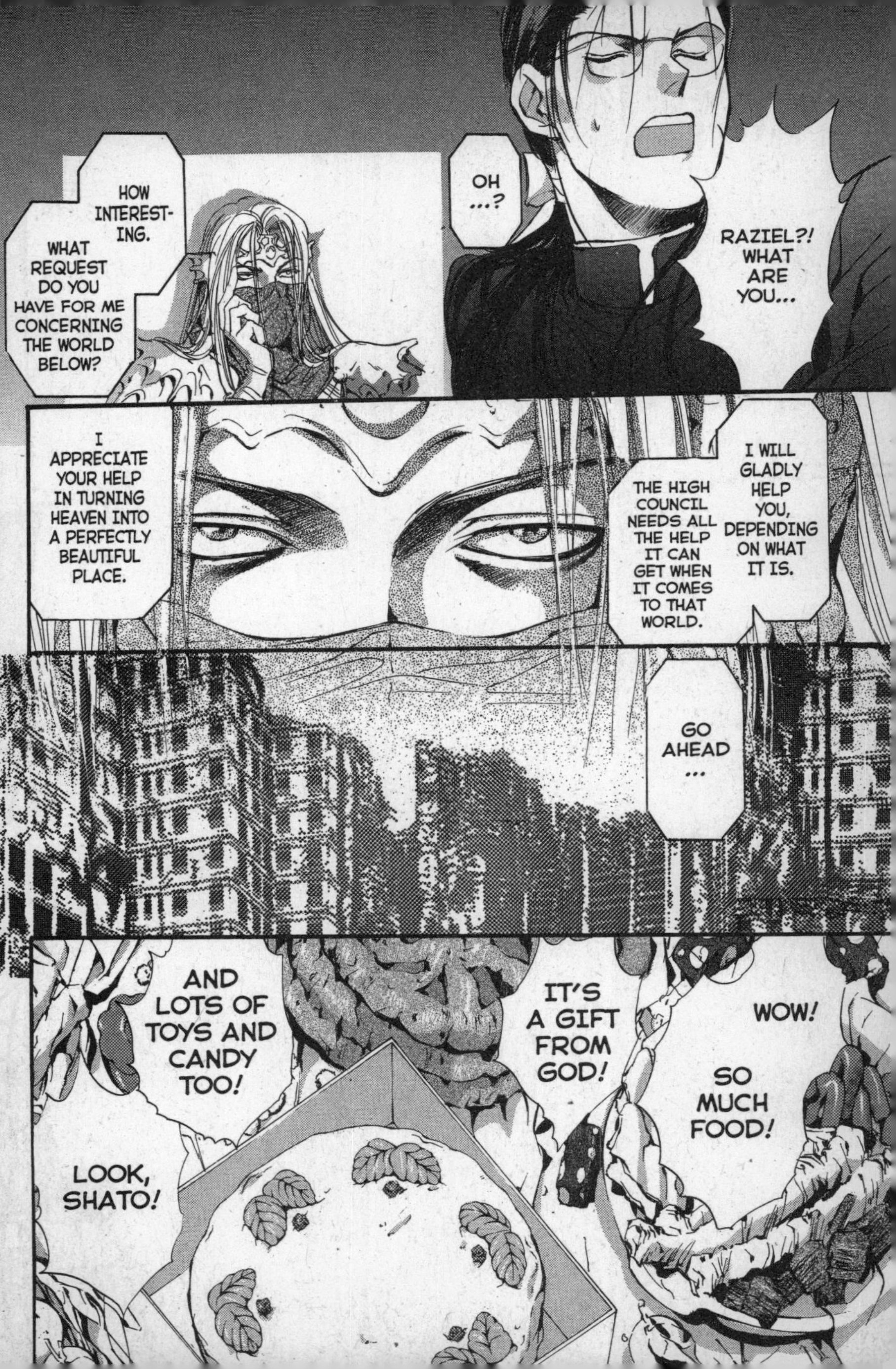
RAZIEL?! WHAT ARE YOU...
OH ...?
HOW INTERESTING.
WHAT REQUEST DO YOU HAVE FOR ME CONCERNING THE WORLD BELOW?
I WILL GLADLY HELP YOU, DEPENDING ON WHAT IT IS.
THE HIGH COUNCIL NEEDS ALL THE HELP IT CAN GET WHEN IT COMES TO THAT WORLD.
I APPRECIATE YOUR HELP IN TURNING HEAVEN INTO A PERFECTLY BEAUTIFUL PLACE.
GO AHEAD ...
WOW!
SO MUCH FOOD!
IT'S A GIFT FROM GOD!
AND LOTS OF TOYS AND CANDY TOO!
LOOK, SHATO!

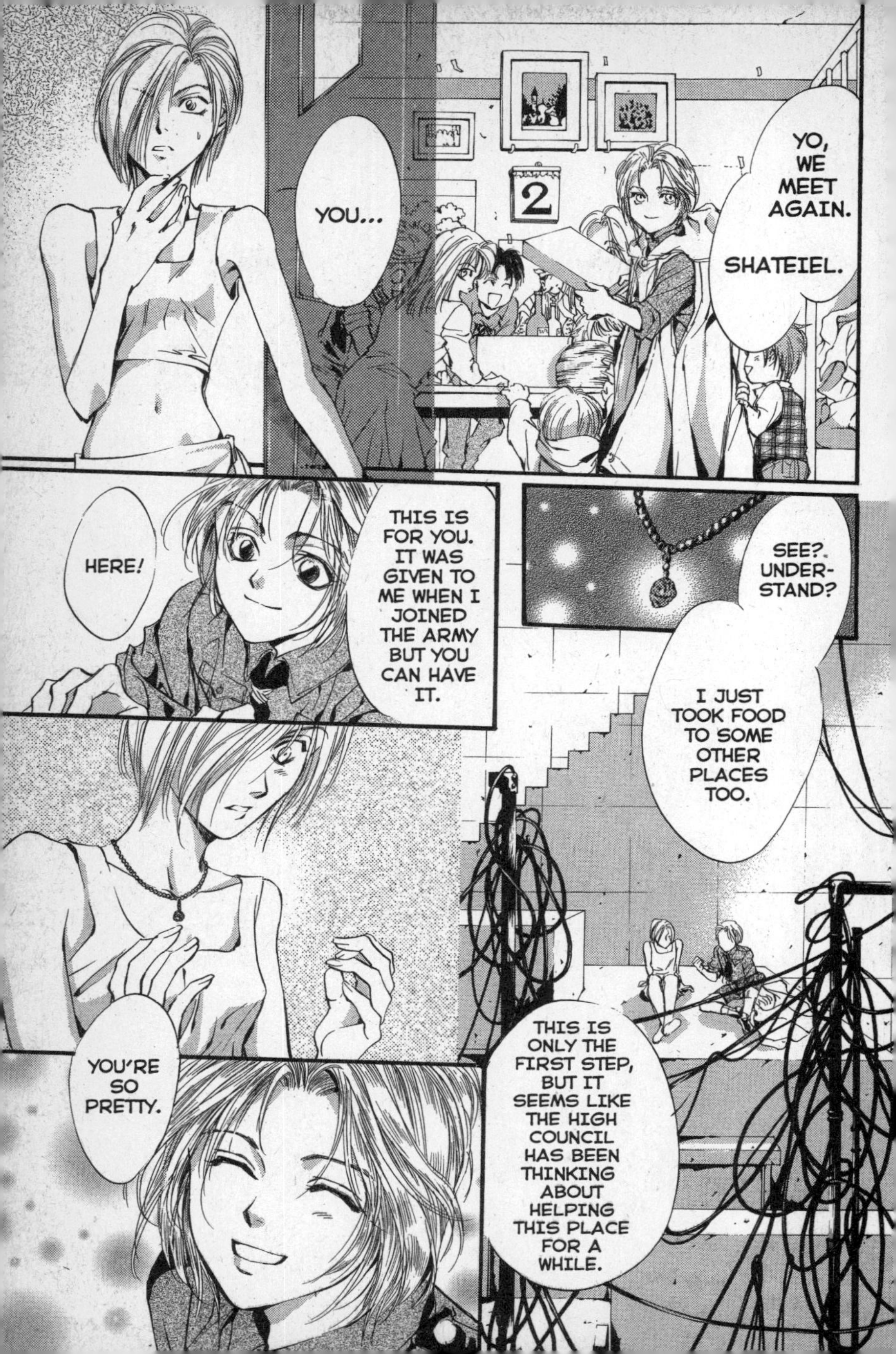
YO, WE MEET AGAIN.
SHATEIEL.
YOU...
2
SEE?. UNDER-STAND?
THIS IS FOR YOU. IT WAS GIVEN TO ME WHEN I JOINED THE ARMY BUT YOU CAN HAVE IT.
HERE!
I JUST TOOK FOOD TO SOME OTHER PLACES TOO.
THIS IS ONLY THE FIRST STEP, BUT IT SEEMS LIKE THE HIGH COUNCIL HAS BEEN THINKING ABOUT HELPING THIS PLACE FOR A WHILE.
YOU'RE SO PRETTY.

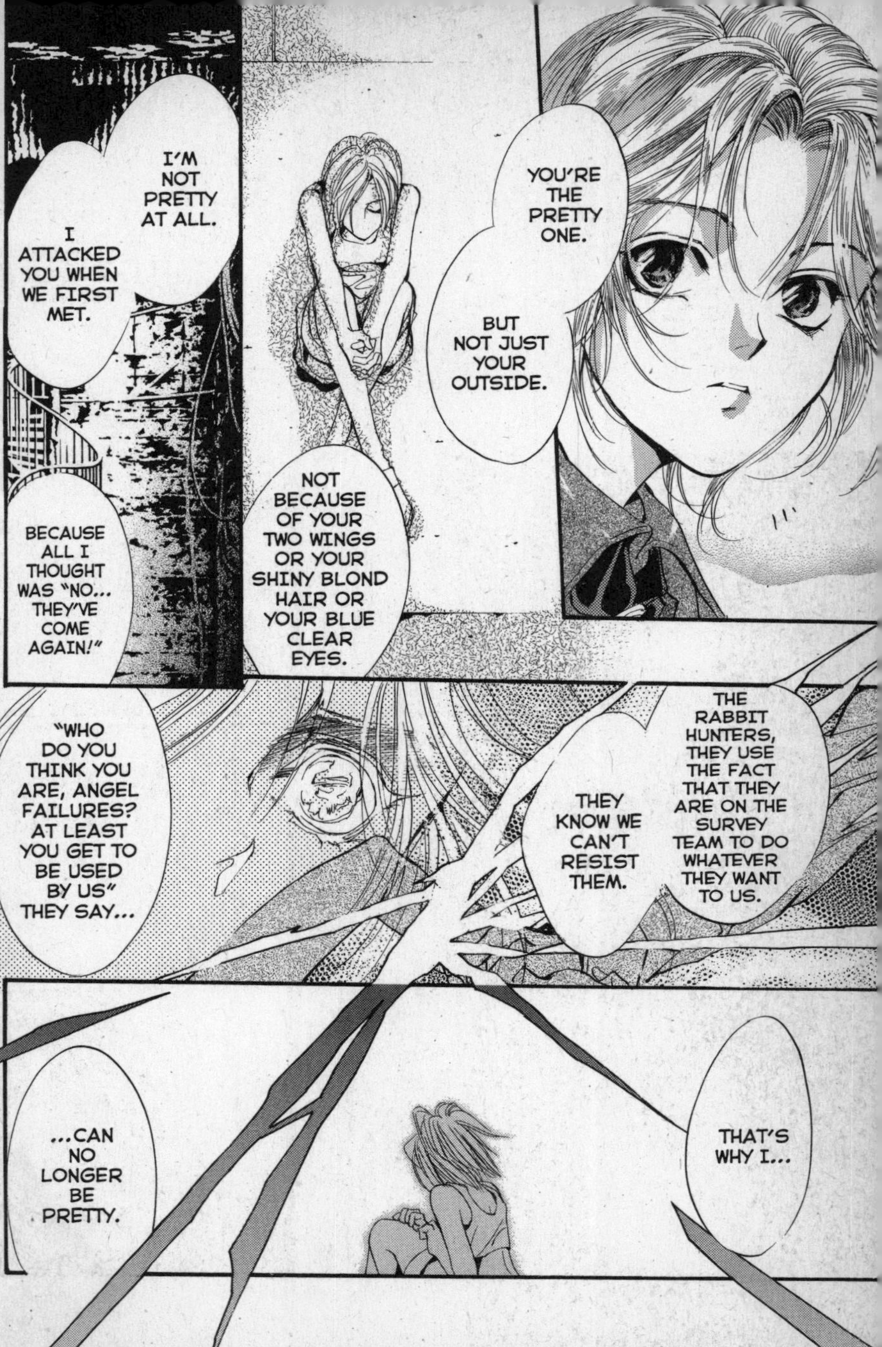
YOU'RE THE PRETTY ONE.
BUT NOT JUST YOUR OUTSIDE.
NOT BECAUSE OF YOUR TWO WINGS OR YOUR SHINY BLOND HAIR OR YOUR BLUE CLEAR EYES.
I'M NOT PRETTY AT ALL.
I ATTACKED YOU WHEN WE FIRST MET.
BECAUSE ALL I THOUGHT WAS "NO... THEY'VE COME AGAIN!"
THE RABBIT HUNTERS, THEY USE THE FACT THAT THEY ARE ON THE SURVEY TEAM TO DO WHATEVER THEY WANT TO US.
THEY KNOW WE CAN'T RESIST THEM.
"WHO DO YOU THINK YOU ARE, ANGEL FAILURES? AT LEAST YOU GET TO BE USED BY US" THEY SAY...
THAT'S WHY I...
...CAN NO LONGER BE PRETTY.

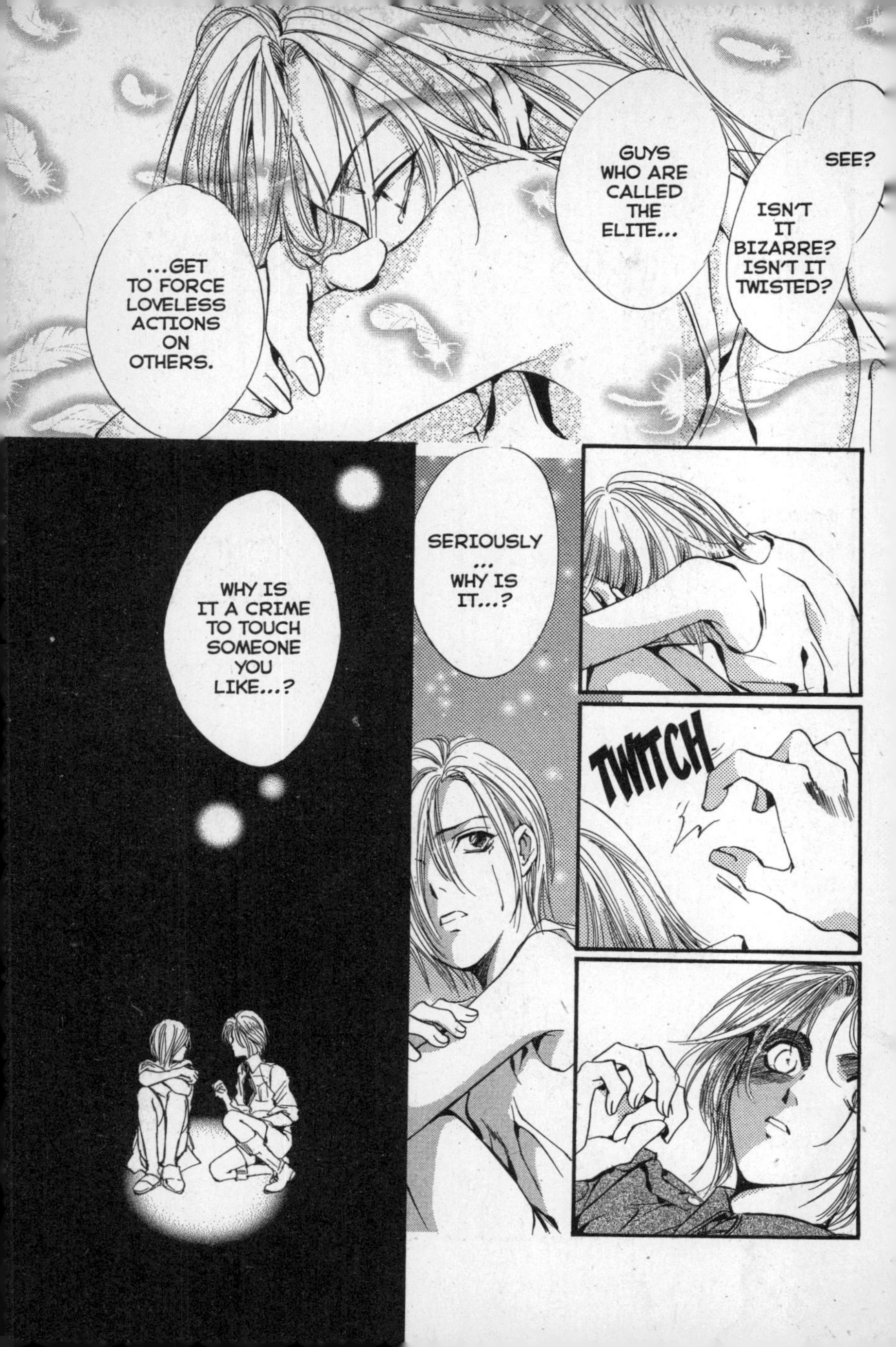
SEE? ISN'T IT BIZARRE? ISN'T IT TWISTED?
GUYS WHO ARE CALLED THE ELITE...
...GET TO FORCE LOVELESS ACTIONS ON OTHERS.
TWITCH
SERIOUSLY... WHY IS IT...?
WHY IS IT A CRIME TO TOUCH SOMEONE YOU LIKE...?

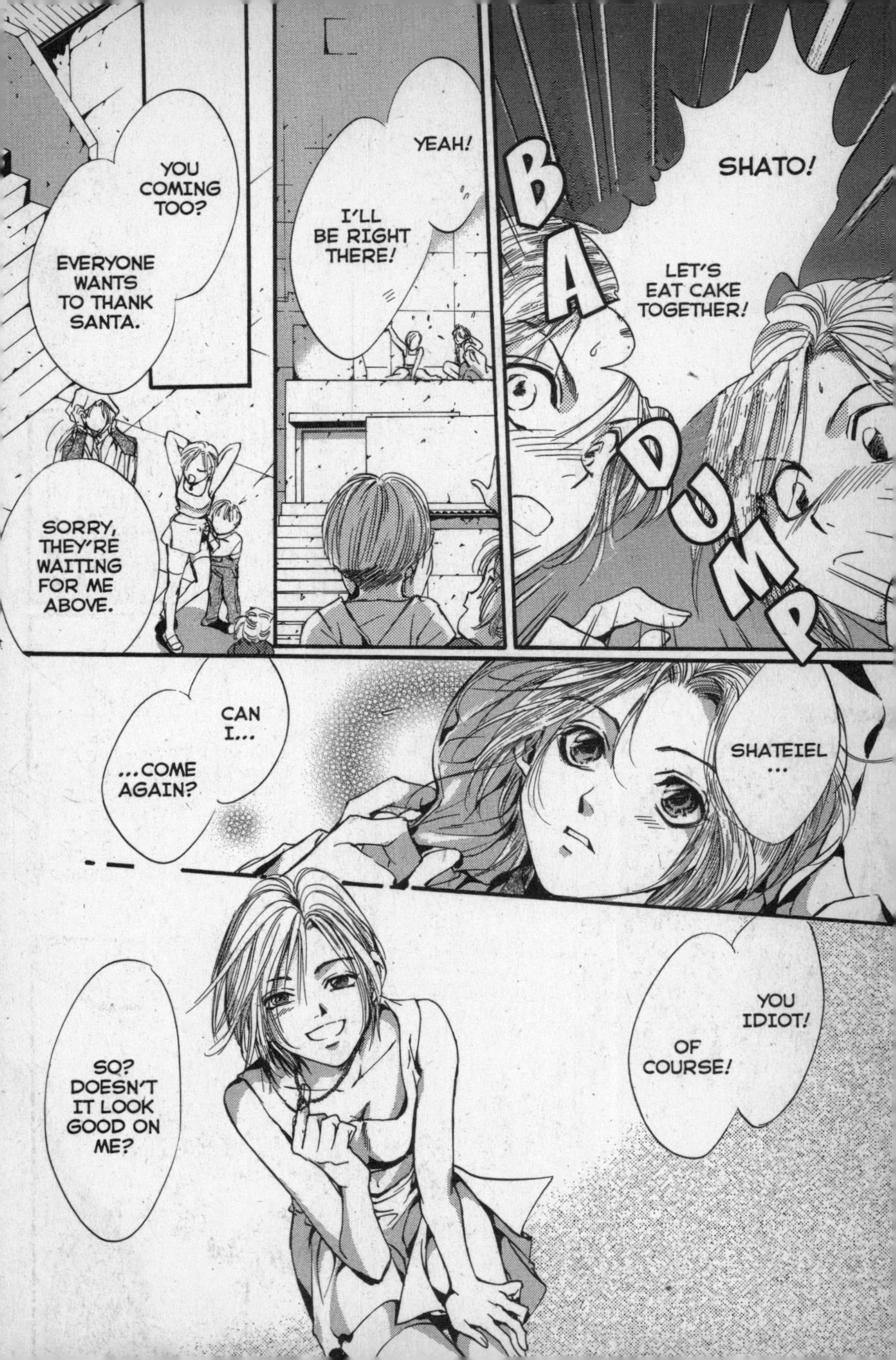
SHATO!
BADUMP
LET'S EAT CAKE TOGETHER!
YEAH!
I'LL BE RIGHT THERE!
YOU COMING TOO?
EVERYONE WANTS TO THANK SANTA.
SORRY, THEY'RE WAITING FOR ME ABOVE.
SHATEIEL ...
CAN I...
...COME AGAIN?
YOU IDIOT!
OF COURSE!
SO? DOESN'T IT LOOK GOOD ON ME?

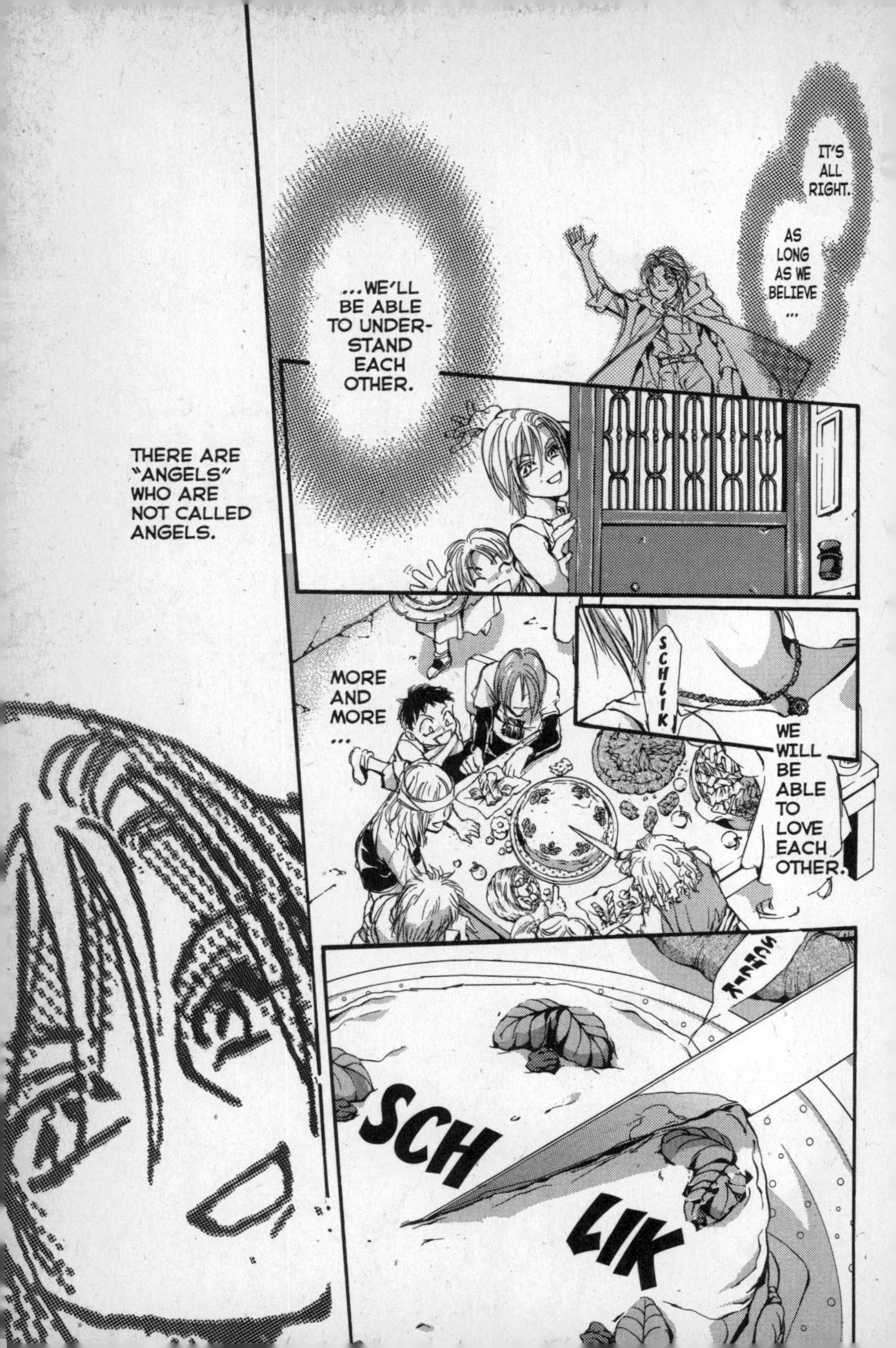
IT'S ALL RIGHT.
AS LONG AS WE BELIEVE ...
...WE'LL BE ABLE TO UNDER-STAND EACH OTHER.
SCHLIK
WE WILL BE ABLE TO LOVE EACH OTHER.
MORE AND MORE ...
SCH LIK
THERE ARE "ANGELS" WHO ARE NOT CALLED ANGELS.

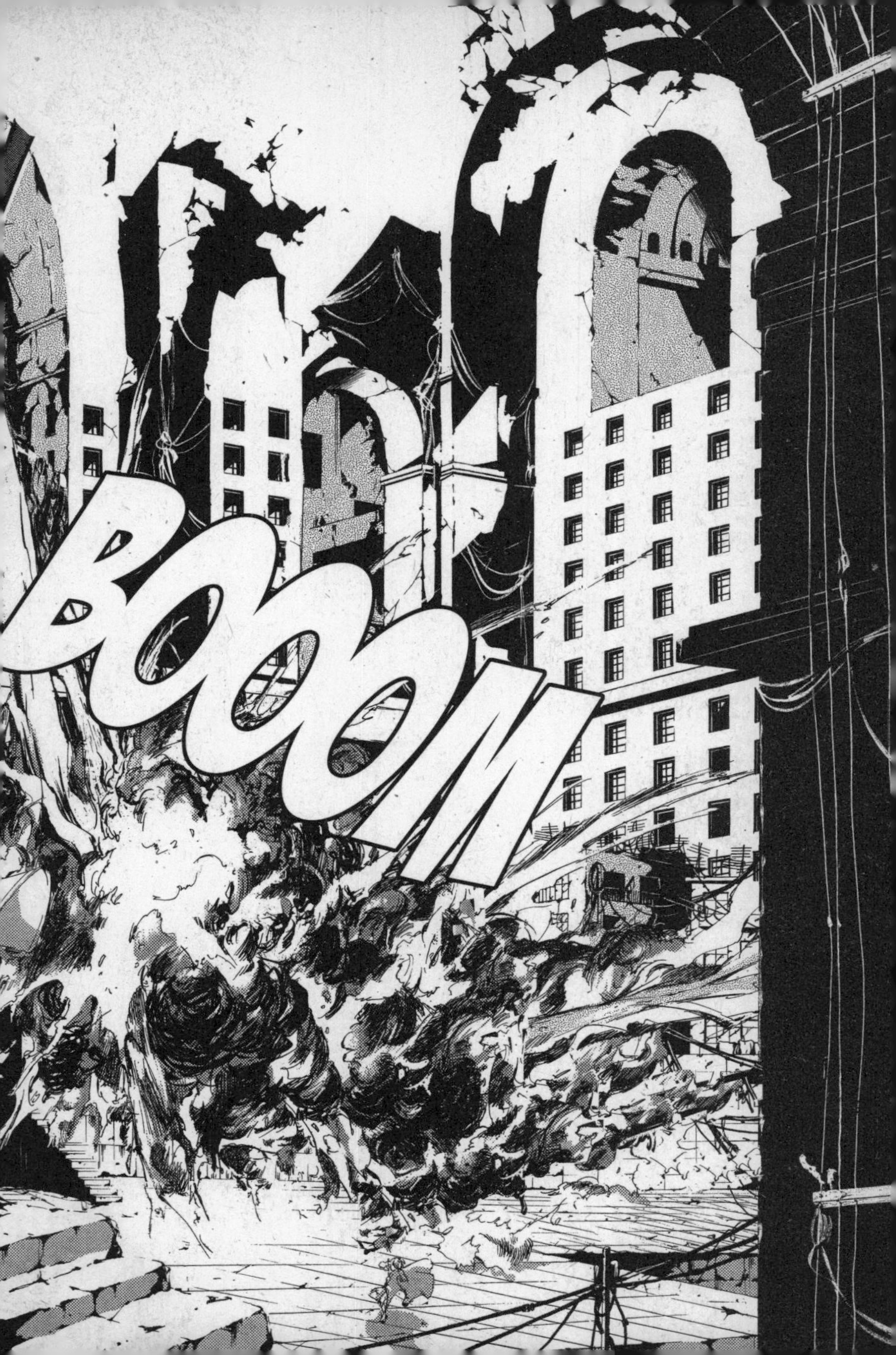
BOOOM

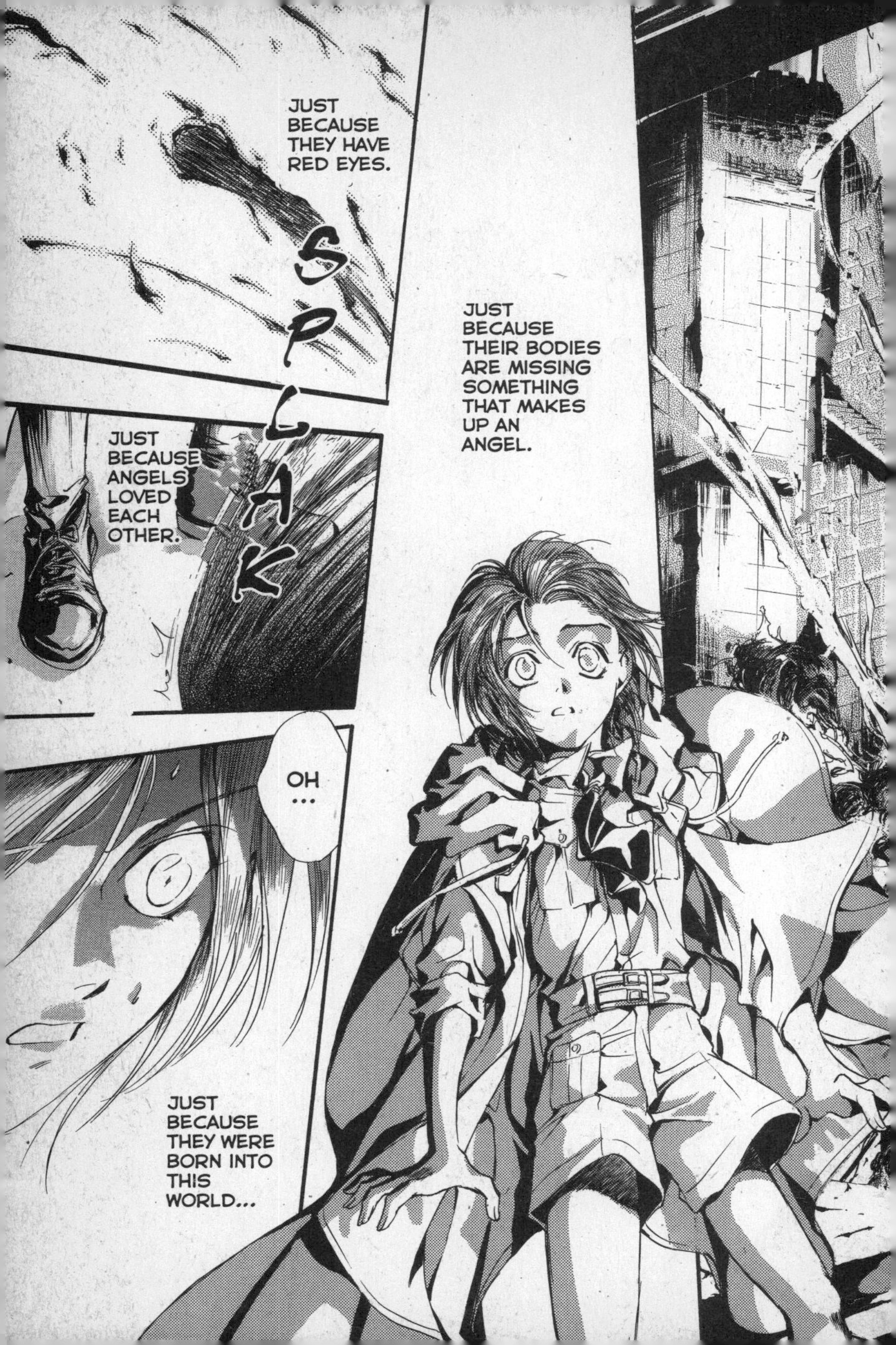
JUST BECAUSE THEIR BODIES ARE MISSING SOMETHING THAT MAKES UP AN ANGEL.
JUST BECAUSE THEY HAVE RED EYES.
SPLAK
JUST BECAUSE ANGELS LOVED EACH OTHER.
OH ...
JUST BECAUSE THEY WERE BORN INTO THIS WORLD...

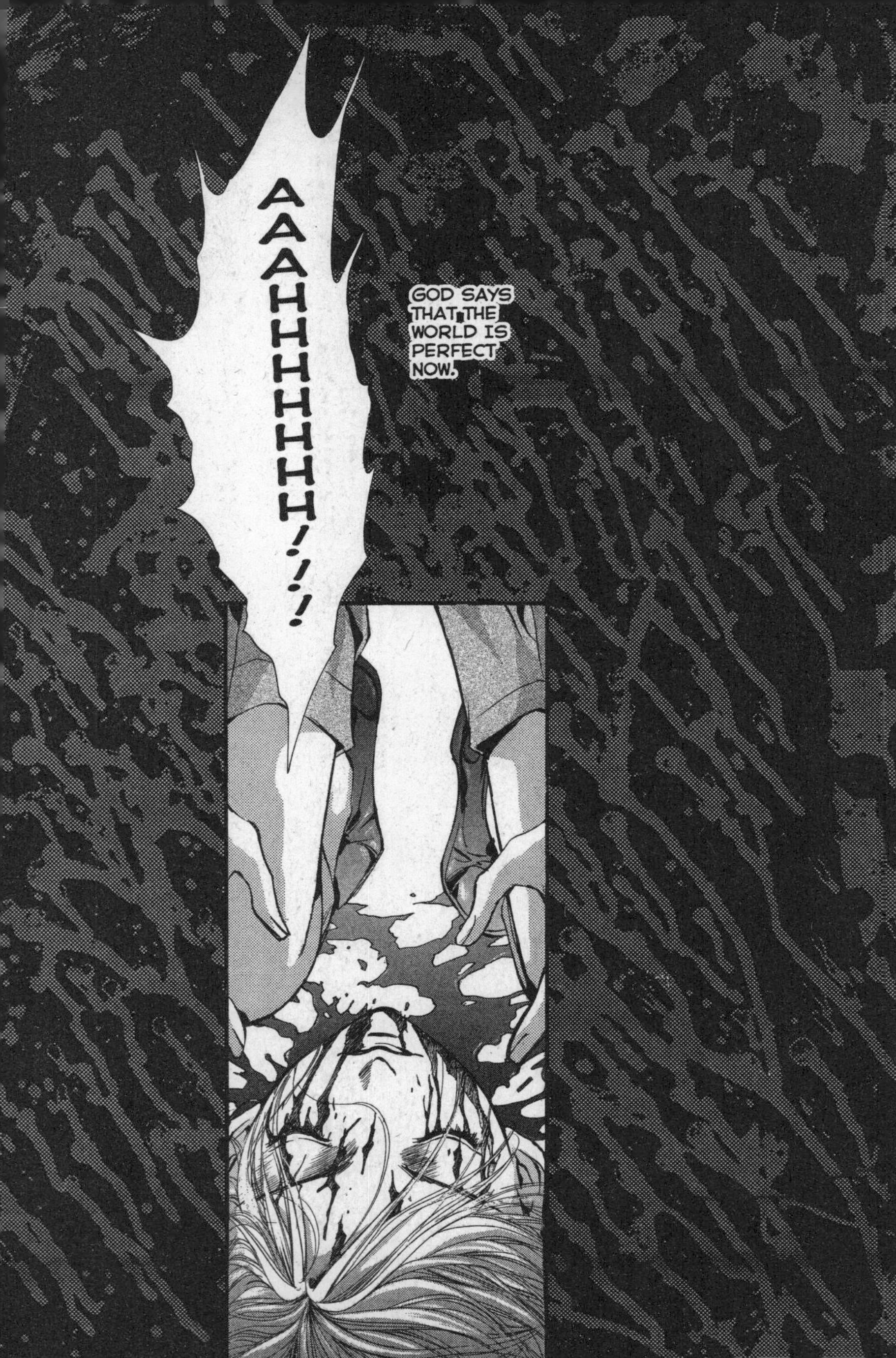
GOD SAYS THAT THE WORLD IS PERFECT NOW.
AAAHHHHHHH!!!

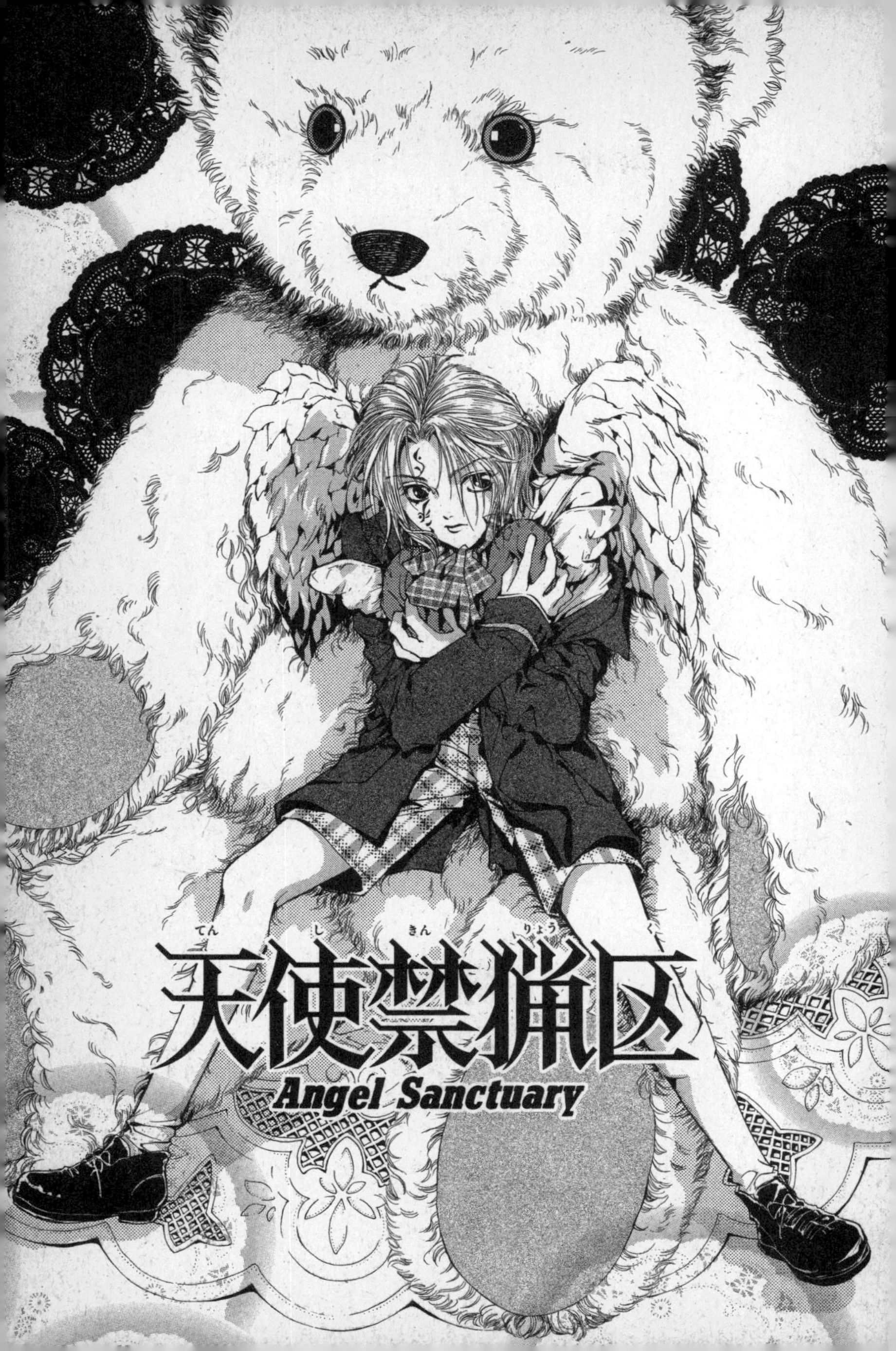
天使禁猟区
Angel Sanctuary

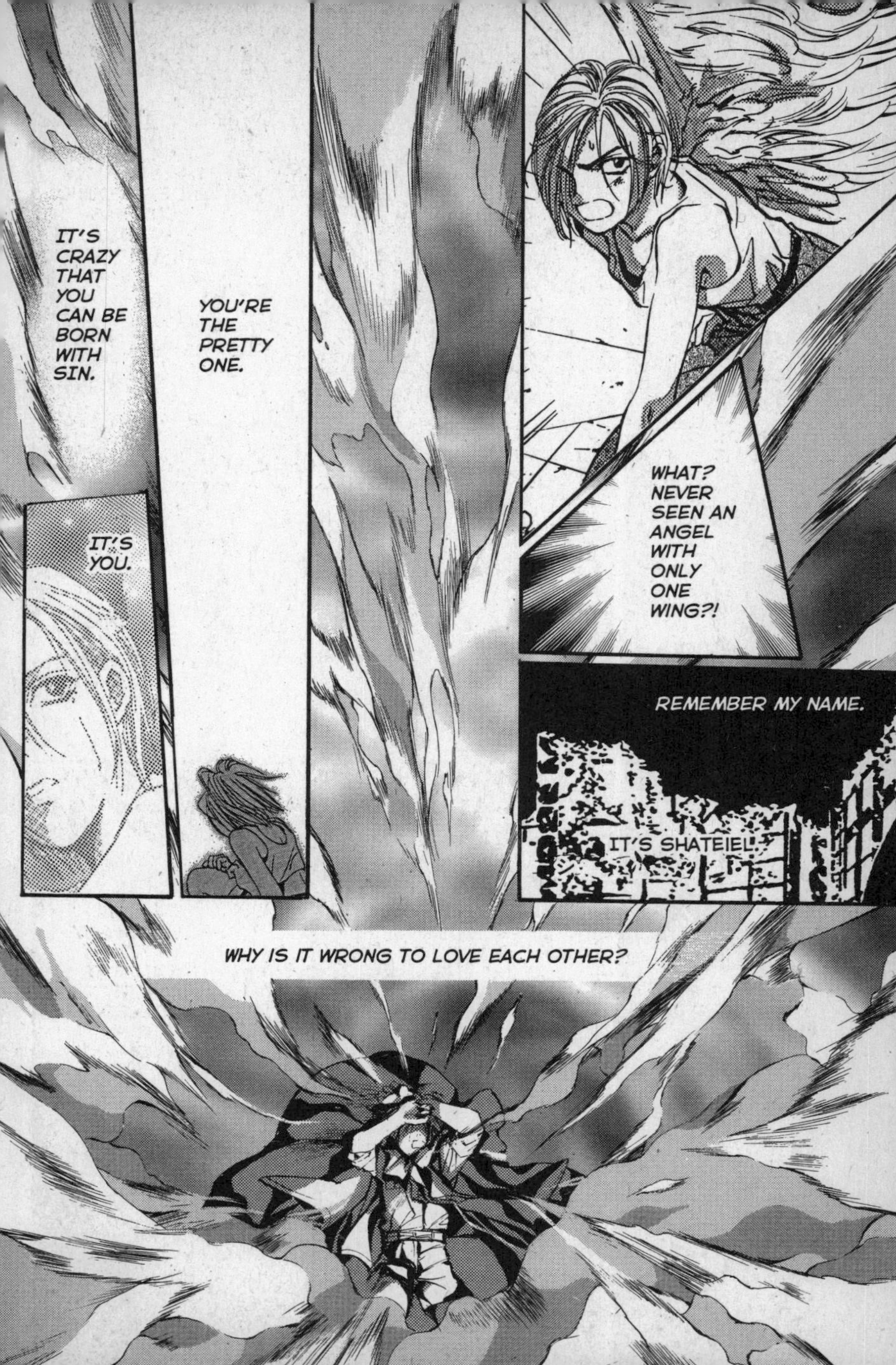
WHAT? NEVER SEEN AN ANGEL WITH ONLY ONE WING?!
REMEMBER MY NAME.
IT'S SHATEIEL.
YOU'RE THE PRETTY ONE.
IT'S CRAZY THAT YOU CAN BE BORN WITH SIN.
IT'S YOU.
WHY IS IT WRONG TO LOVE EACH OTHER?

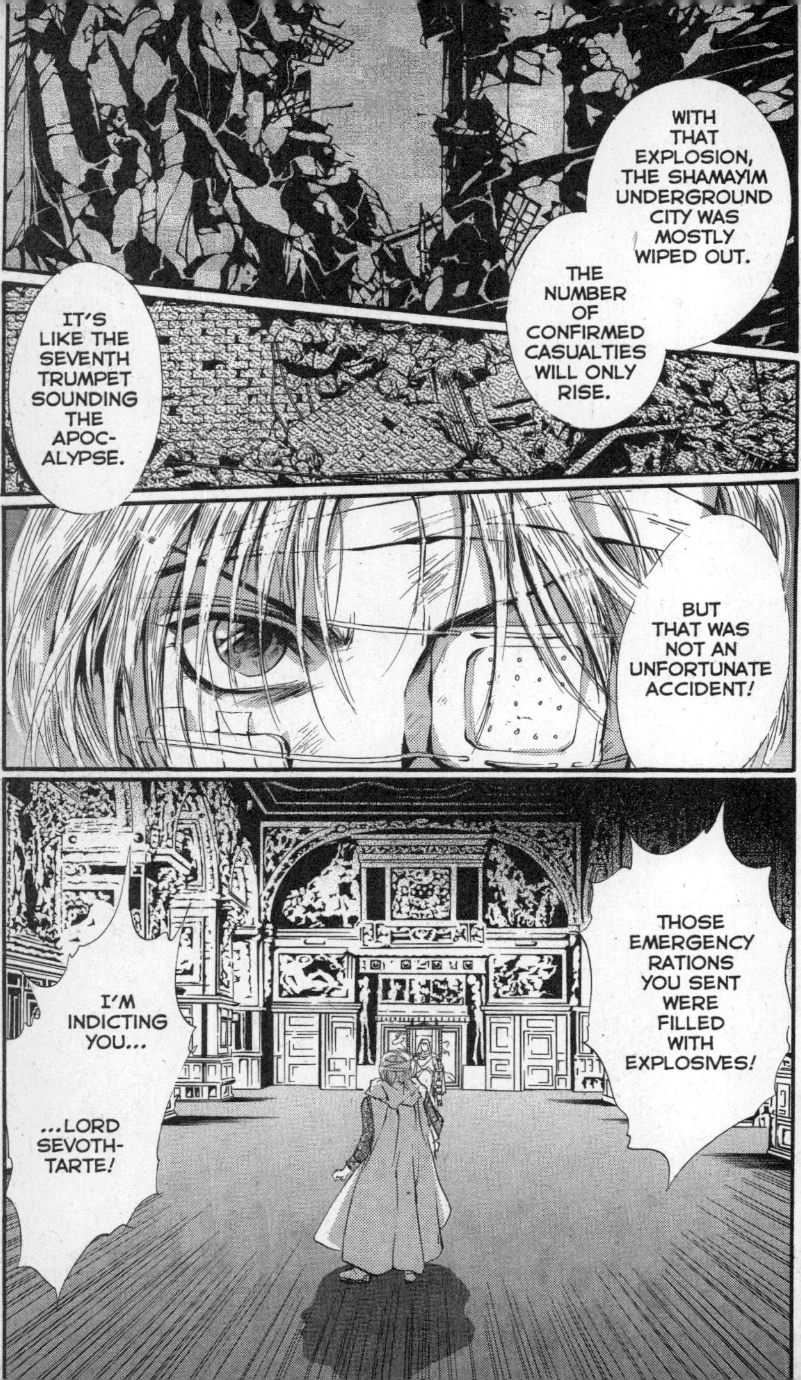
WITH THAT EXPLOSION, THE SHAMAYIM UNDERGROUND CITY WAS MOSTLY WIPED OUT.
THE NUMBER OF CONFIRMED CASUALTIES WILL ONLY RISE.
IT'S LIKE THE SEVENTH TRUMPET SOUNDING THE APOC-ALYPSE.
BUT THAT WAS NOT AN UNFORTUNATE ACCIDENT!
THOSE EMERGENCY RATIONS YOU SENT WERE FILLED WITH EXPLOSIVES!
I'M INDICTING YOU...
...LORD SEVOTH-TARTE!

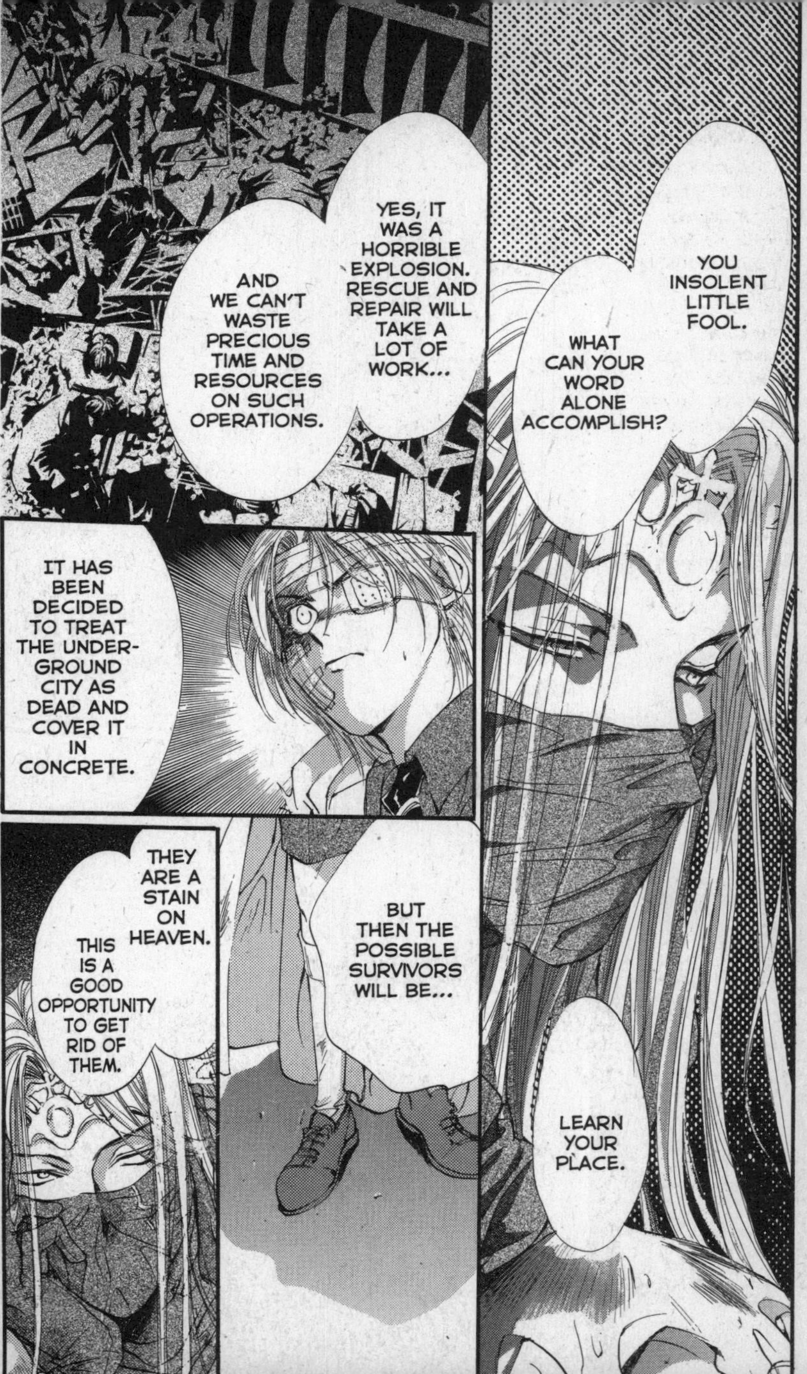
YOU INSOLENT LITTLE FOOL.
WHAT CAN YOUR WORD ALONE ACCOMPLISH?
LEARN YOUR PLACE.
YES, IT WAS A HORRIBLE EXPLOSION. RESCUE AND REPAIR WILL TAKE A LOT OF WORK...
AND WE CAN'T WASTE PRECIOUS TIME AND RESOURCES ON SUCH OPERATIONS.
IT HAS BEEN DECIDED TO TREAT THE UNDER-GROUND CITY AS DEAD AND COVER IT IN CONCRETE.
BUT THEN THE POSSIBLE SURVIVORS WILL BE...
THEY ARE A STAIN ON HEAVEN.
THIS IS A GOOD OPPORTUNITY TO GET RID OF THEM.

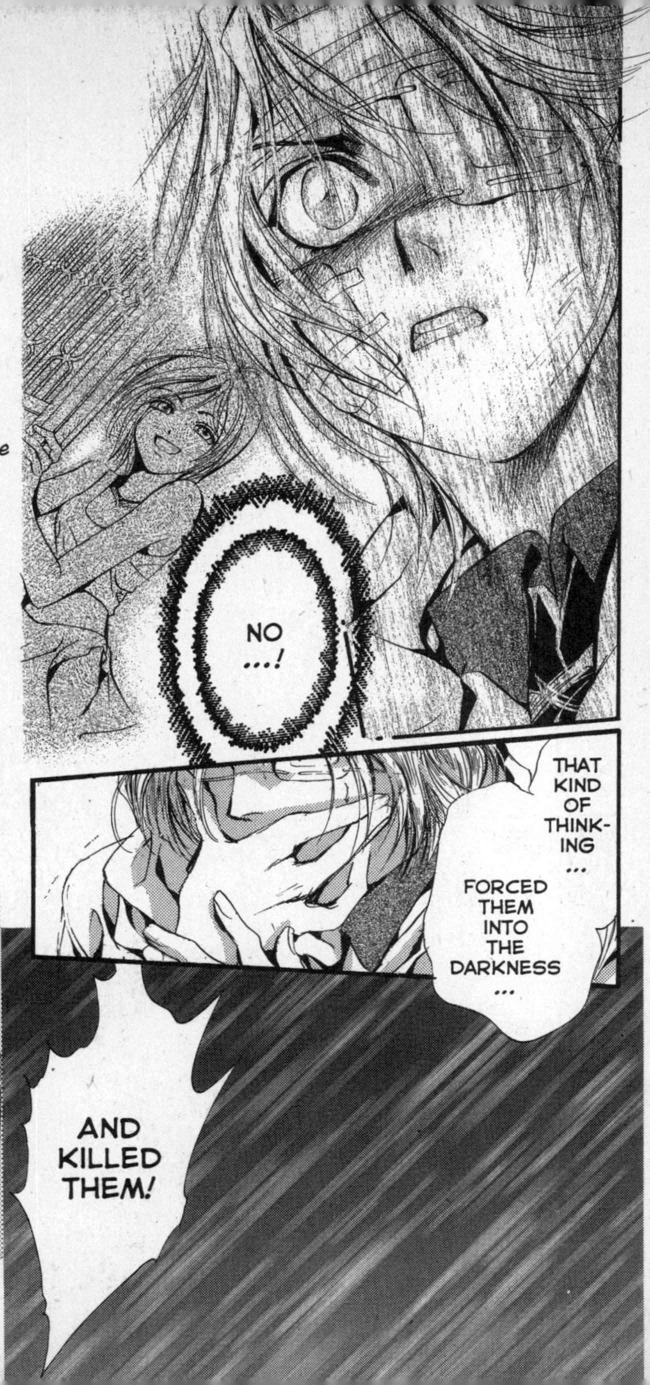
NO ...!
THAT KIND OF THINKING ...
FORCED THEM INTO THE DARKNESS ...
AND KILLED THEM!

I've been really into the PSX game ***Clock Tower: Ghost Head*** lately. I actually bought my PSX just so I could play ***Clock Tower 2.*** I just really like this series of games, the situations, the characters, and the BGM is great. I really liked Shou in this one. I watched all the endings and read the pamphlet... Fujika is... Well, I guess she's all right. It was a pain when you had to go back and save your friends who are surrounded by zombies, but I enjoyed it and hope they make another one.

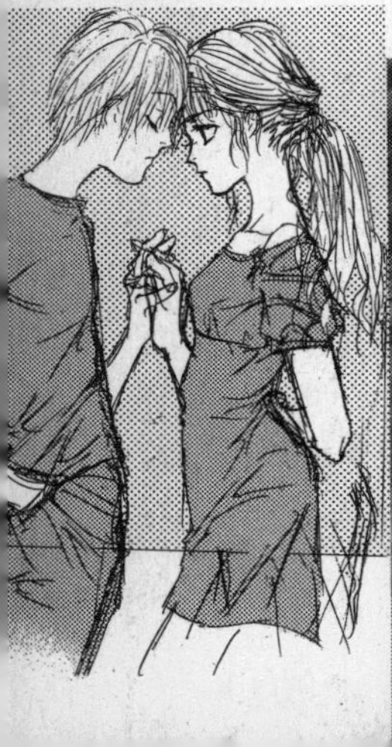

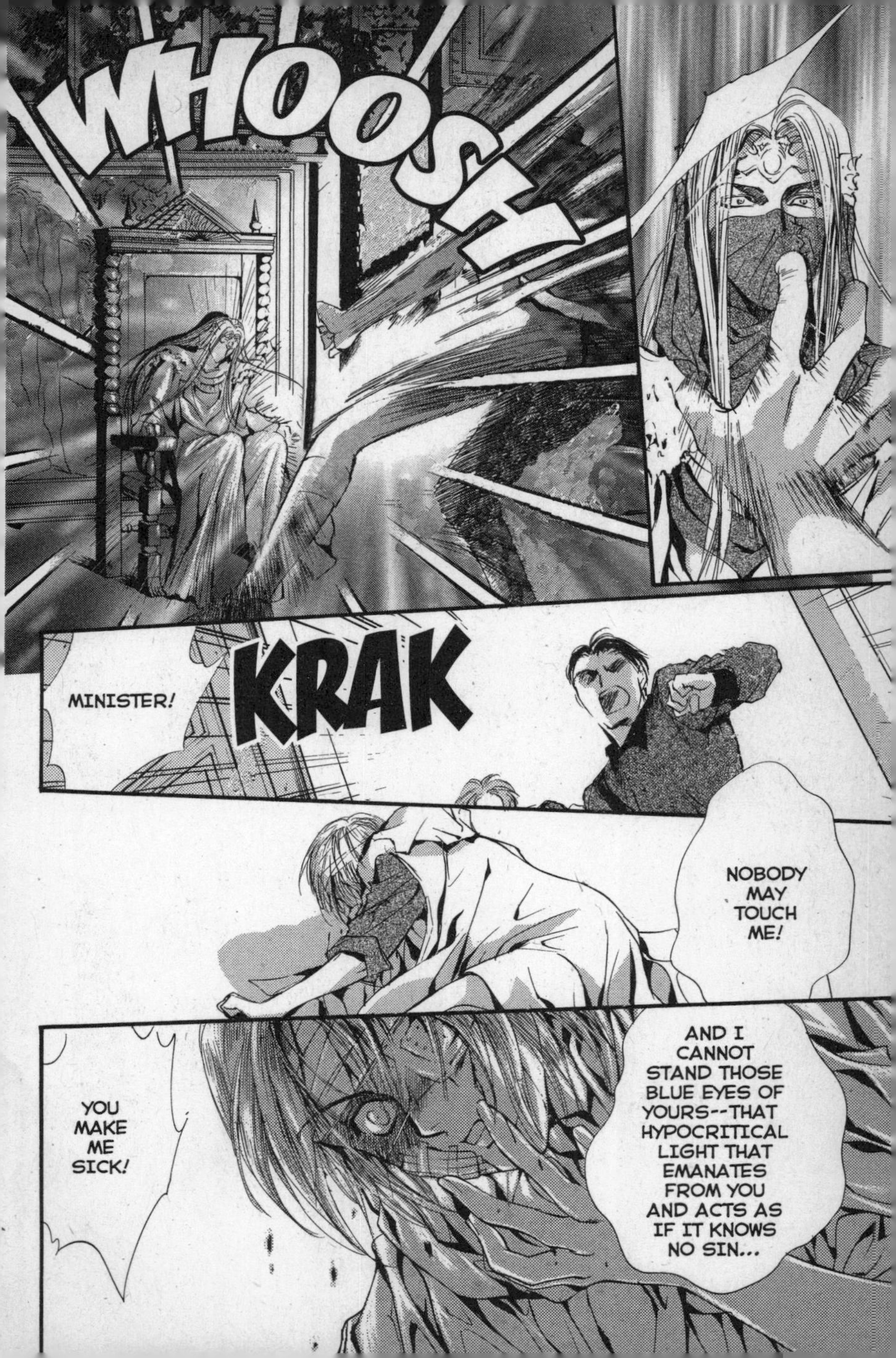
WHOOSH
KRAK
MINISTER!
NOBODY MAY TOUCH ME!
AND I CANNOT STAND THOSE BLUE EYES OF YOURS--THAT HYPOCRITICAL LIGHT THAT EMANATES FROM YOU AND ACTS AS IF IT KNOWS NO SIN...
YOU MAKE ME SICK!

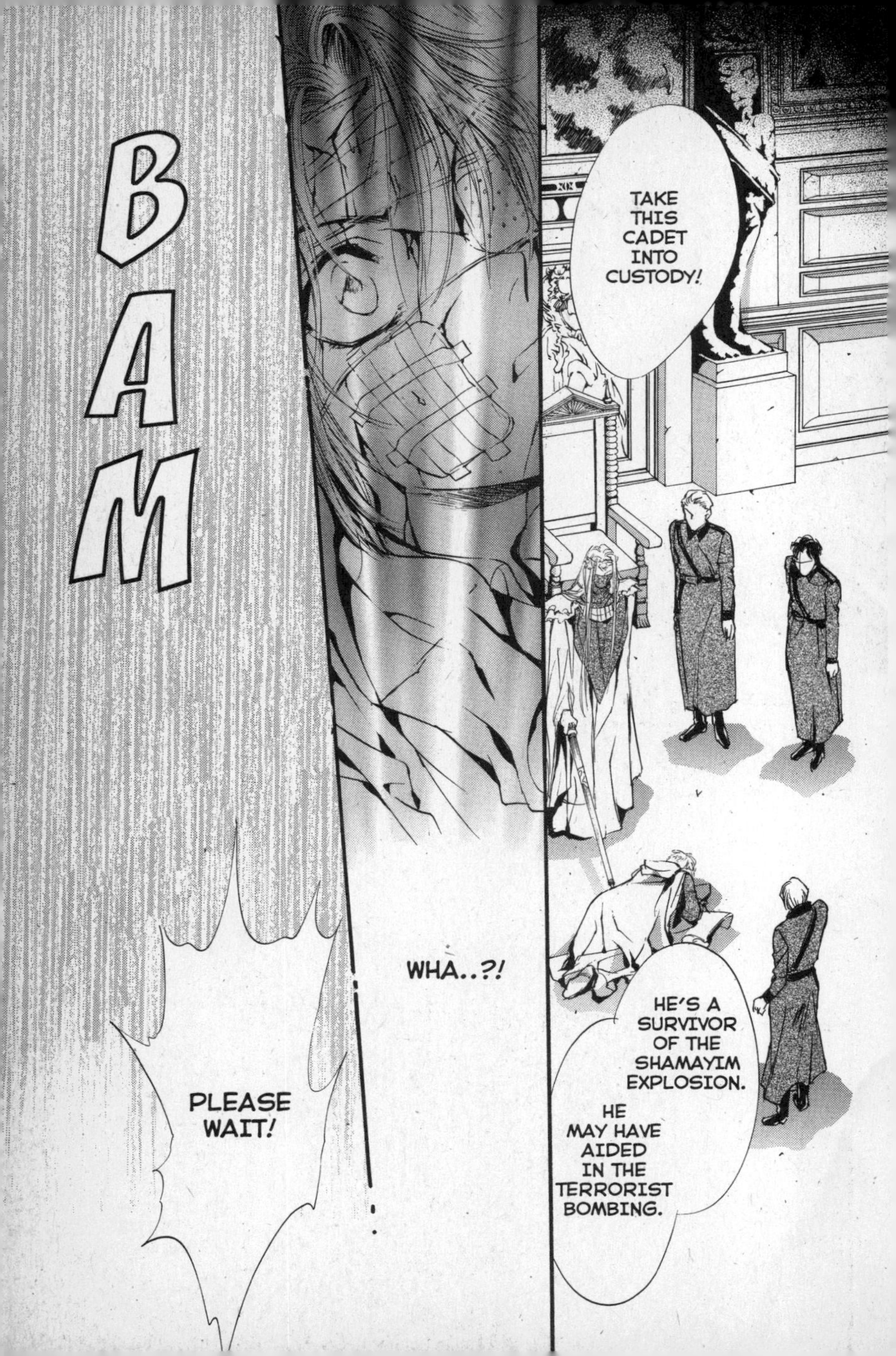
TAKE THIS CADET INTO CUSTODY!
HE'S A SURVIVOR OF THE SHAMAYIM EXPLOSION.
HE MAY HAVE AIDED IN THE TERRORIST BOMBING.
WHA..?!
BAM
PLEASE WAIT!

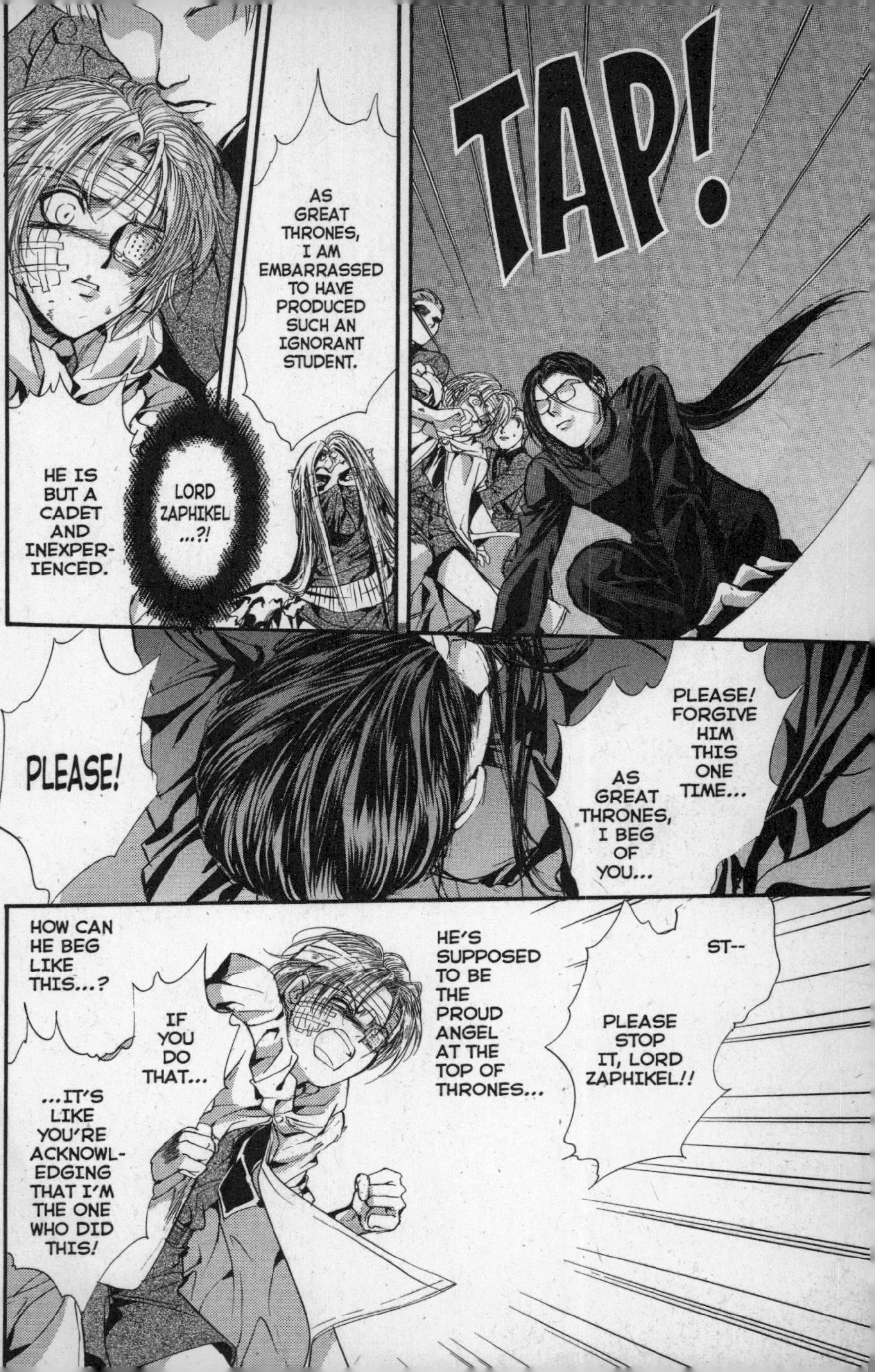
TAP!
AS GREAT THRONES, I AM EMBARRASSED TO HAVE PRODUCED SUCH AN IGNORANT STUDENT.
LORD ZAPHIKEL ...?!
HE IS BUT A CADET AND INEXPERIENCED.
PLEASE! FORGIVE HIM THIS ONE TIME...
AS GREAT THRONES, I BEG OF YOU...
PLEASE!
ST--
PLEASE STOP IT, LORD ZAPHIKEL!!
HE'S SUPPOSED TO BE THE PROUD ANGEL AT THE TOP OF THRONES...
HOW CAN HE BEG LIKE THIS...?
IF YOU DO THAT...
...IT'S LIKE YOU'RE ACKNOWLEDGING THAT I'M THE ONE WHO DID THIS!

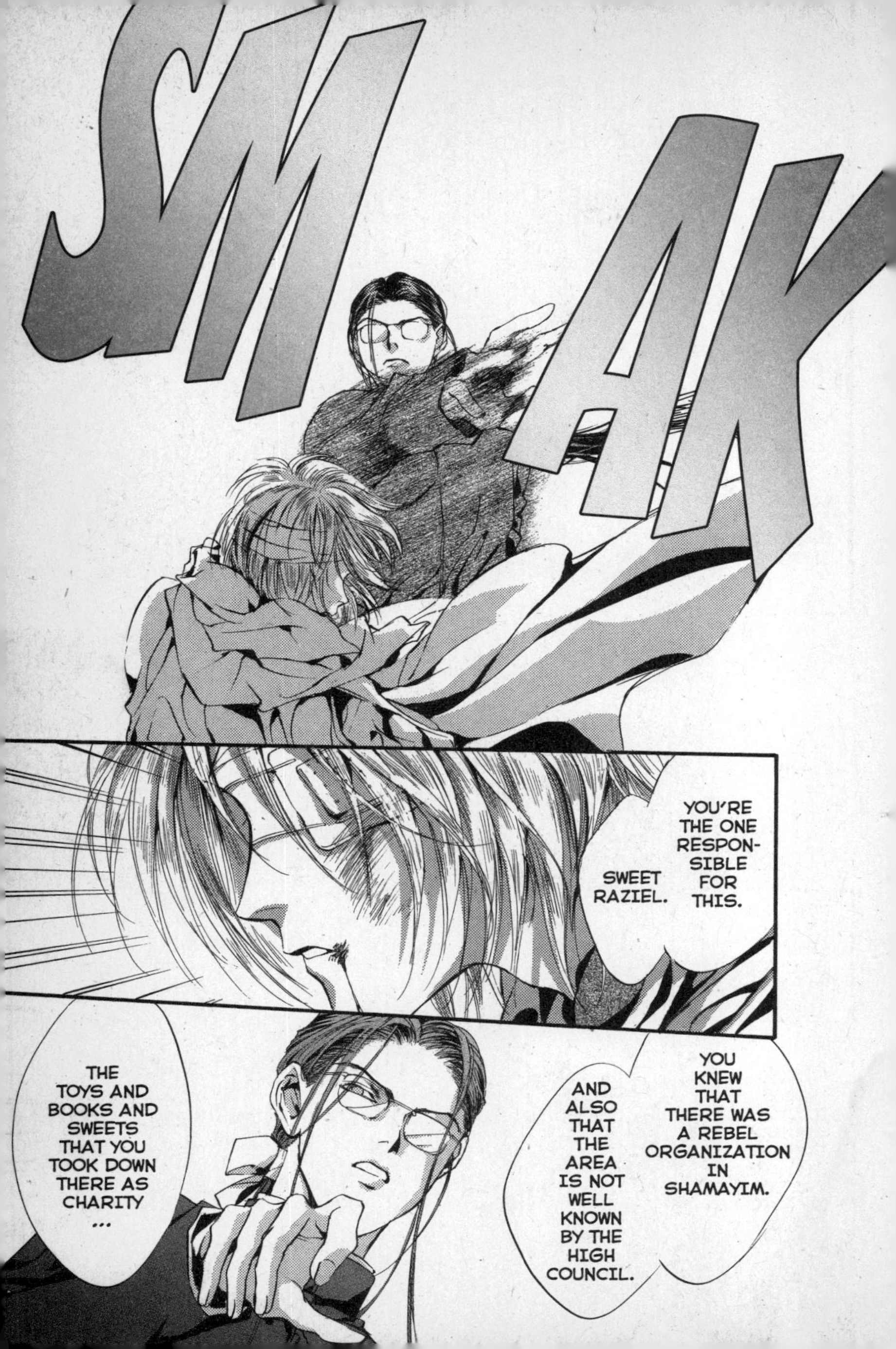
SMAK
YOU'RE THE ONE RESPONSIBLE FOR THIS.
SWEET RAZIEL.
YOU KNEW THAT THERE WAS A REBEL ORGANIZATION IN SHAMAYIM.
AND ALSO THAT THE AREA IS NOT WELL KNOWN BY THE HIGH COUNCIL.
THE TOYS AND BOOKS AND SWEETS THAT YOU TOOK DOWN THERE AS CHARITY ...

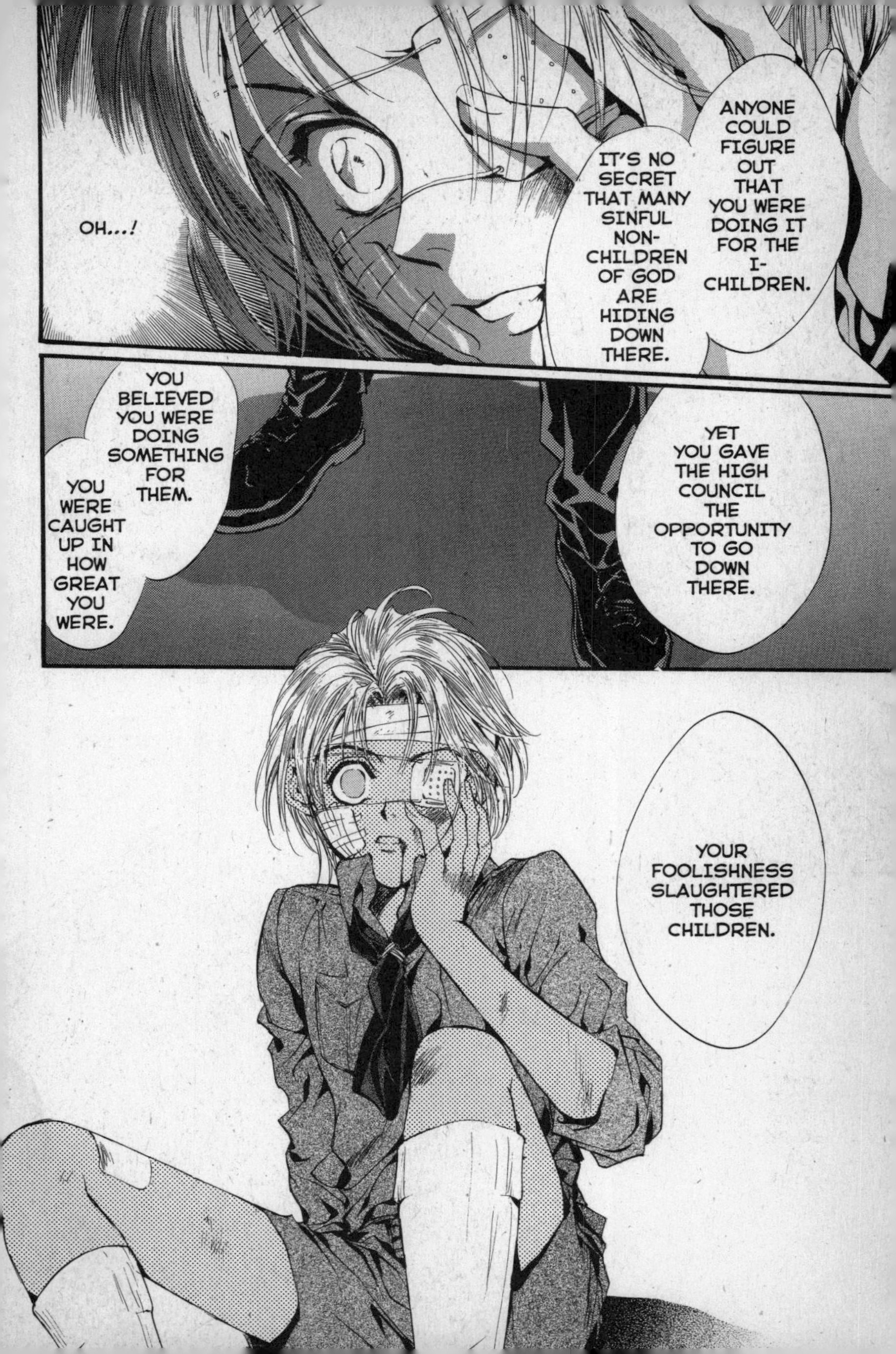
ANYONE COULD FIGURE OUT THAT YOU WERE DOING IT FOR THE I-CHILDREN.
IT'S NO SECRET THAT MANY SINFUL NON-CHILDREN OF GOD ARE HIDING DOWN THERE.
OH...!
YET YOU GAVE THE HIGH COUNCIL THE OPPORTUNITY TO GO DOWN THERE.
YOU BELIEVED YOU WERE DOING SOMETHING FOR THEM.
YOU WERE CAUGHT UP IN HOW GREAT YOU WERE.
YOUR FOOLISHNESS SLAUGHTERED THOSE CHILDREN.

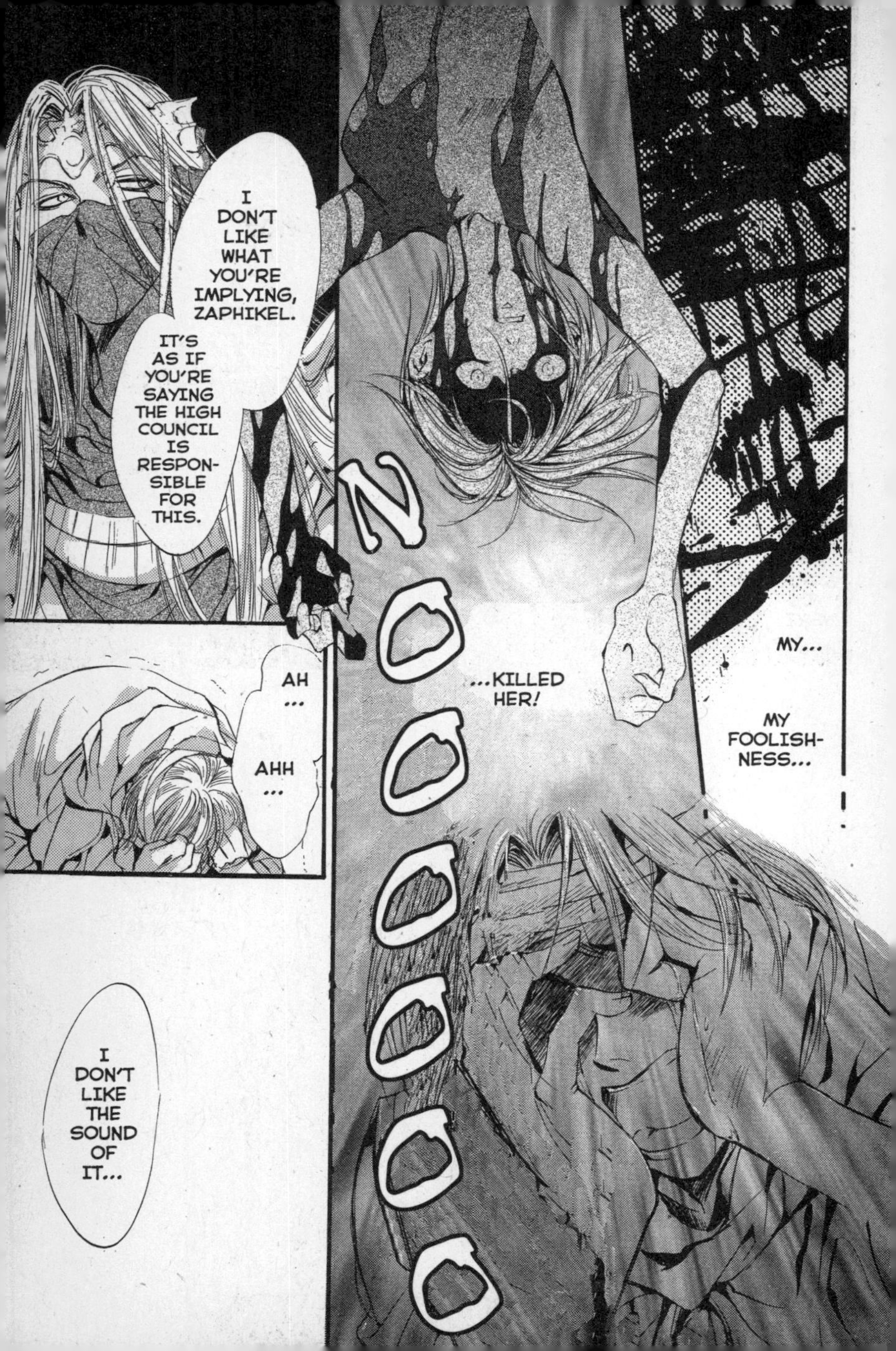
MY...
MY FOOLISHNESS...
...KILLED HER!
ZOOOOOO
I DON'T LIKE WHAT YOU'RE IMPLYING, ZAPHIKEL.
IT'S AS IF YOU'RE SAYING THE HIGH COUNCIL IS RESPONSIBLE FOR THIS.
AH...
AHH...
I DON'T LIKE THE SOUND OF IT...

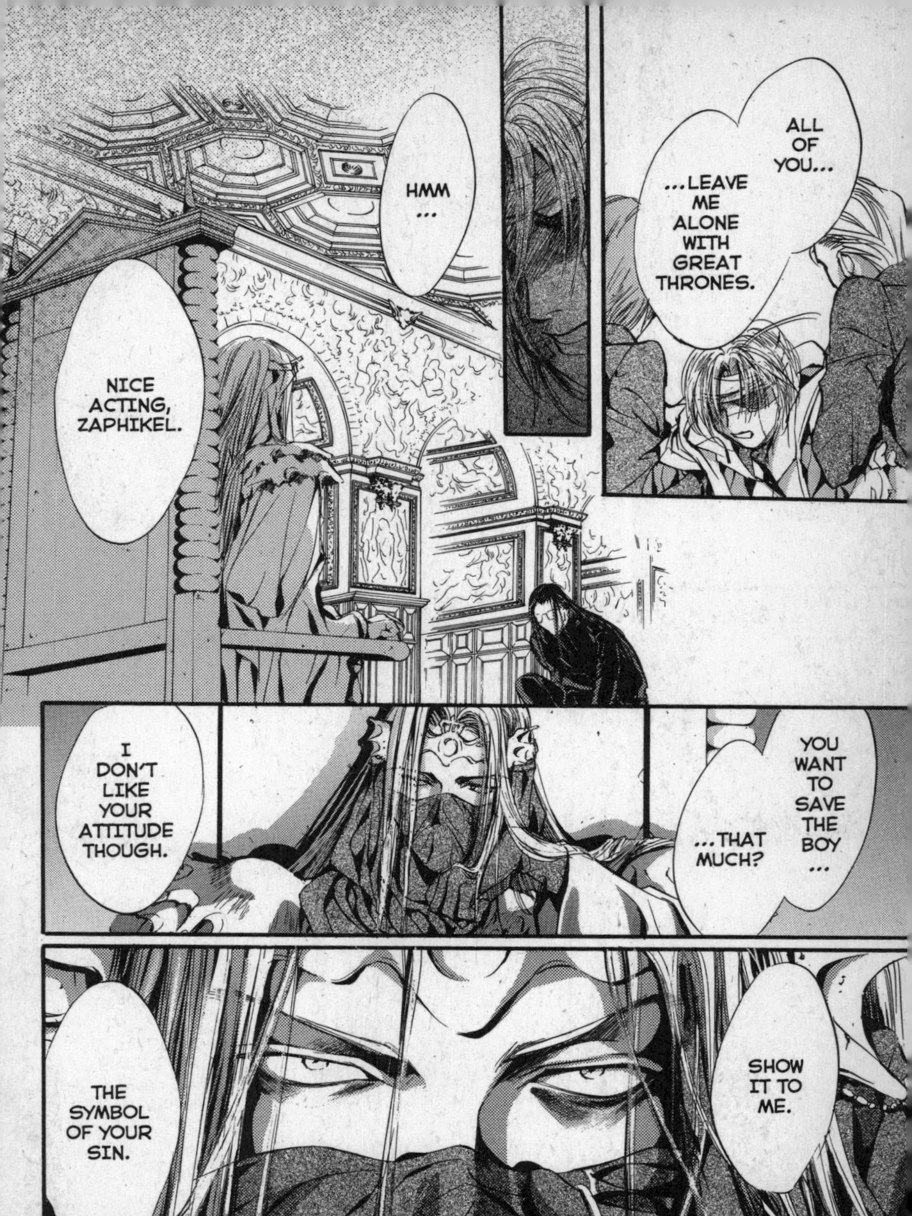

ALL OF YOU...
...LEAVE ME ALONE WITH GREAT THRONES.
HMM...
NICE ACTING, ZAPHIKEL.
YOU WANT TO SAVE THE BOY...
...THAT MUCH?
I DON'T LIKE YOUR ATTITUDE THOUGH.
SHOW IT TO ME.
THE SYMBOL OF YOUR SIN.

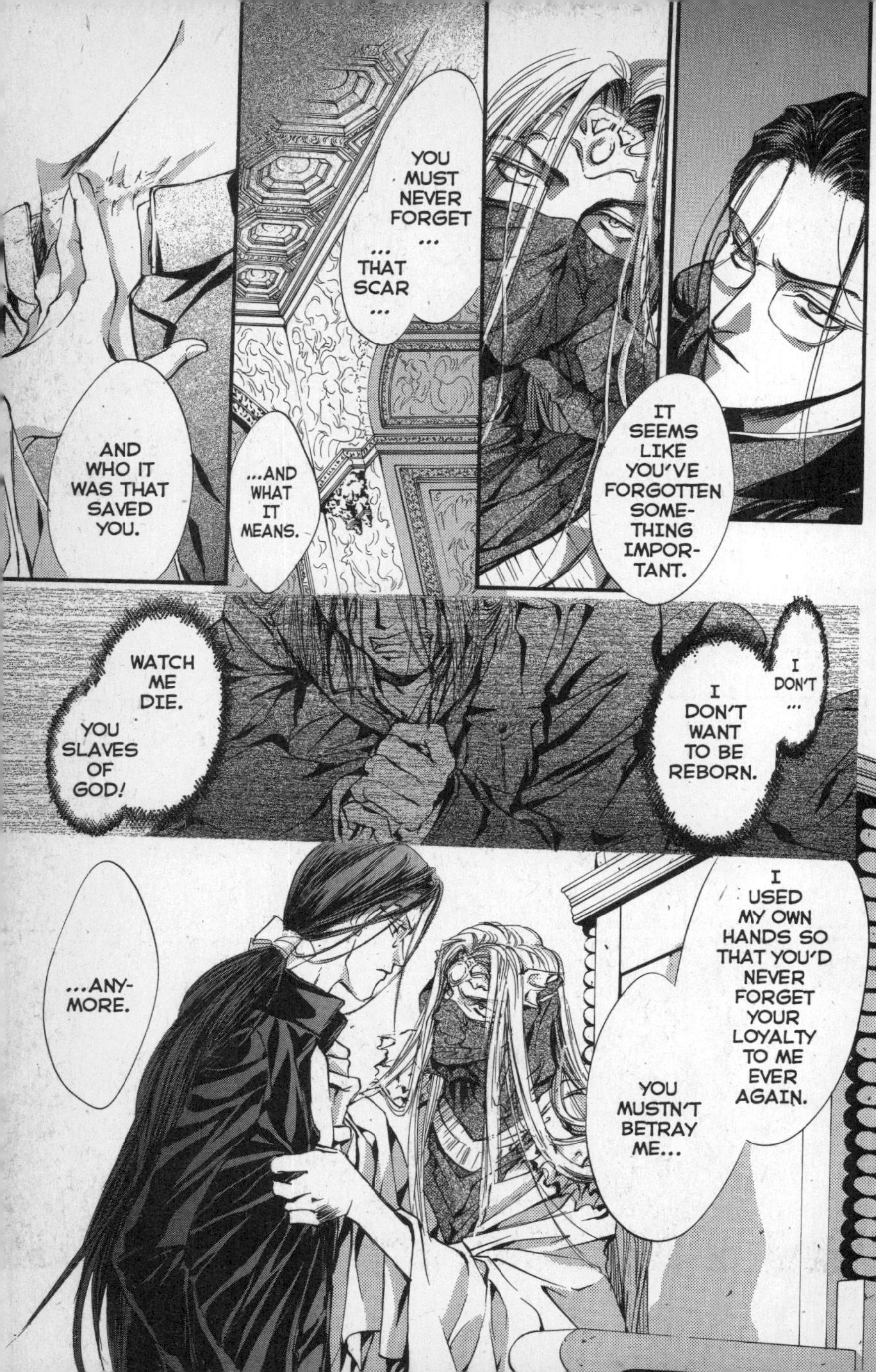
IT SEEMS LIKE YOU'VE FORGOTTEN SOME-THING IMPOR-TANT.
YOU MUST NEVER FORGET ...
... THAT SCAR ...
...AND WHAT IT MEANS.
AND WHO IT WAS THAT SAVED YOU.
I DON'T ...
I DON'T WANT TO BE REBORN.
WATCH ME DIE.
YOU SLAVES OF GOD!
I USED MY OWN HANDS SO THAT YOU'D NEVER FORGET YOUR LOYALTY TO ME EVER AGAIN.
YOU MUSTN'T BETRAY ME...
...ANY-MORE.

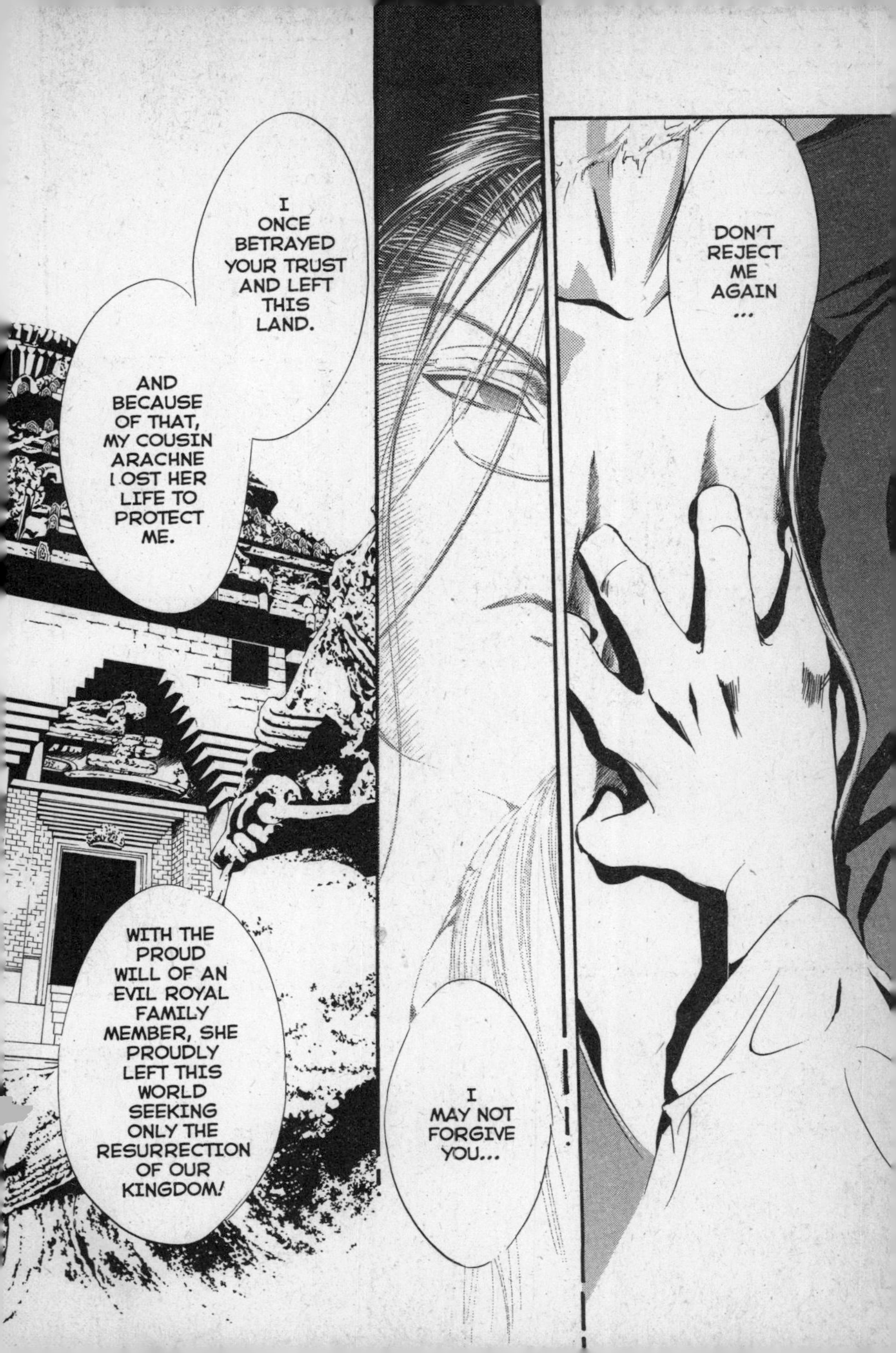
DON'T REJECT ME AGAIN...
I MAY NOT FORGIVE YOU...
I ONCE BETRAYED YOUR TRUST AND LEFT THIS LAND.
AND BECAUSE OF THAT, MY COUSIN ARACHNE LOST HER LIFE TO PROTECT ME.
WITH THE PROUD WILL OF AN EVIL ROYAL FAMILY MEMBER, SHE PROUDLY LEFT THIS WORLD SEEKING ONLY THE RESURRECTION OF OUR KINGDOM!

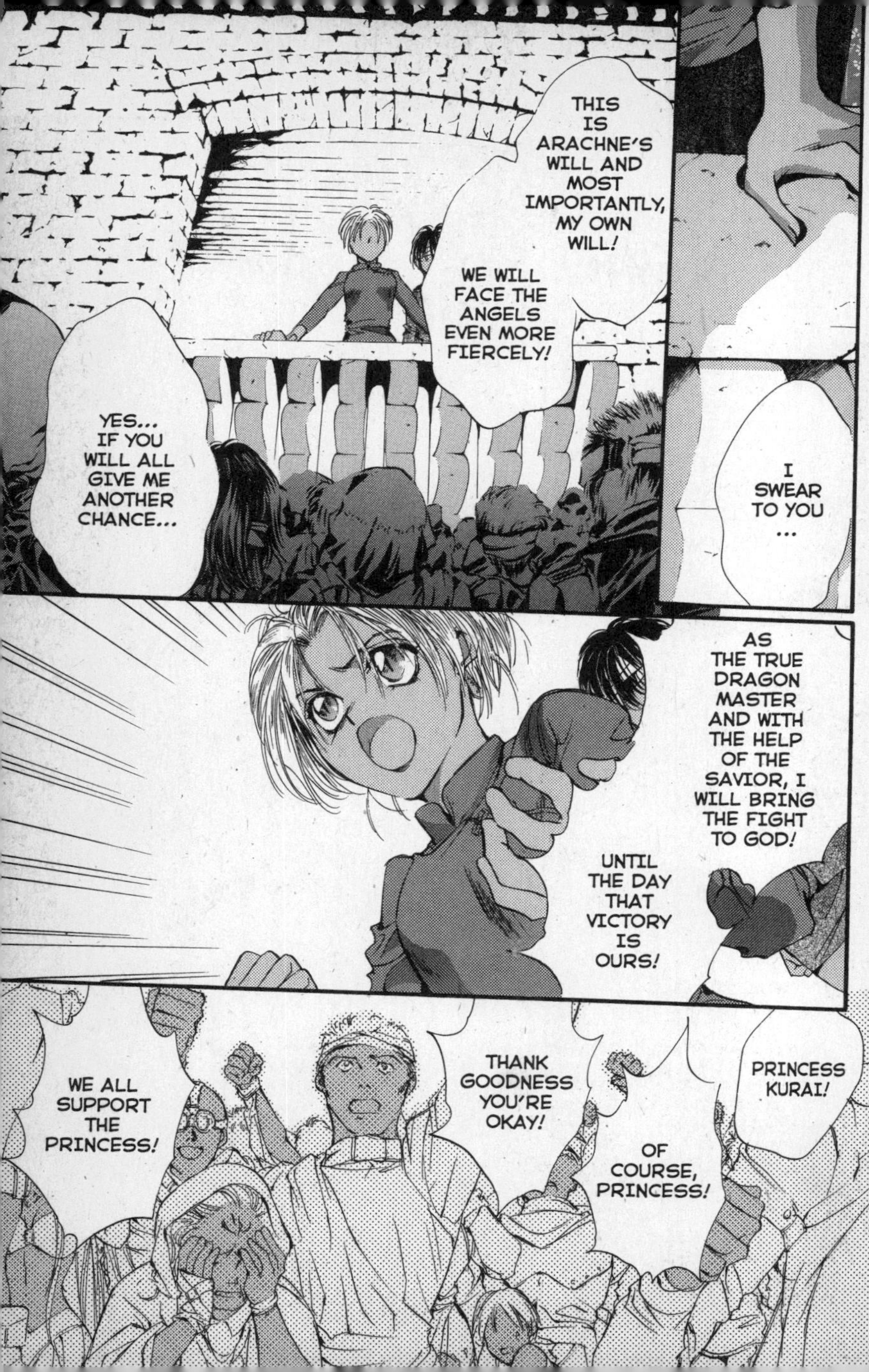
I SWEAR TO YOU ...
THIS IS ARACHNE'S WILL AND MOST IMPORTANTLY, MY OWN WILL!
WE WILL FACE THE ANGELS EVEN MORE FIERCELY!
YES... IF YOU WILL ALL GIVE ME ANOTHER CHANCE...
AS THE TRUE DRAGON MASTER AND WITH THE HELP OF THE SAVIOR, I WILL BRING THE FIGHT TO GOD!
UNTIL THE DAY THAT VICTORY IS OURS!
PRINCESS KURAI!
THANK GOODNESS YOU'RE OKAY!
OF COURSE, PRINCESS!
WE ALL SUPPORT THE PRINCESS!

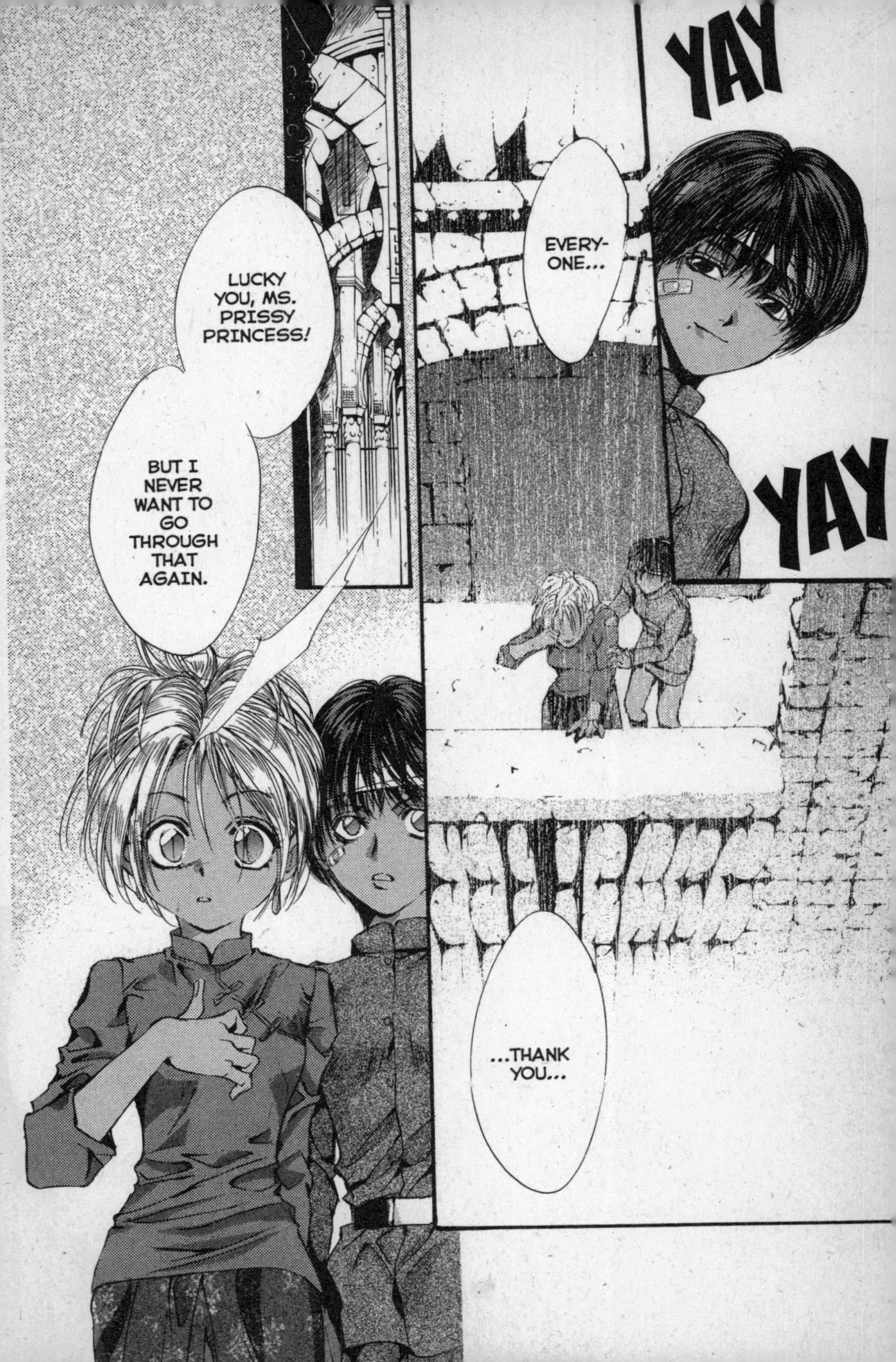
YAY
EVERY-ONE...
YAY
...THANK YOU...
LUCKY YOU, MS. PRISSY PRINCESS!
BUT I NEVER WANT TO GO THROUGH THAT AGAIN.

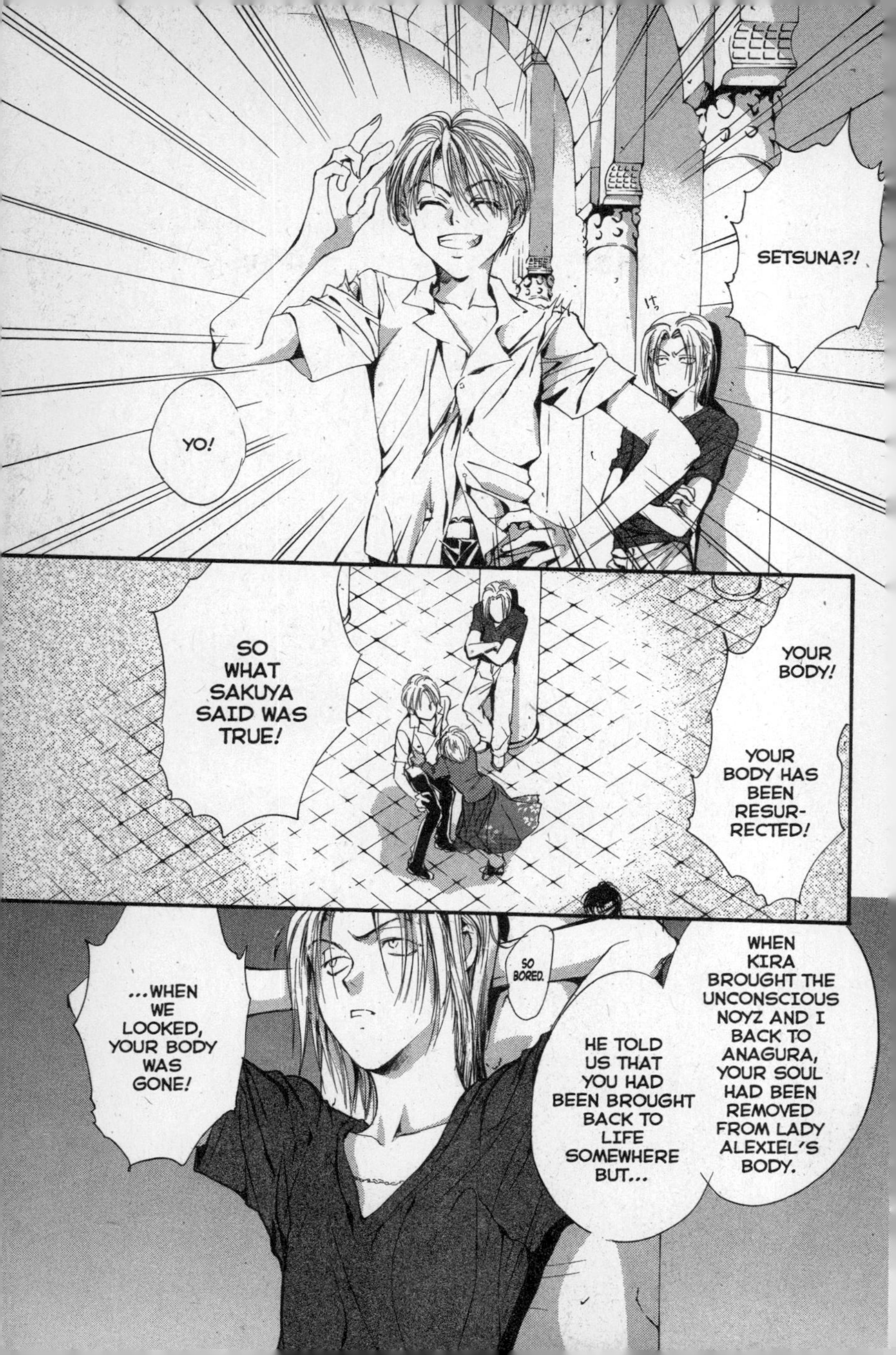
SETSUNA?!
YO!
YOUR BODY!
YOUR BODY HAS BEEN RESURRECTED!
SO WHAT SAKUYA SAID WAS TRUE!
WHEN KIRA BROUGHT THE UNCONSCIOUS NOYZ AND I BACK TO ANAGURA, YOUR SOUL HAD BEEN REMOVED FROM LADY ALEXIEL'S BODY.
HE TOLD US THAT YOU HAD BEEN BROUGHT BACK TO LIFE SOMEWHERE BUT...
SO BORED.
...WHEN WE LOOKED, YOUR BODY WAS GONE!

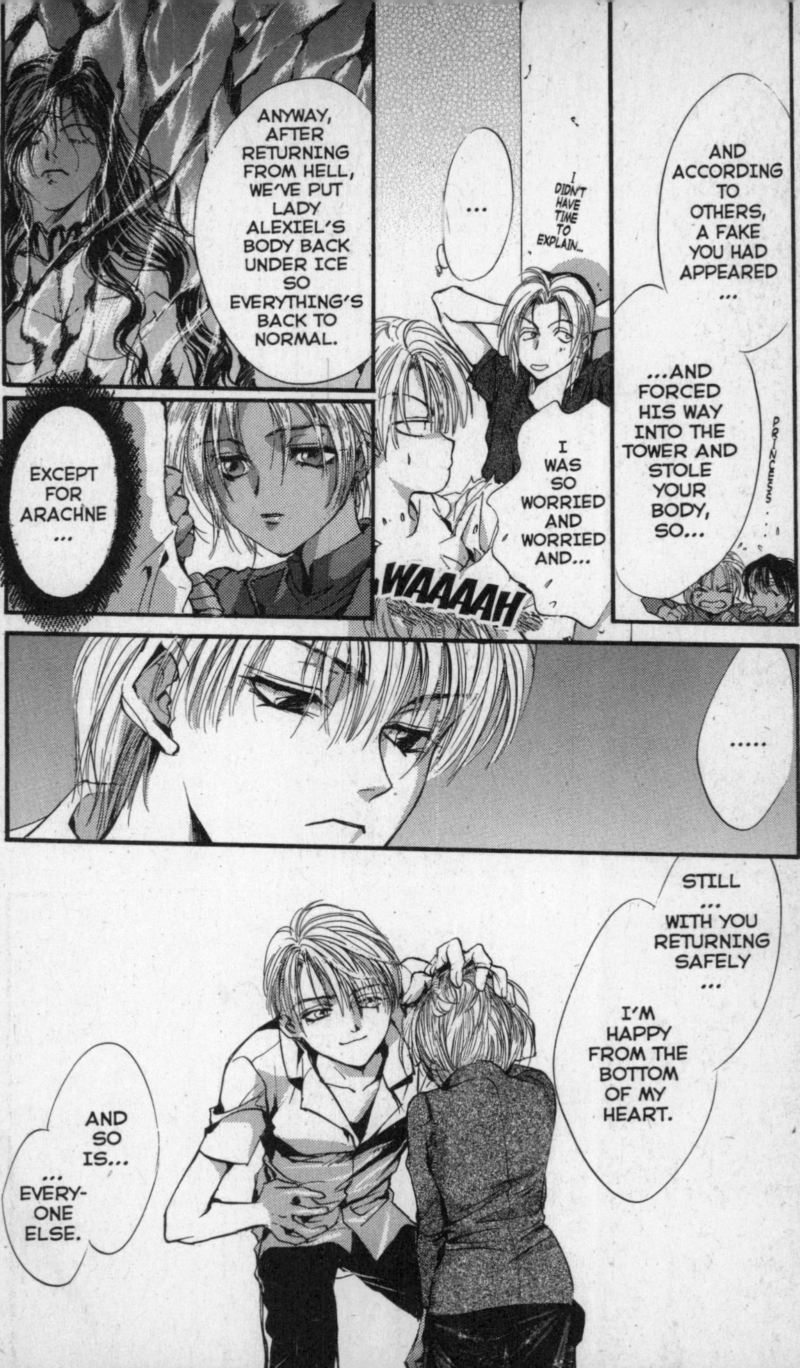
AND ACCORDING TO OTHERS, A FAKE YOU HAD APPEARED...
...AND FORCED HIS WAY INTO THE TOWER AND STOLE YOUR BODY, SO...
PRINCESS...
...
I DIDN'T HAVE TIME TO EXPLAIN...
I WAS SO WORRIED AND WORRIED AND...
WAAAAAH
ANYWAY, AFTER RETURNING FROM HELL, WE'VE PUT LADY ALEXIEL'S BODY BACK UNDER ICE SO EVERYTHING'S BACK TO NORMAL.
EXCEPT FOR ARACHNE...
.....
STILL... WITH YOU RETURNING SAFELY...
I'M HAPPY FROM THE BOTTOM OF MY HEART.
AND SO IS... ...EVERY-ONE ELSE.

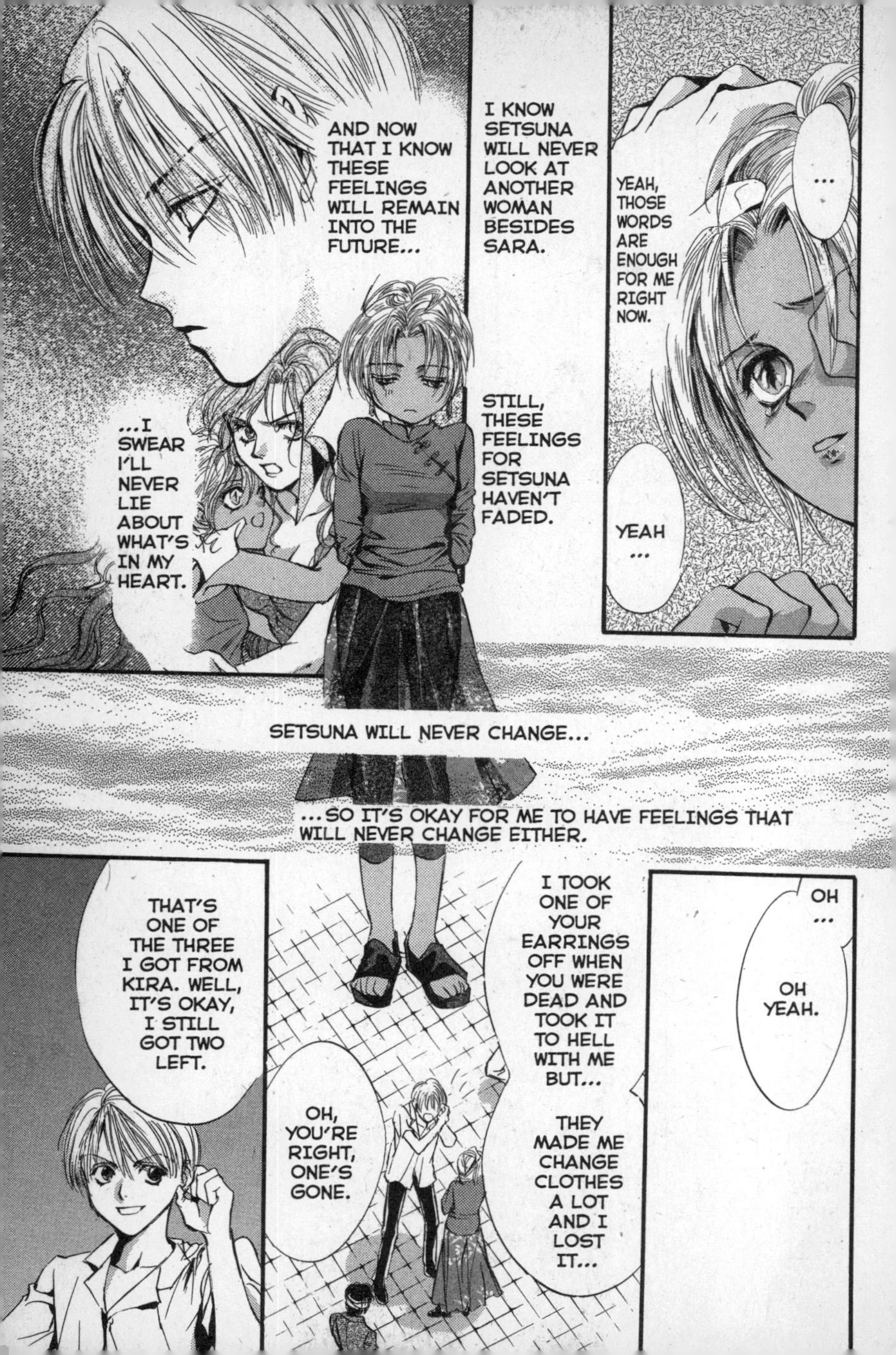
...
YEAH, THOSE WORDS ARE ENOUGH FOR ME RIGHT NOW.
YEAH ...
I KNOW SETSUNA WILL NEVER LOOK AT ANOTHER WOMAN BESIDES SARA.
AND NOW THAT I KNOW THESE FEELINGS WILL REMAIN INTO THE FUTURE...
STILL, THESE FEELINGS FOR SETSUNA HAVEN'T FADED.
...I SWEAR I'LL NEVER LIE ABOUT WHAT'S IN MY HEART.
SETSUNA WILL NEVER CHANGE...
...SO IT'S OKAY FOR ME TO HAVE FEELINGS THAT WILL NEVER CHANGE EITHER.
OH ...
OH YEAH.
I TOOK ONE OF YOUR EARRINGS OFF WHEN YOU WERE DEAD AND TOOK IT TO HELL WITH ME BUT...
THEY MADE ME CHANGE CLOTHES A LOT AND I LOST IT...
OH, YOU'RE RIGHT, ONE'S GONE.
THAT'S ONE OF THE THREE I GOT FROM KIRA. WELL, IT'S OKAY, I STILL GOT TWO LEFT.

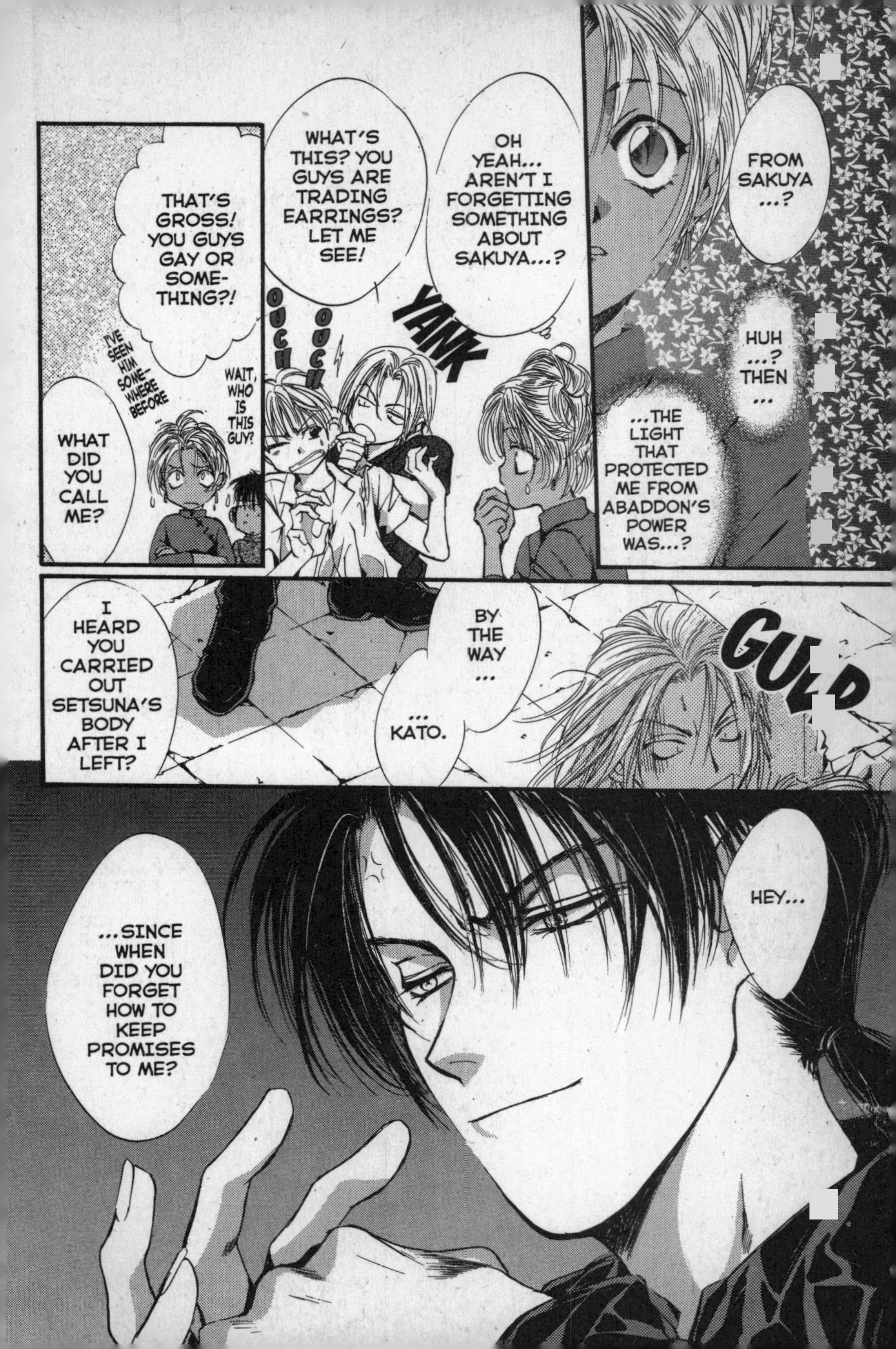
FROM SAKUYA...?
HUH...? THEN...
...THE LIGHT THAT PROTECTED ME FROM ABADDON'S POWER WAS...?
OH YEAH... AREN'T I FORGETTING SOMETHING ABOUT SAKUYA...?
WHAT'S THIS? YOU GUYS ARE TRADING EARRINGS? LET ME SEE!
YANK
OUCH
OUCH
THAT'S GROSS! YOU GUYS GAY OR SOME-THING?!
WAIT, WHO IS THIS GUY?
I'VE SEEN HIM SOME-WHERE BEFORE
WHAT DID YOU CALL ME?
GULP
BY THE WAY...
...KATO.
I HEARD YOU CARRIED OUT SETSUNA'S BODY AFTER I LEFT?
HEY...
...SINCE WHEN DID YOU FORGET HOW TO KEEP PROMISES TO ME?

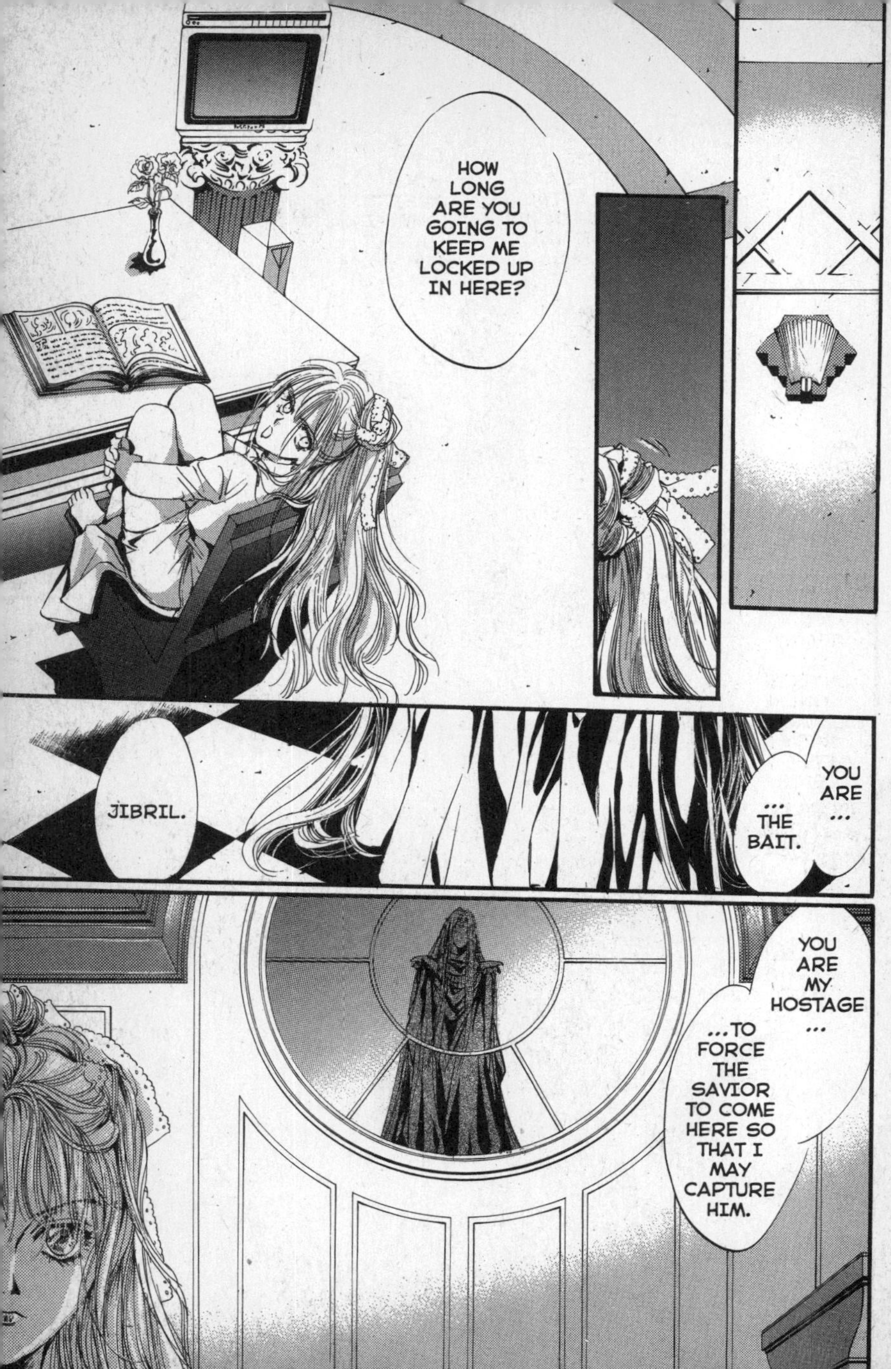
HOW LONG ARE YOU GOING TO KEEP ME LOCKED UP IN HERE?
YOU ARE ...
... THE BAIT.
JIBRIL.
YOU ARE MY HOSTAGE ...
...TO FORCE THE SAVIOR TO COME HERE SO THAT I MAY CAPTURE HIM.

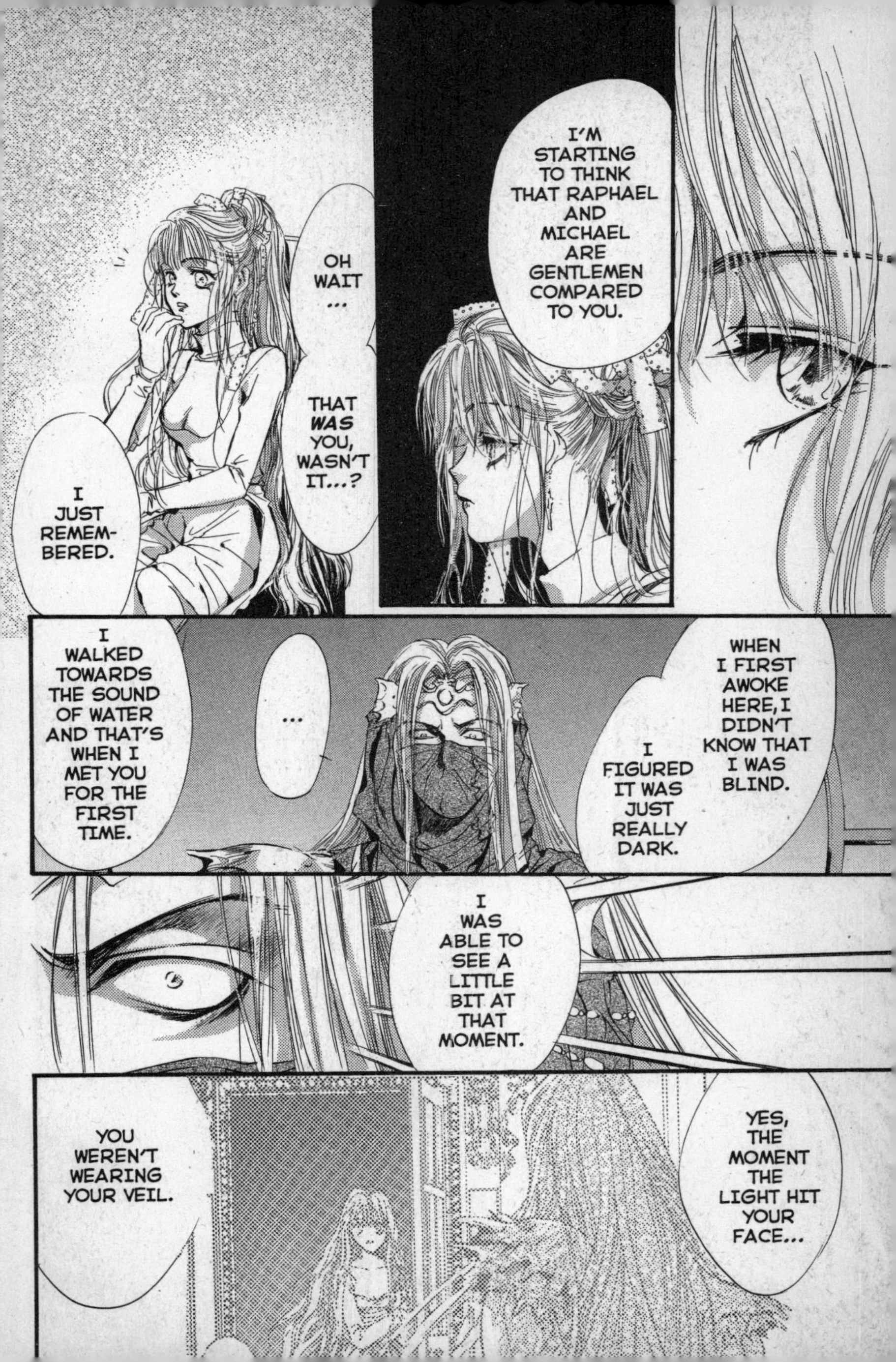
I'M STARTING TO THINK THAT RAPHAEL AND MICHAEL ARE GENTLEMEN COMPARED TO YOU.
OH WAIT ...
THAT *WAS* YOU, WASN'T IT...?
I JUST REMEMBERED.
WHEN I FIRST AWOKE HERE, I DIDN'T KNOW THAT I WAS BLIND.
I FIGURED IT WAS JUST REALLY DARK.
...
I WALKED TOWARDS THE SOUND OF WATER AND THAT'S WHEN I MET YOU FOR THE FIRST TIME.
I WAS ABLE TO SEE A LITTLE BIT AT THAT MOMENT.
YES, THE MOMENT THE LIGHT HIT YOUR FACE...
YOU WEREN'T WEARING YOUR VEIL.

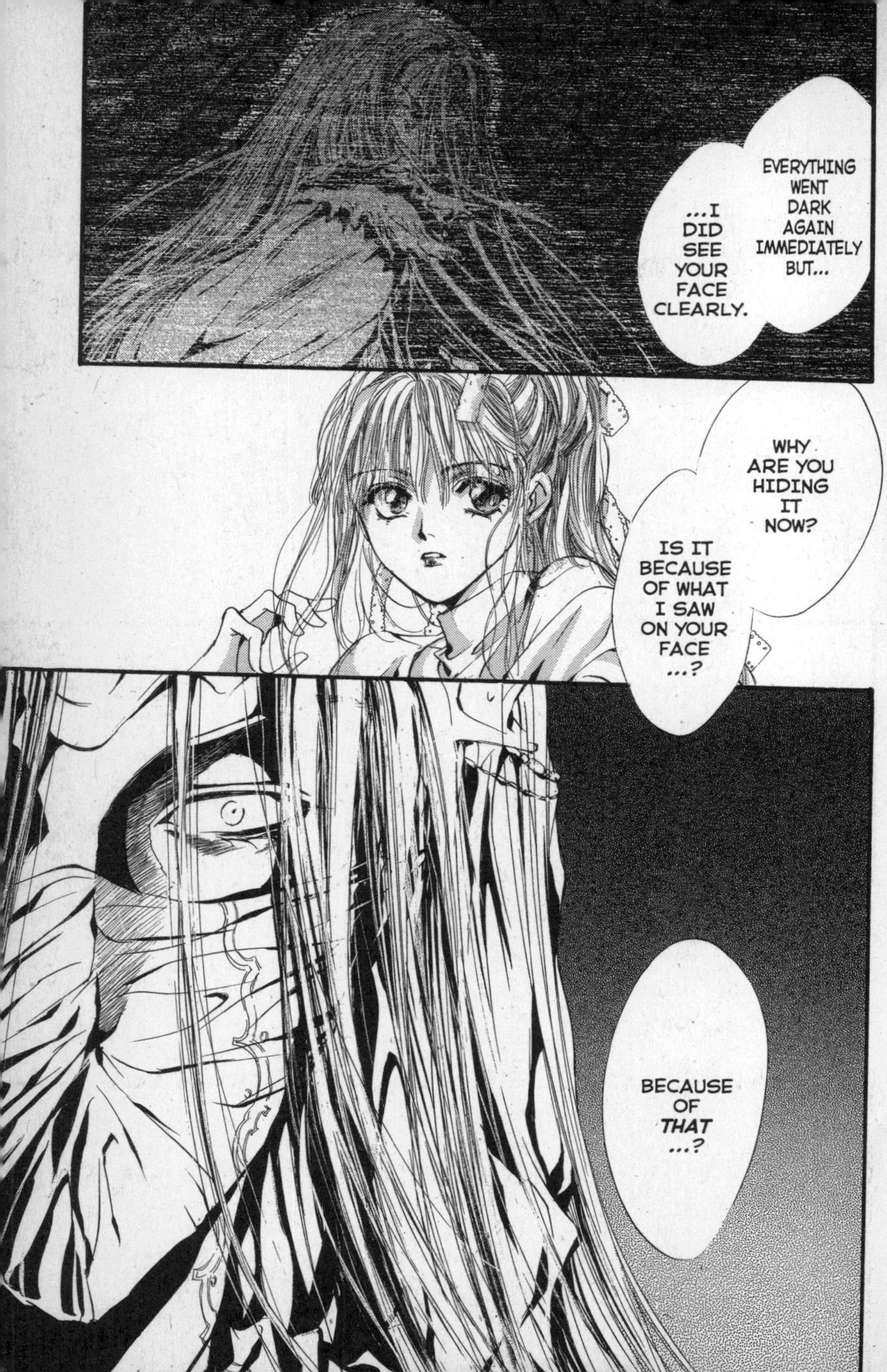
EVERYTHING WENT DARK AGAIN IMMEDIATELY BUT...
...I DID SEE YOUR FACE CLEARLY.
WHY ARE YOU HIDING IT NOW?
IS IT BECAUSE OF WHAT I SAW ON YOUR FACE ...?
BECAUSE OF *THAT* ...?

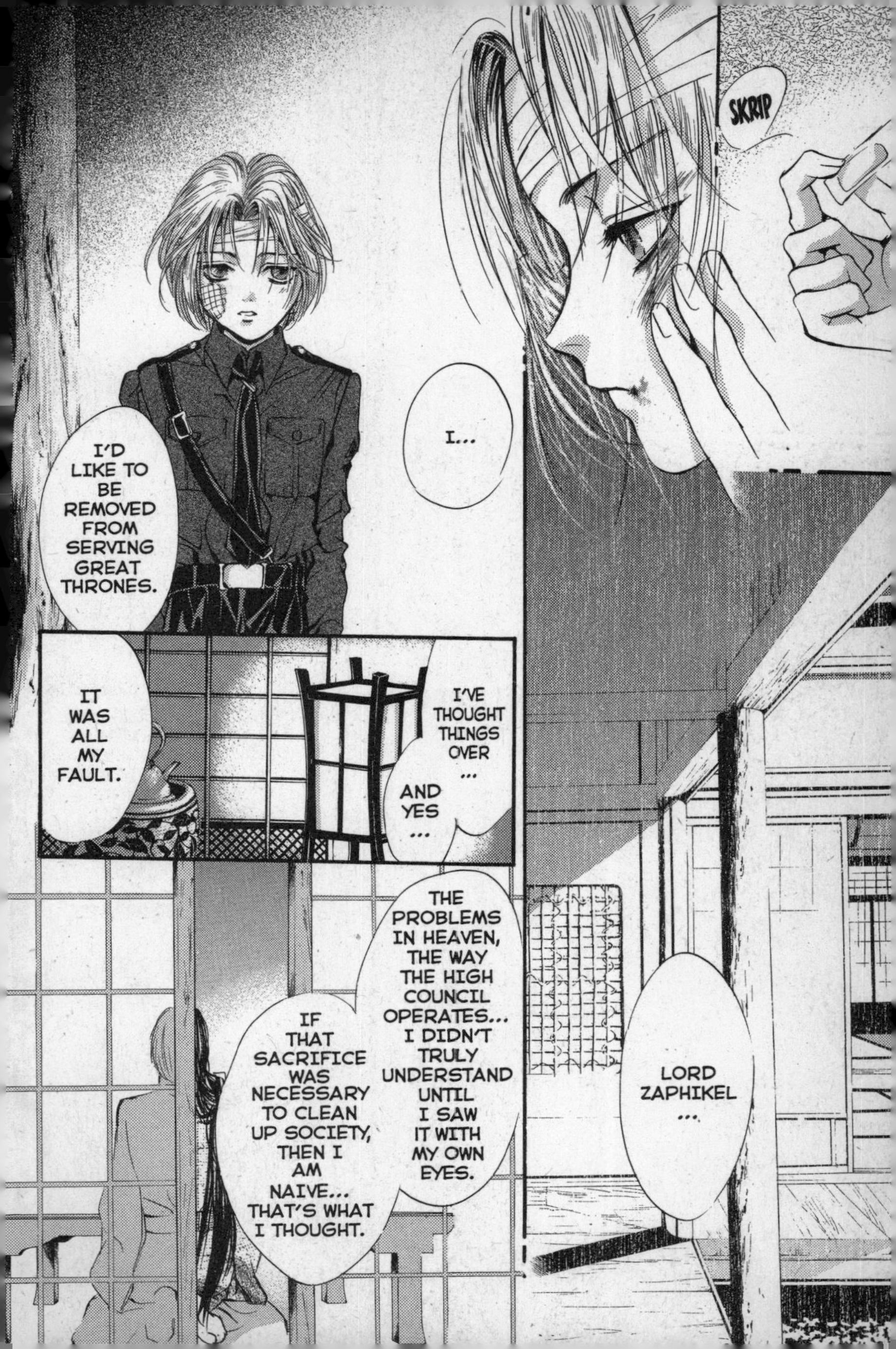
SKRIP
I...
I'D LIKE TO BE REMOVED FROM SERVING GREAT THRONES.
LORD ZAPHIKEL ....
I'VE THOUGHT THINGS OVER ...
AND YES ...
IT WAS ALL MY FAULT.
THE PROBLEMS IN HEAVEN, THE WAY THE HIGH COUNCIL OPERATES... I DIDN'T TRULY UNDERSTAND UNTIL I SAW IT WITH MY OWN EYES.
IF THAT SACRIFICE WAS NECESSARY TO CLEAN UP SOCIETY, THEN I AM NAIVE... THAT'S WHAT I THOUGHT.

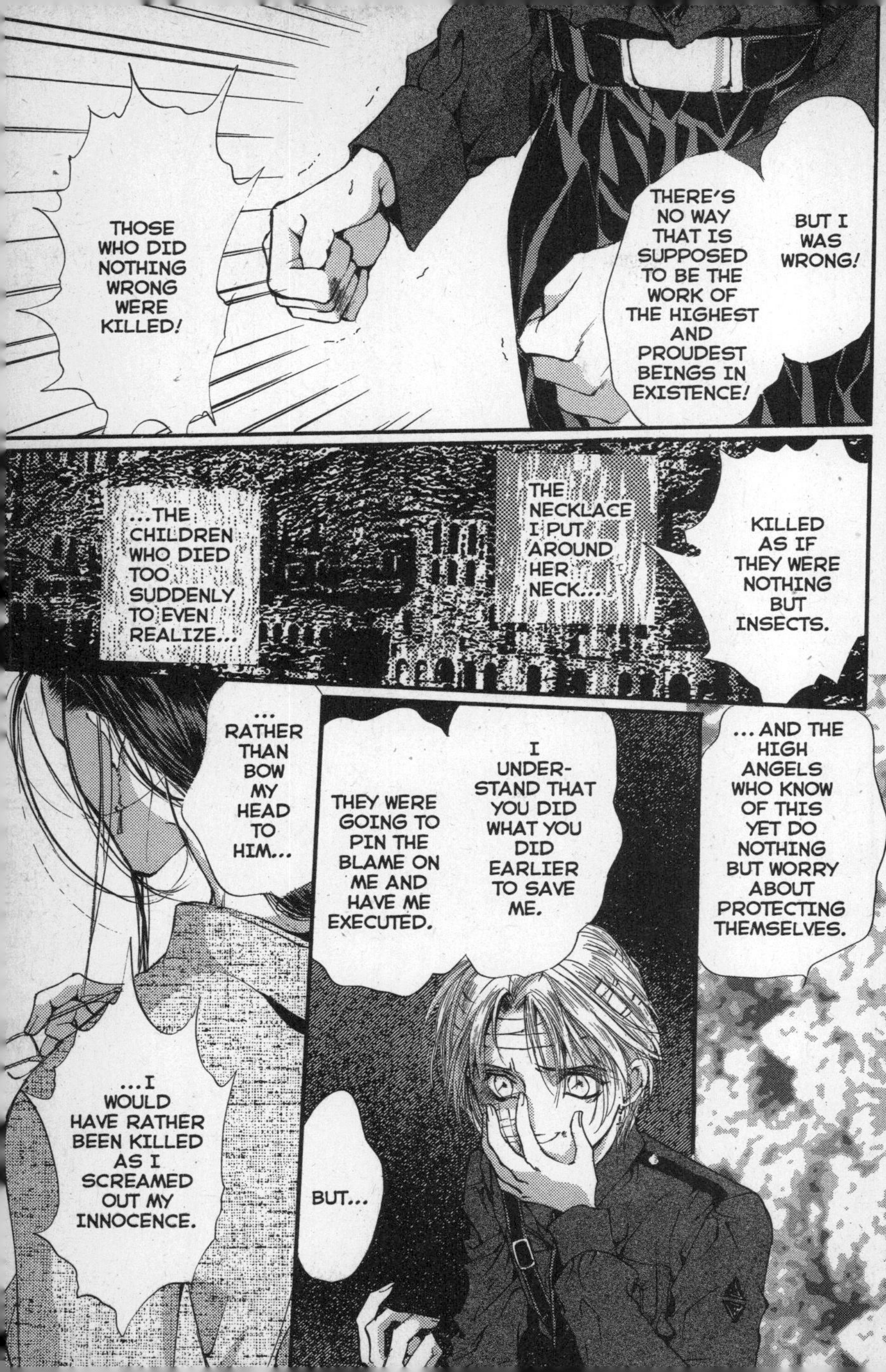
BUT I WAS WRONG!
THERE'S NO WAY THAT IS SUPPOSED TO BE THE WORK OF THE HIGHEST AND PROUDEST BEINGS IN EXISTENCE!
THOSE WHO DID NOTHING WRONG WERE KILLED!
KILLED AS IF THEY WERE NOTHING BUT INSECTS.
THE NECKLACE I PUT AROUND HER NECK...
...THE CHILDREN WHO DIED TOO SUDDENLY TO EVEN REALIZE...
...AND THE HIGH ANGELS WHO KNOW OF THIS YET DO NOTHING BUT WORRY ABOUT PROTECTING THEMSELVES.
I UNDER-STAND THAT YOU DID WHAT YOU DID EARLIER TO SAVE ME.
THEY WERE GOING TO PIN THE BLAME ON ME AND HAVE ME EXECUTED.
BUT...
... RATHER THAN BOW MY HEAD TO HIM...
...I WOULD HAVE RATHER BEEN KILLED AS I SCREAMED OUT MY INNOCENCE.

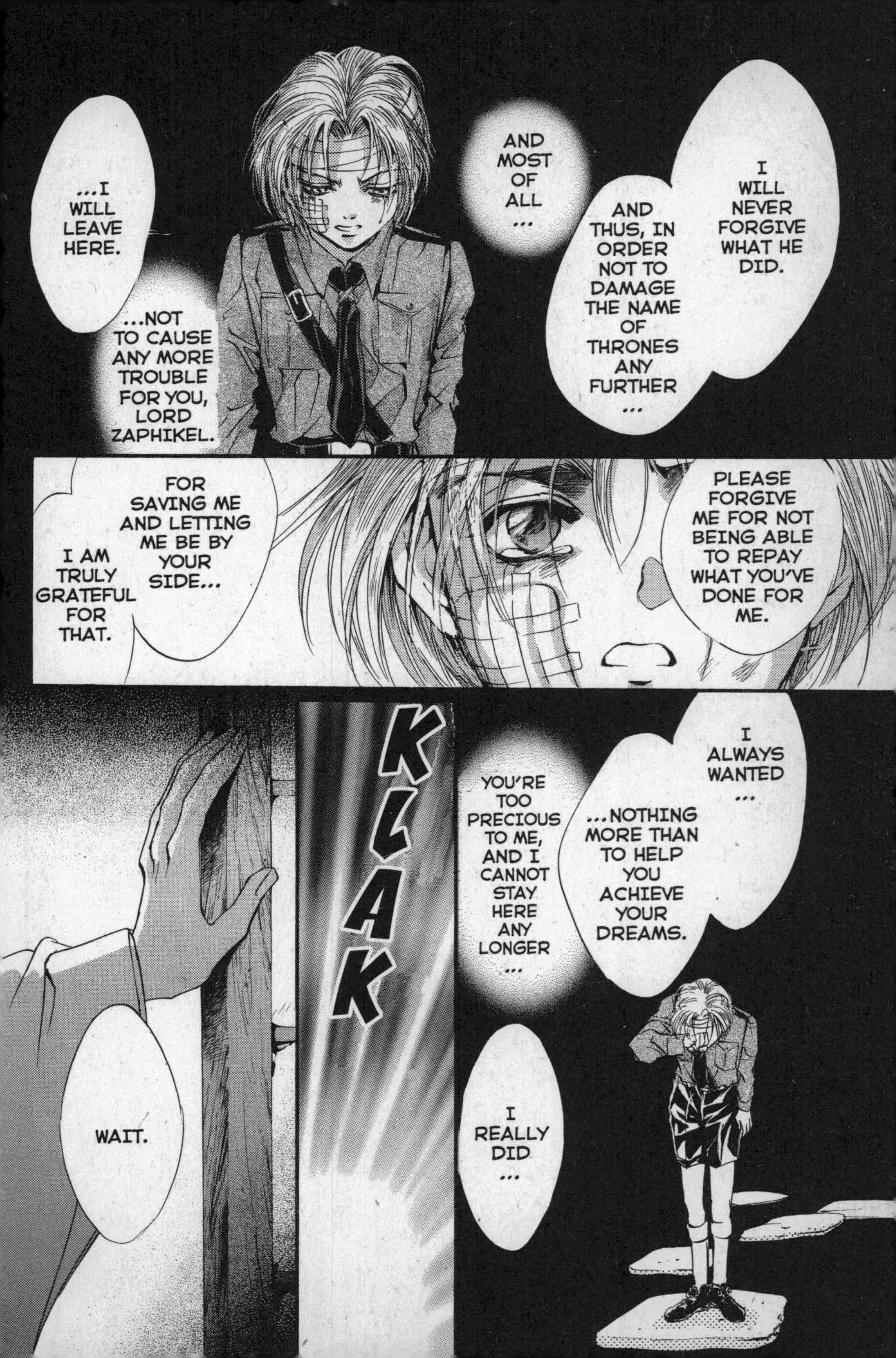
I WILL NEVER FORGIVE WHAT HE DID.
AND THUS, IN ORDER NOT TO DAMAGE THE NAME OF THRONES ANY FURTHER...
AND MOST OF ALL...
...NOT TO CAUSE ANY MORE TROUBLE FOR YOU, LORD ZAPHIKEL.
...I WILL LEAVE HERE.
PLEASE FORGIVE ME FOR NOT BEING ABLE TO REPAY WHAT YOU'VE DONE FOR ME.
FOR SAVING ME AND LETTING ME BE BY YOUR SIDE...
I AM TRULY GRATEFUL FOR THAT.
I ALWAYS WANTED...
...NOTHING MORE THAN TO HELP YOU ACHIEVE YOUR DREAMS.
YOU'RE TOO PRECIOUS TO ME, AND I CANNOT STAY HERE ANY LONGER...
I REALLY DID...
KLAK
WAIT.

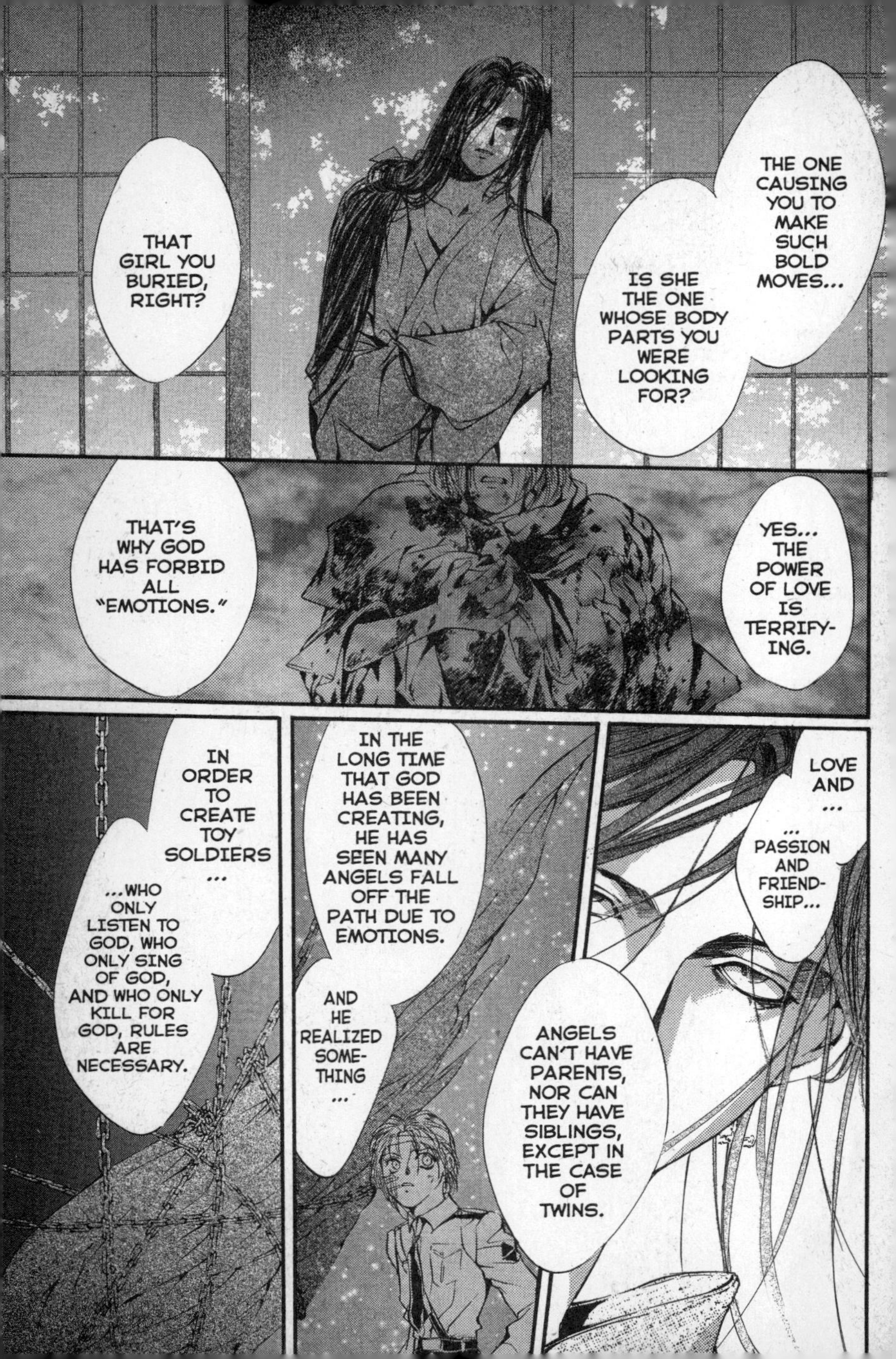
THE ONE CAUSING YOU TO MAKE SUCH BOLD MOVES...
IS SHE THE ONE WHOSE BODY PARTS YOU WERE LOOKING FOR?
THAT GIRL YOU BURIED, RIGHT?
YES... THE POWER OF LOVE IS TERRIFYING.
THAT'S WHY GOD HAS FORBID ALL "EMOTIONS."
LOVE AND ...
... PASSION AND FRIENDSHIP...
ANGELS CAN'T HAVE PARENTS, NOR CAN THEY HAVE SIBLINGS, EXCEPT IN THE CASE OF TWINS.
IN THE LONG TIME THAT GOD HAS BEEN CREATING, HE HAS SEEN MANY ANGELS FALL OFF THE PATH DUE TO EMOTIONS.
AND HE REALIZED SOMETHING ...
IN ORDER TO CREATE TOY SOLDIERS ...
...WHO ONLY LISTEN TO GOD, WHO ONLY SING OF GOD, AND WHO ONLY KILL FOR GOD, RULES ARE NECESSARY.

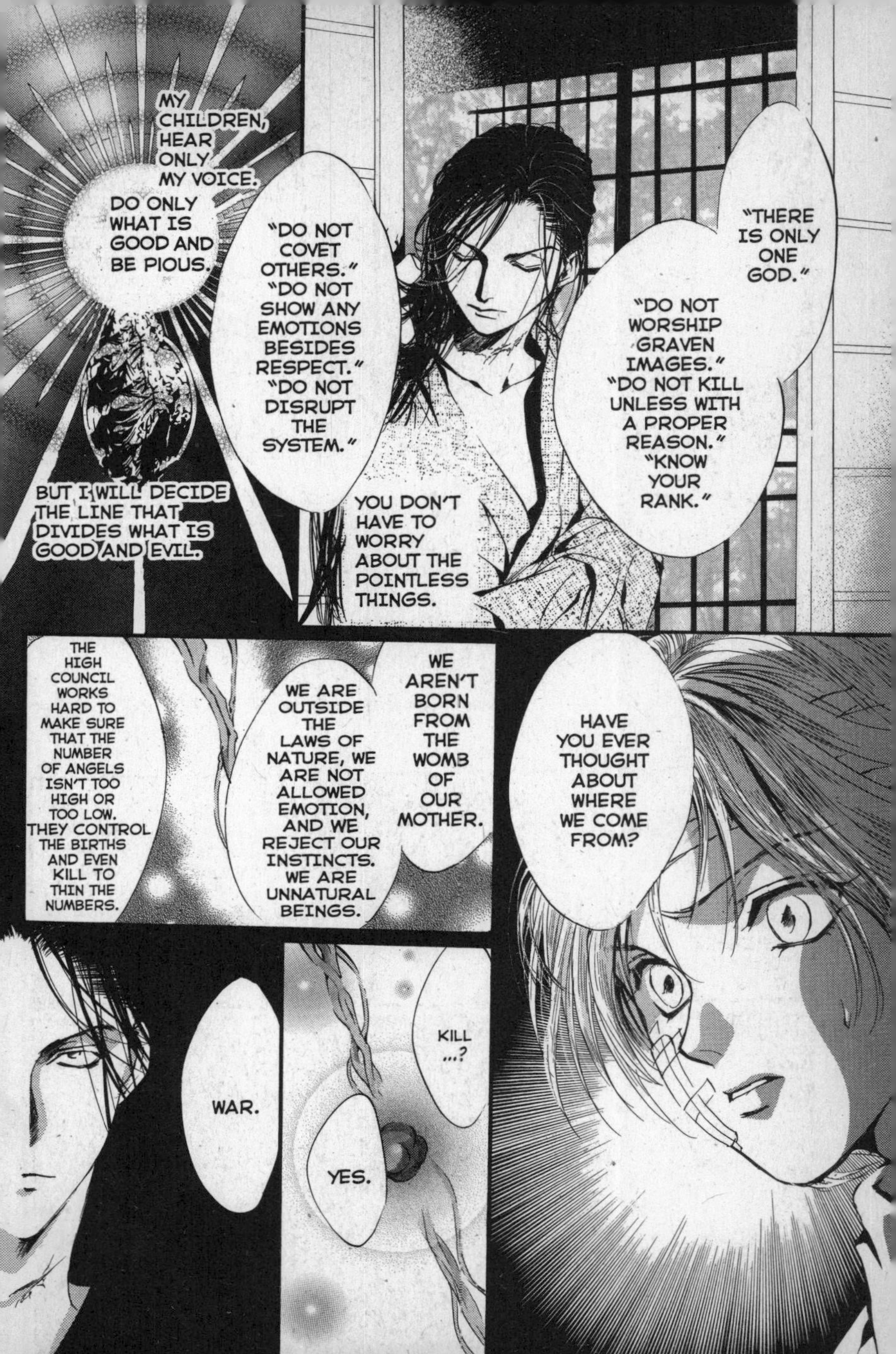
"THERE IS ONLY ONE GOD."
"DO NOT WORSHIP GRAVEN IMAGES." "DO NOT KILL UNLESS WITH A PROPER REASON." "KNOW YOUR RANK."
YOU DON'T HAVE TO WORRY ABOUT THE POINTLESS THINGS.
"DO NOT COVET OTHERS." "DO NOT SHOW ANY EMOTIONS BESIDES RESPECT." "DO NOT DISRUPT THE SYSTEM."
MY CHILDREN, HEAR ONLY MY VOICE.
DO ONLY WHAT IS GOOD AND BE PIOUS.
BUT I WILL DECIDE THE LINE THAT DIVIDES WHAT IS GOOD AND EVIL.
HAVE YOU EVER THOUGHT ABOUT WHERE WE COME FROM?
WE AREN'T BORN FROM THE WOMB OF OUR MOTHER.
WE ARE OUTSIDE THE LAWS OF NATURE, WE ARE NOT ALLOWED EMOTION, AND WE REJECT OUR INSTINCTS. WE ARE UNNATURAL BEINGS.
THE HIGH COUNCIL WORKS HARD TO MAKE SURE THAT THE NUMBER OF ANGELS ISN'T TOO HIGH OR TOO LOW. THEY CONTROL THE BIRTHS AND EVEN KILL TO THIN THE NUMBERS.
KILL ...?
YES.
WAR.

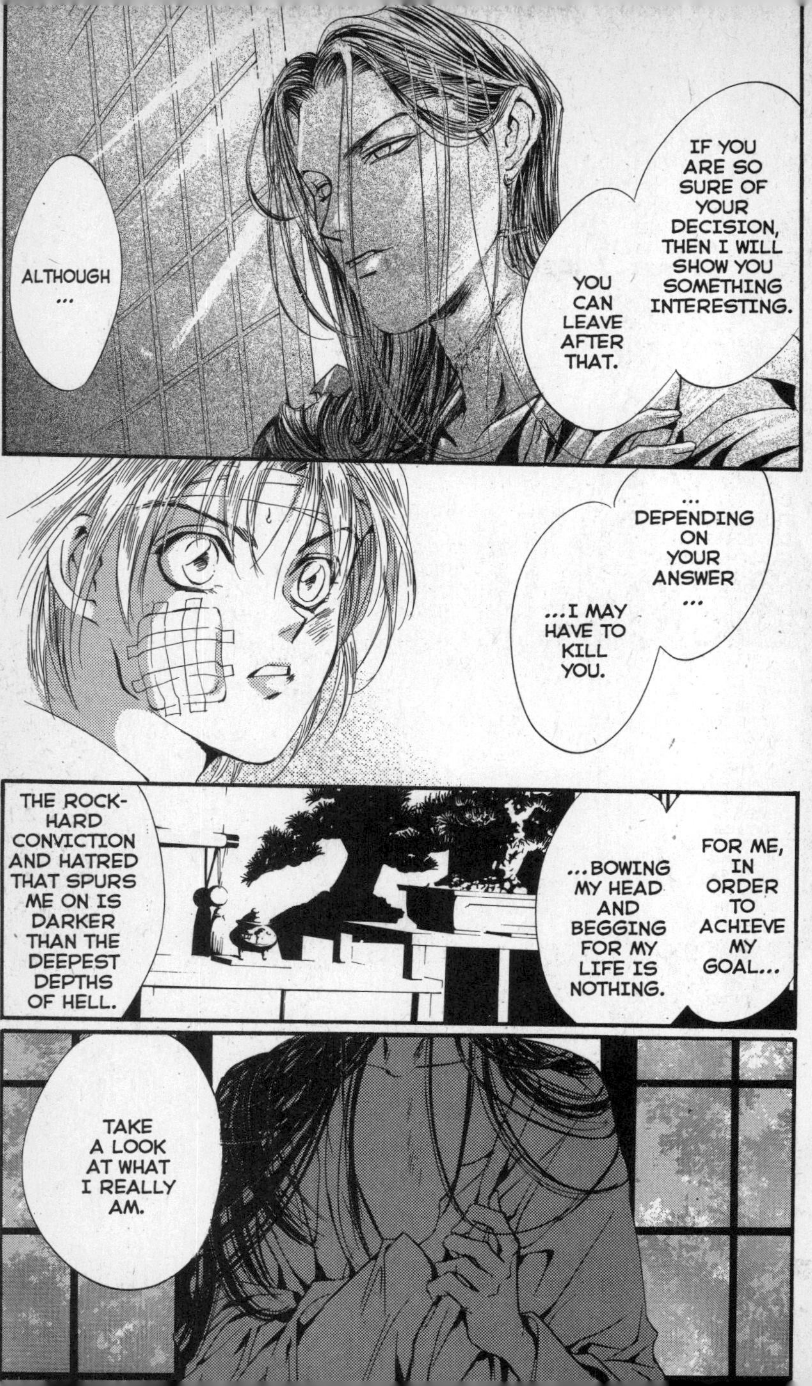
IF YOU ARE SO SURE OF YOUR DECISION, THEN I WILL SHOW YOU SOMETHING INTERESTING.
YOU CAN LEAVE AFTER THAT.
ALTHOUGH ...
... DEPENDING ON YOUR ANSWER ...
...I MAY HAVE TO KILL YOU.
FOR ME, IN ORDER TO ACHIEVE MY GOAL...
...BOWING MY HEAD AND BEGGING FOR MY LIFE IS NOTHING.
THE ROCK-HARD CONVICTION AND HATRED THAT SPURS ME ON IS DARKER THAN THE DEEPEST DEPTHS OF HELL.
TAKE A LOOK AT WHAT I REALLY AM.

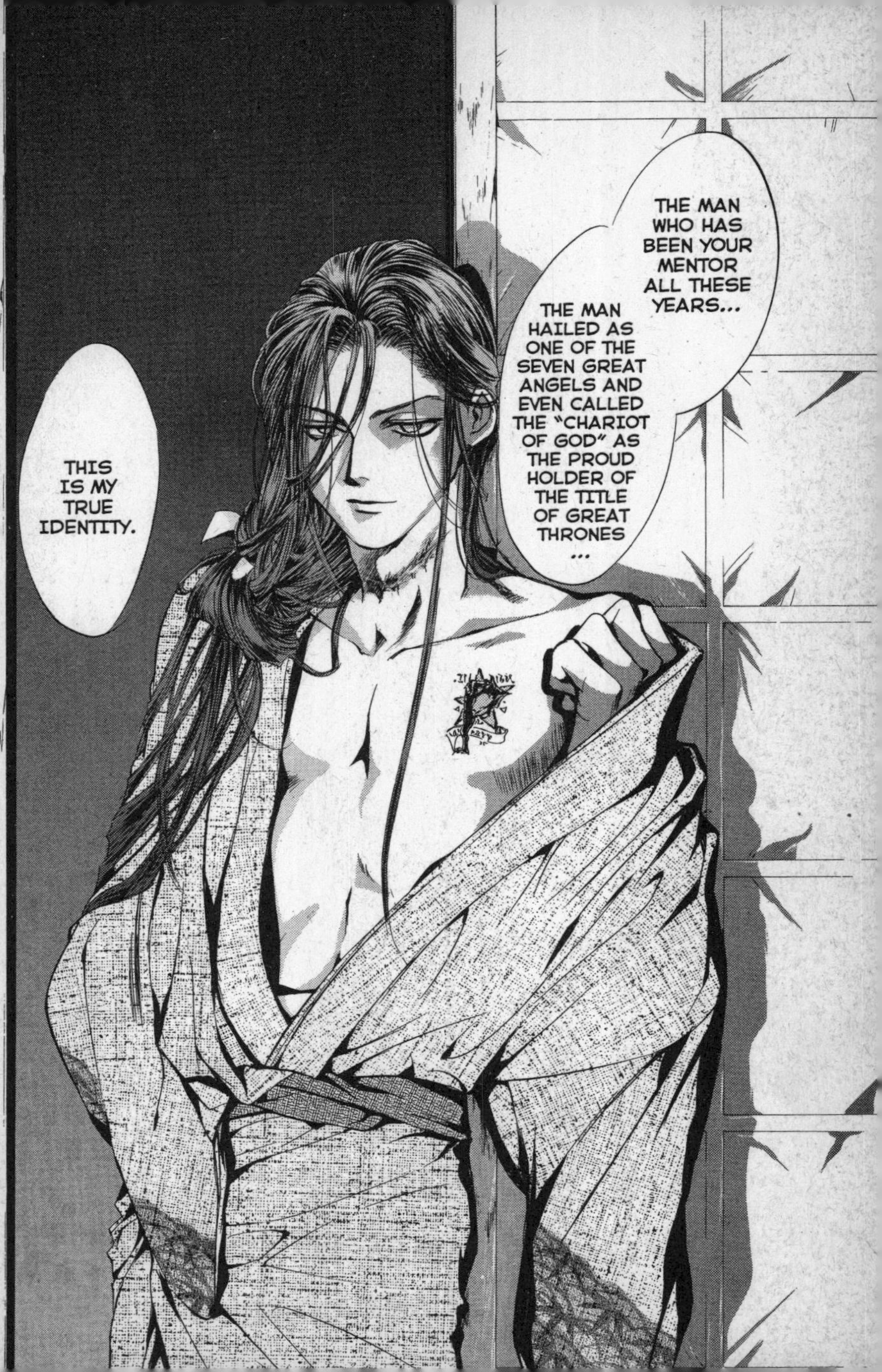
THE MAN WHO HAS BEEN YOUR MENTOR ALL THESE YEARS...
THE MAN HAILED AS ONE OF THE SEVEN GREAT ANGELS AND EVEN CALLED THE "CHARIOT OF GOD" AS THE PROUD HOLDER OF THE TITLE OF GREAT THRONES ...
THIS IS MY TRUE IDENTITY.

天使禁猟区
Angel Sanctuary

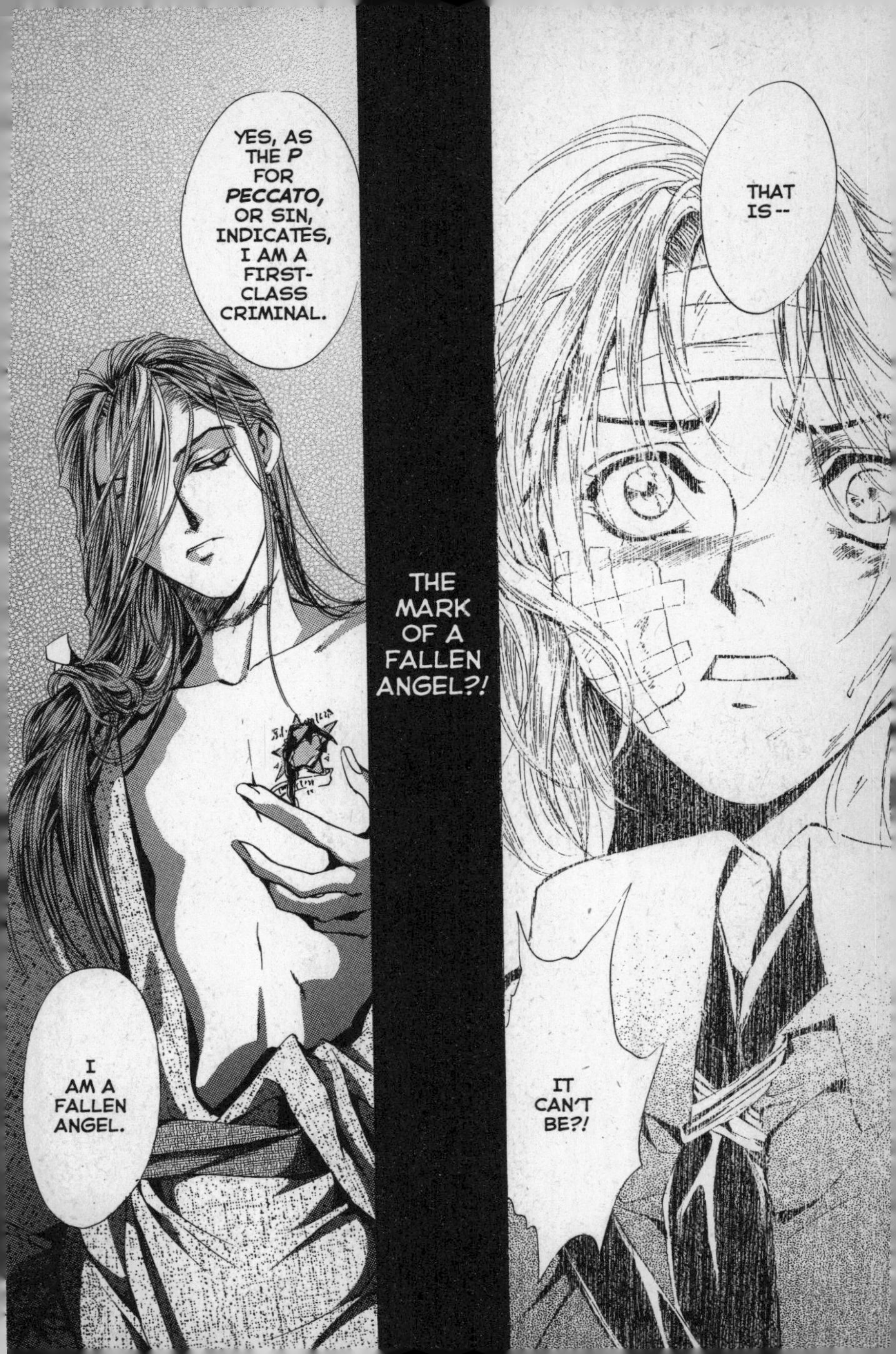
THAT IS --
IT CAN'T BE?!
THE MARK OF A FALLEN ANGEL?!
YES, AS THE *P* FOR *PECCATO*, OR SIN, INDICATES, I AM A FIRST-CLASS CRIMINAL.
I AM A FALLEN ANGEL.

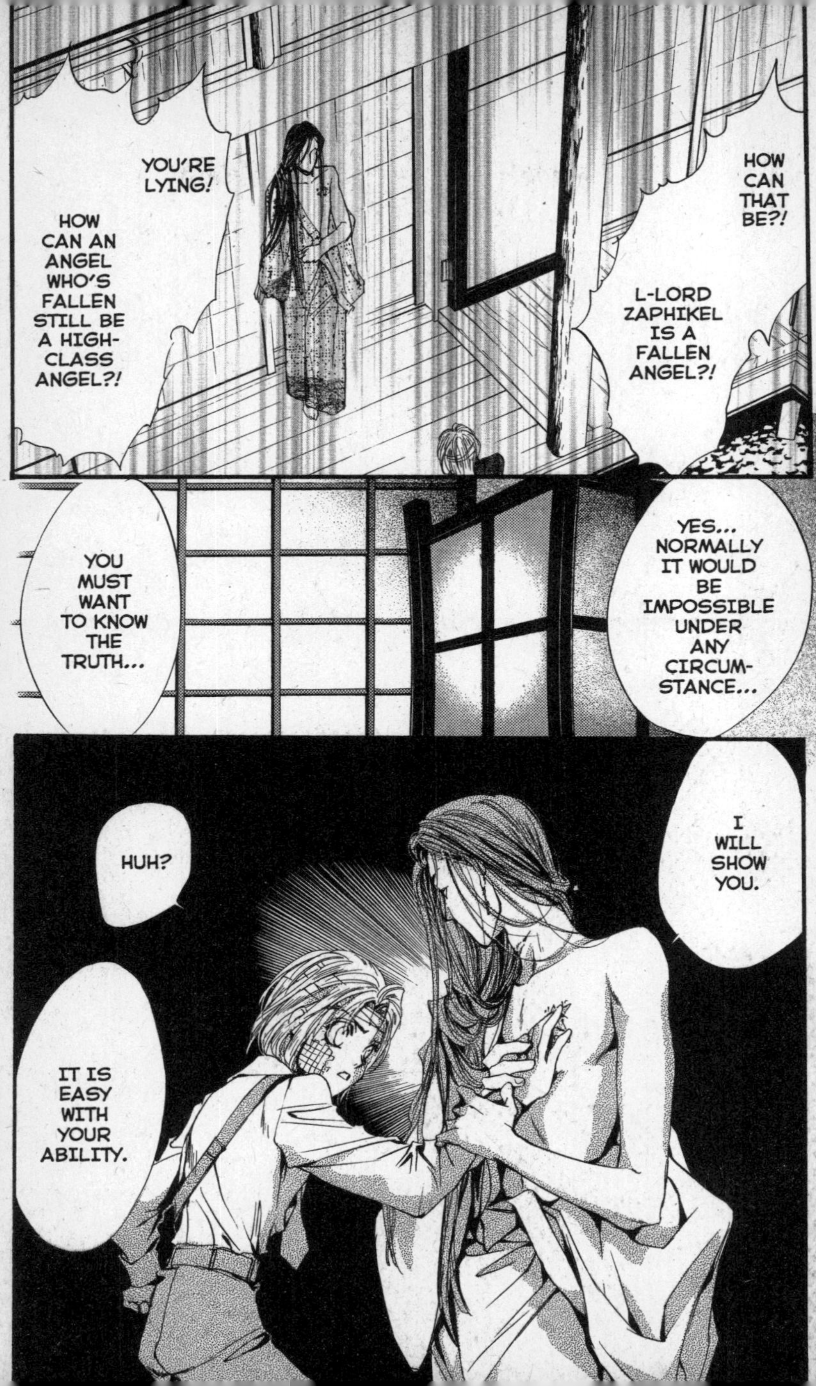
HOW CAN THAT BE?!
L-LORD ZAPHIKEL IS A FALLEN ANGEL?!
YOU'RE LYING!
HOW CAN AN ANGEL WHO'S FALLEN STILL BE A HIGH-CLASS ANGEL?!
YES... NORMALLY IT WOULD BE IMPOSSIBLE UNDER ANY CIRCUMSTANCE...
YOU MUST WANT TO KNOW THE TRUTH...
I WILL SHOW YOU.
HUH?
IT IS EASY WITH YOUR ABILITY.

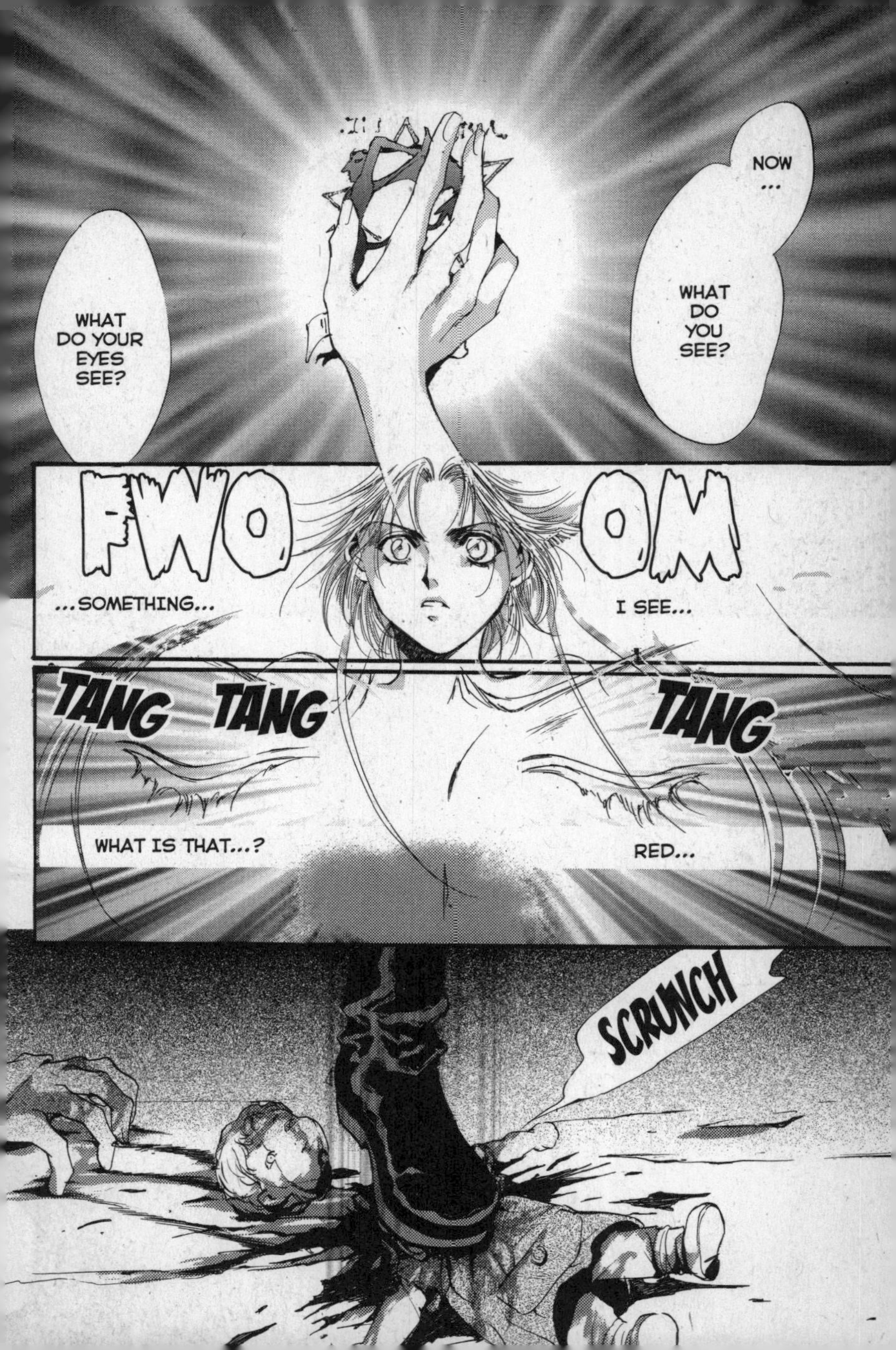
NOW ... WHAT DO YOU SEE?
WHAT DO YOUR EYES SEE?
FWOOM
I SEE...
...SOMETHING...
TANG TANG TANG
RED...
WHAT IS THAT...?
SCRUNCH

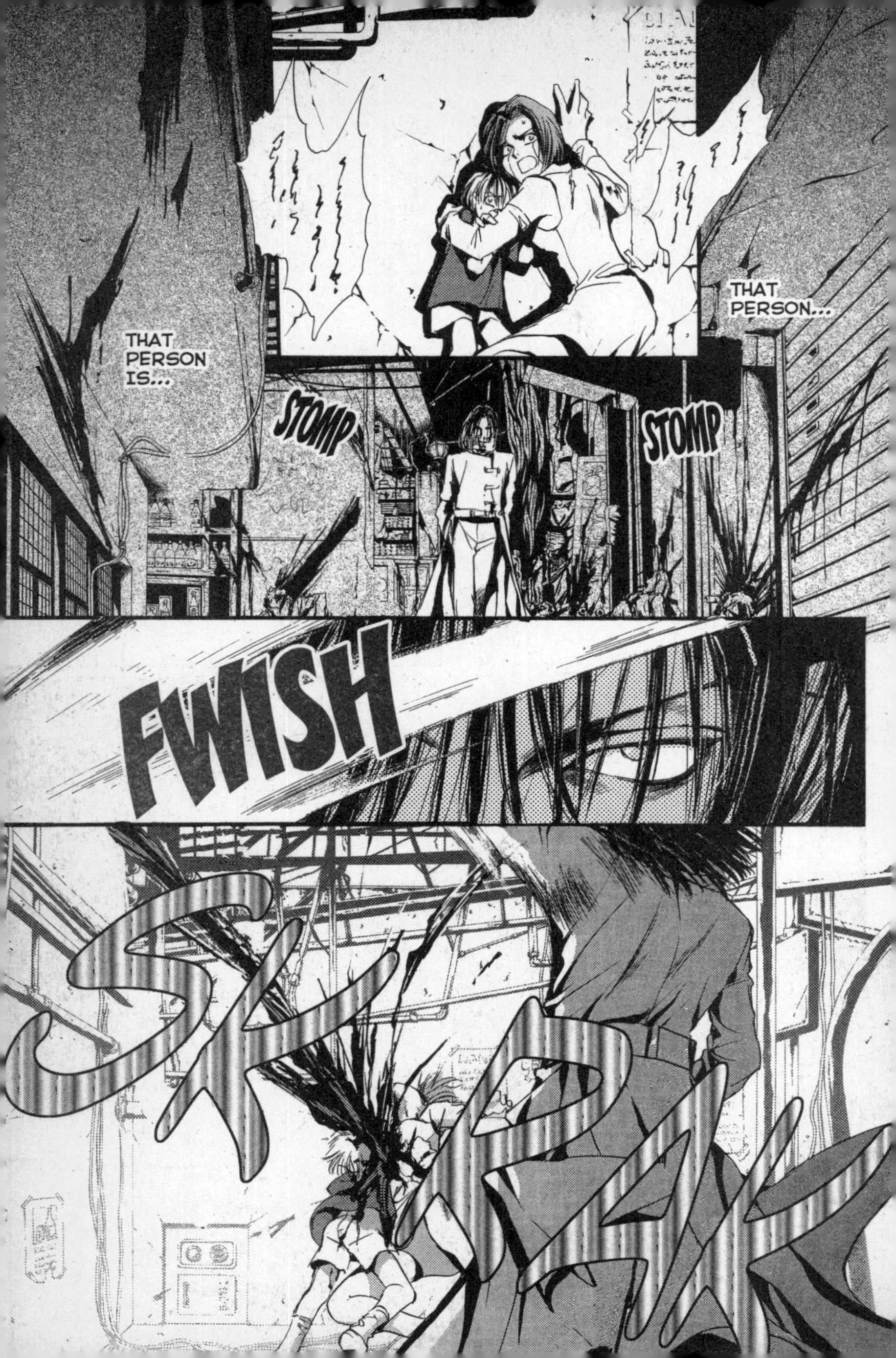
THAT PERSON...
THAT PERSON IS...
STOMP
STOMP
FWISH
SKRAK

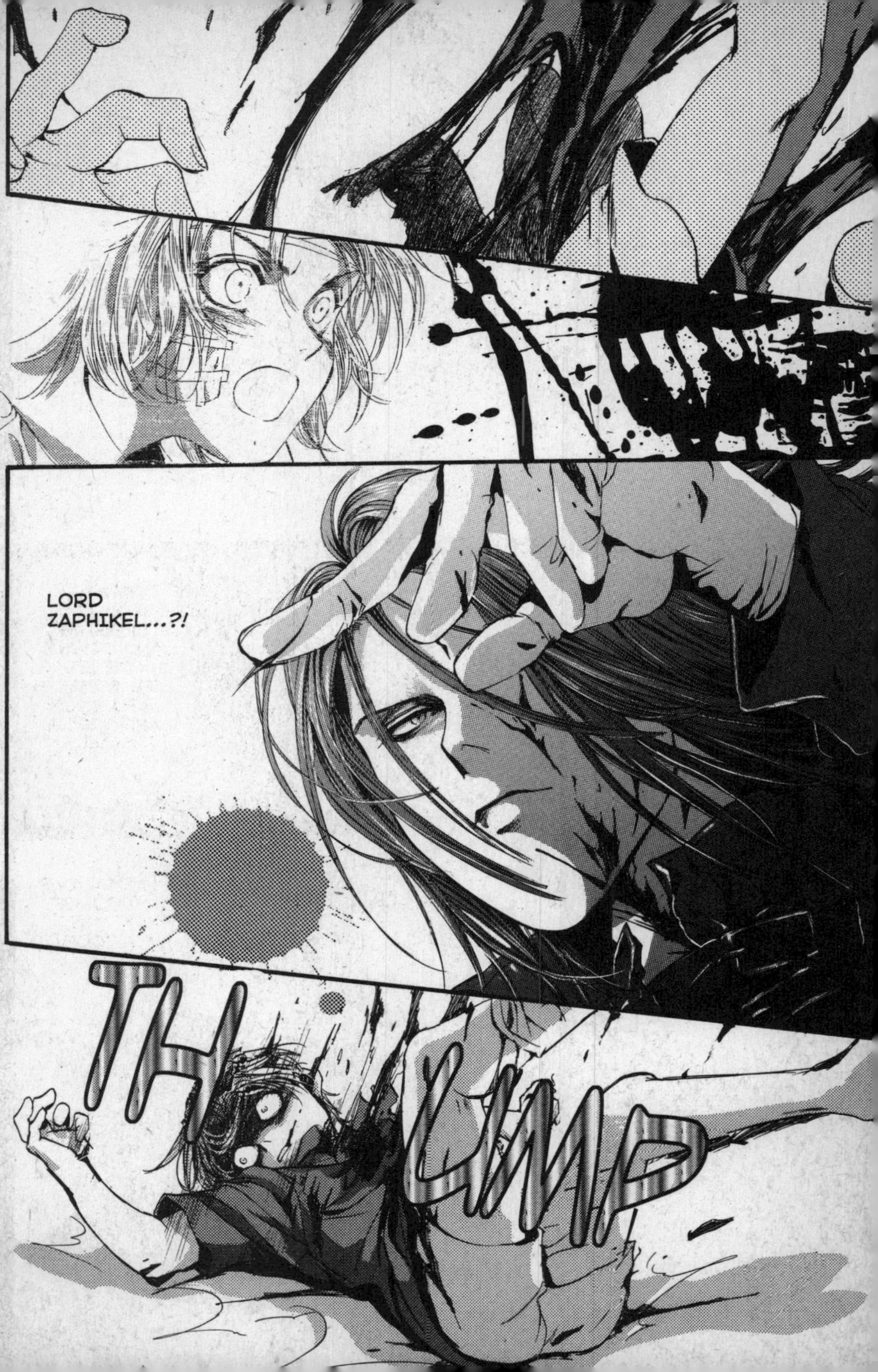
LORD ZAPHIKEL...?!
THUMP

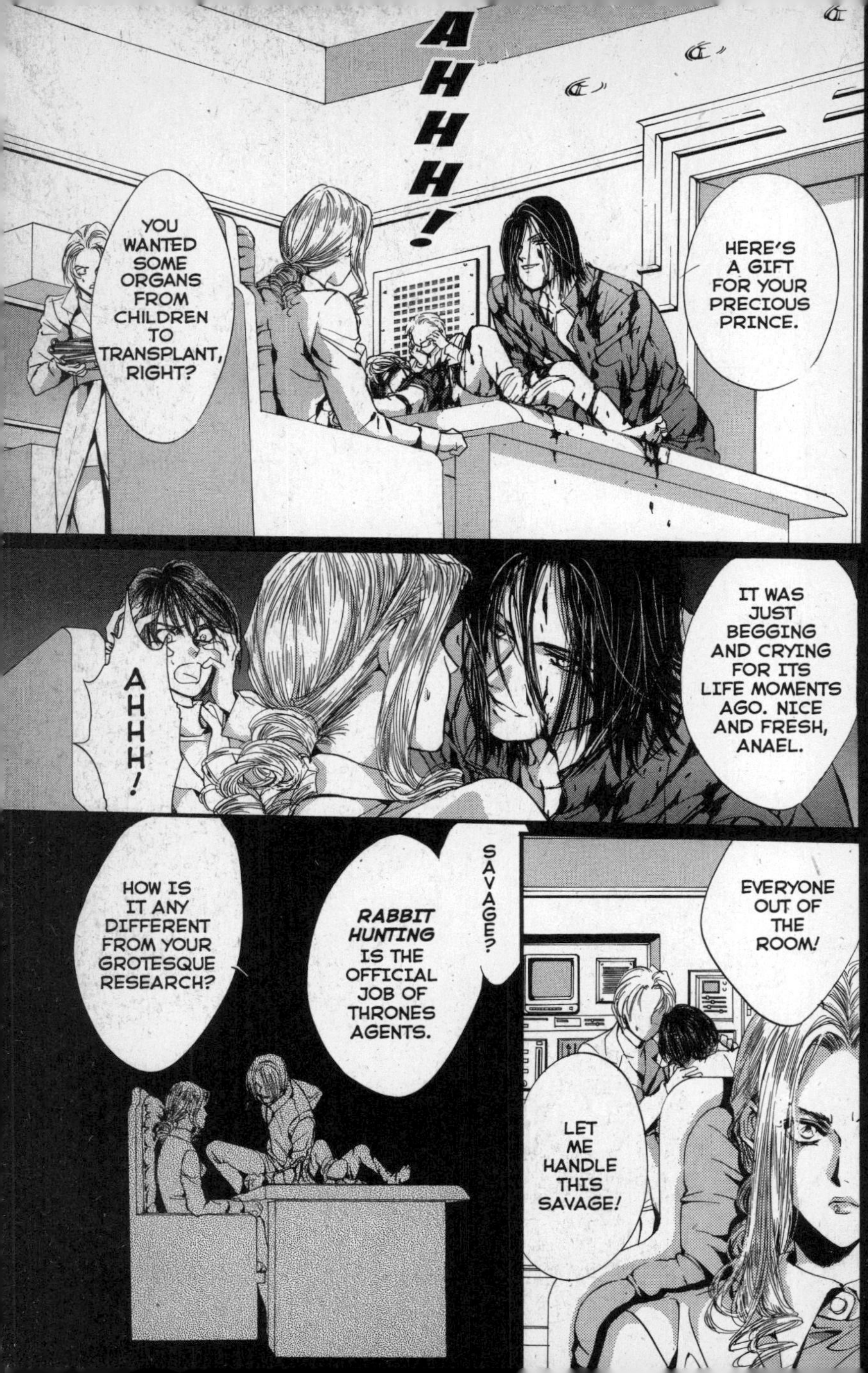
HERE'S A GIFT FOR YOUR PRECIOUS PRINCE.
AHHHH!
YOU WANTED SOME ORGANS FROM CHILDREN TO TRANSPLANT, RIGHT?
IT WAS JUST BEGGING AND CRYING FOR ITS LIFE MOMENTS AGO. NICE AND FRESH, ANAEL.
AHHH!
EVERYONE OUT OF THE ROOM!
LET ME HANDLE THIS SAVAGE!
SAVAGE?
RABBIT HUNTING IS THE OFFICIAL JOB OF THRONES AGENTS.
HOW IS IT ANY DIFFERENT FROM YOUR GROTESQUE RESEARCH?

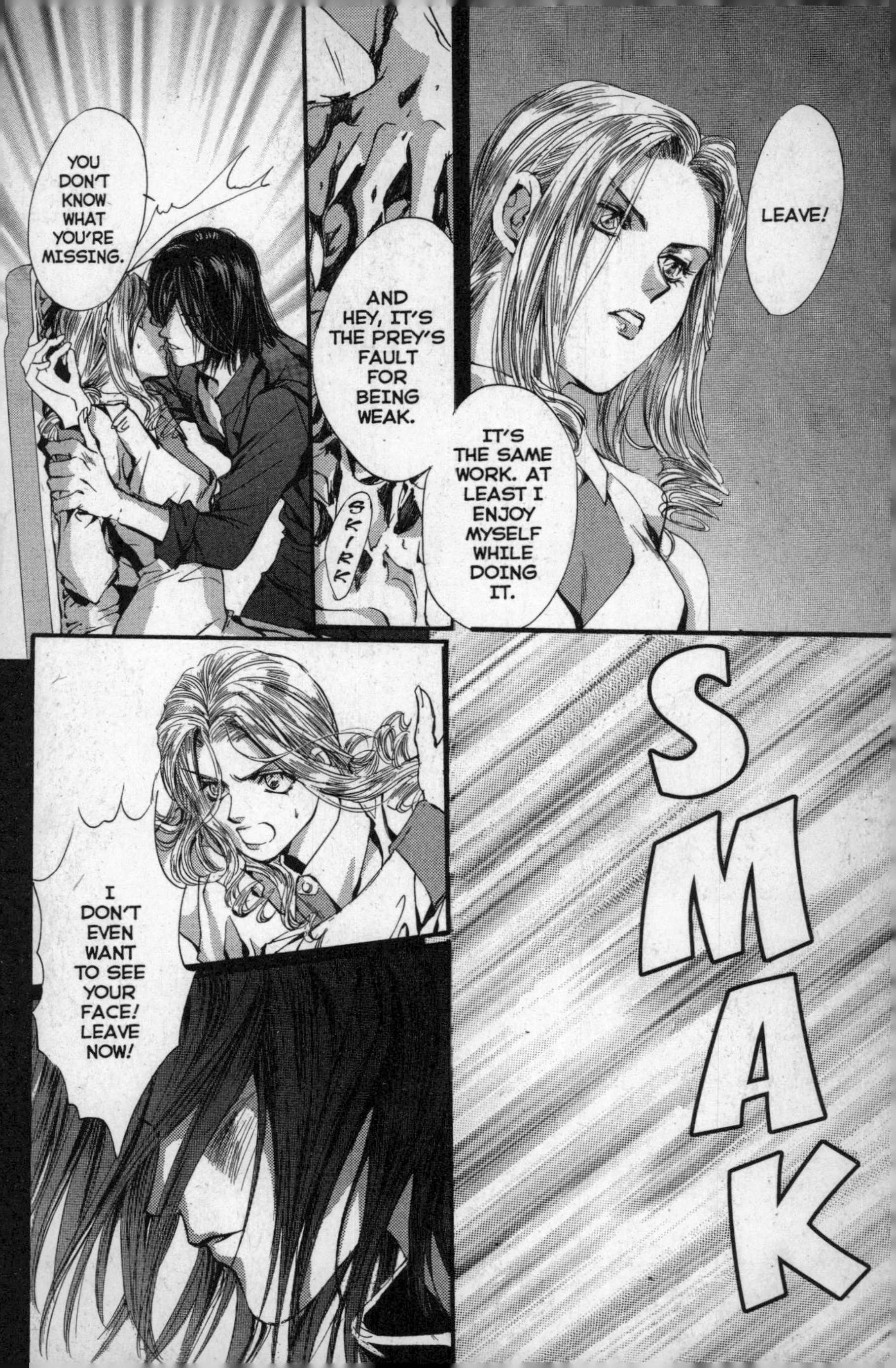
LEAVE!
IT'S THE SAME WORK. AT LEAST I ENJOY MYSELF WHILE DOING IT.
AND HEY, IT'S THE PREY'S FAULT FOR BEING WEAK.
SKIRK
YOU DON'T KNOW WHAT YOU'RE MISSING.
SMAK
I DON'T EVEN WANT TO SEE YOUR FACE! LEAVE NOW!

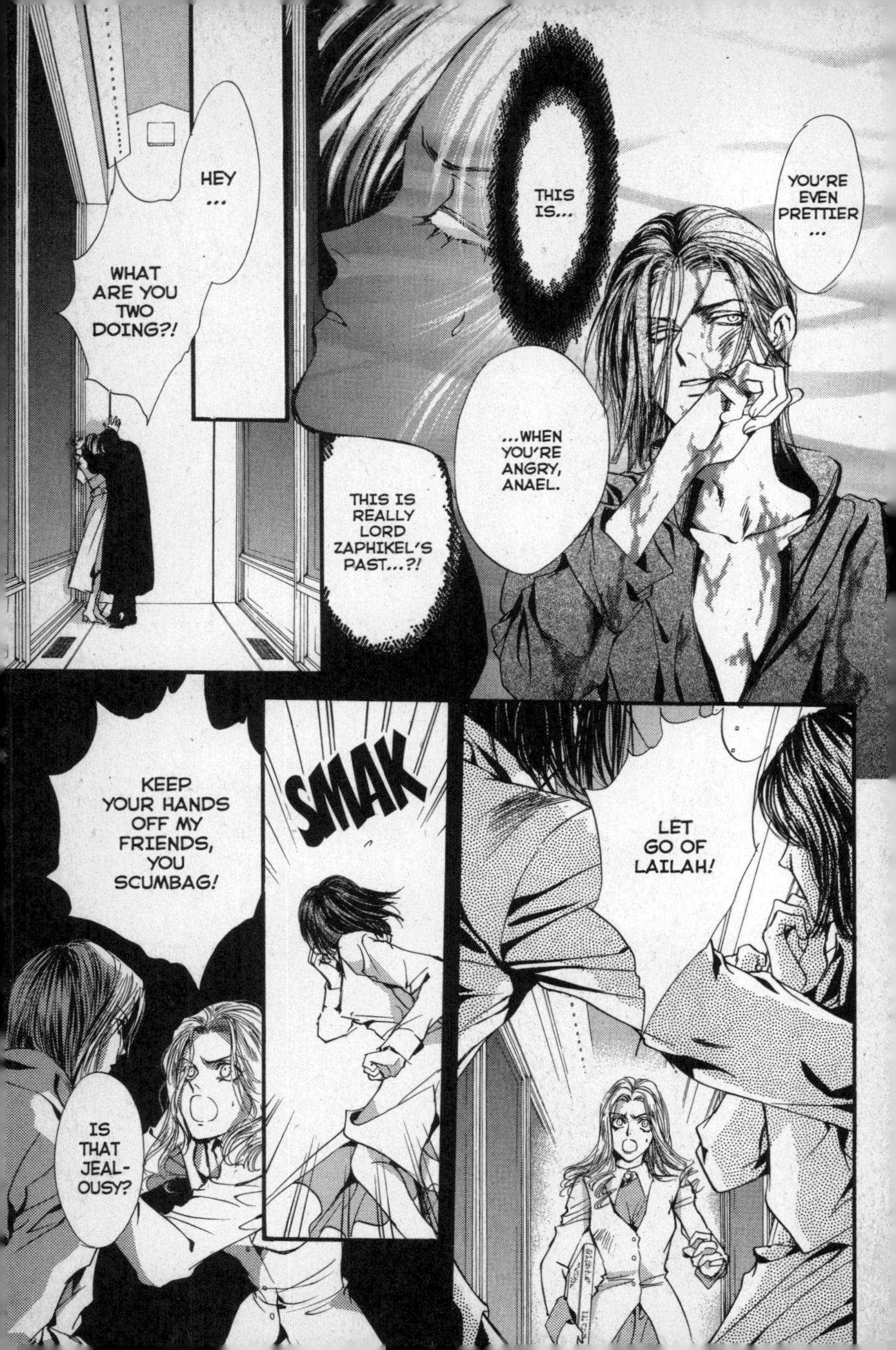
YOU'RE EVEN PRETTIER ...
...WHEN YOU'RE ANGRY, ANAEL.
THIS IS...
THIS IS REALLY LORD ZAPHIKEL'S PAST...?!
HEY ...
WHAT ARE YOU TWO DOING?!
LET GO OF LAILAH!
SMAK
KEEP YOUR HANDS OFF MY FRIENDS, YOU SCUMBAG!
IS THAT JEAL-OUSY?

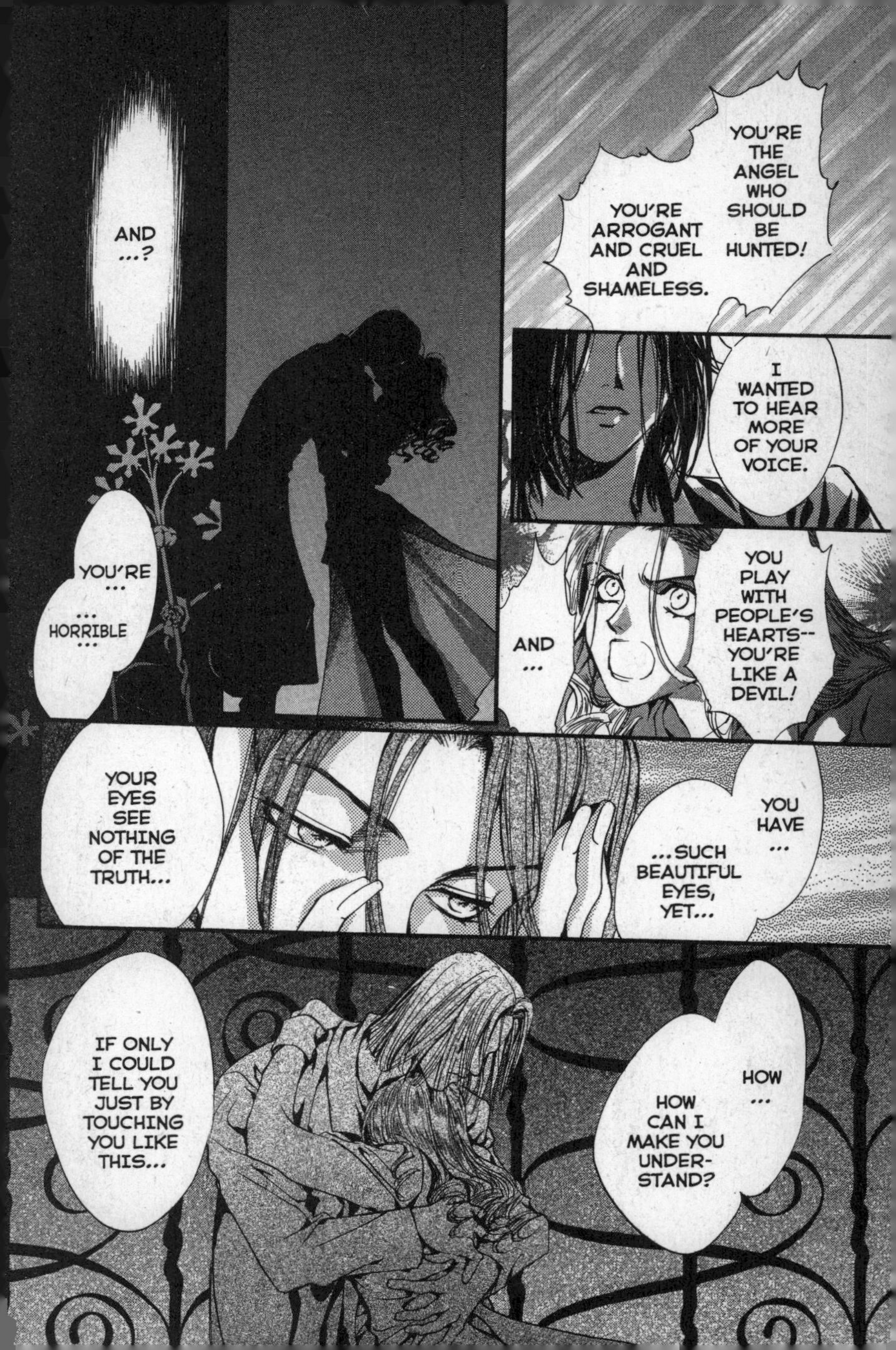
YOU'RE THE ANGEL WHO SHOULD BE HUNTED!
YOU'RE ARROGANT AND CRUEL AND SHAMELESS.
I WANTED TO HEAR MORE OF YOUR VOICE.
YOU PLAY WITH PEOPLE'S HEARTS-- YOU'RE LIKE A DEVIL!
AND ...
AND ...?
YOU'RE ...
... HORRIBLE ...
YOU HAVE ...
... SUCH BEAUTIFUL EYES, YET...
YOUR EYES SEE NOTHING OF THE TRUTH...
HOW ...
HOW CAN I MAKE YOU UNDER- STAND?
IF ONLY I COULD TELL YOU JUST BY TOUCHING YOU LIKE THIS...

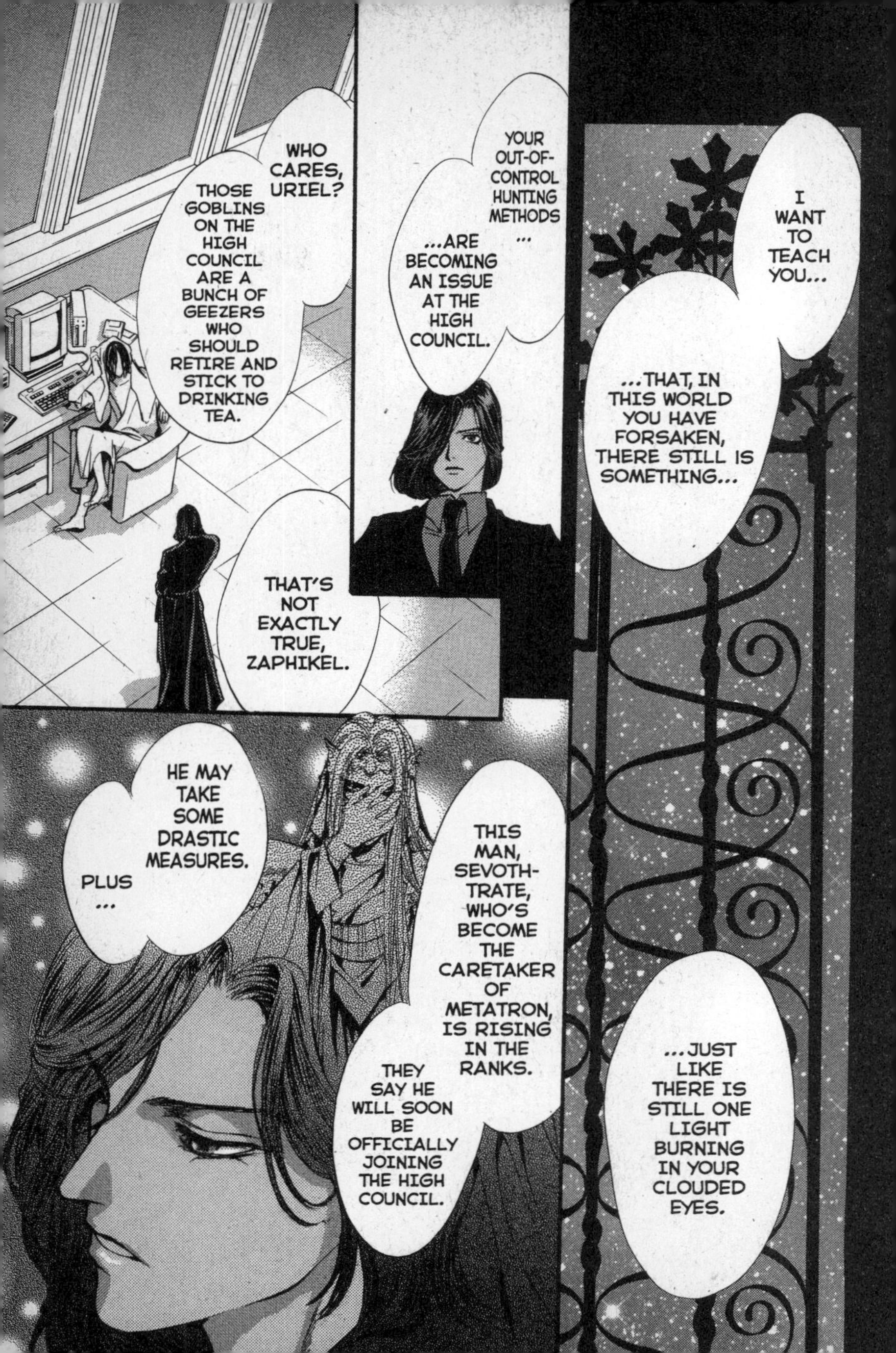
I WANT TO TEACH YOU...
...THAT, IN THIS WORLD YOU HAVE FORSAKEN, THERE STILL IS SOMETHING...
...JUST LIKE THERE IS STILL ONE LIGHT BURNING IN YOUR CLOUDED EYES.
YOUR OUT-OF-CONTROL HUNTING METHODS ...
...ARE BECOMING AN ISSUE AT THE HIGH COUNCIL.
WHO CARES, URIEL?
THOSE GOBLINS ON THE HIGH COUNCIL ARE A BUNCH OF GEEZERS WHO SHOULD RETIRE AND STICK TO DRINKING TEA.
THAT'S NOT EXACTLY TRUE, ZAPHIKEL.
THIS MAN, SEVOTH-TRATE, WHO'S BECOME THE CARETAKER OF METATRON, IS RISING IN THE RANKS.
THEY SAY HE WILL SOON BE OFFICIALLY JOINING THE HIGH COUNCIL.
HE MAY TAKE SOME DRASTIC MEASURES.
PLUS ...

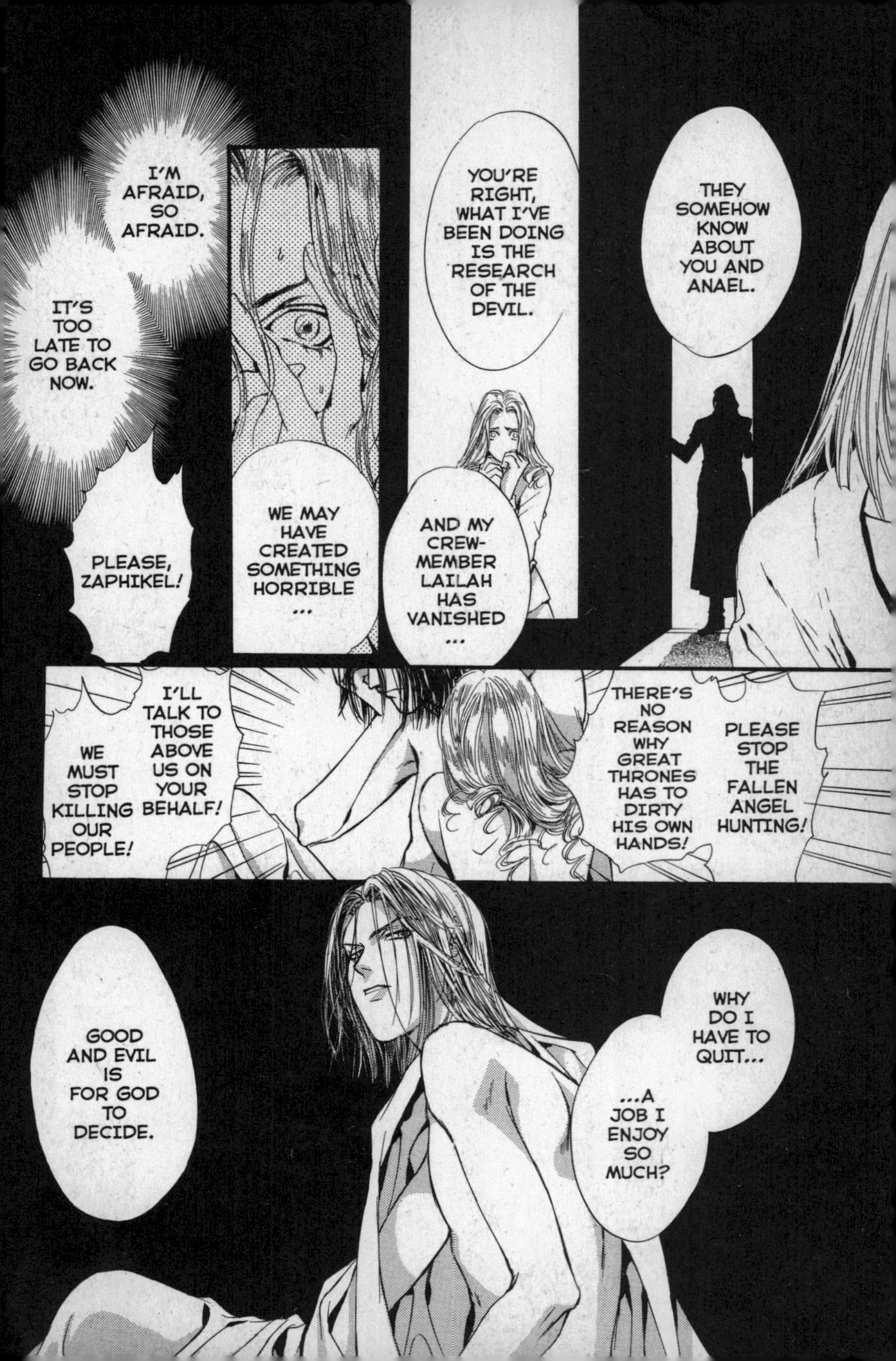
THEY SOMEHOW KNOW ABOUT YOU AND ANAEL.
YOU'RE RIGHT, WHAT I'VE BEEN DOING IS THE RESEARCH OF THE DEVIL.
AND MY CREW-MEMBER LAILAH HAS VANISHED...
WE MAY HAVE CREATED SOMETHING HORRIBLE...
I'M AFRAID, SO AFRAID.
IT'S TOO LATE TO GO BACK NOW.
PLEASE, ZAPHIKEL!
PLEASE STOP THE FALLEN ANGEL HUNTING!
THERE'S NO REASON WHY GREAT THRONES HAS TO DIRTY HIS OWN HANDS!
I'LL TALK TO THOSE ABOVE US ON YOUR BEHALF!
WE MUST STOP KILLING OUR PEOPLE!
WHY DO I HAVE TO QUIT...
...A JOB I ENJOY SO MUCH?
GOOD AND EVIL IS FOR GOD TO DECIDE.

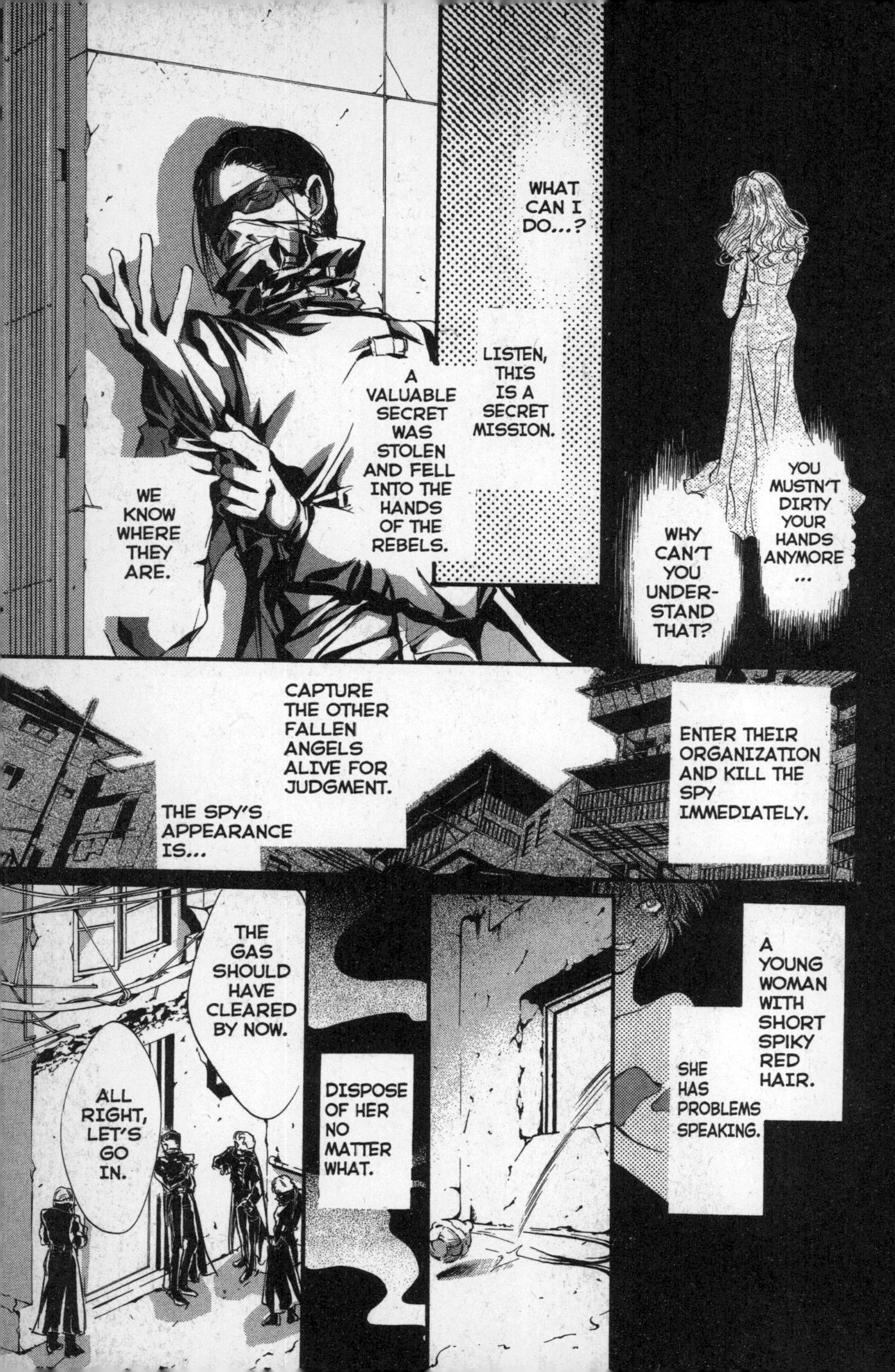
YOU MUSTN'T DIRTY YOUR HANDS ANYMORE...
WHY CAN'T YOU UNDERSTAND THAT?
WHAT CAN I DO...?
LISTEN, THIS IS A SECRET MISSION.
A VALUABLE SECRET WAS STOLEN AND FELL INTO THE HANDS OF THE REBELS.
WE KNOW WHERE THEY ARE.
ENTER THEIR ORGANIZATION AND KILL THE SPY IMMEDIATELY.
CAPTURE THE OTHER FALLEN ANGELS ALIVE FOR JUDGMENT.
THE SPY'S APPEARANCE IS...
A YOUNG WOMAN WITH SHORT SPIKY RED HAIR.
SHE HAS PROBLEMS SPEAKING.
DISPOSE OF HER NO MATTER WHAT.
THE GAS SHOULD HAVE CLEARED BY NOW.
ALL RIGHT, LET'S GO IN.

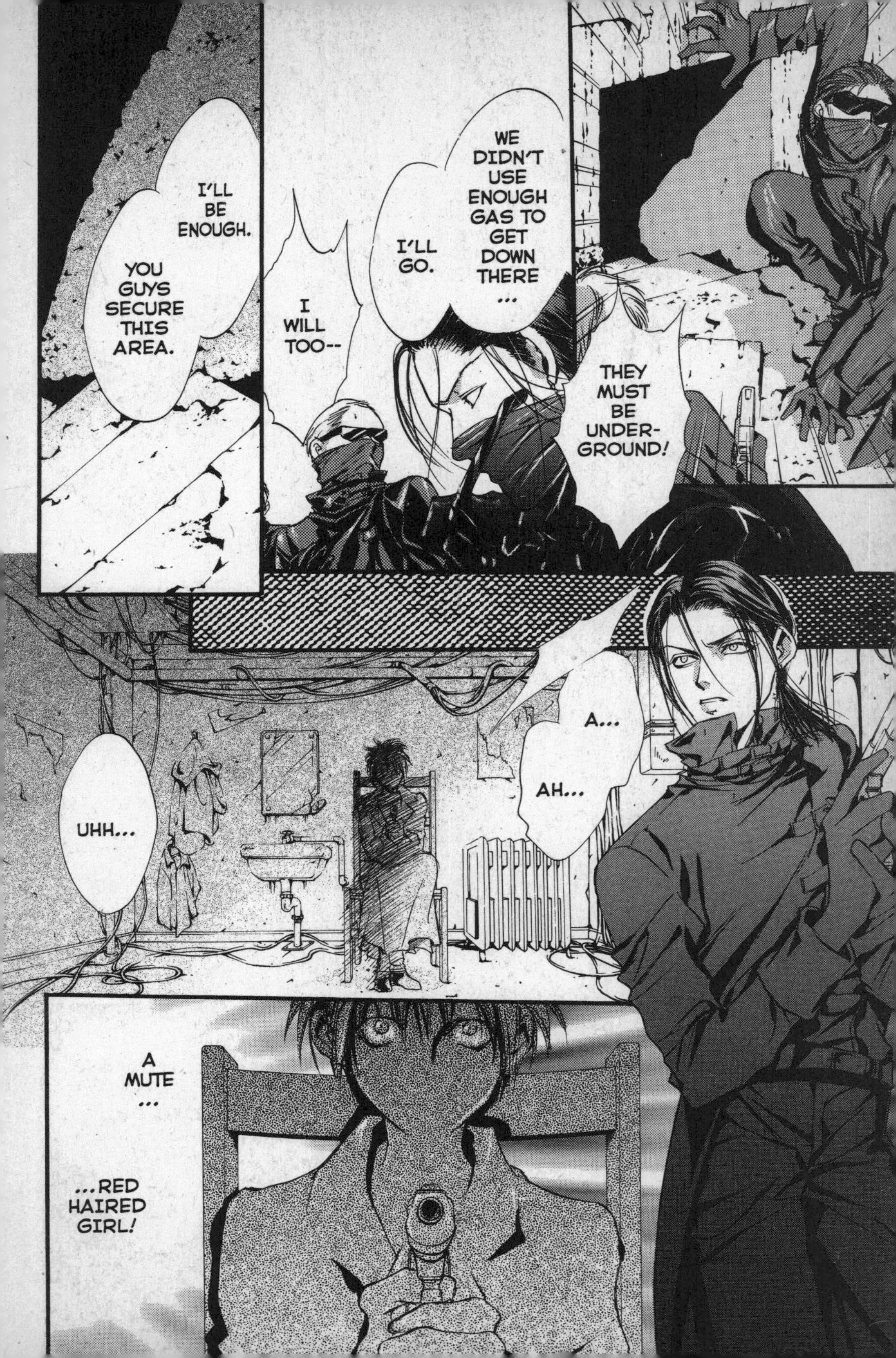
THEY MUST BE UNDERGROUND!
WE DIDN'T USE ENOUGH GAS TO GET DOWN THERE ...
I'LL GO.
I WILL TOO--
I'LL BE ENOUGH.
YOU GUYS SECURE THIS AREA.
A...
AH...
UHH...
A MUTE ...
...RED HAIRED GIRL!

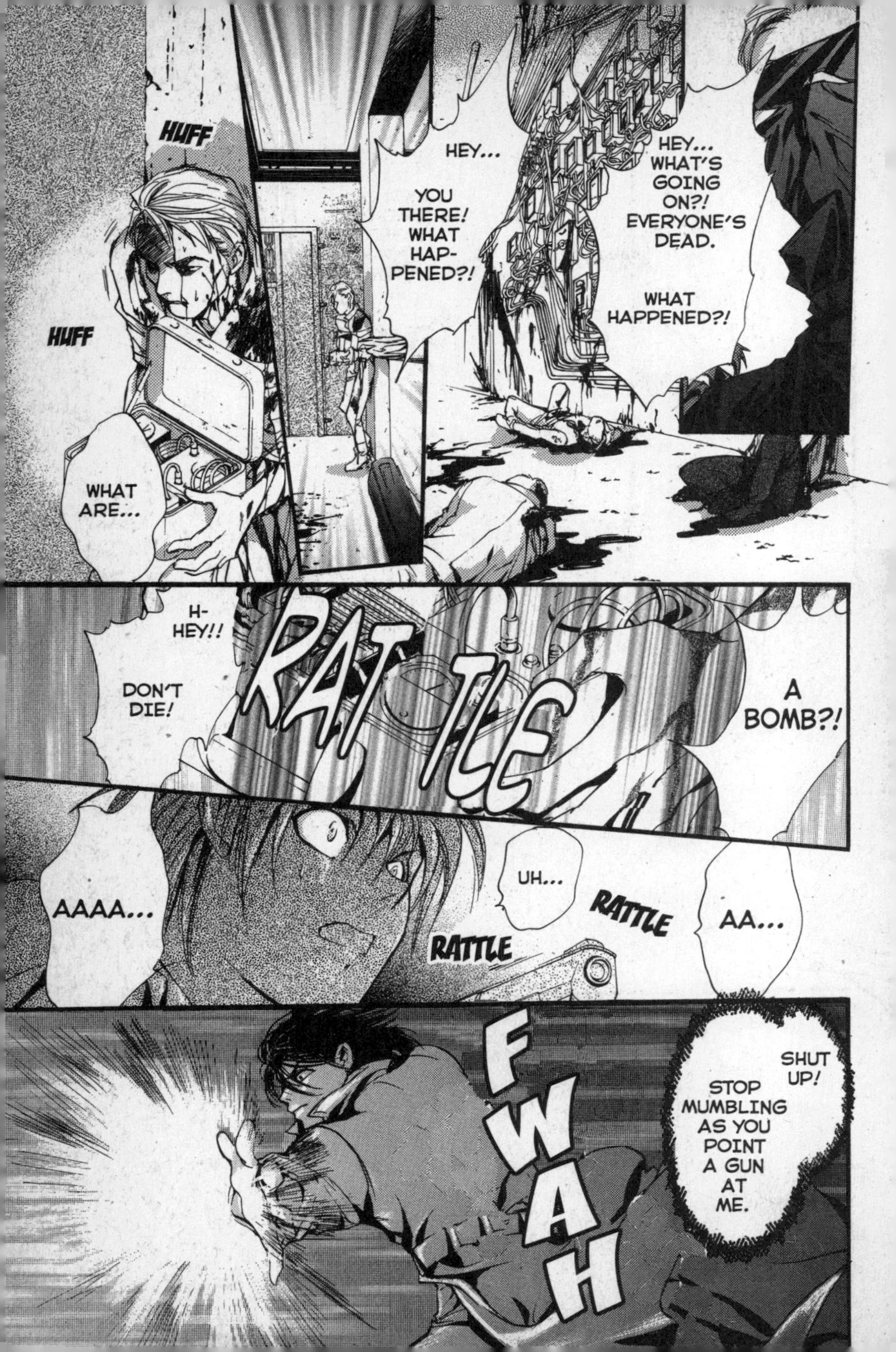
HEY... WHAT'S GOING ON?! EVERYONE'S DEAD.
WHAT HAPPENED?!
HEY...
YOU THERE! WHAT HAP-PENED?!
HUFF
HUFF
WHAT ARE...
A BOMB?!
RATTLE
H-HEY!!
DON'T DIE!
AA...
RATTLE
UH...
RATTLE
AAAA...
SHUT UP!
STOP MUMBLING AS YOU POINT A GUN AT ME.
FWAH

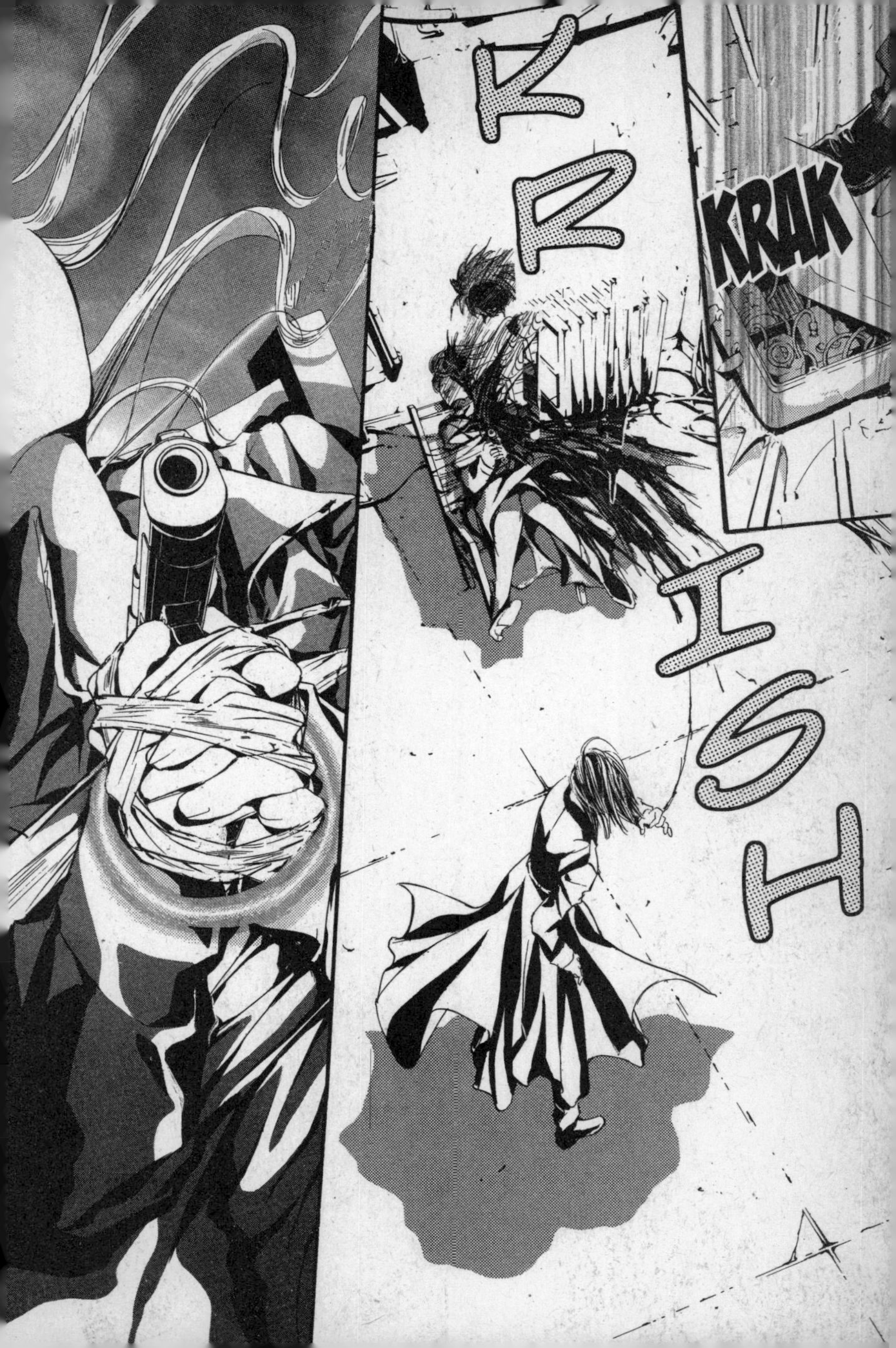
KRAK
KRISH

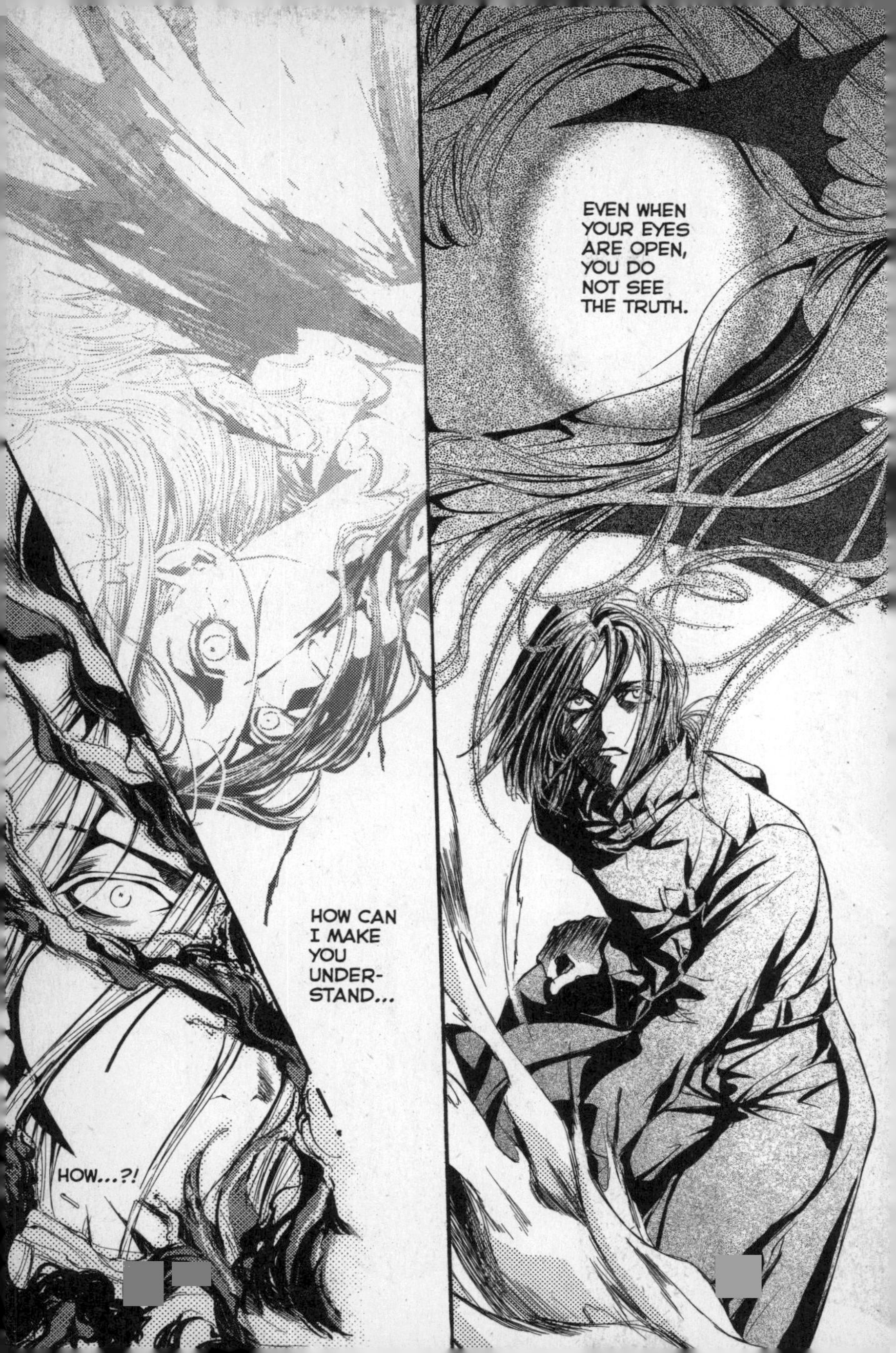
EVEN WHEN YOUR EYES ARE OPEN, YOU DO NOT SEE THE TRUTH.
HOW CAN I MAKE YOU UNDER-STAND...
HOW...?!

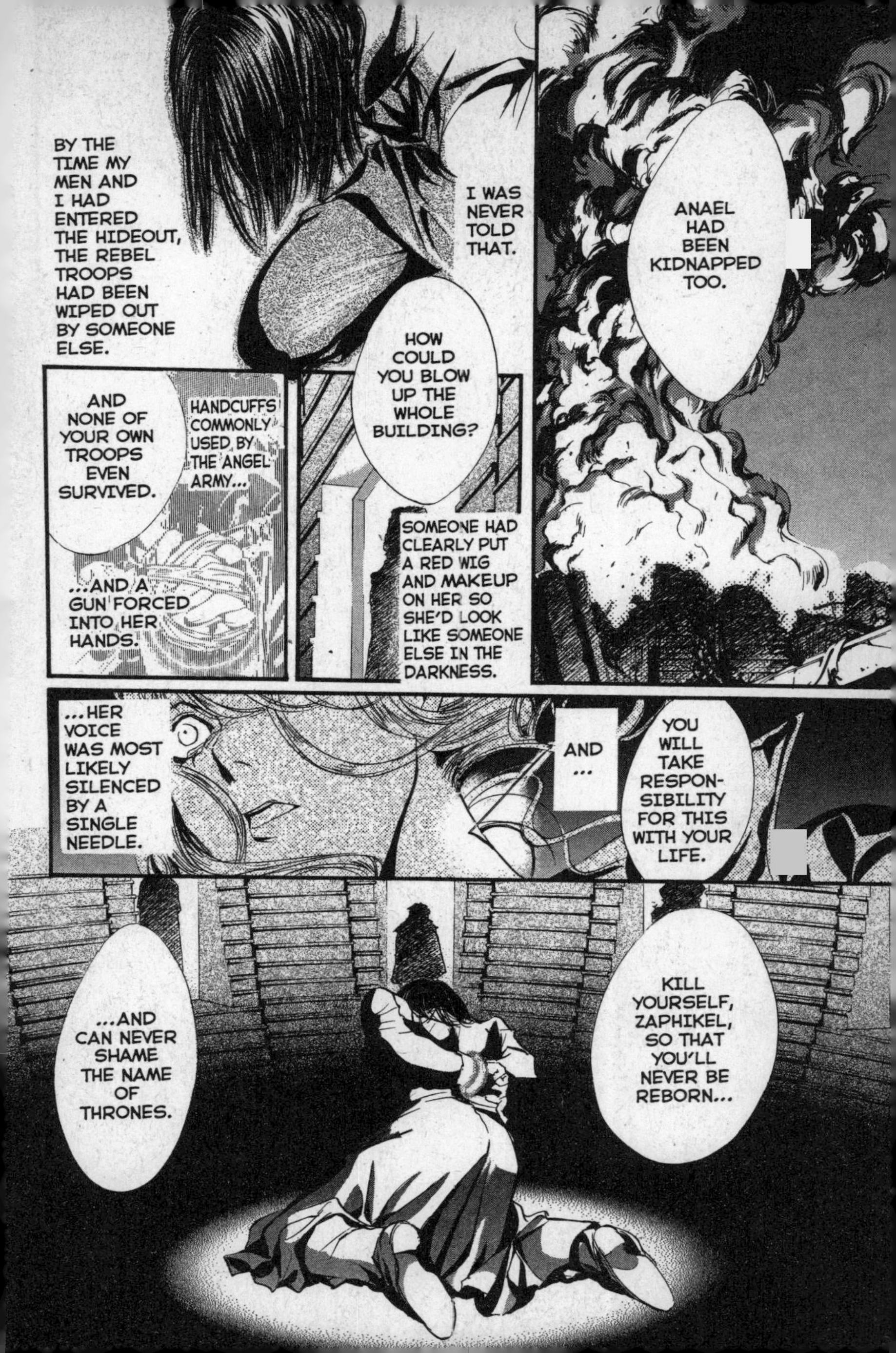
ANAEL HAD BEEN KIDNAPPED TOO.
I WAS NEVER TOLD THAT.
BY THE TIME MY MEN AND I HAD ENTERED THE HIDEOUT, THE REBEL TROOPS HAD BEEN WIPED OUT BY SOMEONE ELSE.
HOW COULD YOU BLOW UP THE WHOLE BUILDING?
SOMEONE HAD CLEARLY PUT A RED WIG AND MAKEUP ON HER SO SHE'D LOOK LIKE SOMEONE ELSE IN THE DARKNESS.
HANDCUFFS COMMONLY USED BY THE ANGEL ARMY...
AND NONE OF YOUR OWN TROOPS EVEN SURVIVED.
...AND A GUN FORCED INTO HER HANDS.
YOU WILL TAKE RESPONSIBILITY FOR THIS WITH YOUR LIFE.
AND ...
...HER VOICE WAS MOST LIKELY SILENCED BY A SINGLE NEEDLE.
KILL YOURSELF, ZAPHIKEL, SO THAT YOU'LL NEVER BE REBORN...
...AND CAN NEVER SHAME THE NAME OF THRONES.

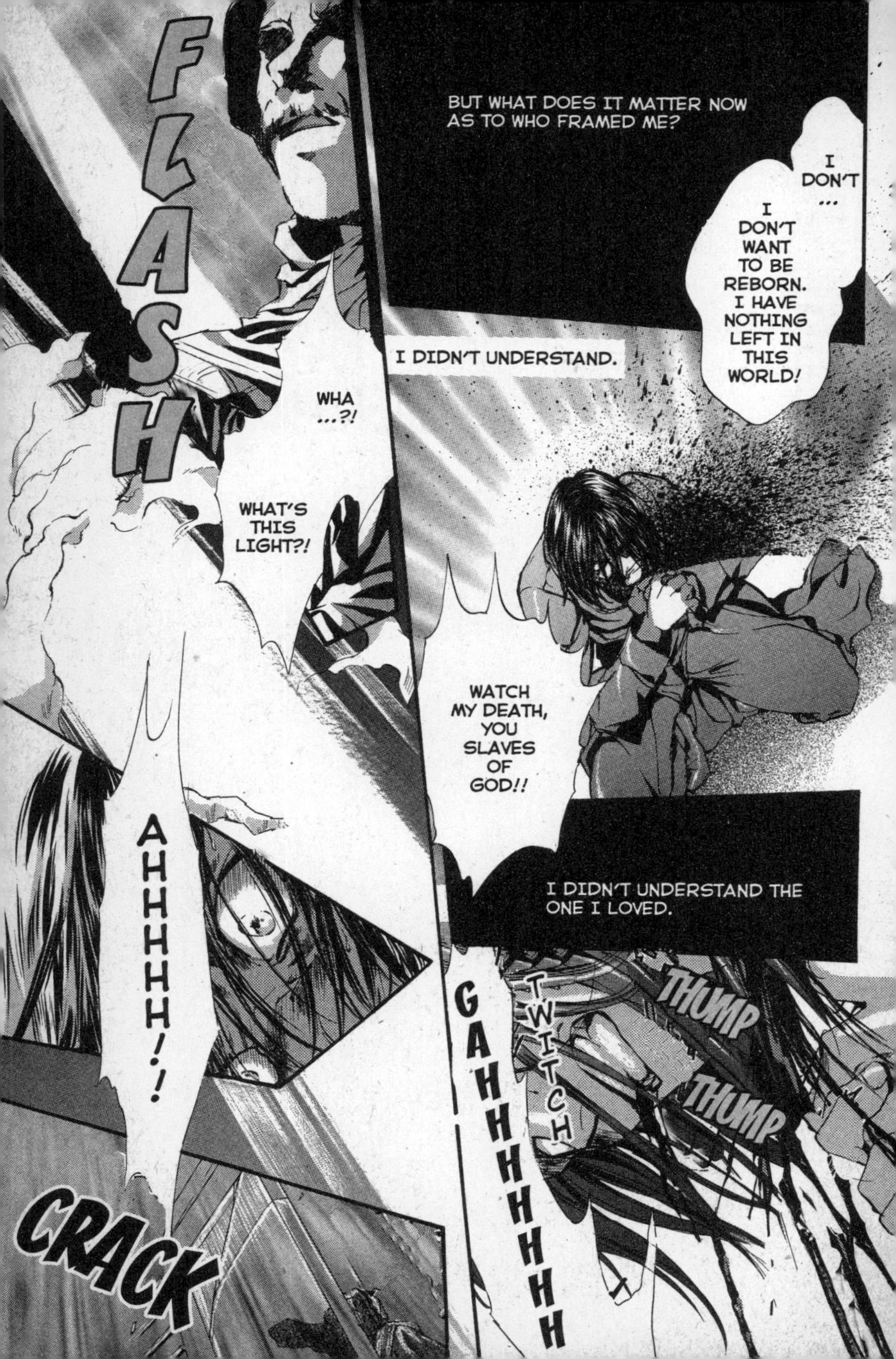
BUT WHAT DOES IT MATTER NOW AS TO WHO FRAMED ME?
I DON'T ...
I DON'T WANT TO BE REBORN. I HAVE NOTHING LEFT IN THIS WORLD!
I DIDN'T UNDERSTAND.
WATCH MY DEATH, YOU SLAVES OF GOD!!
I DIDN'T UNDERSTAND THE ONE I LOVED.
THUMP
THUMP
TWITCH
GAHHHHHHHH
FLASH
WHA ...?!
WHAT'S THIS LIGHT?!
AHHHHH!!
CRACK

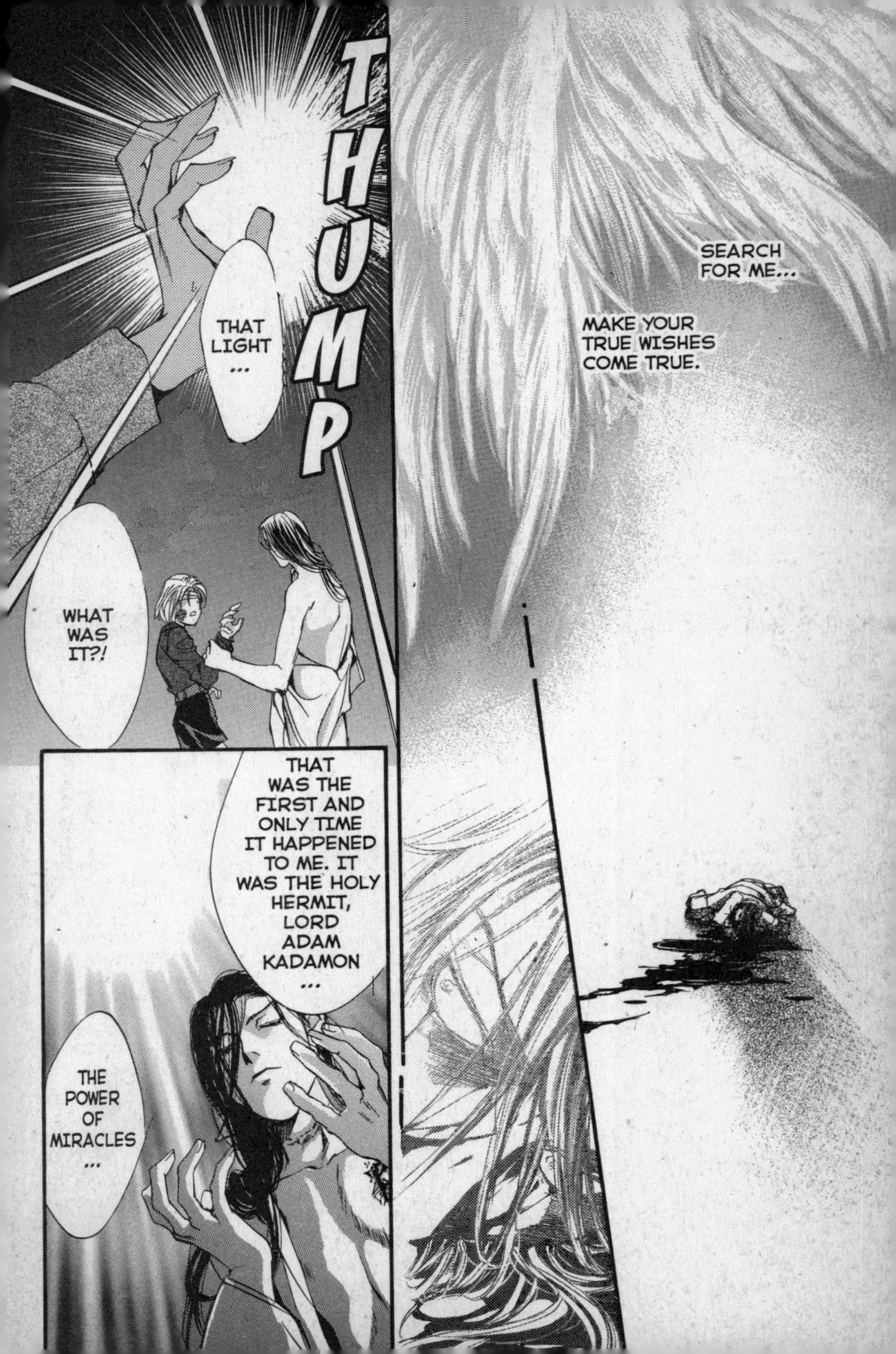
SEARCH FOR ME...
MAKE YOUR TRUE WISHES COME TRUE.
THUMP
THAT LIGHT ...
WHAT WAS IT?!
THAT WAS THE FIRST AND ONLY TIME IT HAPPENED TO ME. IT WAS THE HOLY HERMIT, LORD ADAM KADAMON ...
THE POWER OF MIRACLES ...

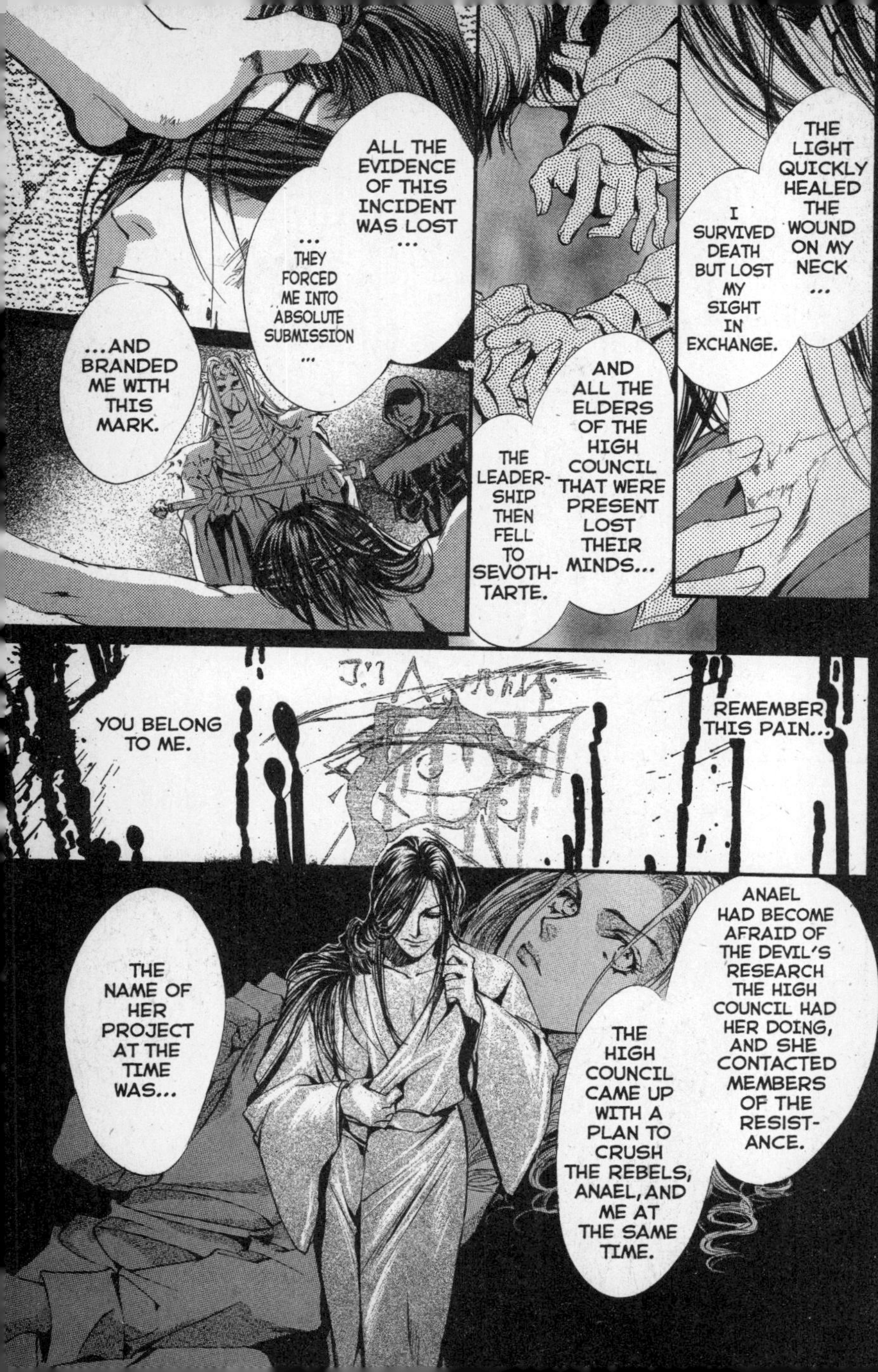
THE LIGHT QUICKLY HEALED THE WOUND ON MY NECK...
I SURVIVED DEATH BUT LOST MY SIGHT IN EXCHANGE.
AND ALL THE ELDERS OF THE HIGH COUNCIL THAT WERE PRESENT LOST THEIR MINDS...
THE LEADERSHIP THEN FELL TO SEVOTHTARTE.
ALL THE EVIDENCE OF THIS INCIDENT WAS LOST...
...THEY FORCED ME INTO ABSOLUTE SUBMISSION...
...AND BRANDED ME WITH THIS MARK.
REMEMBER THIS PAIN...
YOU BELONG TO ME.
ANAEL HAD BECOME AFRAID OF THE DEVIL'S RESEARCH THE HIGH COUNCIL HAD HER DOING, AND SHE CONTACTED MEMBERS OF THE RESISTANCE.
THE HIGH COUNCIL CAME UP WITH A PLAN TO CRUSH THE REBELS, ANAEL, AND ME AT THE SAME TIME.
THE NAME OF HER PROJECT AT THE TIME WAS...

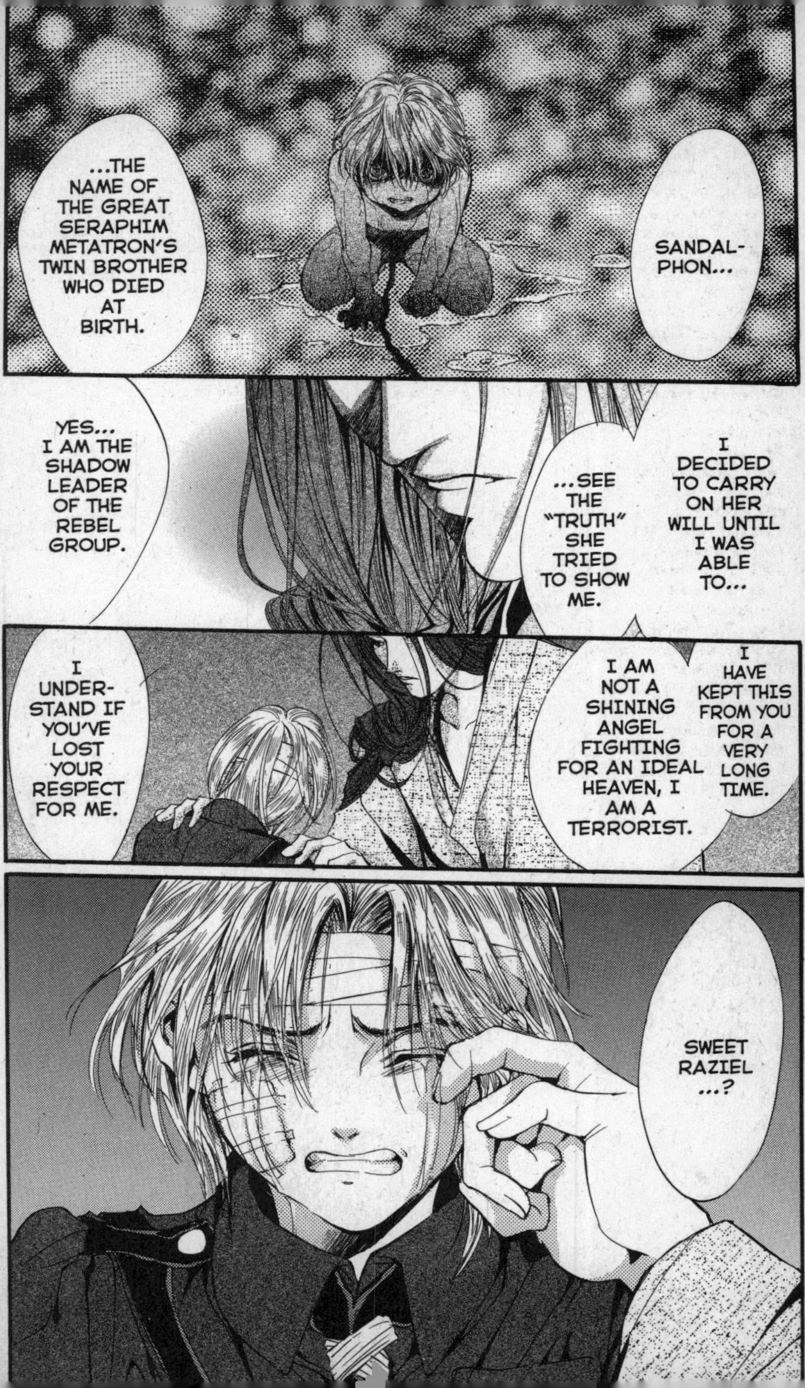
SANDALPHON...
...THE NAME OF THE GREAT SERAPHIM METATRON'S TWIN BROTHER WHO DIED AT BIRTH.
I DECIDED TO CARRY ON HER WILL UNTIL I WAS ABLE TO...
...SEE THE "TRUTH" SHE TRIED TO SHOW ME.
YES... I AM THE SHADOW LEADER OF THE REBEL GROUP.
I HAVE KEPT THIS FROM YOU FOR A VERY LONG TIME.
I AM NOT A SHINING ANGEL FIGHTING FOR AN IDEAL HEAVEN, I AM A TERRORIST.
I UNDERSTAND IF YOU'VE LOST YOUR RESPECT FOR ME.
SWEET RAZIEL ...?

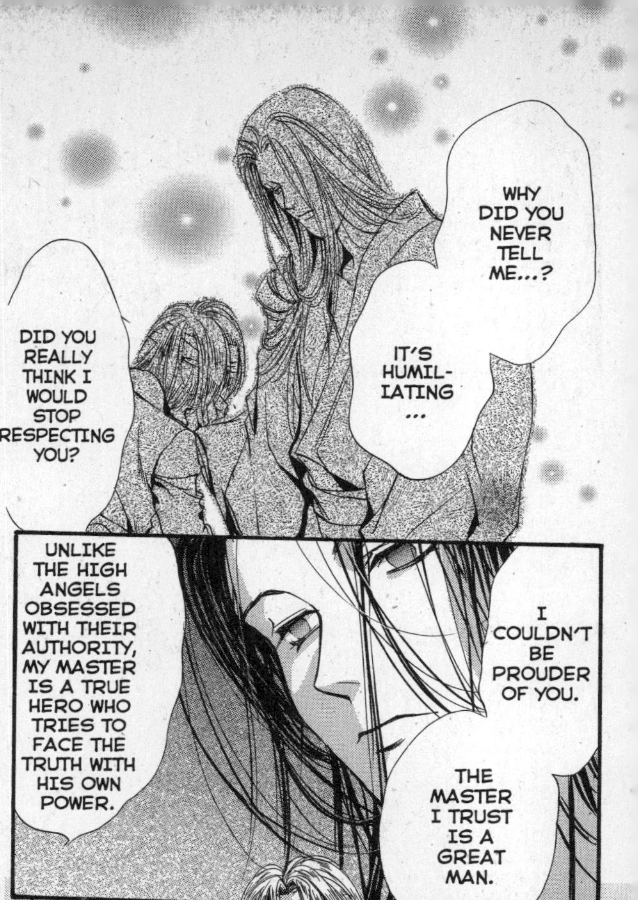
WHY DID YOU NEVER TELL ME...?
IT'S HUMILIATING...
DID YOU REALLY THINK I WOULD STOP RESPECTING YOU?
I COULDN'T BE PROUDER OF YOU.
THE MASTER I TRUST IS A GREAT MAN.
UNLIKE THE HIGH ANGELS OBSESSED WITH THEIR AUTHORITY, MY MASTER IS A TRUE HERO WHO TRIES TO FACE THE TRUTH WITH HIS OWN POWER.

I was often asked "Why is Zaphikel in a Japanese-style house wearing a kimono?" There's a real reason... I just figured he'd look good doing so. This episode with Anael is totally different from what I originally planned. But I may use my original idea for something else... The "enemy or ally" line at the end might not make sense years from now, but I'm a huge fan of the variety show Downtown. (small, huge Matsu fan!) I'm actually the kind of girl who rented every episode of "If we met in a dream" and watched them late into the night. I've used dialog from that for Zaphikel in the past.

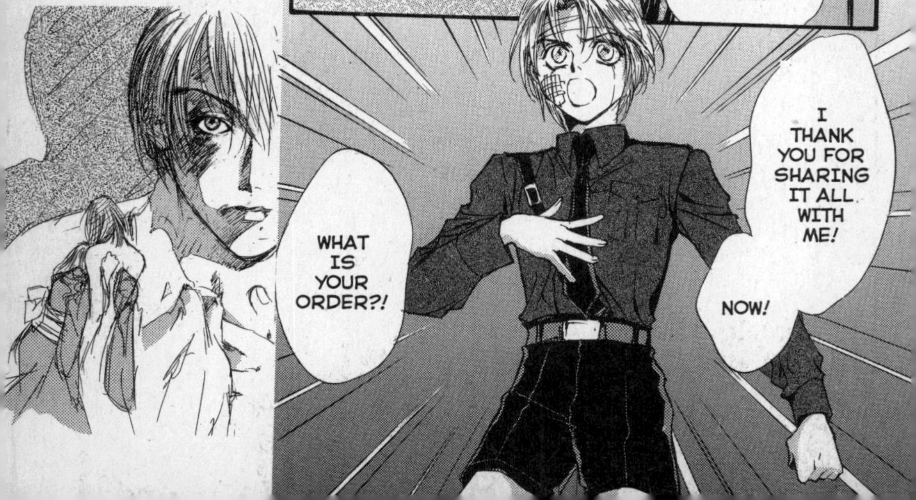
I THANK YOU FOR SHARING IT ALL WITH ME!
NOW!
WHAT IS YOUR ORDER?!

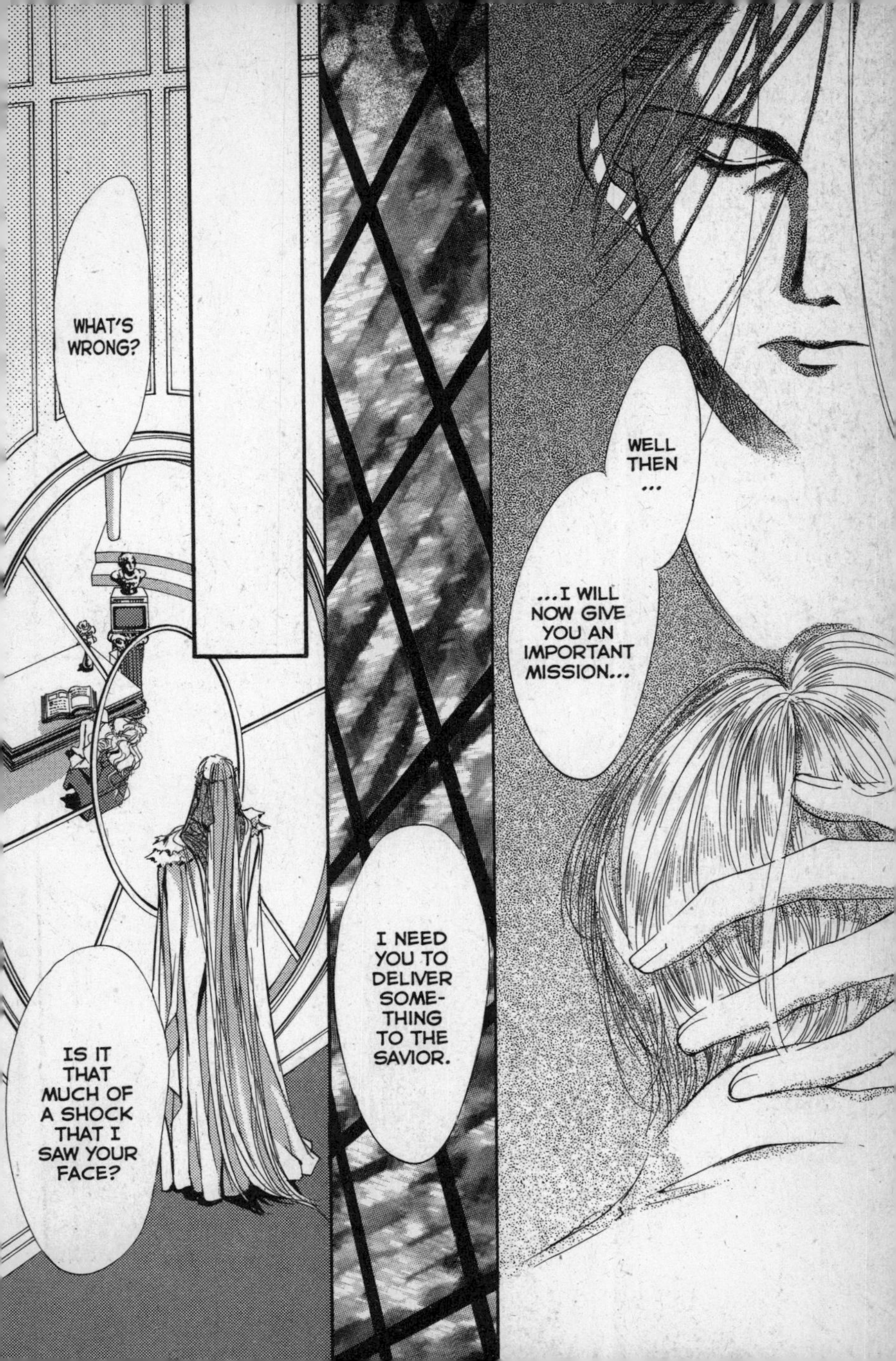
WELL THEN ...
...I WILL NOW GIVE YOU AN IMPORTANT MISSION...
I NEED YOU TO DELIVER SOME-THING TO THE SAVIOR.
WHAT'S WRONG?
IS IT THAT MUCH OF A SHOCK THAT I SAW YOUR FACE?

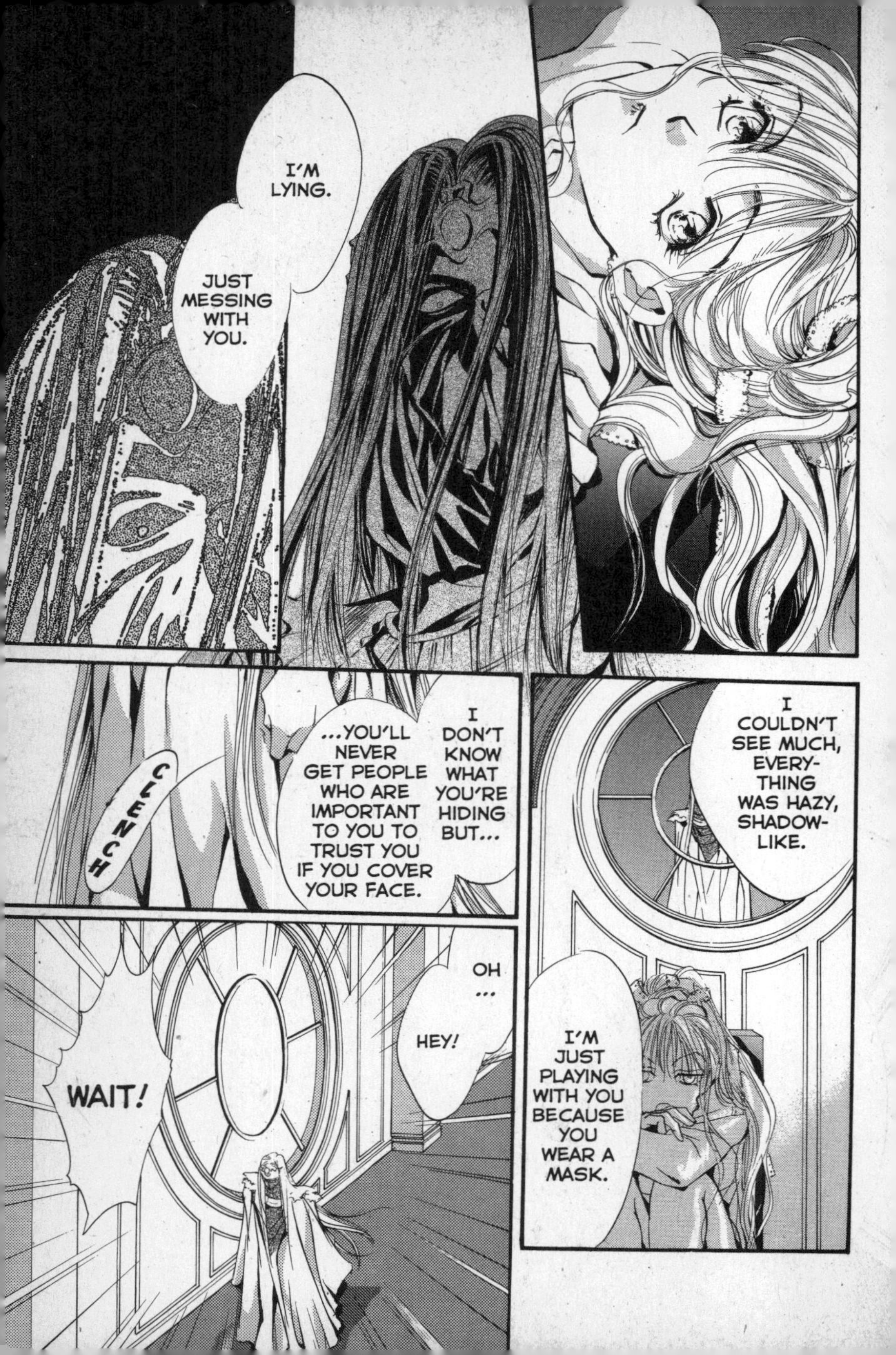
I'M LYING.
JUST MESSING WITH YOU.
I COULDN'T SEE MUCH, EVERY-THING WAS HAZY, SHADOW-LIKE.
I'M JUST PLAYING WITH YOU BECAUSE YOU WEAR A MASK.
I DON'T KNOW WHAT YOU'RE HIDING BUT...
...YOU'LL NEVER GET PEOPLE WHO ARE IMPORTANT TO YOU TO TRUST YOU IF YOU COVER YOUR FACE.
CLENCH
OH...
HEY!
WAIT!

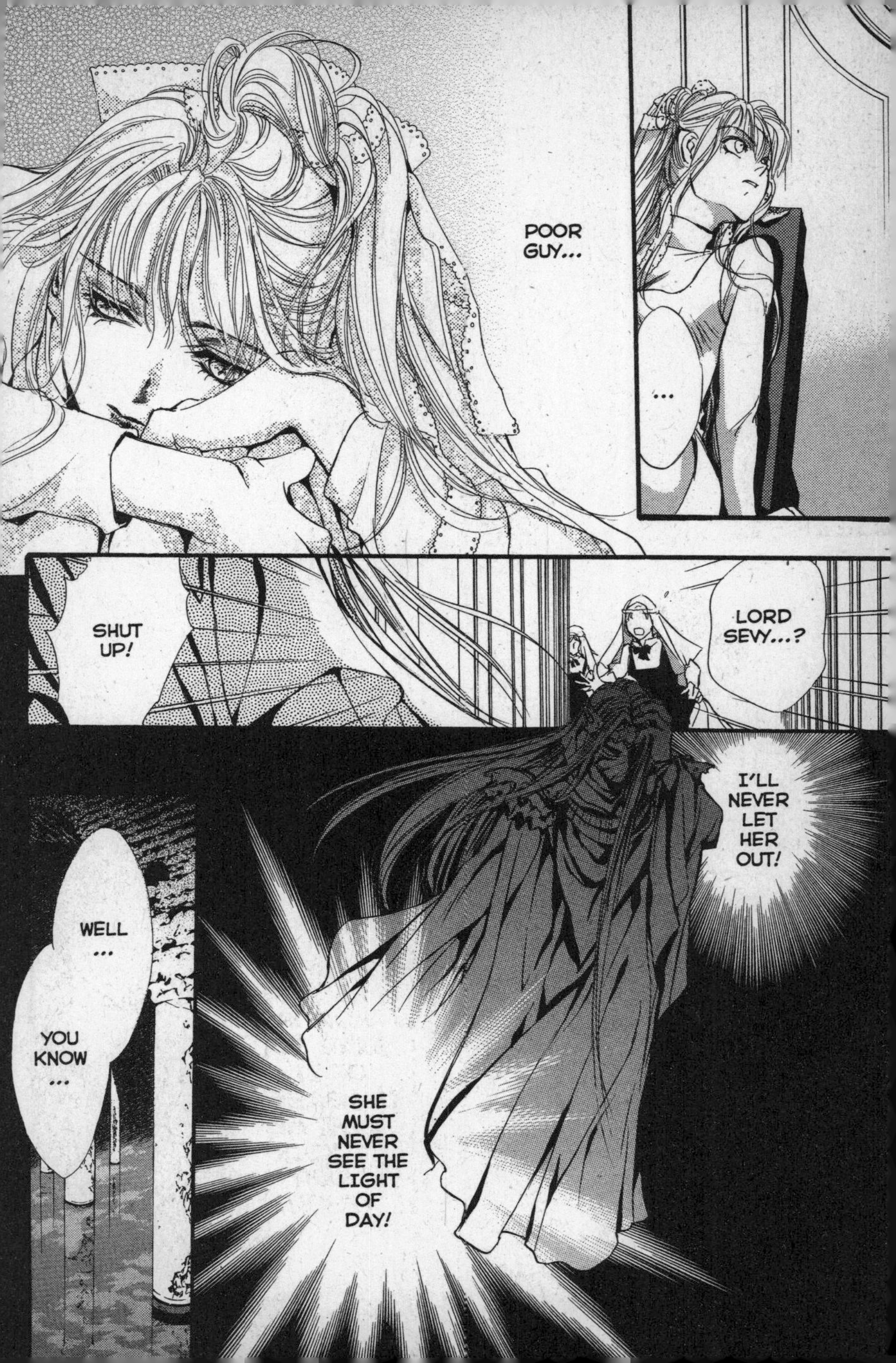
...
POOR GUY...
LORD SEVY...?
SHUT UP!
I'LL NEVER LET HER OUT!
SHE MUST NEVER SEE THE LIGHT OF DAY!
WELL ...
YOU KNOW ...

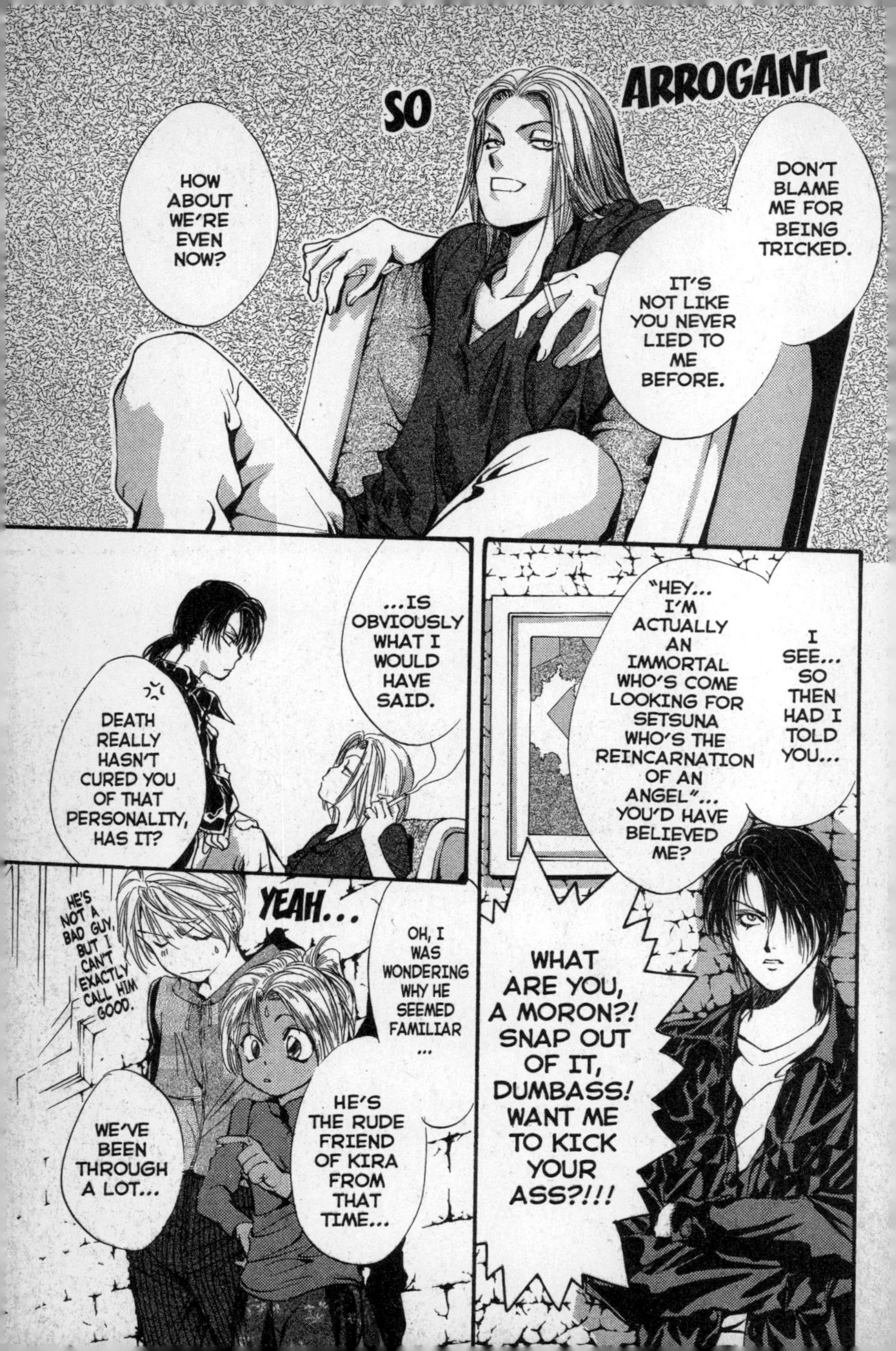
SO ARROGANT
DON'T BLAME ME FOR BEING TRICKED.
IT'S NOT LIKE YOU NEVER LIED TO ME BEFORE.
HOW ABOUT WE'RE EVEN NOW?
I SEE... SO THEN HAD I TOLD YOU...
"HEY... I'M ACTUALLY AN IMMORTAL WHO'S COME LOOKING FOR SETSUNA WHO'S THE REINCARNATION OF AN ANGEL"... YOU'D HAVE BELIEVED ME?
WHAT ARE YOU, A MORON?! SNAP OUT OF IT, DUMBASS! WANT ME TO KICK YOUR ASS?!!!
...IS OBVIOUSLY WHAT I WOULD HAVE SAID.
DEATH REALLY HASN'T CURED YOU OF THAT PERSONALITY, HAS IT?
OH, I WAS WONDERING WHY HE SEEMED FAMILIAR...
YEAH...
HE'S NOT A BAD GUY, BUT I CAN'T EXACTLY CALL HIM GOOD.
HE'S THE RUDE FRIEND OF KIRA FROM THAT TIME...
WE'VE BEEN THROUGH A LOT...

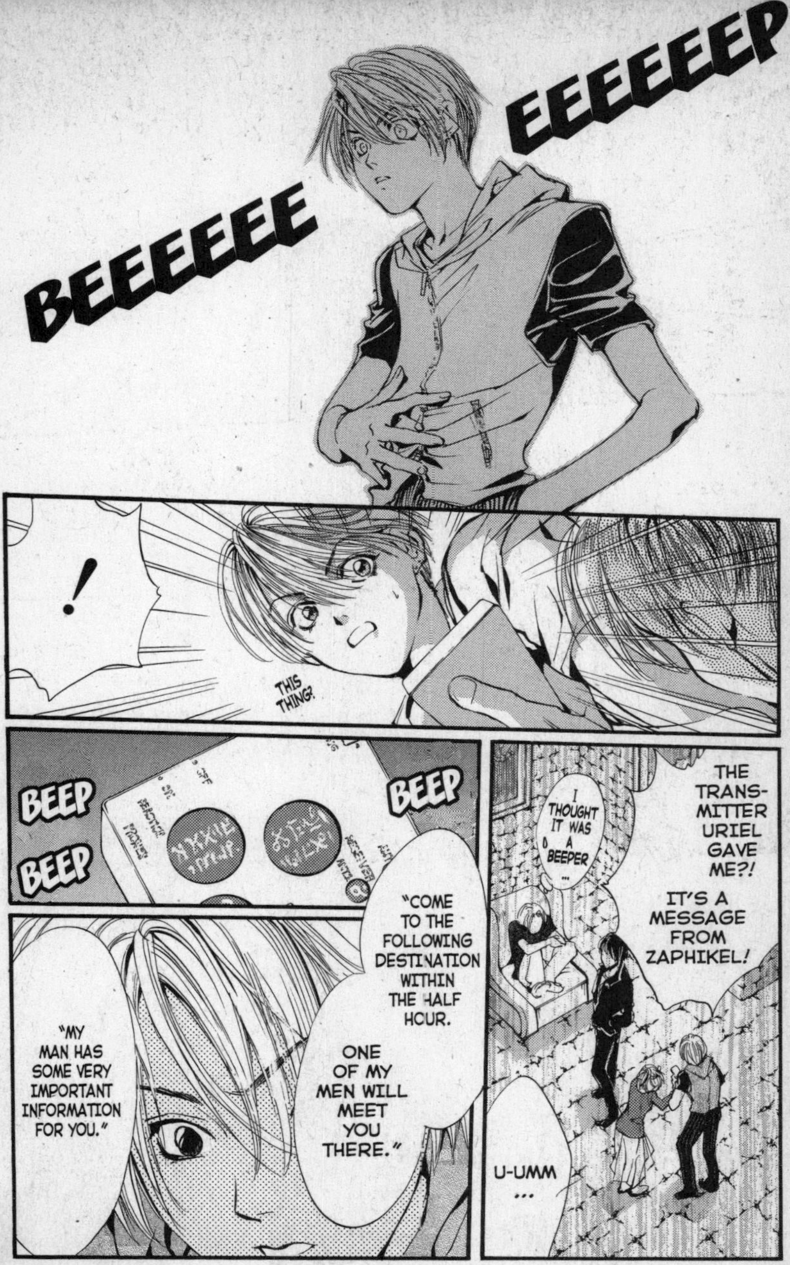
BEEEEEEEEEEEEEP
!
THIS THING?
THE TRANS-MITTER URIEL GAVE ME?!
I THOUGHT IT WAS A BEEPER...
IT'S A MESSAGE FROM ZAPHIKEL!
U-UMM...
BEEP
BEEP
BEEP
"COME TO THE FOLLOWING DESTINATION WITHIN THE HALF HOUR.
ONE OF MY MEN WILL MEET YOU THERE."
"MY MAN HAS SOME VERY IMPORTANT INFORMATION FOR YOU."

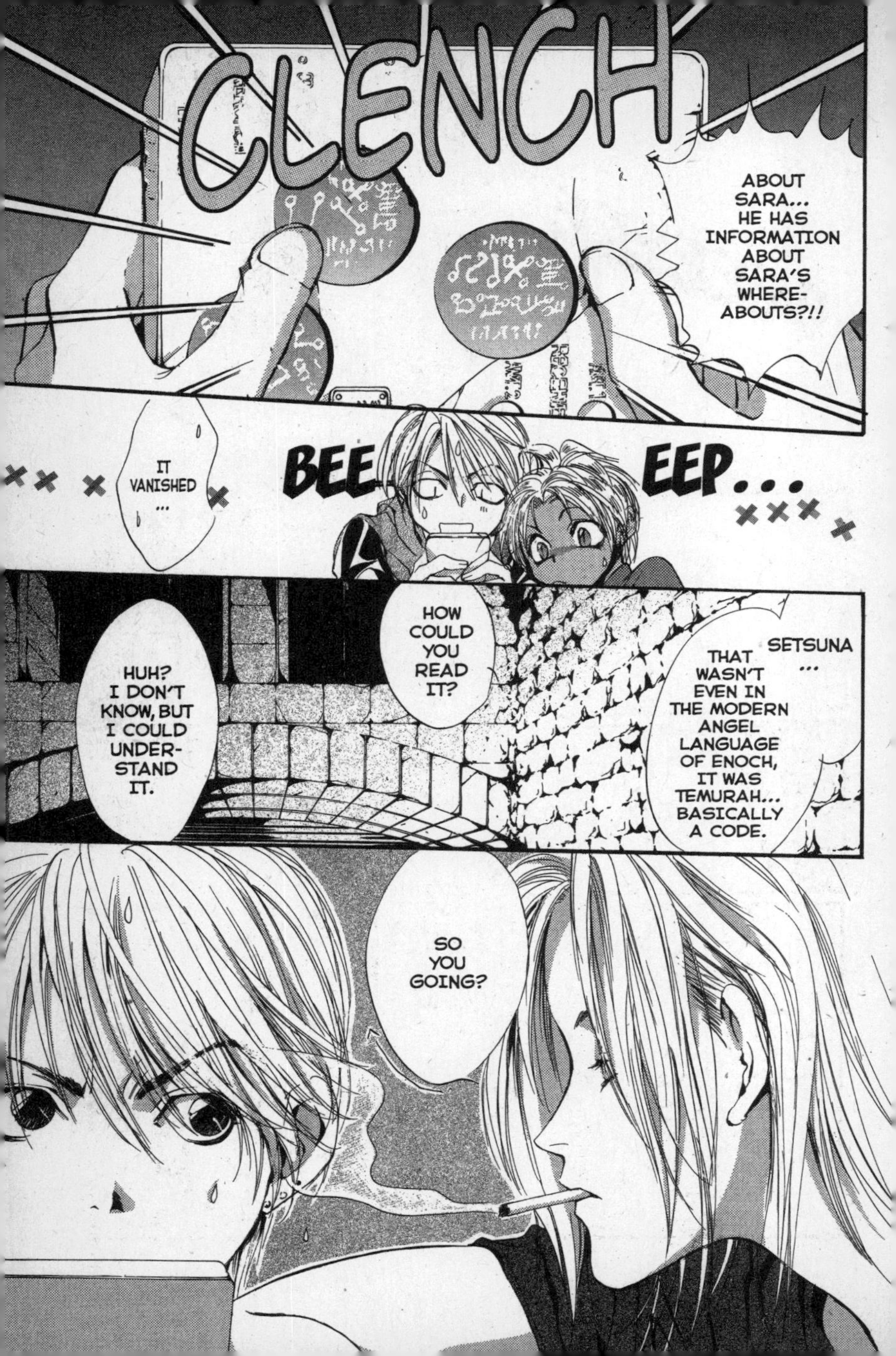
ABOUT SARA... HE HAS INFORMATION ABOUT SARA'S WHERE-ABOUTS?!!
CLENCH
BEE EEP...
IT VANISHED...
SETSUNA...
THAT WASN'T EVEN IN THE MODERN ANGEL LANGUAGE OF ENOCH, IT WAS TEMURAH... BASICALLY A CODE.
HOW COULD YOU READ IT?
HUH? I DON'T KNOW, BUT I COULD UNDER-STAND IT.
SO YOU GOING?

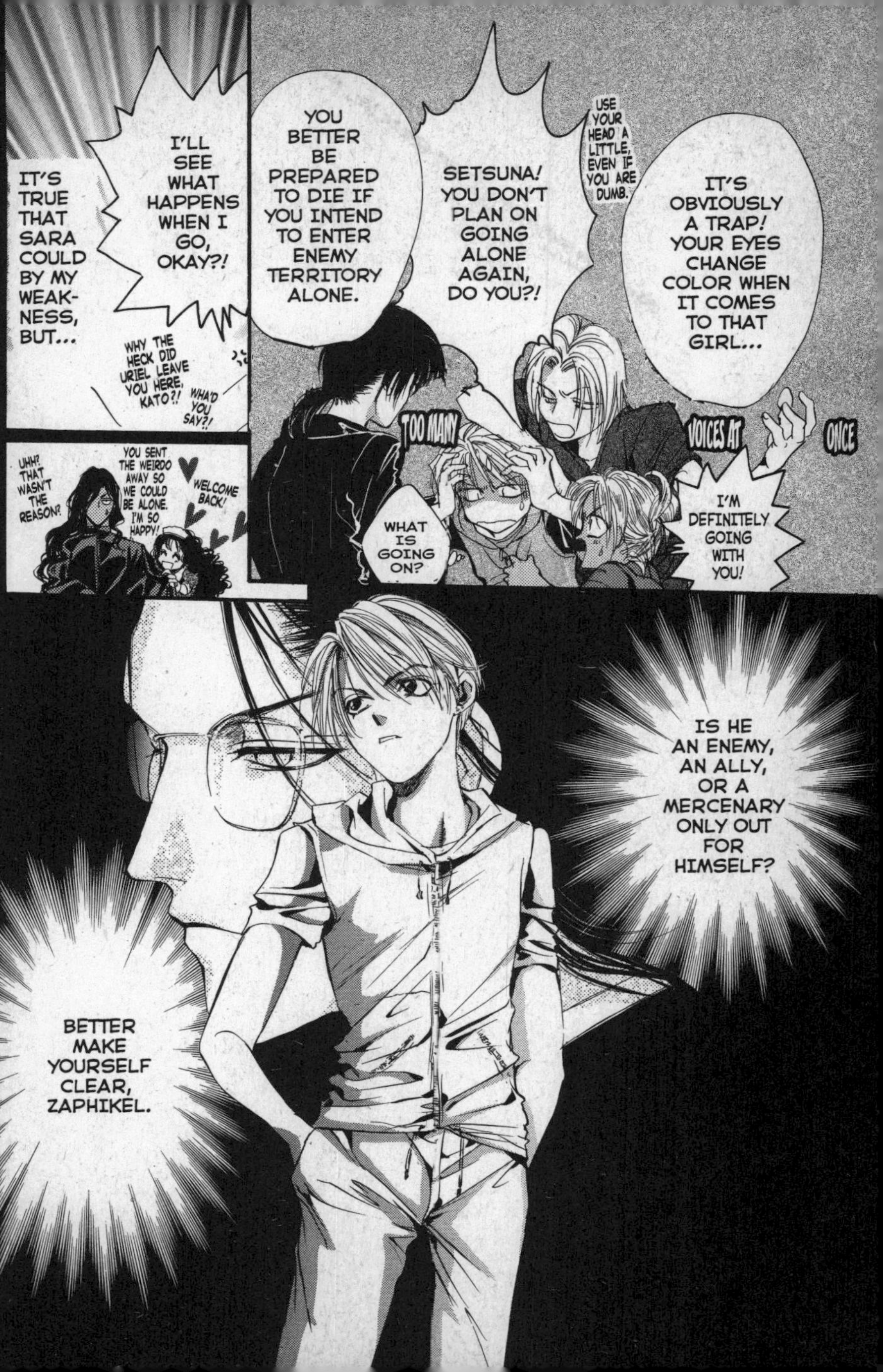
IT'S OBVIOUSLY A TRAP! YOUR EYES CHANGE COLOR WHEN IT COMES TO THAT GIRL...
USE YOUR HEAD A LITTLE, EVEN IF YOU ARE DUMB.
SETSUNA! YOU DON'T PLAN ON GOING ALONE AGAIN, DO YOU?!
YOU BETTER BE PREPARED TO DIE IF YOU INTEND TO ENTER ENEMY TERRITORY ALONE.
TOO MANY VOICES AT ONCE
I'M DEFINITELY GOING WITH YOU!
WHAT IS GOING ON?
I'LL SEE WHAT HAPPENS WHEN I GO, OKAY?!
IT'S TRUE THAT SARA COULD BY MY WEAKNESS, BUT...
WHY THE HECK DID URIEL LEAVE YOU HERE, KATO?!
WHA'D YOU SAY?!
WELCOME BACK!
YOU SENT THE WEIRDO AWAY SO WE COULD BE ALONE. I'M SO HAPPY!
UHH? THAT WASN'T THE REASON?
IS HE AN ENEMY, AN ALLY, OR A MERCENARY ONLY OUT FOR HIMSELF?
BETTER MAKE YOURSELF CLEAR, ZAPHIKEL.

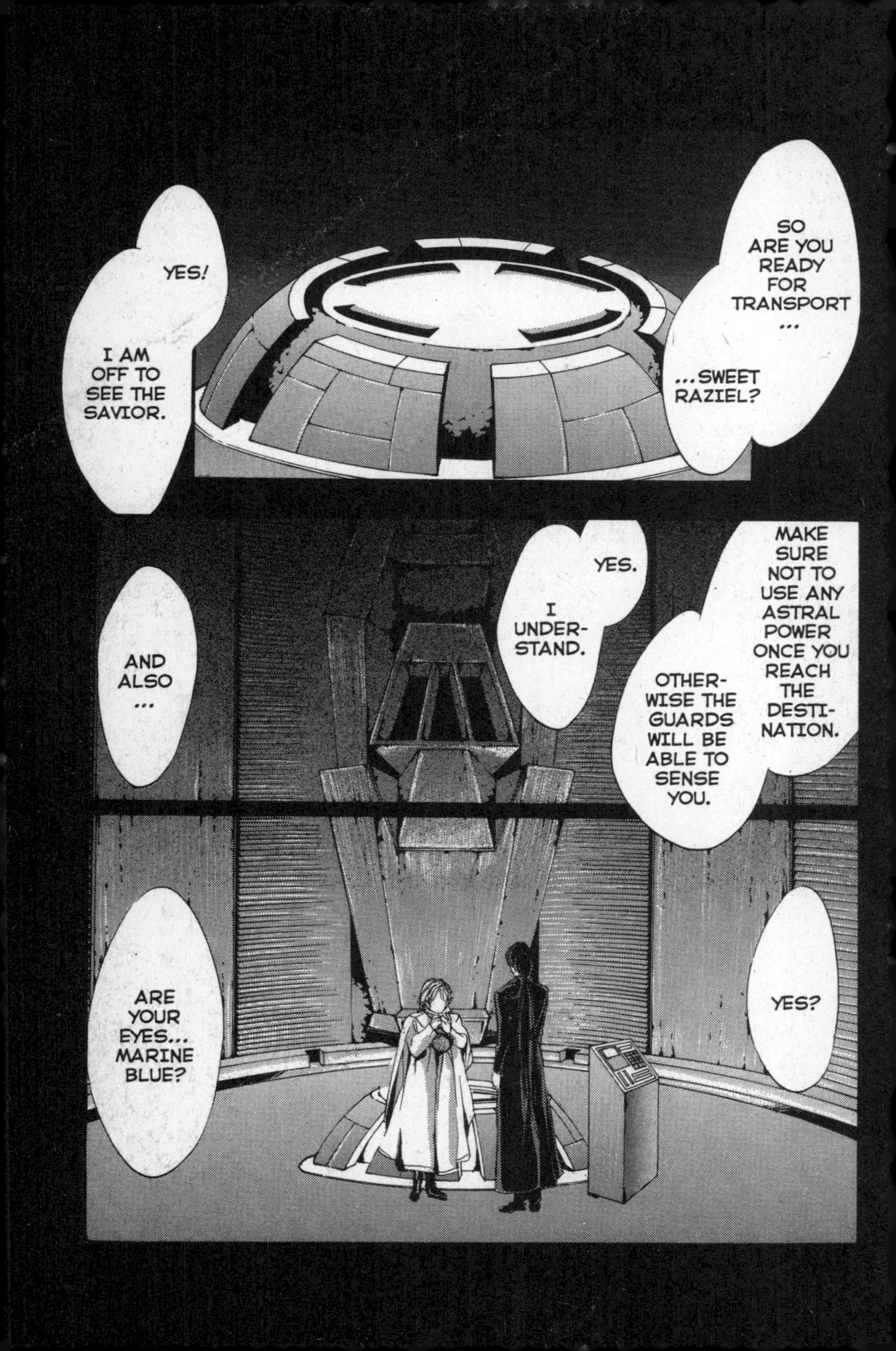
SO ARE YOU READY FOR TRANSPORT ...
...SWEET RAZIEL?
YES!
I AM OFF TO SEE THE SAVIOR.
MAKE SURE NOT TO USE ANY ASTRAL POWER ONCE YOU REACH THE DESTI-NATION.
OTHER-WISE THE GUARDS WILL BE ABLE TO SENSE YOU.
YES.
I UNDER-STAND.
AND ALSO ...
YES?
ARE YOUR EYES... MARINE BLUE?

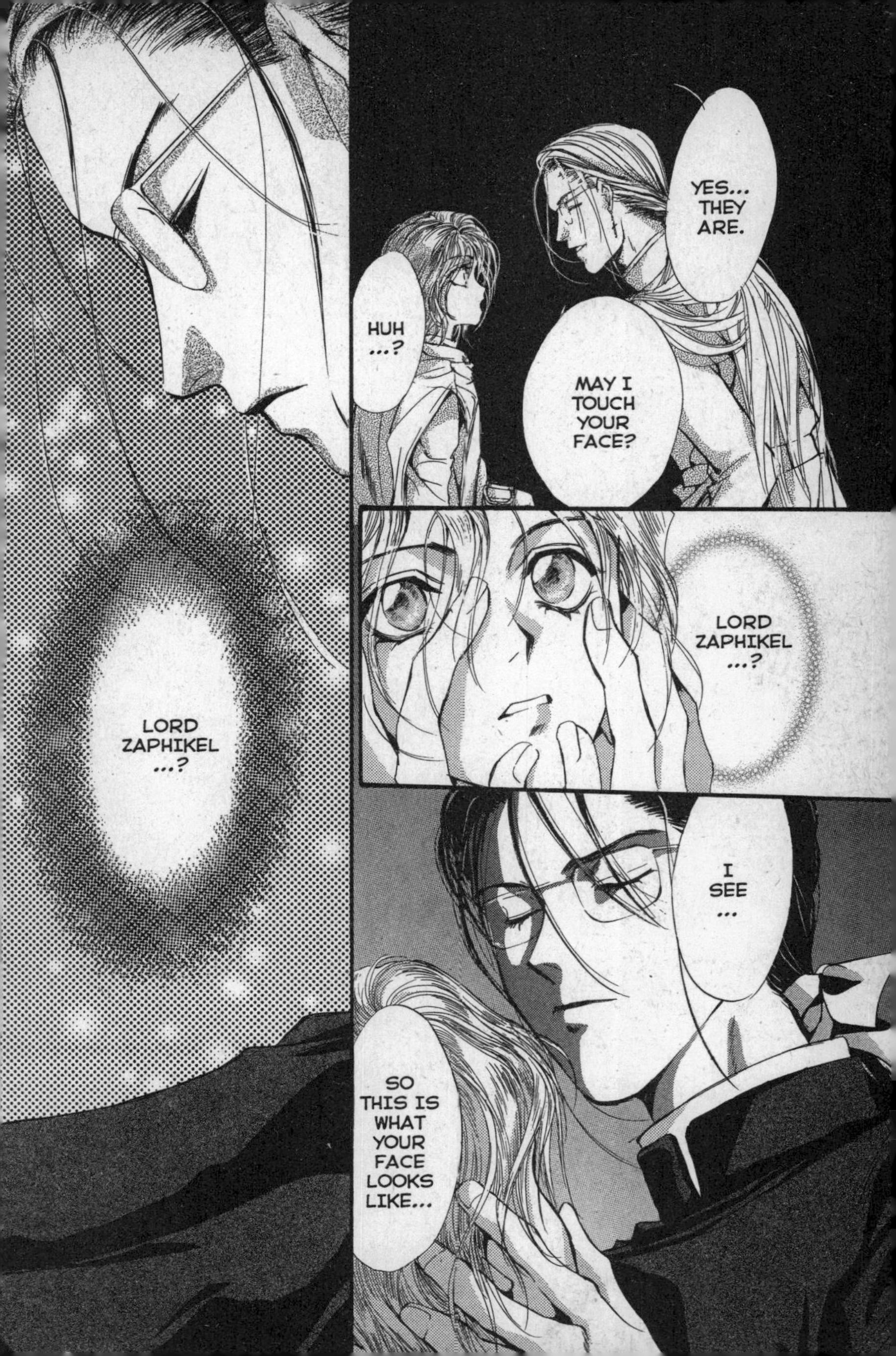
YES... THEY ARE.
HUH ...?
MAY I TOUCH YOUR FACE?
LORD ZAPHIKEL ...?
I SEE ...
SO THIS IS WHAT YOUR FACE LOOKS LIKE...
LORD ZAPHIKEL ...?

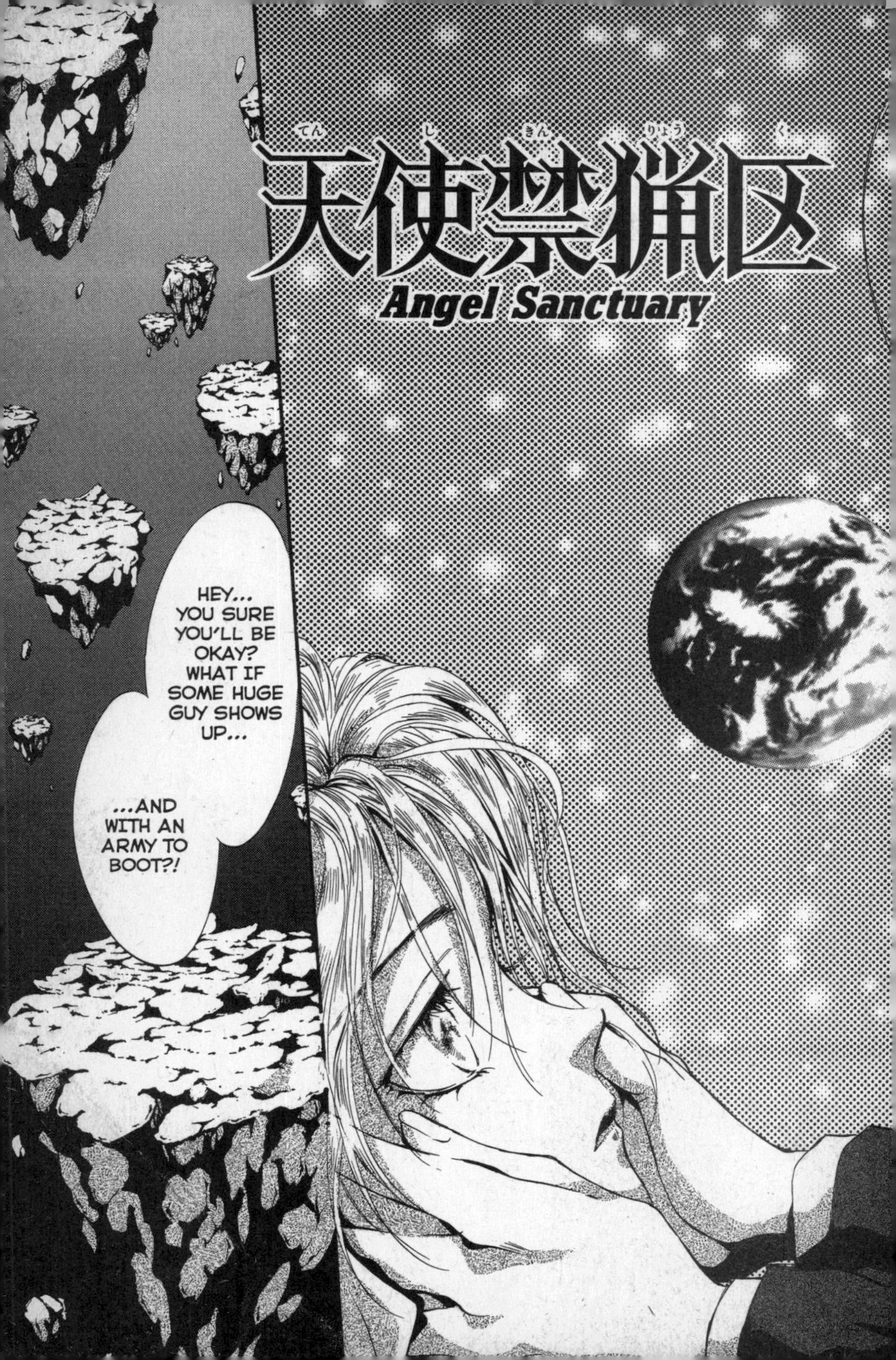

てんしきんりょうく
天使禁猟区
Angel Sanctuary
HEY... YOU SURE YOU'LL BE OKAY? WHAT IF SOME HUGE GUY SHOWS UP...
...AND WITH AN ARMY TO BOOT?!

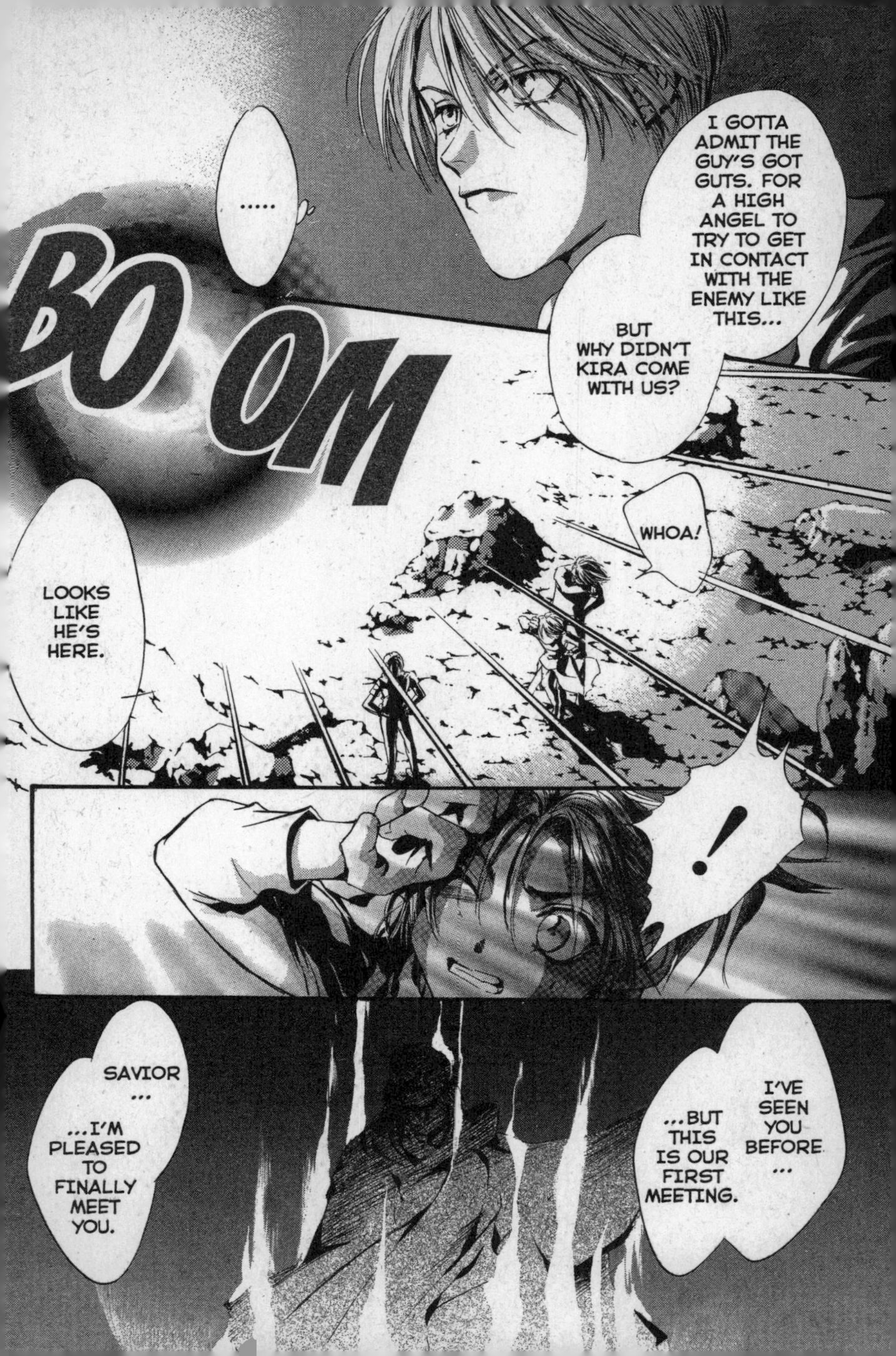

I GOTTA ADMIT THE GUY'S GOT GUTS. FOR A HIGH ANGEL TO TRY TO GET IN CONTACT WITH THE ENEMY LIKE THIS...
.....
BUT WHY DIDN'T KIRA COME WITH US?
BOOM
WHOA!
LOOKS LIKE HE'S HERE.
!
I'VE SEEN YOU BEFORE...
...BUT THIS IS OUR FIRST MEETING.
SAVIOR...
...I'M PLEASED TO FINALLY MEET YOU.

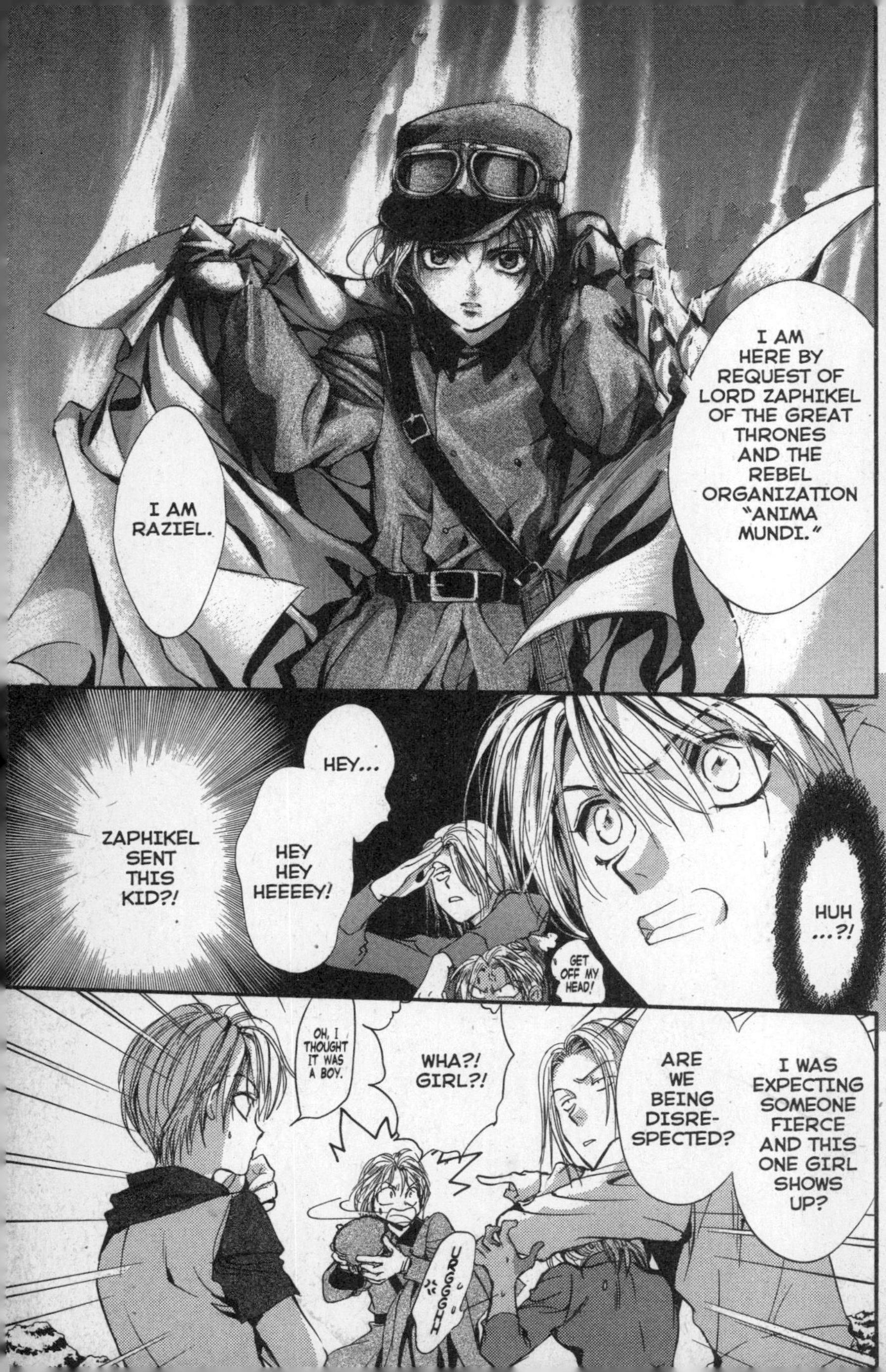
I AM HERE BY REQUEST OF LORD ZAPHIKEL OF THE GREAT THRONES AND THE REBEL ORGANIZATION "ANIMA MUNDI."
I AM RAZIEL.
HUH ...?!
HEY...
HEY HEY HEEEEY!
GET OFF MY HEAD!
ZAPHIKEL SENT THIS KID?!
I WAS EXPECTING SOMEONE FIERCE AND THIS ONE GIRL SHOWS UP?
ARE WE BEING DISRE-SPECTED?
WHA?! GIRL?!
OH, I THOUGHT IT WAS A BOY.
URGGGGH

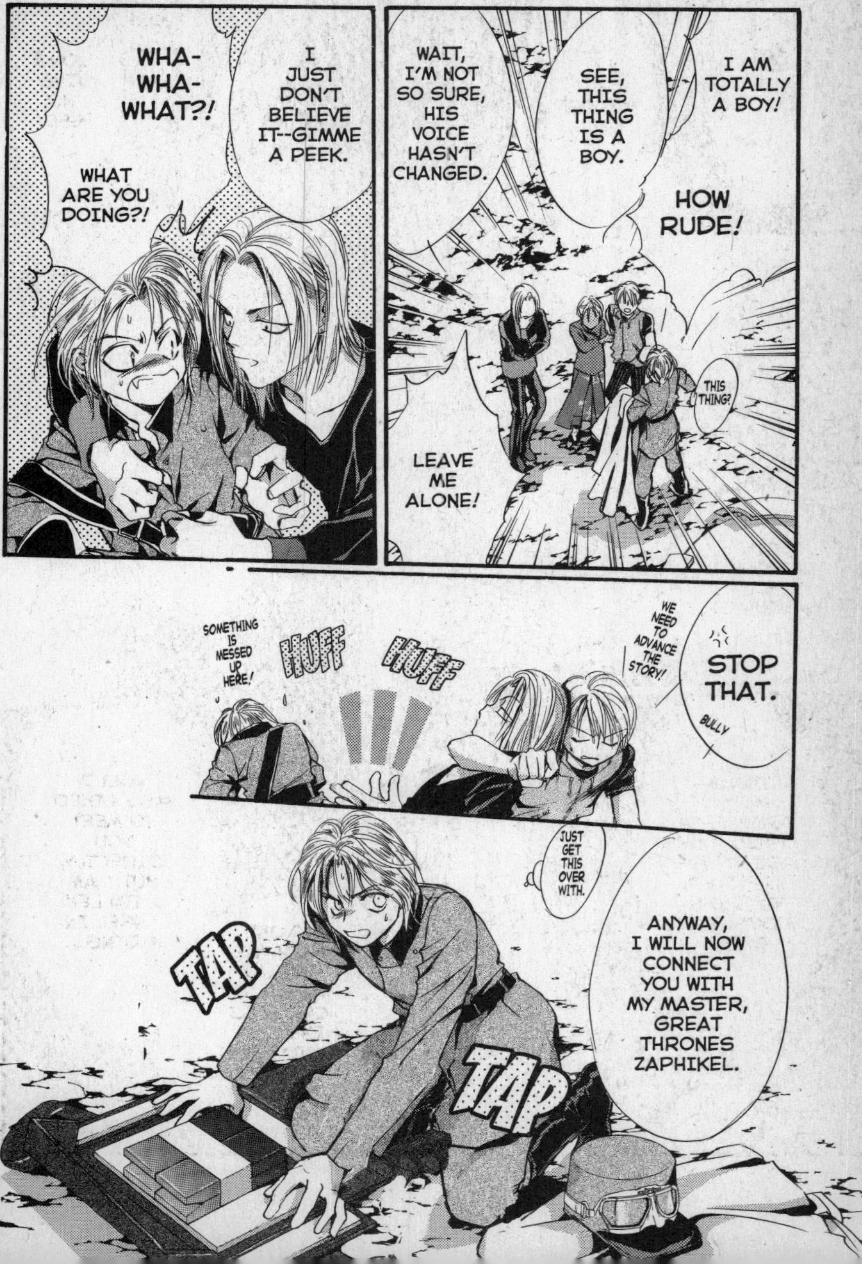
I AM TOTALLY A BOY!
SEE, THIS THING IS A BOY.
WAIT, I'M NOT SO SURE, HIS VOICE HASN'T CHANGED.
HOW RUDE!
THIS THING?
LEAVE ME ALONE!
I JUST DON'T BELIEVE IT--GIMME A PEEK.
WHA-WHA-WHAT?!
WHAT ARE YOU DOING?!
STOP THAT.
BULLY
WE NEED TO ADVANCE THE STORY!
HUFF
HUFF
SOMETHING IS MESSED UP HERE!
ANYWAY, I WILL NOW CONNECT YOU WITH MY MASTER, GREAT THRONES ZAPHIKEL.
JUST GET THIS OVER WITH.
TAP
TAP

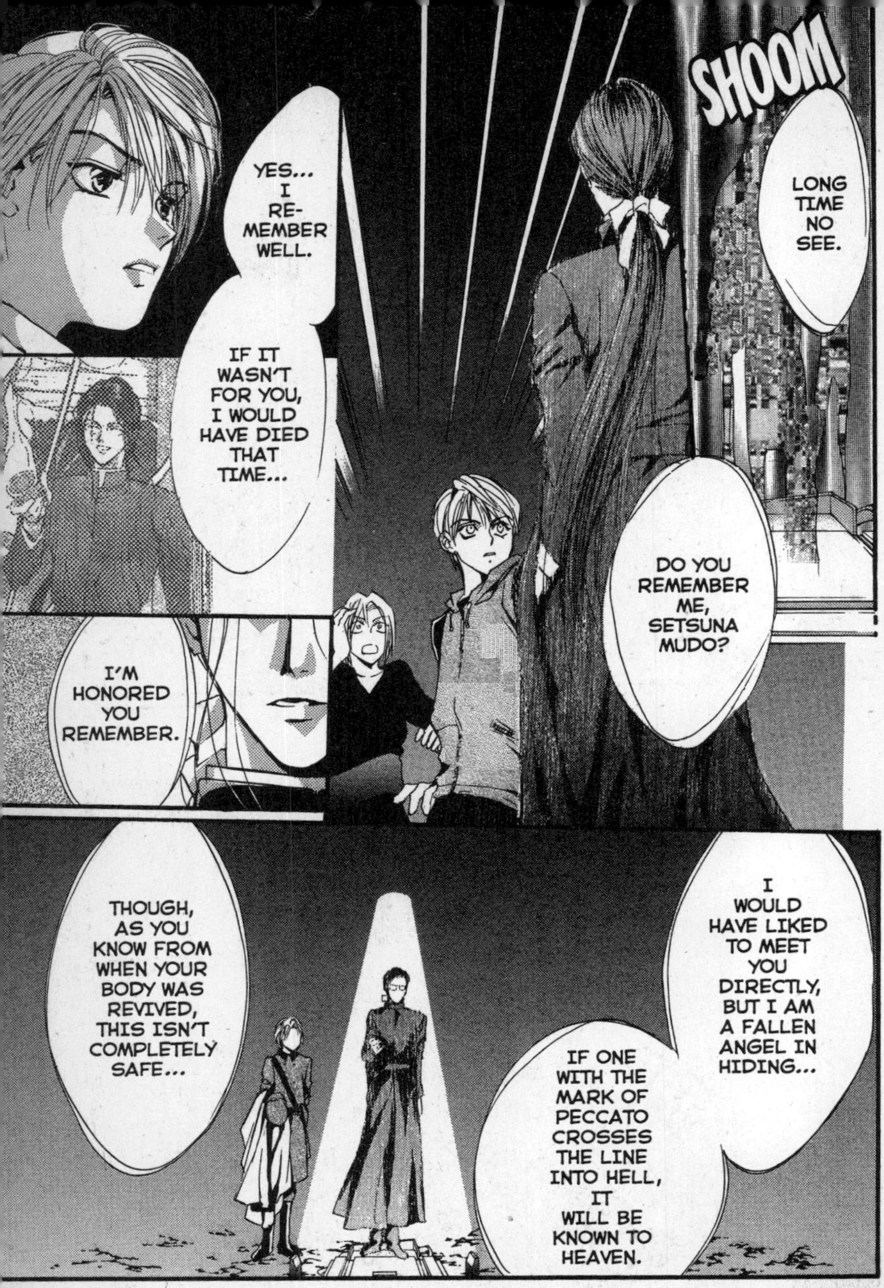

SHOOM
LONG TIME NO SEE.
DO YOU REMEMBER ME, SETSUNA MUDO?
YES... I RE-MEMBER WELL.
IF IT WASN'T FOR YOU, I WOULD HAVE DIED THAT TIME...
I'M HONORED YOU REMEMBER.
I WOULD HAVE LIKED TO MEET YOU DIRECTLY, BUT I AM A FALLEN ANGEL IN HIDING...
IF ONE WITH THE MARK OF PECCATO CROSSES THE LINE INTO HELL, IT WILL BE KNOWN TO HEAVEN.
THOUGH, AS YOU KNOW FROM WHEN YOUR BODY WAS REVIVED, THIS ISN'T COMPLETELY SAFE...

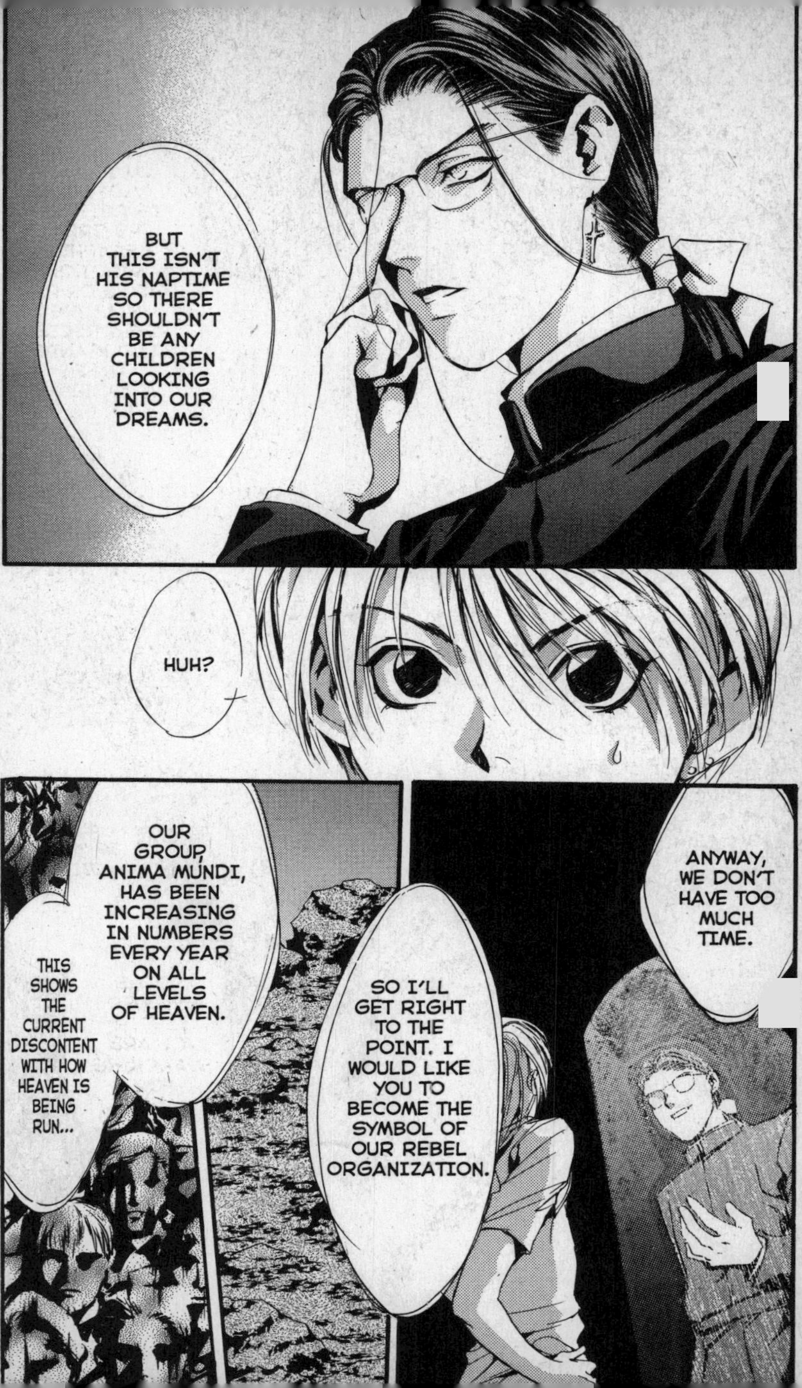
BUT THIS ISN'T HIS NAPTIME SO THERE SHOULDN'T BE ANY CHILDREN LOOKING INTO OUR DREAMS.
HUH?
ANYWAY, WE DON'T HAVE TOO MUCH TIME.
SO I'LL GET RIGHT TO THE POINT. I WOULD LIKE YOU TO BECOME THE SYMBOL OF OUR REBEL ORGANIZATION.
OUR GROUP, ANIMA MUNDI, HAS BEEN INCREASING IN NUMBERS EVERY YEAR ON ALL LEVELS OF HEAVEN.
THIS SHOWS THE CURRENT DISCONTENT WITH HOW HEAVEN IS BEING RUN...

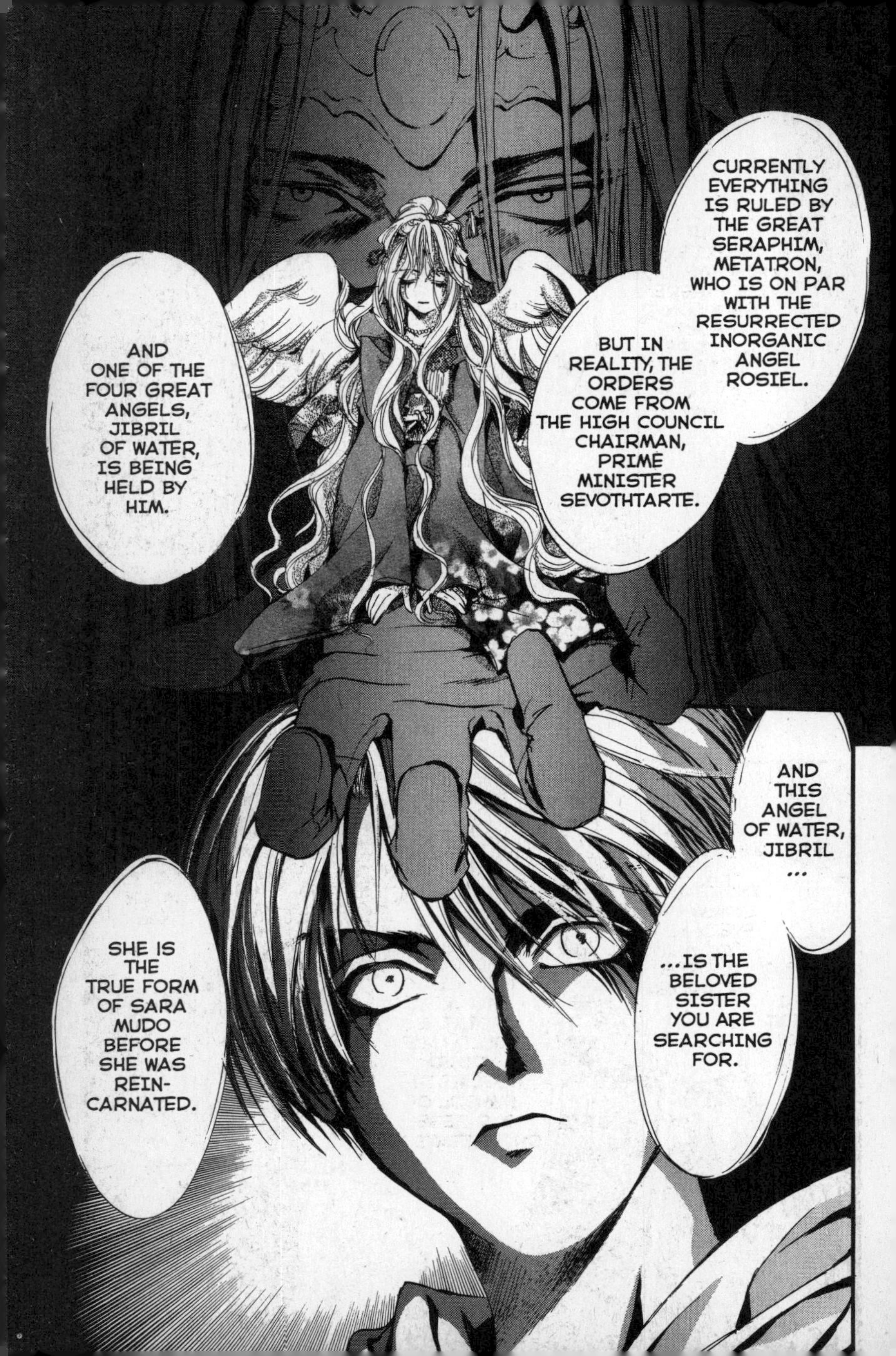
CURRENTLY EVERYTHING IS RULED BY THE GREAT SERAPHIM, METATRON, WHO IS ON PAR WITH THE RESURRECTED INORGANIC ANGEL ROSIEL.
BUT IN REALITY, THE ORDERS COME FROM THE HIGH COUNCIL CHAIRMAN, PRIME MINISTER SEVOTHTARTE.
AND ONE OF THE FOUR GREAT ANGELS, JIBRIL OF WATER, IS BEING HELD BY HIM.
AND THIS ANGEL OF WATER, JIBRIL ...
...IS THE BELOVED SISTER YOU ARE SEARCHING FOR.
SHE IS THE TRUE FORM OF SARA MUDO BEFORE SHE WAS REIN-CARNATED.

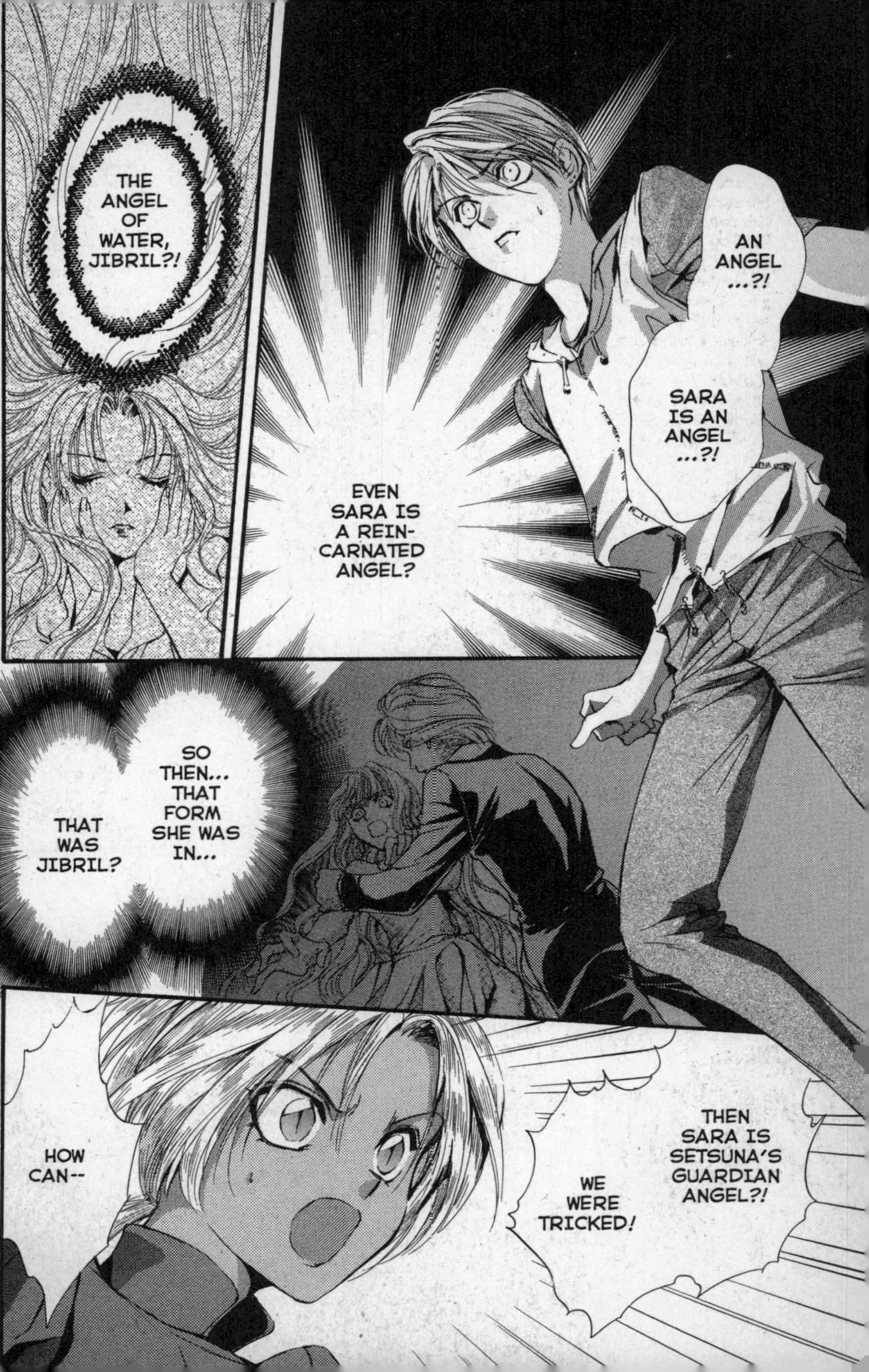
AN ANGEL ...?!
SARA IS AN ANGEL ...?!
EVEN SARA IS A REIN-CARNATED ANGEL?
THE ANGEL OF WATER, JIBRIL?!
SO THEN... THAT FORM SHE WAS IN...
THAT WAS JIBRIL?
THEN SARA IS SETSUNA'S GUARDIAN ANGEL?!
WE WERE TRICKED!
HOW CAN--

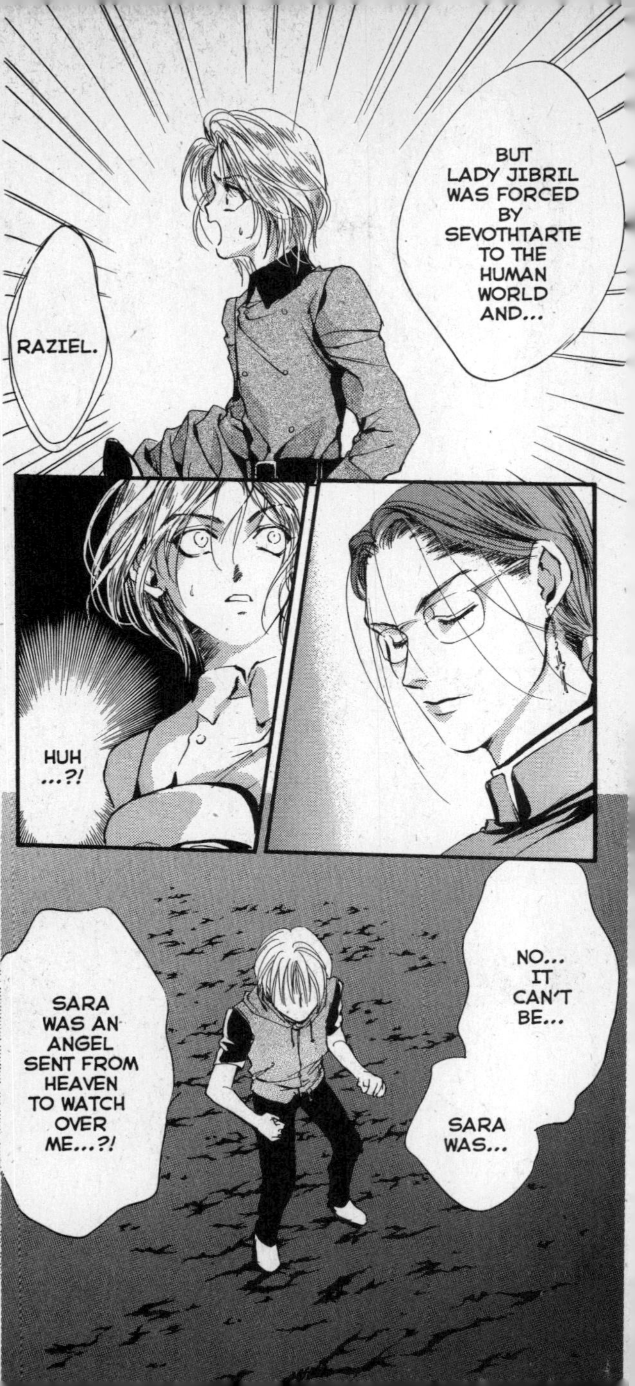
BUT LADY JIBRIL WAS FORCED BY SEVOTHTARTE TO THE HUMAN WORLD AND...
RAZIEL.
HUH ...?!
NO... IT CAN'T BE...
SARA WAS...
SARA WAS AN ANGEL SENT FROM HEAVEN TO WATCH OVER ME...?!

The small spirit girl, Lil, who appears in the second half of this chapter, was well-liked by my assistants who called her Lil-Lil. It can be fun drawing girls. I modeled her after idol singer Hirosue but you can't see it at all in this chapter. Isn't her catlike mouth when she smiles really cute? Also, there is no such flower as the Moonlil. If only there was a pretty small flower that would bloom in the moonlight... I did base it off a flower called Mugisennou (Agrostemma). It's a very lovely pink flower. Also, Zaphy is goofy in this chapter for the first time in a while.

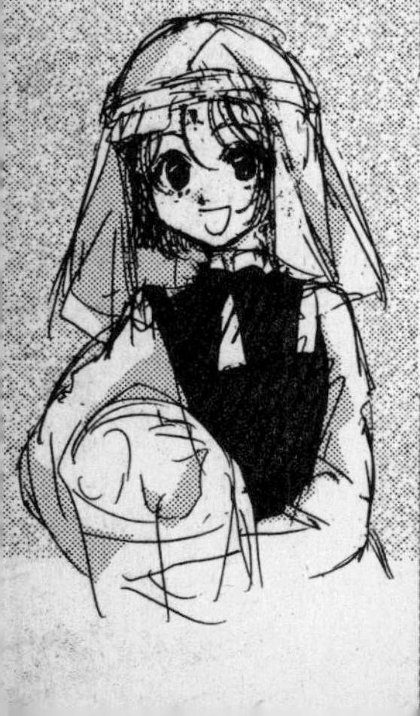

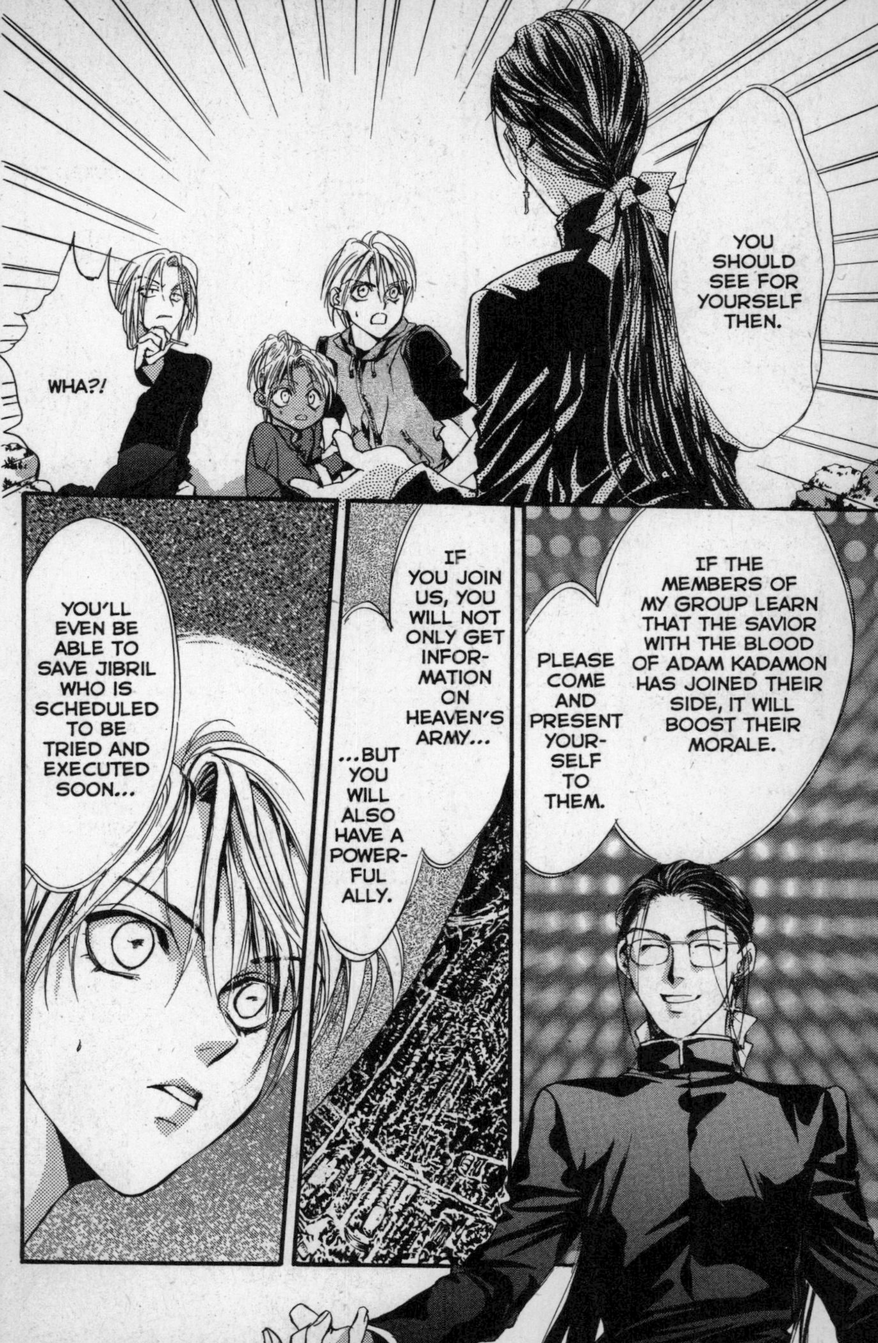
YOU SHOULD SEE FOR YOURSELF THEN.
WHA?!
IF THE MEMBERS OF MY GROUP LEARN THAT THE SAVIOR WITH THE BLOOD OF ADAM KADAMON HAS JOINED THEIR SIDE, IT WILL BOOST THEIR MORALE.
PLEASE COME AND PRESENT YOUR-SELF TO THEM.
IF YOU JOIN US, YOU WILL NOT ONLY GET INFOR-MATION ON HEAVEN'S ARMY...
...BUT YOU WILL ALSO HAVE A POWER-FUL ALLY.
YOU'LL EVEN BE ABLE TO SAVE JIBRIL WHO IS SCHEDULED TO BE TRIED AND EXECUTED SOON...

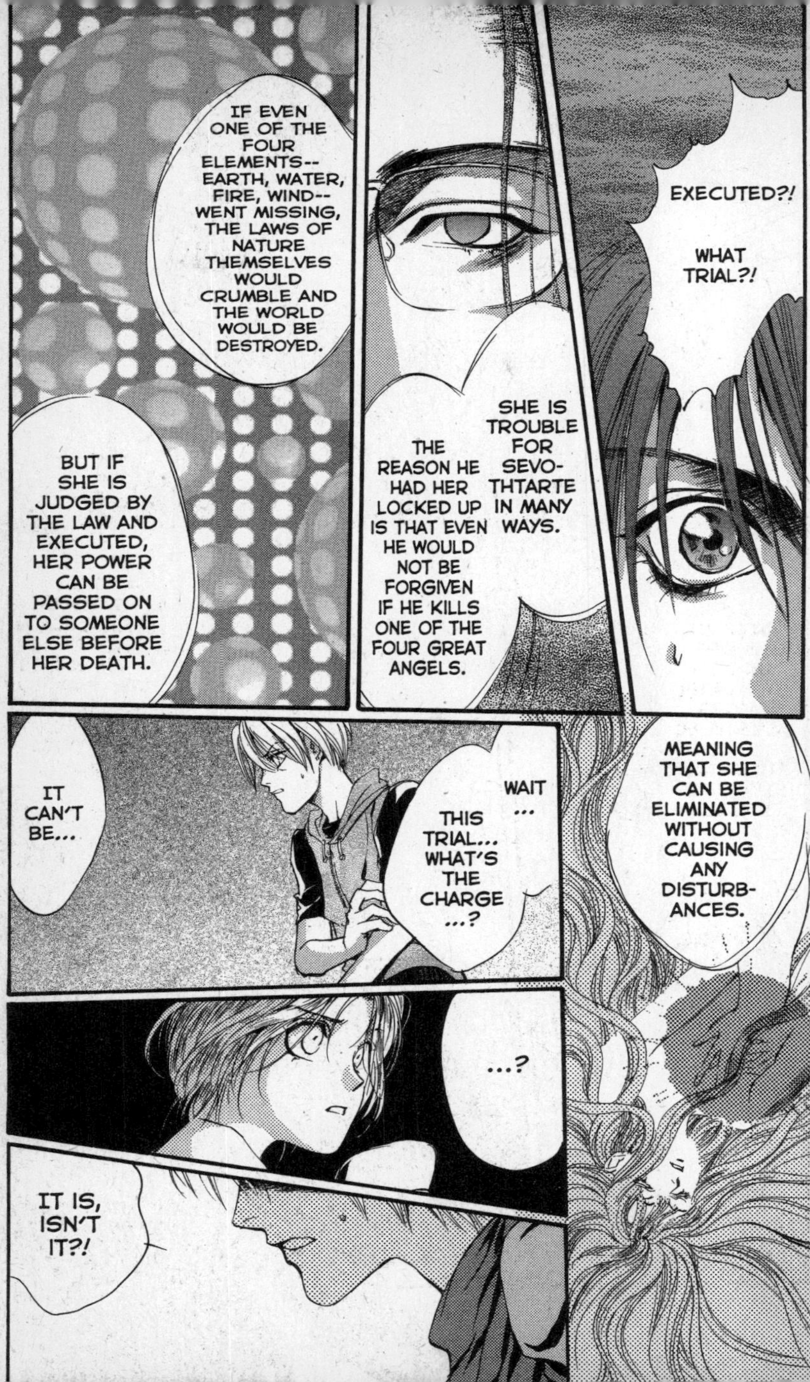
EXECUTED?!
WHAT TRIAL?!
SHE IS TROUBLE FOR SEVOTHTARTE IN MANY WAYS.
THE REASON HE HAD HER LOCKED UP IS THAT EVEN HE WOULD NOT BE FORGIVEN IF HE KILLS ONE OF THE FOUR GREAT ANGELS.
IF EVEN ONE OF THE FOUR ELEMENTS--EARTH, WATER, FIRE, WIND--WENT MISSING, THE LAWS OF NATURE THEMSELVES WOULD CRUMBLE AND THE WORLD WOULD BE DESTROYED.
BUT IF SHE IS JUDGED BY THE LAW AND EXECUTED, HER POWER CAN BE PASSED ON TO SOMEONE ELSE BEFORE HER DEATH.
MEANING THAT SHE CAN BE ELIMINATED WITHOUT CAUSING ANY DISTURBANCES.
WAIT...
THIS TRIAL... WHAT'S THE CHARGE...?
IT CAN'T BE...
...?
IT IS, ISN'T IT?!

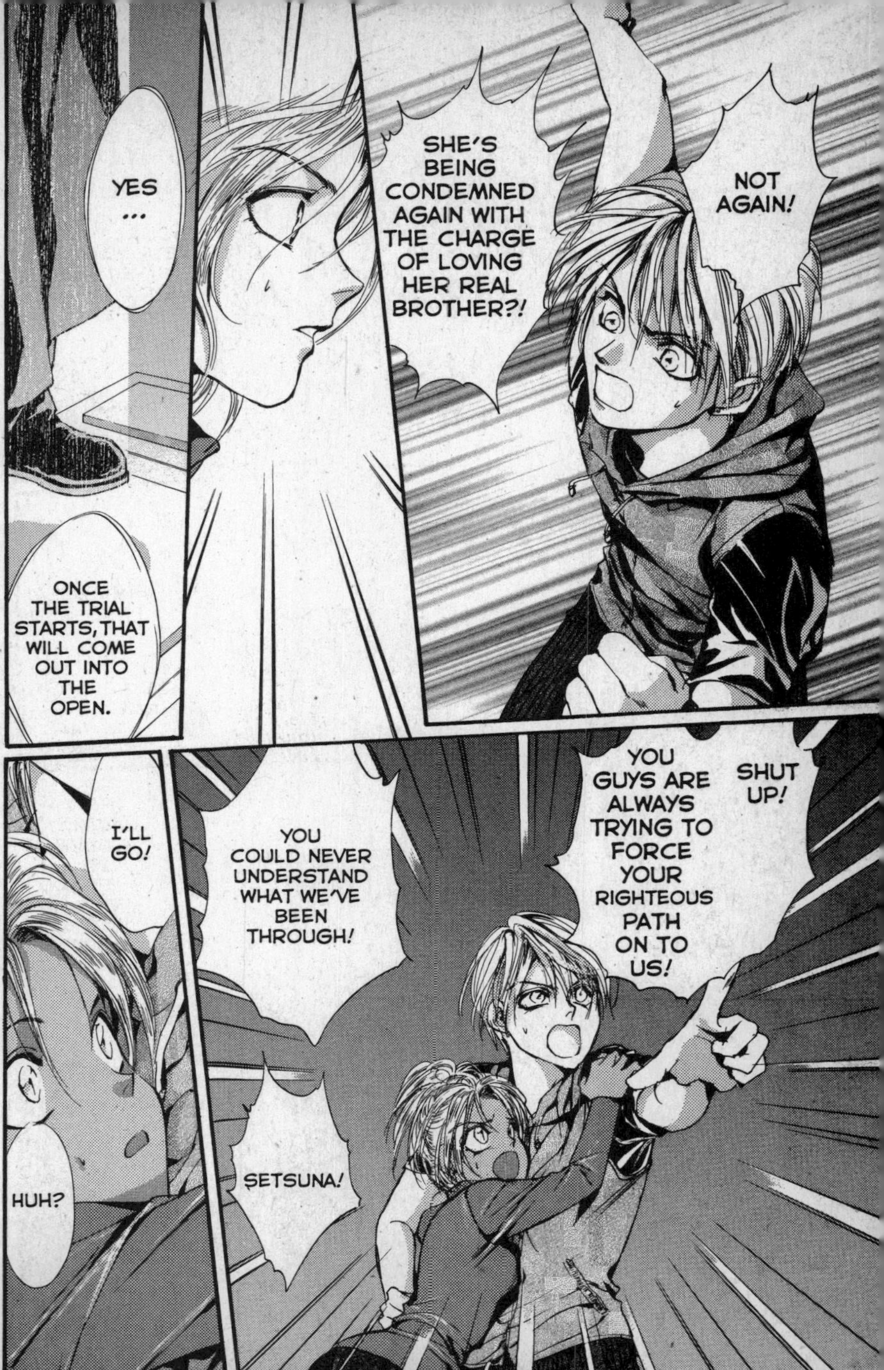
NOT AGAIN!
SHE'S BEING CONDEMNED AGAIN WITH THE CHARGE OF LOVING HER REAL BROTHER?!
YES ...
ONCE THE TRIAL STARTS, THAT WILL COME OUT INTO THE OPEN.
SHUT UP!
YOU GUYS ARE ALWAYS TRYING TO FORCE YOUR RIGHTEOUS PATH ON TO US!
YOU COULD NEVER UNDERSTAND WHAT WE'VE BEEN THROUGH!
SETSUNA!
I'LL GO!
HUH?

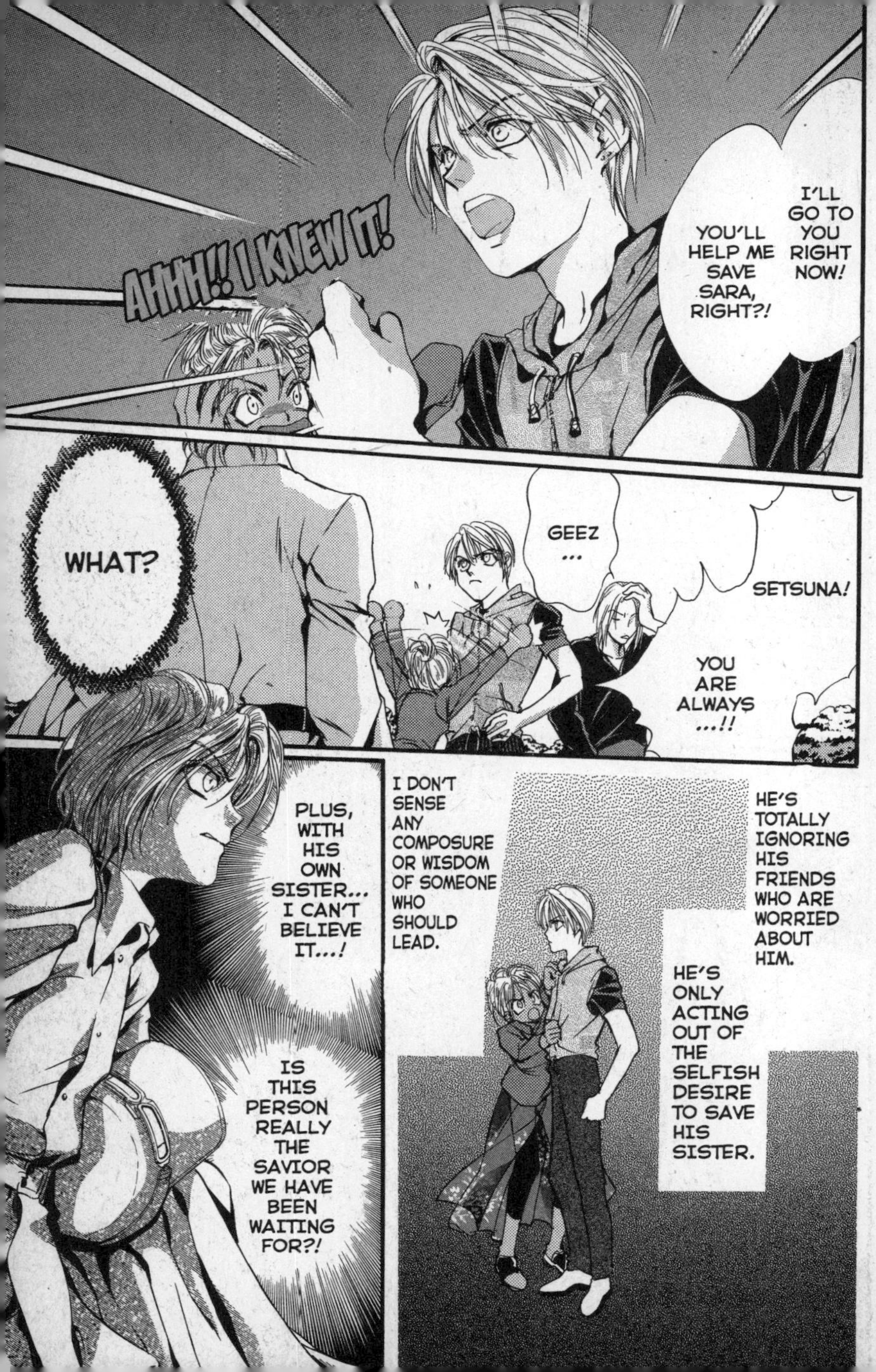
I'LL GO TO YOU RIGHT NOW!
YOU'LL HELP ME SAVE SARA, RIGHT?!
AHHH!! I KNEW IT!
SETSUNA!
YOU ARE ALWAYS ...!!
GEEZ ...
WHAT?
HE'S TOTALLY IGNORING HIS FRIENDS WHO ARE WORRIED ABOUT HIM.
HE'S ONLY ACTING OUT OF THE SELFISH DESIRE TO SAVE HIS SISTER.
I DON'T SENSE ANY COMPOSURE OR WISDOM OF SOMEONE WHO SHOULD LEAD.
PLUS, WITH HIS OWN SISTER... I CAN'T BELIEVE IT...!
IS THIS PERSON REALLY THE SAVIOR WE HAVE BEEN WAITING FOR?!

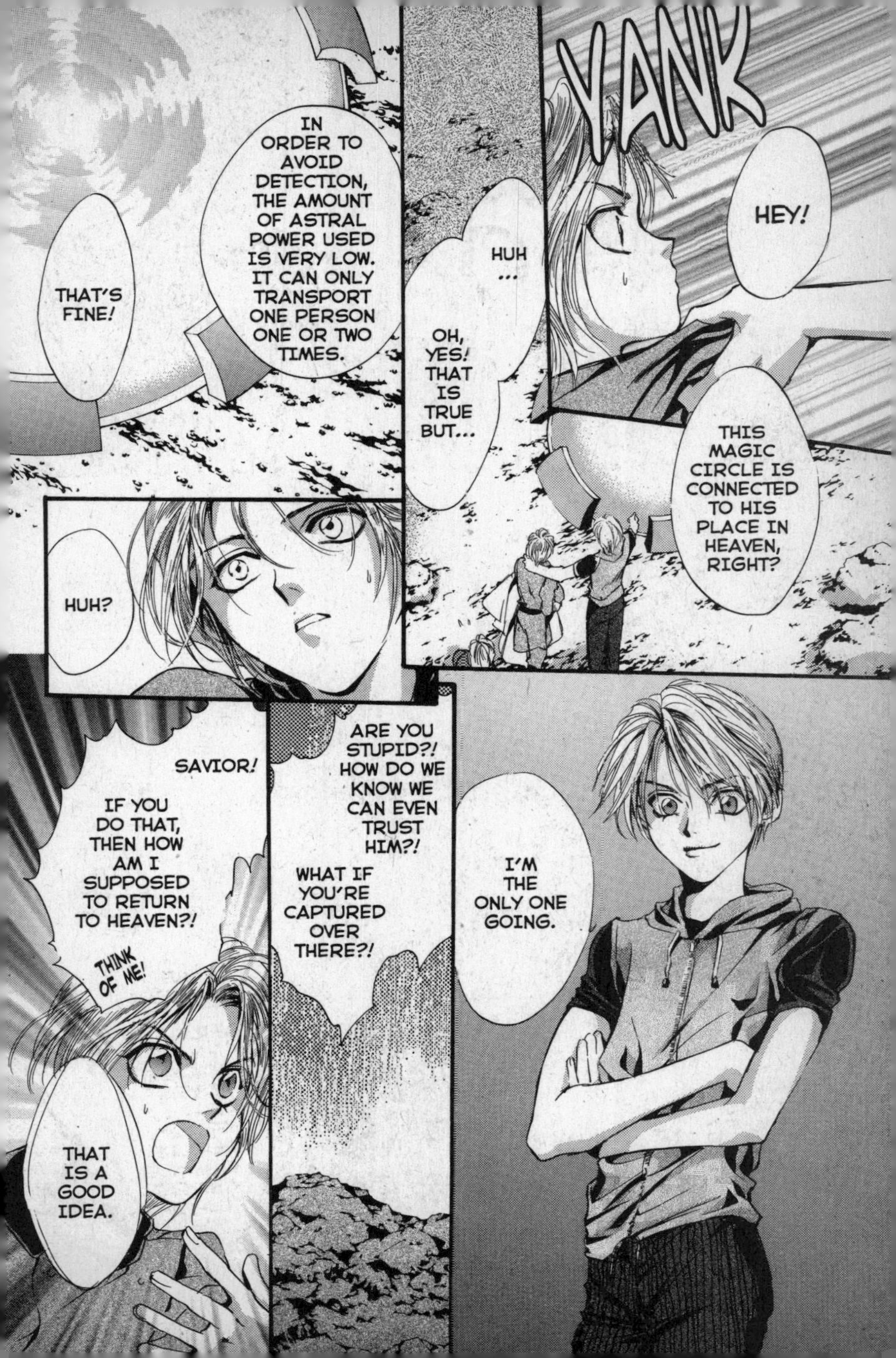
YANK
HEY!
THIS MAGIC CIRCLE IS CONNECTED TO HIS PLACE IN HEAVEN, RIGHT?
HUH ...
OH, YES! THAT IS TRUE BUT...
IN ORDER TO AVOID DETECTION, THE AMOUNT OF ASTRAL POWER USED IS VERY LOW. IT CAN ONLY TRANSPORT ONE PERSON ONE OR TWO TIMES.
THAT'S FINE!
HUH?
I'M THE ONLY ONE GOING.
ARE YOU STUPID?! HOW DO WE KNOW WE CAN EVEN TRUST HIM?!
WHAT IF YOU'RE CAPTURED OVER THERE?!
SAVIOR!
IF YOU DO THAT, THEN HOW AM I SUPPOSED TO RETURN TO HEAVEN?!
THINK OF ME!
THAT IS A GOOD IDEA.

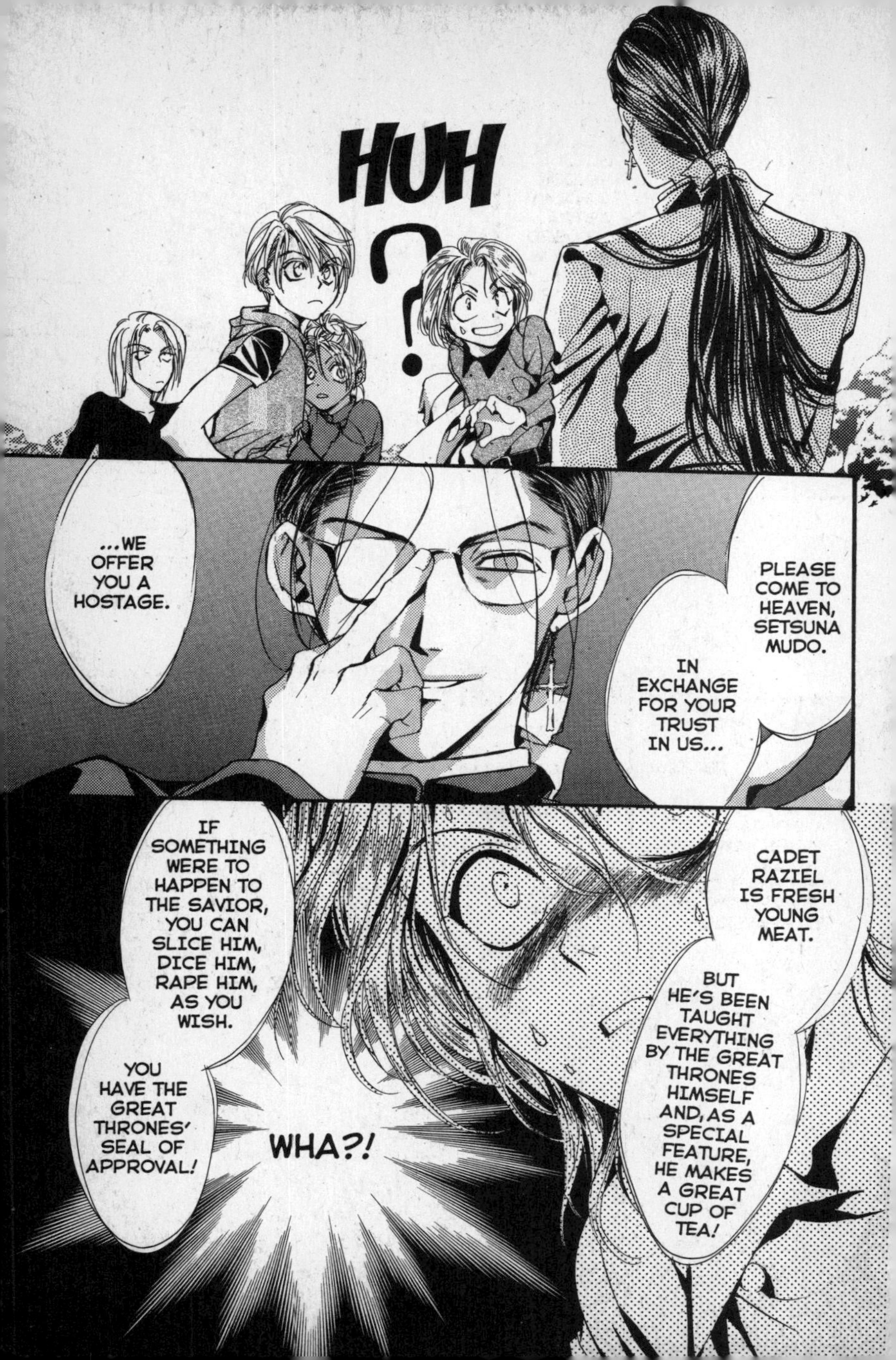
HUH
?
PLEASE COME TO HEAVEN, SETSUNA MUDO.
IN EXCHANGE FOR YOUR TRUST IN US...
...WE OFFER YOU A HOSTAGE.
CADET RAZIEL IS FRESH YOUNG MEAT.
BUT HE'S BEEN TAUGHT EVERYTHING BY THE GREAT THRONES HIMSELF AND, AS A SPECIAL FEATURE, HE MAKES A GREAT CUP OF TEA!
IF SOMETHING WERE TO HAPPEN TO THE SAVIOR, YOU CAN SLICE HIM, DICE HIM, RAPE HIM, AS YOU WISH.
WHA?!
YOU HAVE THE GREAT THRONES' SEAL OF APPROVAL!

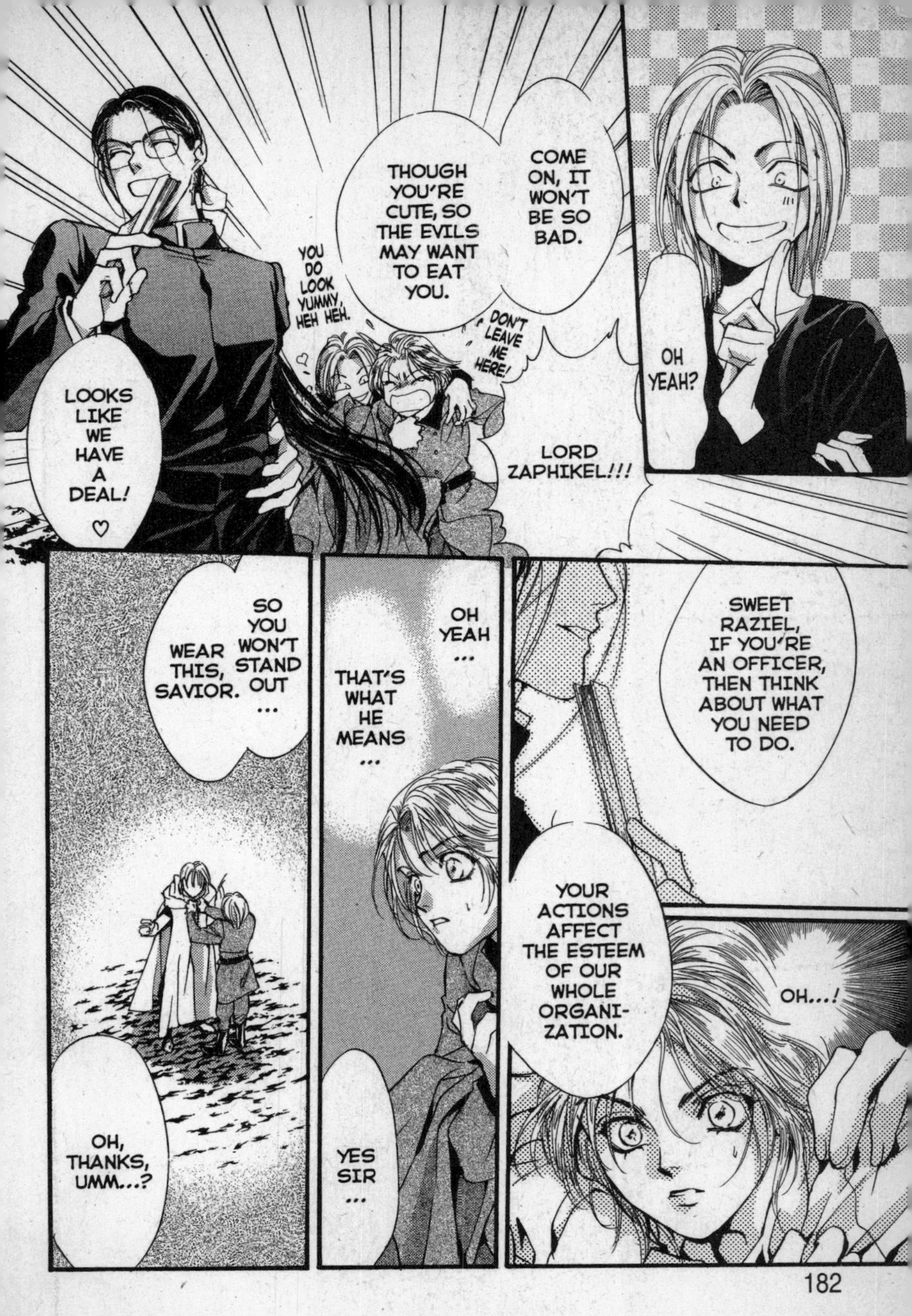
OH YEAH?
COME ON, IT WON'T BE SO BAD.
THOUGH YOU'RE CUTE, SO THE EVILS MAY WANT TO EAT YOU.
DON'T LEAVE ME HERE!
LORD ZAPHIKEL!!!
YOU DO LOOK YUMMY, HEH HEH.
LOOKS LIKE WE HAVE A DEAL! ♡
SWEET RAZIEL, IF YOU'RE AN OFFICER, THEN THINK ABOUT WHAT YOU NEED TO DO.
YOUR ACTIONS AFFECT THE ESTEEM OF OUR WHOLE ORGANIZATION.
OH...!
OH YEAH...
THAT'S WHAT HE MEANS...
YES SIR...
SO YOU WON'T STAND OUT...
WEAR THIS, SAVIOR.
OH, THANKS, UMM...?

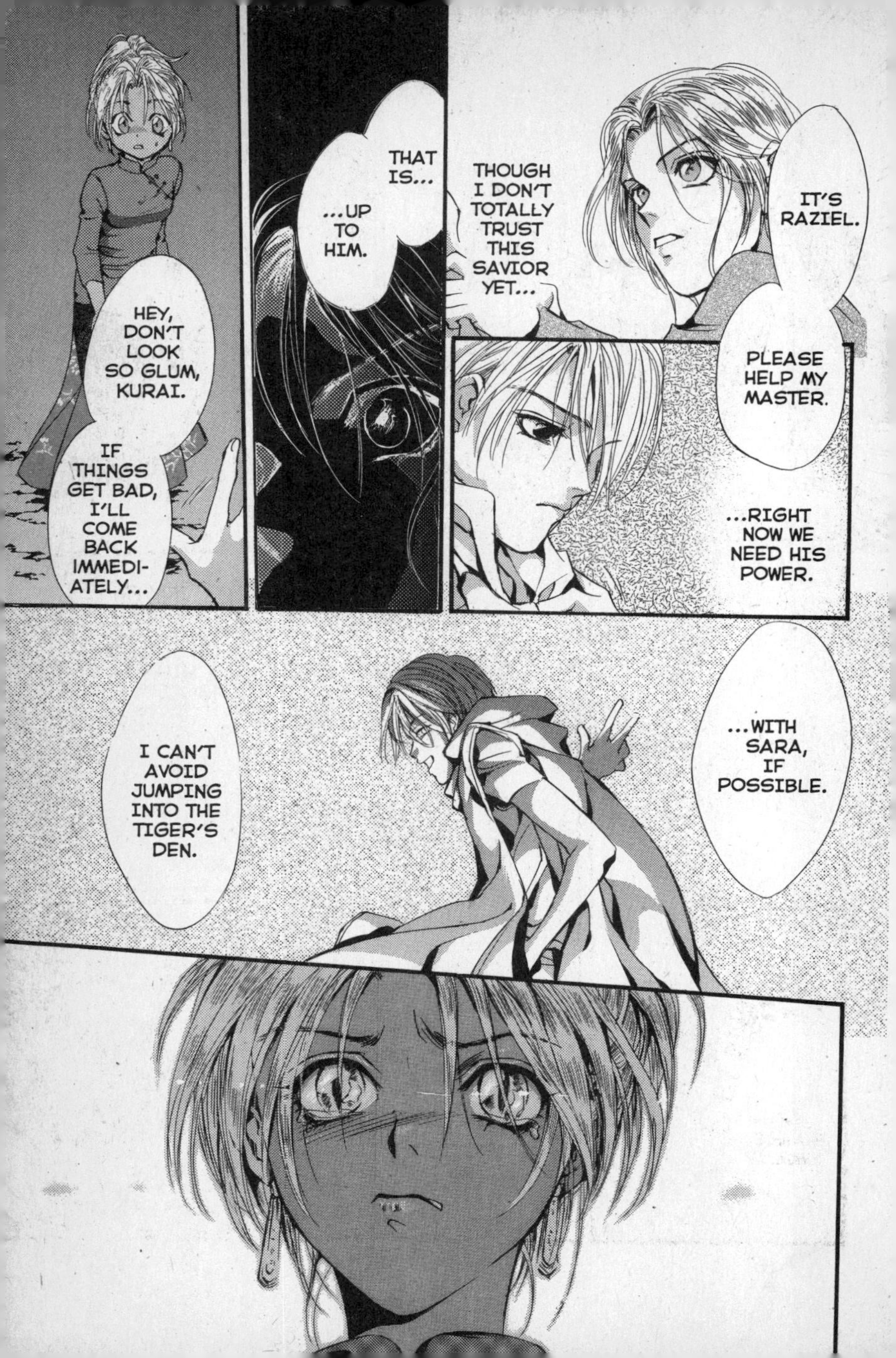
IT'S RAZIEL.
THOUGH I DON'T TOTALLY TRUST THIS SAVIOR YET...
PLEASE HELP MY MASTER.
...RIGHT NOW WE NEED HIS POWER.
THAT IS...
...UP TO HIM.
HEY, DON'T LOOK SO GLUM, KURAI.
IF THINGS GET BAD, I'LL COME BACK IMMEDI-ATELY...
...WITH SARA, IF POSSIBLE.
I CAN'T AVOID JUMPING INTO THE TIGER'S DEN.

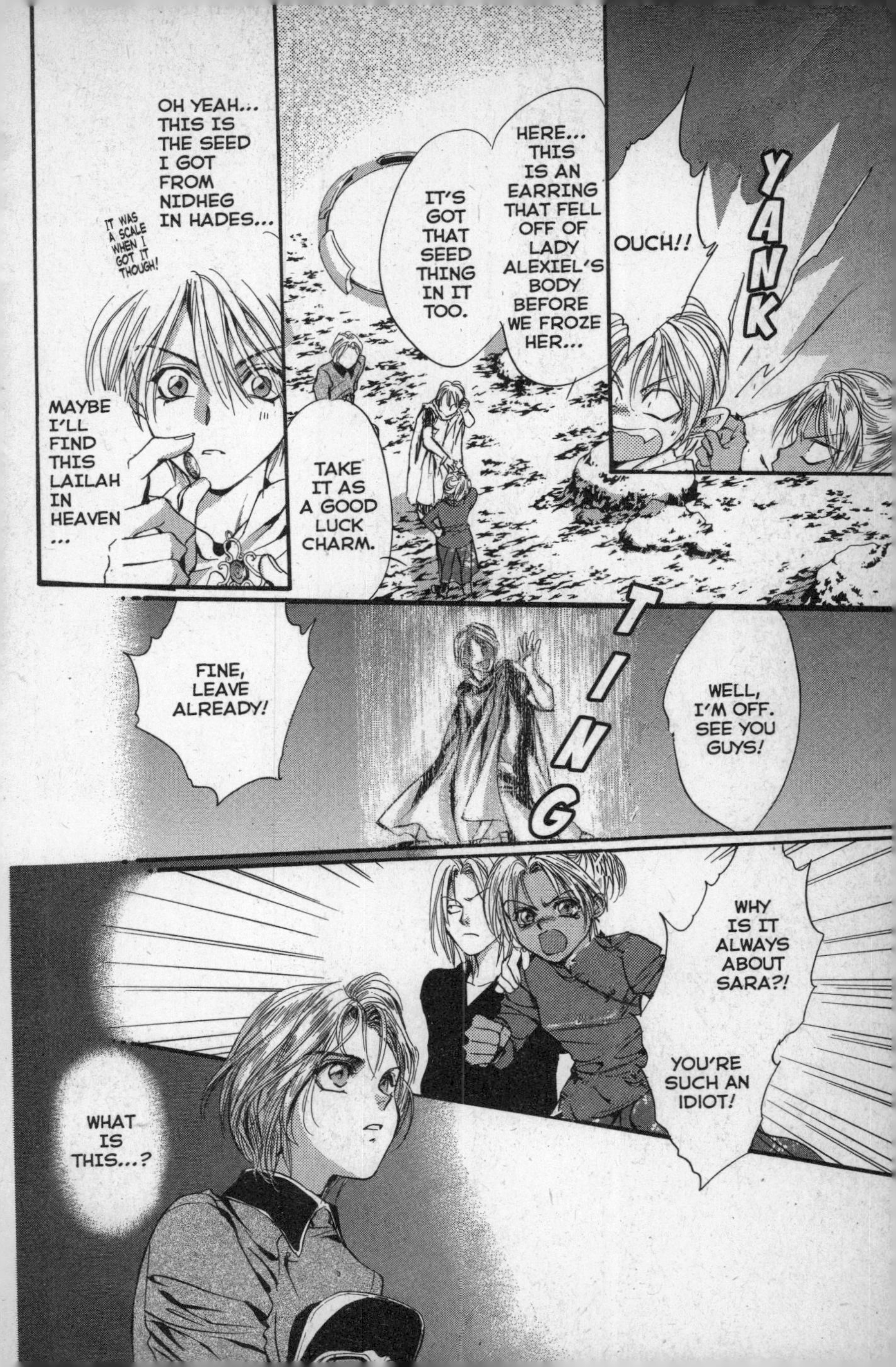
YANK
OUCH!!
HERE... THIS IS AN EARRING THAT FELL OFF OF LADY ALEXIEL'S BODY BEFORE WE FROZE HER...
IT'S GOT THAT SEED THING IN IT TOO.
TAKE IT AS A GOOD LUCK CHARM.
OH YEAH... THIS IS THE SEED I GOT FROM NIDHEG IN HADES...
IT WAS A SCALE WHEN I GOT IT THOUGH!
MAYBE I'LL FIND THIS LAILAH IN HEAVEN...
WELL, I'M OFF. SEE YOU GUYS!
TING
FINE, LEAVE ALREADY!
WHY IS IT ALWAYS ABOUT SARA?!
YOU'RE SUCH AN IDIOT!
WHAT IS THIS...?

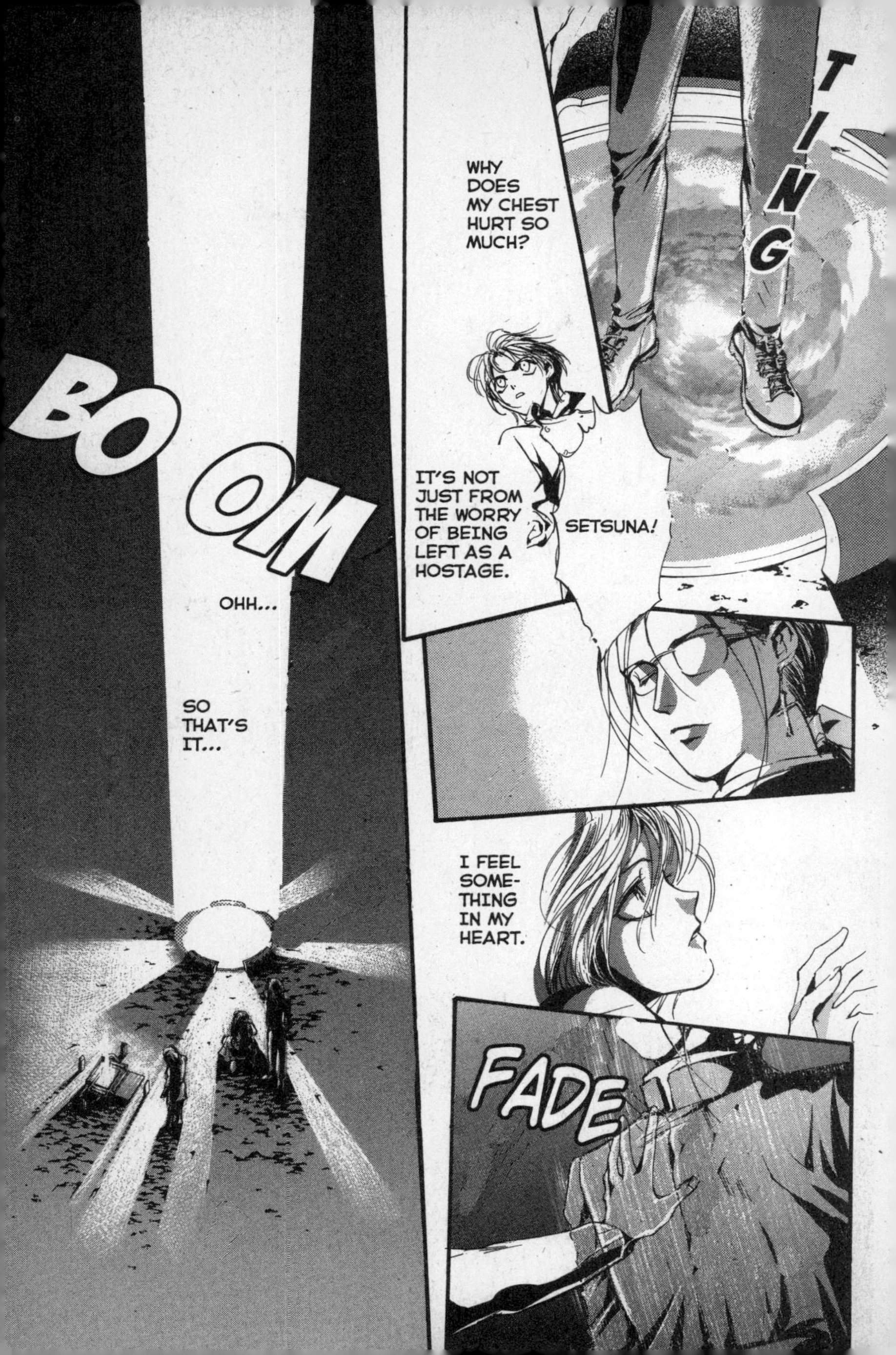
TING
WHY DOES MY CHEST HURT SO MUCH?
IT'S NOT JUST FROM THE WORRY OF BEING LEFT AS A HOSTAGE.
SETSUNA!
I FEEL SOME-THING IN MY HEART.
FADE
BOOM
OHH...
SO THAT'S IT...

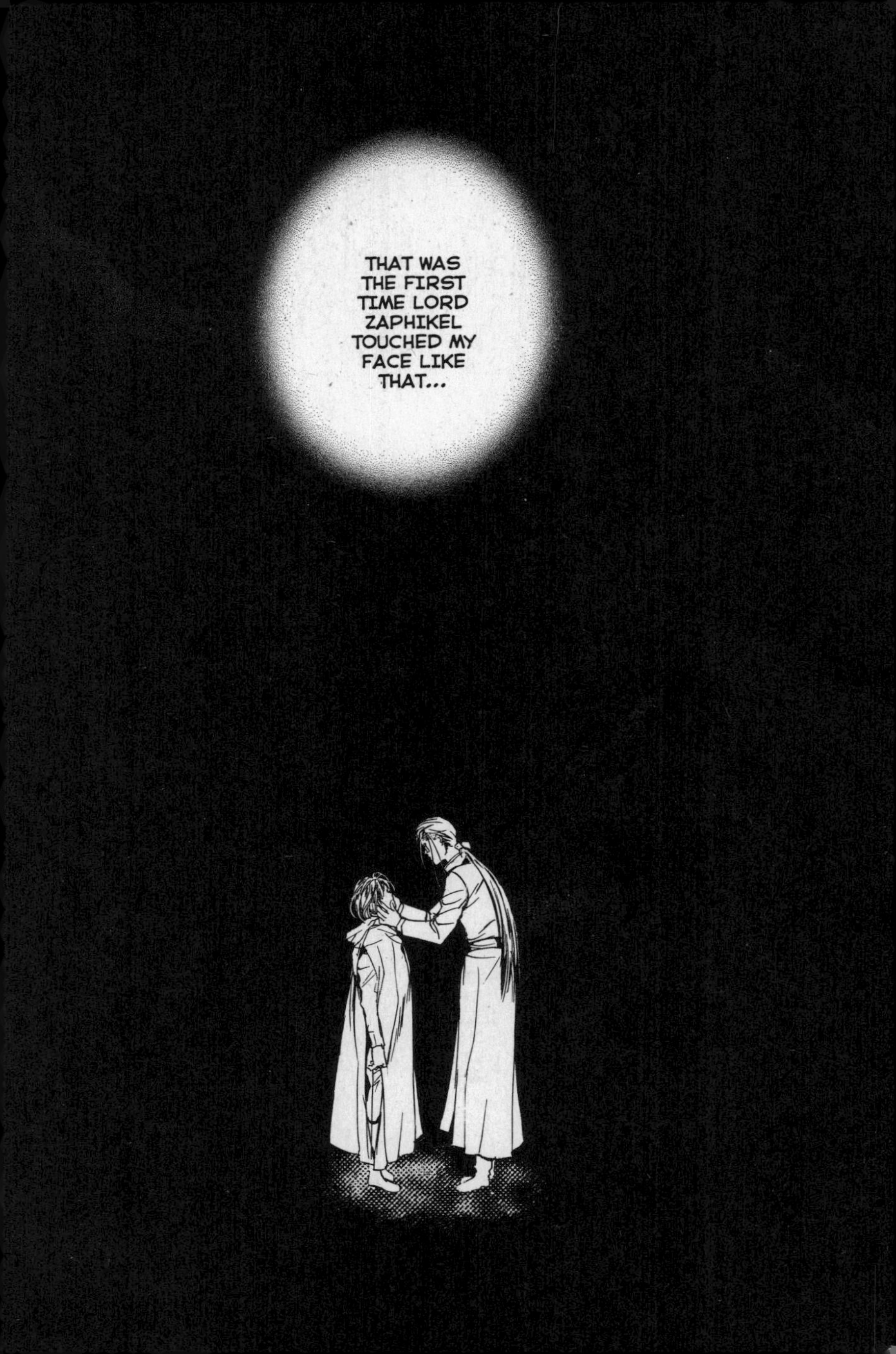
THAT WAS THE FIRST TIME LORD ZAPHIKEL TOUCHED MY FACE LIKE THAT...

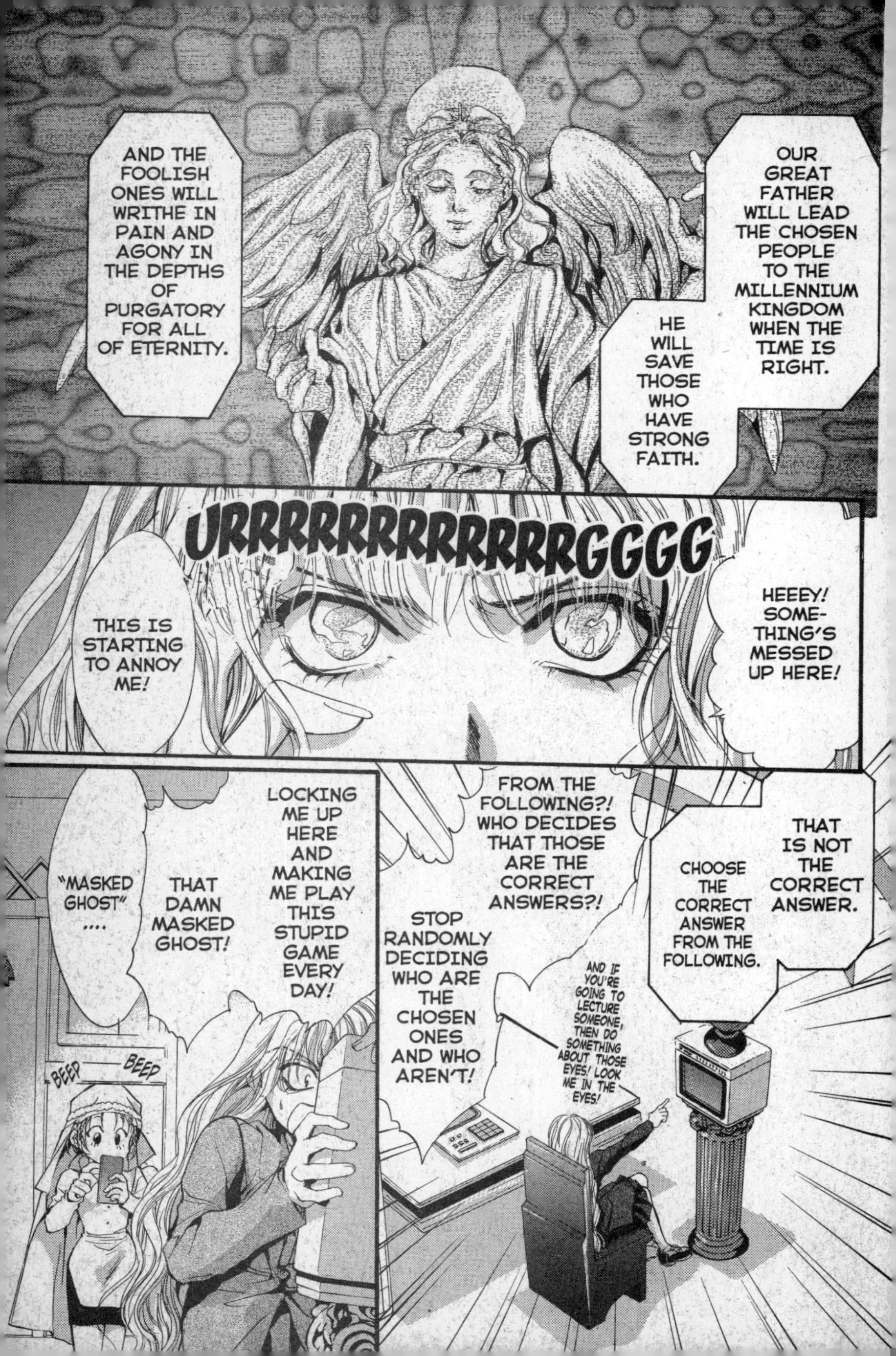
OUR GREAT FATHER WILL LEAD THE CHOSEN PEOPLE TO THE MILLENNIUM KINGDOM WHEN THE TIME IS RIGHT.
HE WILL SAVE THOSE WHO HAVE STRONG FAITH.
AND THE FOOLISH ONES WILL WRITHE IN PAIN AND AGONY IN THE DEPTHS OF PURGATORY FOR ALL OF ETERNITY.
URRRRRRRRRRRRRRGGGG
HEEEY! SOME-THING'S MESSED UP HERE!
THIS IS STARTING TO ANNOY ME!
THAT IS NOT THE CORRECT ANSWER.
CHOOSE THE CORRECT ANSWER FROM THE FOLLOWING.
AND IF YOU'RE GOING TO LECTURE SOMEONE, THEN DO SOMETHING ABOUT THOSE EYES! LOOK ME IN THE EYES!
FROM THE FOLLOWING?! WHO DECIDES THAT THOSE ARE THE CORRECT ANSWERS?!
STOP RANDOMLY DECIDING WHO ARE THE CHOSEN ONES AND WHO AREN'T!
LOCKING ME UP HERE AND MAKING ME PLAY THIS STUPID GAME EVERY DAY!
THAT DAMN MASKED GHOST!
"MASKED GHOST" ....
BEEP
BEEP

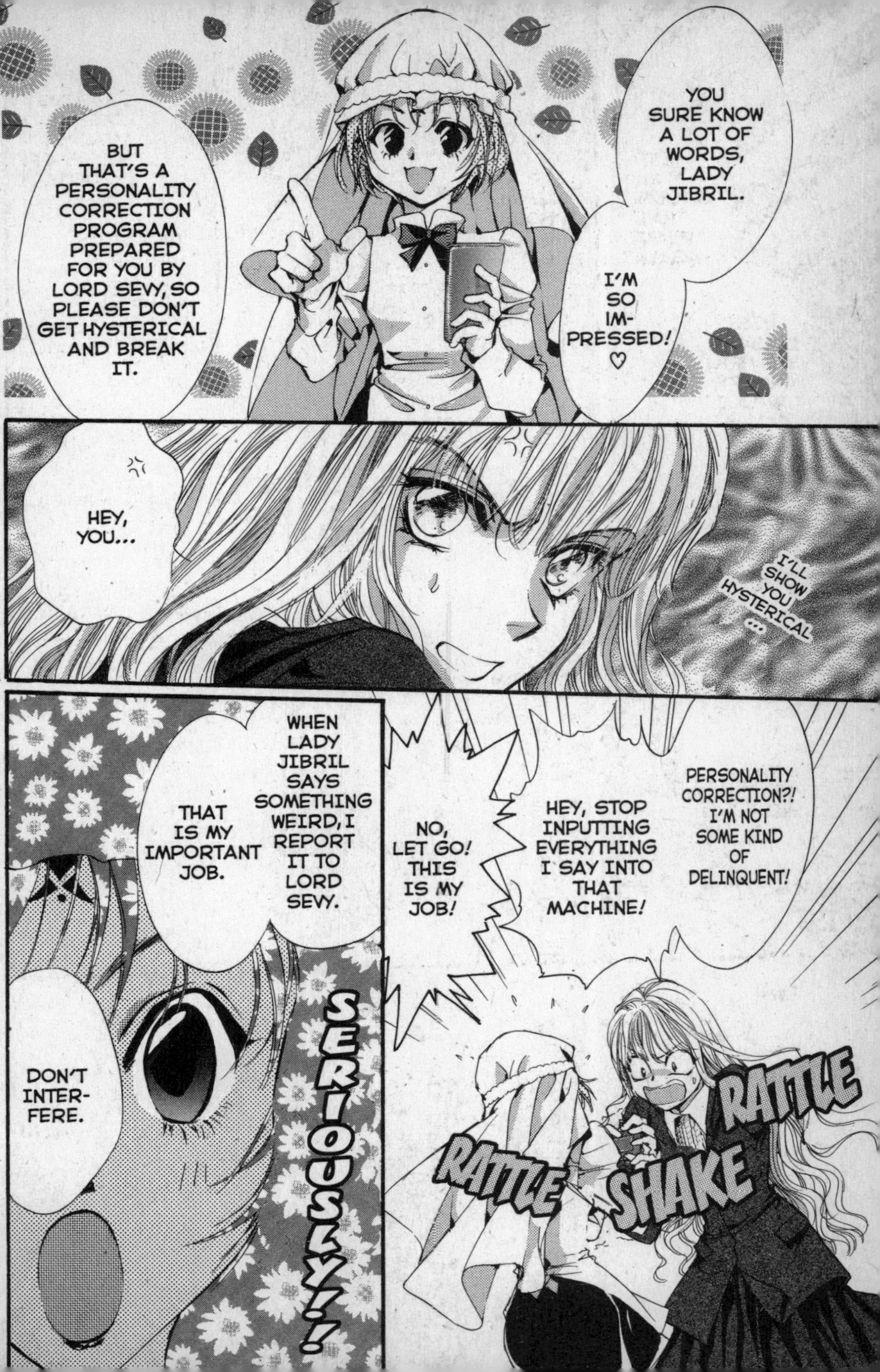
YOU SURE KNOW A LOT OF WORDS, LADY JIBRIL.
I'M SO IM-PRESSED! ♡
BUT THAT'S A PERSONALITY CORRECTION PROGRAM PREPARED FOR YOU BY LORD SEVY, SO PLEASE DON'T GET HYSTERICAL AND BREAK IT.
I'LL SHOW YOU HYSTERICAL...
HEY, YOU...
PERSONALITY CORRECTION?! I'M NOT SOME KIND OF DELINQUENT!
HEY, STOP INPUTTING EVERYTHING I SAY INTO THAT MACHINE!
NO, LET GO! THIS IS MY JOB!
RATTLE
SHAKE
RATTLE
WHEN LADY JIBRIL SAYS SOMETHING WEIRD, I REPORT IT TO LORD SEVY.
THAT IS MY IMPORTANT JOB.
SERIOUSLY!!
DON'T INTERFERE.

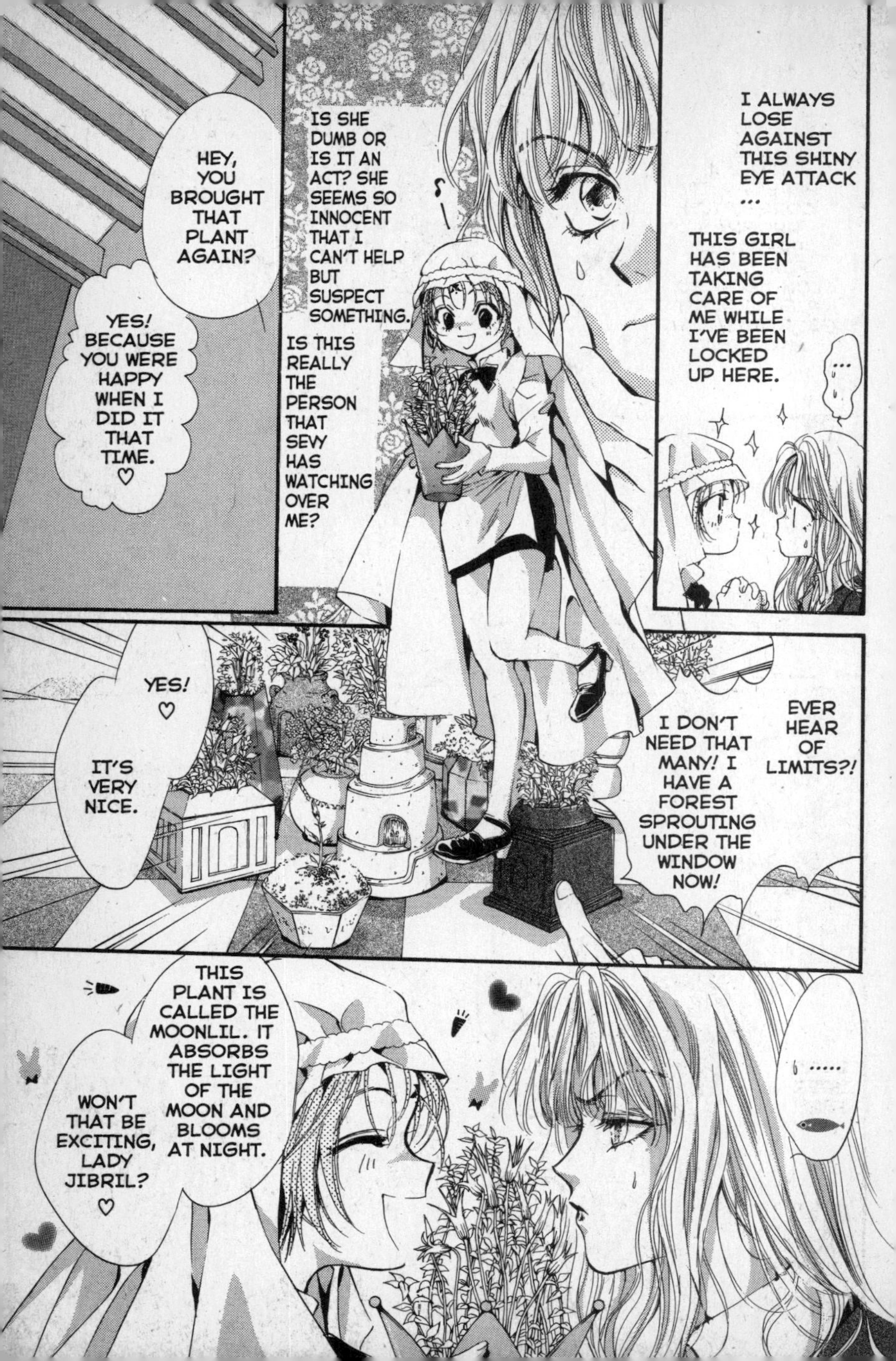
I ALWAYS LOSE AGAINST THIS SHINY EYE ATTACK ...
THIS GIRL HAS BEEN TAKING CARE OF ME WHILE I'VE BEEN LOCKED UP HERE.
...
IS SHE DUMB OR IS IT AN ACT? SHE SEEMS SO INNOCENT THAT I CAN'T HELP BUT SUSPECT SOMETHING.
IS THIS REALLY THE PERSON THAT SEVY HAS WATCHING OVER ME?
HEY, YOU BROUGHT THAT PLANT AGAIN?
YES! BECAUSE YOU WERE HAPPY WHEN I DID IT THAT TIME. ♡
EVER HEAR OF LIMITS?!
I DON'T NEED THAT MANY! I HAVE A FOREST SPROUTING UNDER THE WINDOW NOW!
YES! ♡
IT'S VERY NICE.
......
THIS PLANT IS CALLED THE MOONLIL. IT ABSORBS THE LIGHT OF THE MOON AND BLOOMS AT NIGHT.
WON'T THAT BE EXCITING, LADY JIBRIL? ♡

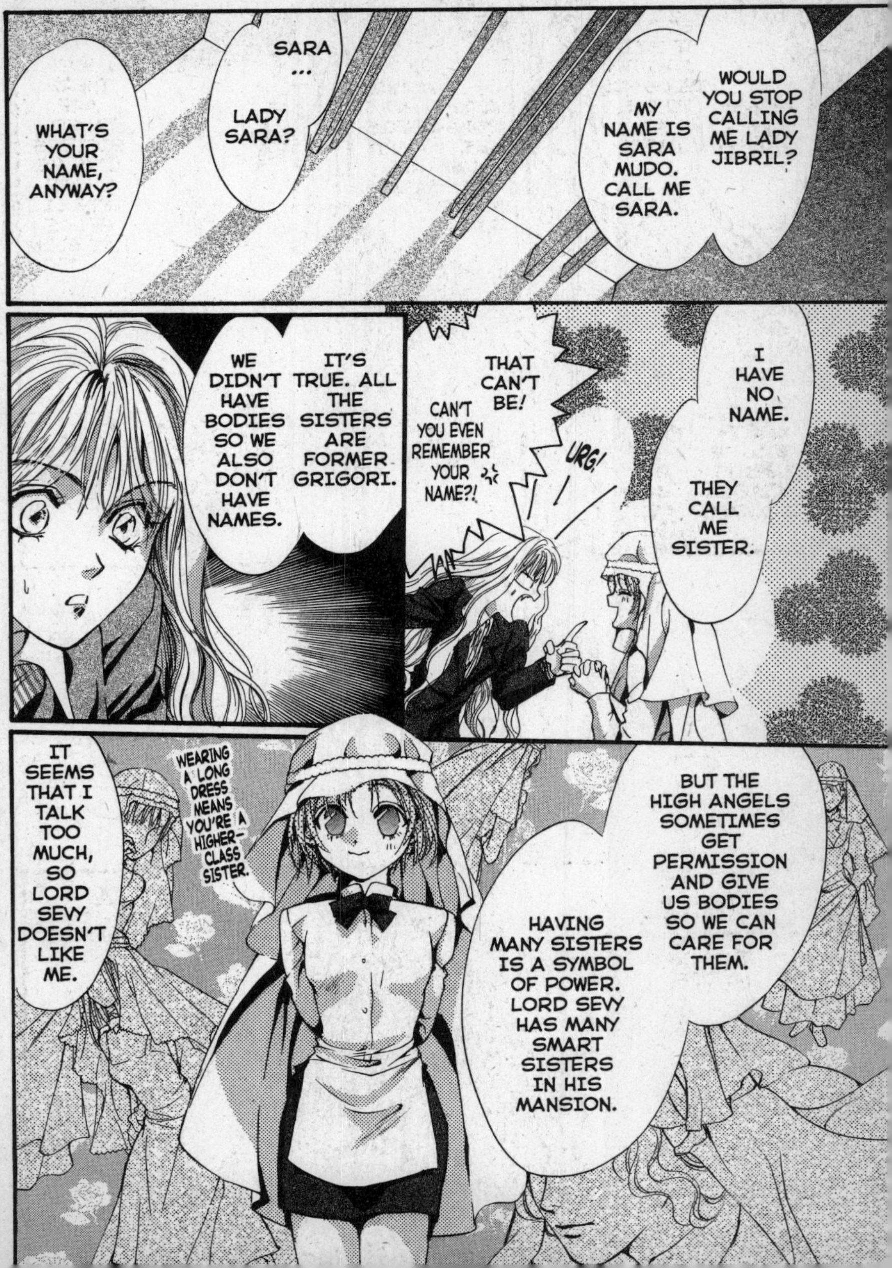

WOULD YOU STOP CALLING ME LADY JIBRIL?
MY NAME IS SARA MUDO. CALL ME SARA.
SARA... LADY SARA?
WHAT'S YOUR NAME, ANYWAY?
I HAVE NO NAME.
THEY CALL ME SISTER.
THAT CAN'T BE!
CAN'T YOU EVEN REMEMBER YOUR NAME?!
URG!
IT'S TRUE. ALL THE SISTERS ARE FORMER GRIGORI.
WE DIDN'T HAVE BODIES SO WE ALSO DON'T HAVE NAMES.
BUT THE HIGH ANGELS SOMETIMES GET PERMISSION AND GIVE US BODIES SO WE CAN CARE FOR THEM.
HAVING MANY SISTERS IS A SYMBOL OF POWER. LORD SEVY HAS MANY SMART SISTERS IN HIS MANSION.
WEARING A LONG DRESS MEANS YOU'RE A HIGHER-CLASS SISTER.
IT SEEMS THAT I TALK TOO MUCH, SO LORD SEVY DOESN'T LIKE ME.

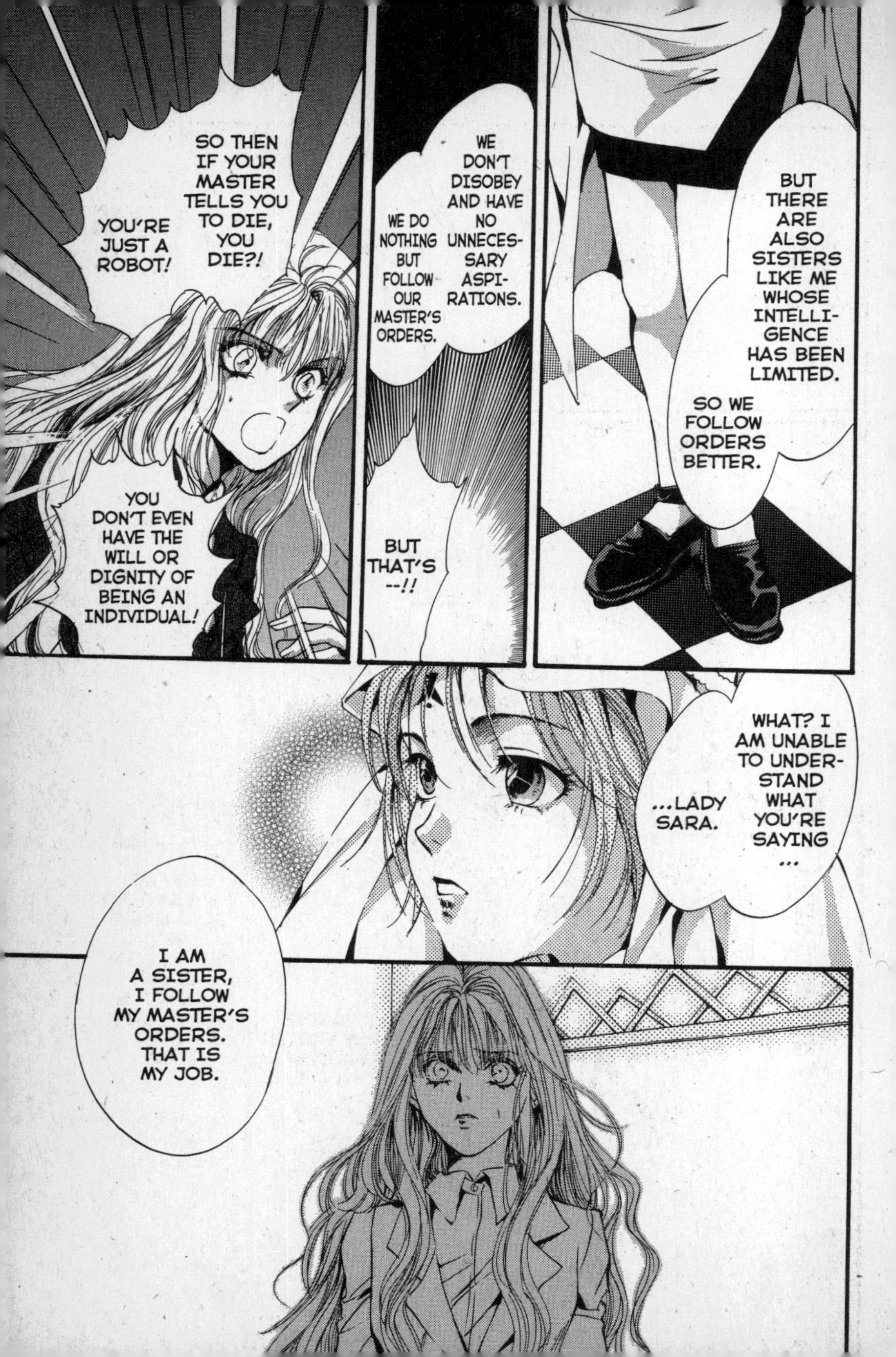
BUT THERE ARE ALSO SISTERS LIKE ME WHOSE INTELLIGENCE HAS BEEN LIMITED.
SO WE FOLLOW ORDERS BETTER.
WE DON'T DISOBEY AND HAVE NO UNNECESSARY ASPIRATIONS.
WE DO NOTHING BUT FOLLOW OUR MASTER'S ORDERS.
BUT THAT'S --!!
SO THEN IF YOUR MASTER TELLS YOU TO DIE, YOU DIE?!
YOU'RE JUST A ROBOT!
YOU DON'T EVEN HAVE THE WILL OR DIGNITY OF BEING AN INDIVIDUAL!
WHAT? I AM UNABLE TO UNDERSTAND WHAT YOU'RE SAYING ...
...LADY SARA.
I AM A SISTER, I FOLLOW MY MASTER'S ORDERS. THAT IS MY JOB.

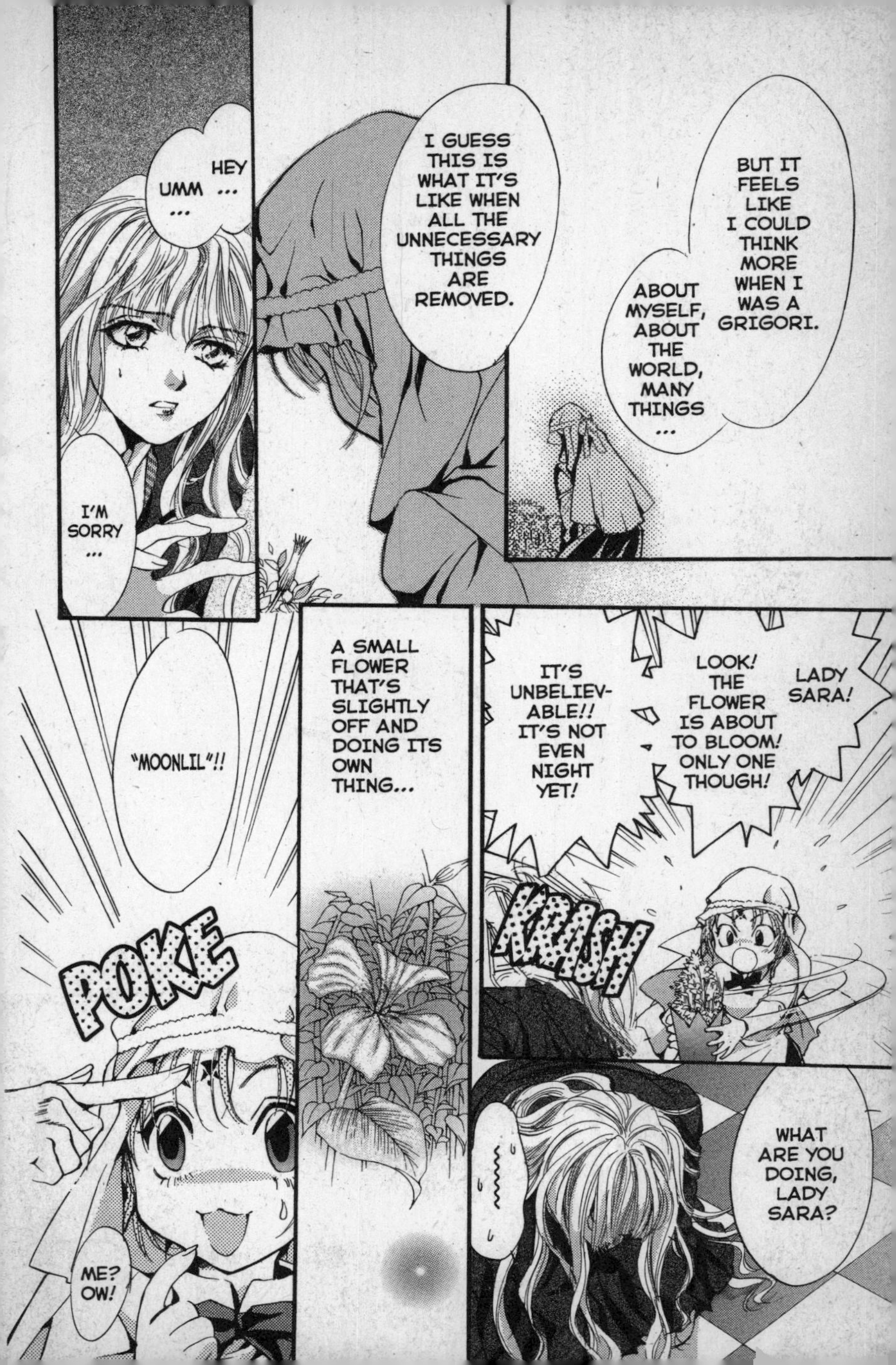
BUT IT FEELS LIKE I COULD THINK MORE WHEN I WAS A GRIGORI.
ABOUT MYSELF, ABOUT THE WORLD, MANY THINGS ...
I GUESS THIS IS WHAT IT'S LIKE WHEN ALL THE UNNECESSARY THINGS ARE REMOVED.
HEY ... UMM ...
I'M SORRY ...
LADY SARA!
LOOK! THE FLOWER IS ABOUT TO BLOOM! ONLY ONE THOUGH!
IT'S UNBELIEVABLE!! IT'S NOT EVEN NIGHT YET!
KRASH
WHAT ARE YOU DOING, LADY SARA?
A SMALL FLOWER THAT'S SLIGHTLY OFF AND DOING ITS OWN THING...
"MOONLIL"!!
POKE
ME? OW!

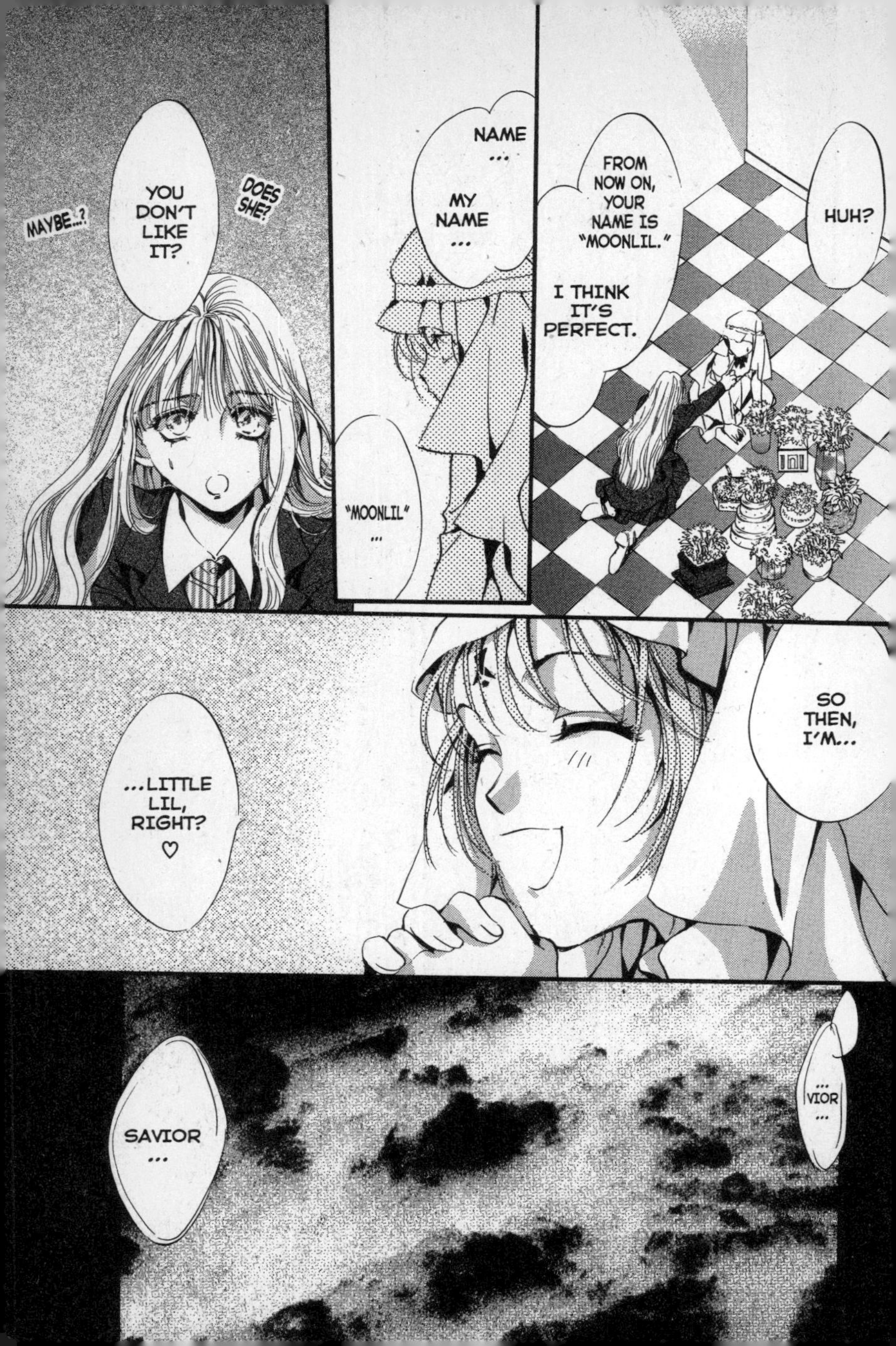
HUH?
FROM NOW ON, YOUR NAME IS "MOONLIL."
I THINK IT'S PERFECT.
NAME ...
MY NAME ...
"MOONLIL" ...
YOU DON'T LIKE IT?
DOES SHE?
MAYBE...?
SO THEN, I'M...
...LITTLE LIL, RIGHT? ♡
... VIOR ...
SAVIOR ...

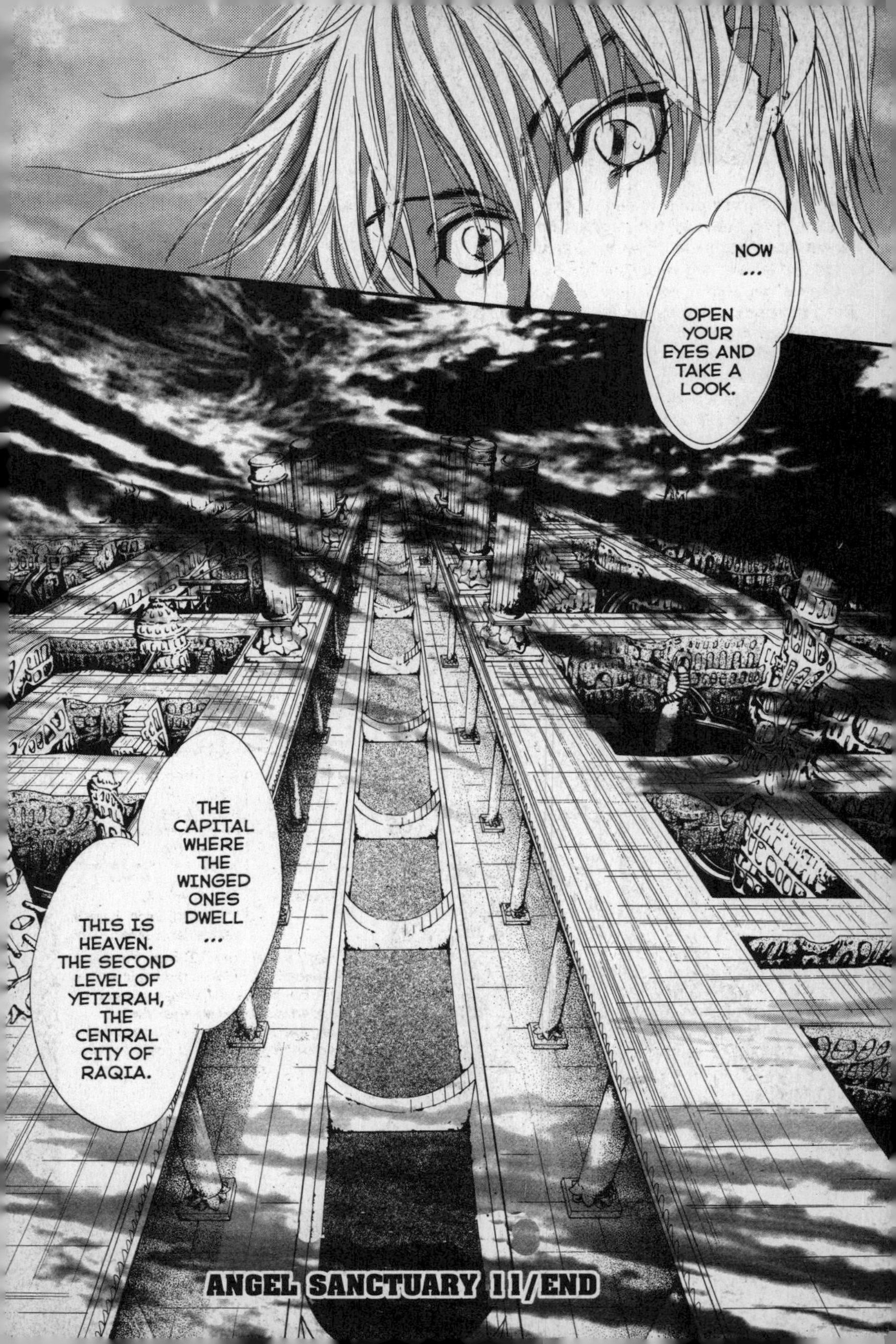
NOW ...
OPEN YOUR EYES AND TAKE A LOOK.
THE CAPITAL WHERE THE WINGED ONES DWELL ...
THIS IS HEAVEN. THE SECOND LEVEL OF YETZIRAH, THE CENTRAL CITY OF RAQIA.
ANGEL SANCTUARY 11/END

There's not much point in saying this here, but I wanted to thank all the people who wrote to me about my short "Shonen Zantou." I received a very big reaction for such a short manga story and it really surprised me. I'd like to thank everyone who read it regardless if you liked it or not. I figured I'd get letters just liking the fact that there were gay characters in it. I was very happy that so many people could enjoy it in a pure sense as a complete story.

This is sudden, but we had a popularity poll in the magazine and I've listed the rankings here. The poll was only open for a short time, but we received many replies. I think this can be trusted even though some people sent in dozens of votes. We counted those as one. Someone is a huge Rosiel fan...

#1 Setsuna Mudo
Easily
#2 Sakuya Kira
#3 Yue Kato
#4 Michael
Very small margin
#5 Sara
Good, she is the heroine.
#6 Kurai
#7 Mad Hatter
Because I'm always talking about him?
#8 Rosiel
He's hasn't appeared in Forever!
#9 Zaphikel
They are on top of each other...
#10 Raziel
#11 Alexiel
#12 Katan
#13 Raphael
Kinda low
#14 Arachne
Her too
#15 Astaroth
Wow
#16 Jibril
#17 Uriel
Well I like Uri...
#18 Boyz
#19 Lil
Good for being so new.
#20 Metatron
#21 Teiaiel
#22 Adam Kadamon
Really?

#23 Asmodeus
Hot...
#24 Kirie
Brings back memories...
#25 Sevothtarte
I like him...
#26 Noyz
#27 Shateiel
#28 Sandalphon
#29 Ruri Aoki
So old...
#30 Astarte
Sorry for turning you into that snake...
#31 Doll
#32 Anael
#33 Lucifer
#34 Okazaki
Thank you for remembering
#35 Kamael
I kind of like him too
#36 Nidheg
...?
#37 Abaddon
#38 Lailah
#39 Kira's dad
The old guy
#40 Beelzebub
He never appeared!
#41 Barbiel
#42 Agat
Most popular of the three
#43 Aunt Afu
#44 Dobiel, Jade, Mamnon, Asmo's Pet, Barbelo, Bobby

...So what do you think? I know there's a lot of "what the...?!" Who the heck is Bobby?! Barbelo and Beelzebub never even appeared in the manga... And obviously the characters that were being focused on at the time the poll was taken did well.

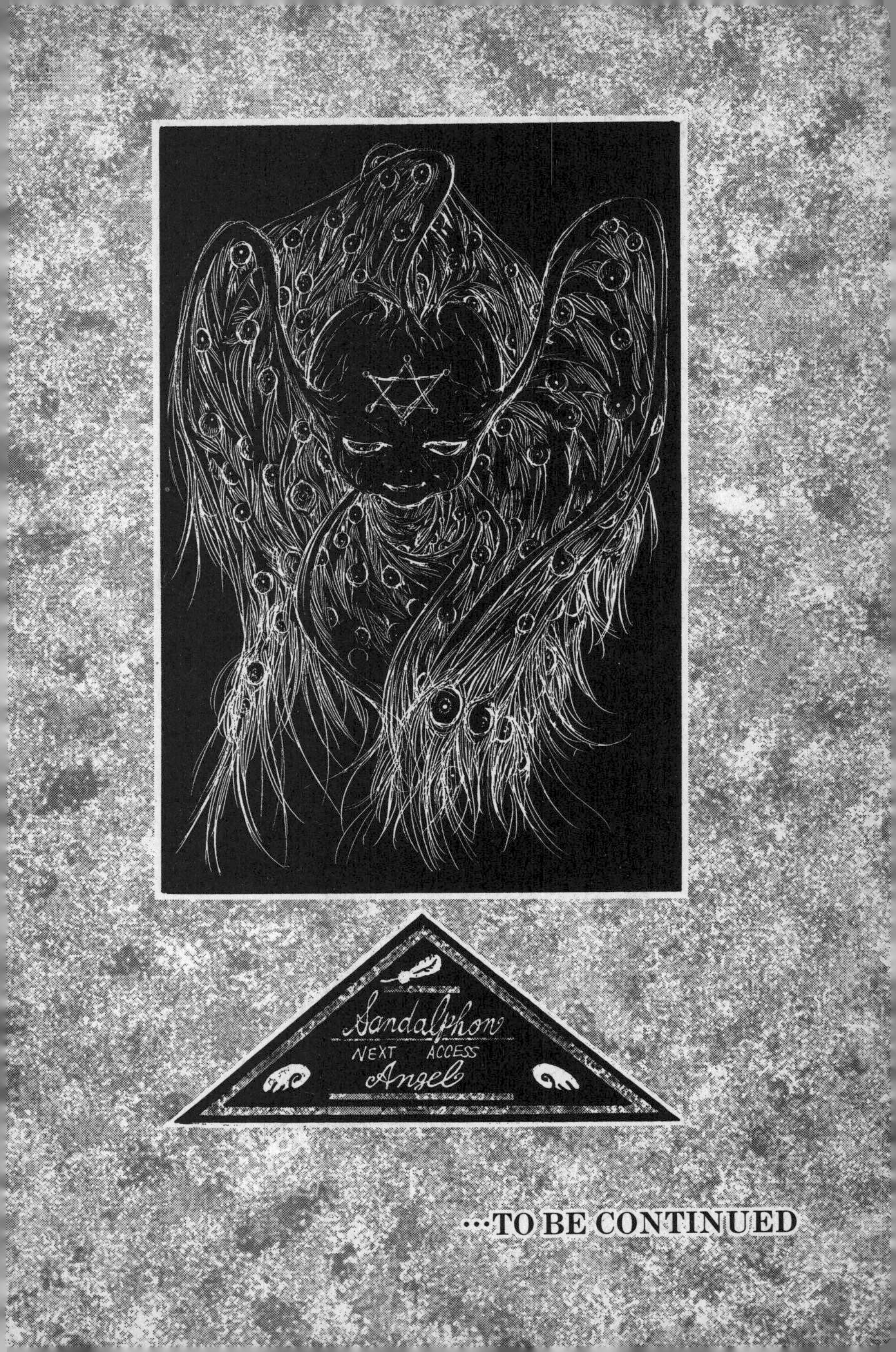
Sandalphon
NEXT ACCESS
Angel
...TO BE CONTINUED

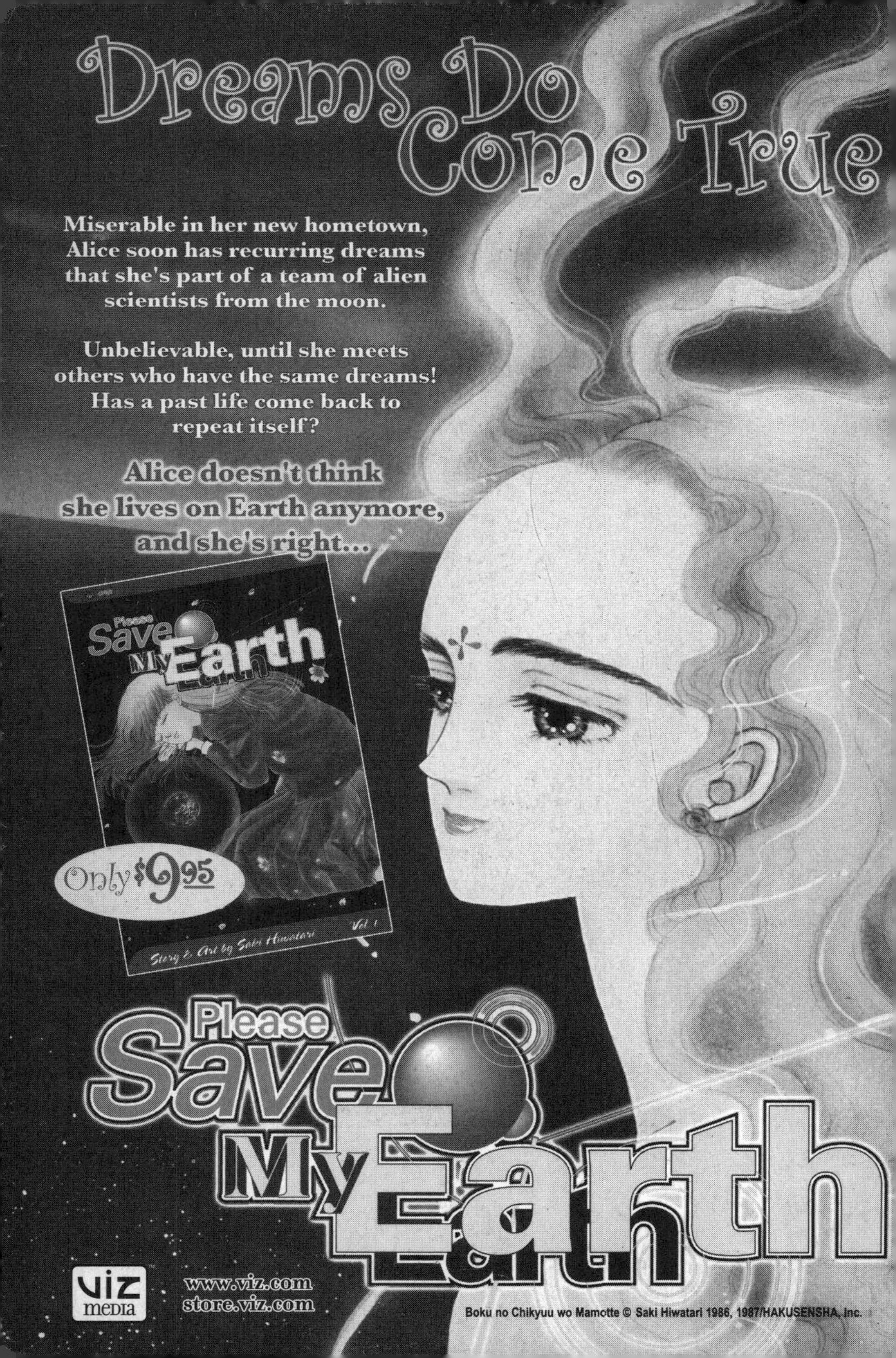
Dreams Do Come True
Miserable in her new hometown, Alice soon has recurring dreams that she's part of a team of alien scientists from the moon.
Unbelievable, until she meets others who have the same dreams! Has a past life come back to repeat itself?
Alice doesn't think she lives on Earth anymore, and she's right...
Please Save My Earth
Story & Art by Saki Hiwatari
Vol. 1
Only $9.95
Please Save My Earth
viz media
www.viz.com
store.viz.com
Boku no Chikyuu wo Mamotte © Saki Hiwatari 1986, 1987/HAKUSENSHA, Inc.

LOVE SHOJO? LET US KNOW!

☐ Please do NOT send me information about VIZ Media products, news and events, special offers, or other information.

☐ Please do NOT send me information from VIZ' trusted business partners.

Name: _____

Address: _____

City: _____ State: _____ Zip: _____

E-mail: _____

☐ Male   ☐ Female   Date of Birth (mm/dd/yyyy): ___ / ___ / ___   (Under 13? Parental consent required)

What race/ethnicity do you consider yourself? (check all that apply)

☐ White/Caucasian   ☐ Black/African American   ☐ Hispanic/Latino

☐ Asian/Pacific Islander ☐ Native American/Alaskan Native ☐ Other: _____

What VIZ shojo title(s) did you purchase? (indicate title(s) purchased)

_____

What other shojo titles from other publishers do you own? _____

_____

Reason for purchase: (check all that apply)

☐ Special offer   ☐ Favorite title / author / artist / genre
☐ Gift   ☐ Recommendation   ☐ Collection
☐ Read excerpt in VIZ manga sampler   ☐ Other _____

Where did you make your purchase? (please check one)

☐ Comic store   ☐ Bookstore   ☐ Mass/Grocery Store
☐ Newsstand   ☐ Video/Video Game Store
☐ Online (site:_____)   ☐ Other _____

How many shojo titles have you purchased in the last year? How many were VIZ shojo titles?
(please check one from each column)

SHOJO MANGA

- ☐ None
- ☐ 1 – 4
- ☐ 5 – 10
- ☐ 11+

VIZ SHOJO MANGA

- ☐ None
- ☐ 1 – 4
- ☐ 5 – 10
- ☐ 11+

What do you like most about shojo graphic novels? (check all that apply)

- ☐ Romance
- ☐ Drama / conflict
- ☐ Fantasy
- ☐ Comedy
- ☐ Real-life storylines
- ☐ Relatable characters
- ☐ Other ______________________

Do you purchase every volume of your favorite shojo series?

- ☐ Yes! Gotta have 'em as my own
- ☐ No. Please explain: ______________________

Who are your favorite shojo authors / artists? ______________________

____

What shojo titles would like you translated and sold in English? ______________________

____

THANK YOU! Please send the completed form to:

VIZ media

NJW Research
ATTN: VIZ Media Shojo Survey
42 Catharine Street
Poughkeepsie, NY 12601

Your privacy is very important to us. All information provided will be used for internal purposes only and will not be sold or otherwise divulged.